I'm Not a Film Star

I'm Not a Film Star

David Bowie as Actor

Edited by
Ian Dixon and Brendan Black

BLOOMSBURY ACADEMIC
NEW YORK · LONDON · OXFORD · NEW DELHI · SYDNEY

BLOOMSBURY ACADEMIC
Bloomsbury Publishing Inc
1385 Broadway, New York, NY 10018, USA
50 Bedford Square, London, WC1B 3DP, UK
29 Earlsfort Terrace, Dublin 2, Ireland

BLOOMSBURY, BLOOMSBURY ACADEMIC and the Diana logo are trademarks of
Bloomsbury Publishing Plc

First published in the United States of America 2022
Paperback edition published 2024

Volume Editor's Part of the Work © Ian Dixon and Brendan Black
Each chapter © of Contributors

For legal purposes the Acknowledgements on pp. xxiii-xxvi constitute an extension
of this copyright page.

Cover design: Eleanor Rose
Cover image: David Bowie in *The Man Who Fell to Earth*, 1976, Dir. Nicolas Roeg
© Ronald Grant Archive / ArenaPAL

All rights reserved. No part of this publication may be reproduced or transmitted in any form or by any means, electronic or mechanical, including photocopying, recording, or any information storage or retrieval system, without prior permission in writing from the publishers.

Bloomsbury Publishing Inc does not have any control over, or responsibility for, any third-party websites referred to or in this book. All internet addresses given in this book were correct at the time of going to press. The author and publisher regret any inconvenience caused if addresses have changed or sites have ceased to exist, but can accept no responsibility for any such changes.

Library of Congress Cataloging-in-Publication Data
Names: Dixon, Ian (College teacher), editor. | Black, Brendan, editor.
Title: I'm not a film star: David Bowie as actor / edited by Ian Dixon and Brendan Black.
Description: New York : Bloomsbury Academic, 2022. | Includes bibliographical references and index. | Summary: "A critical exploration of David Bowie's varied works as an actor, revealing who 'Bowie' is while affording the reader keen insights into the nuances of performance studies"-- Provided by publisher.
Identifiers: LCCN 2022006049 (print) | LCCN 2022006050 (ebook) | ISBN 9781501368684 (hardback) | ISBN 9781501370489 (paperback) | ISBN 9781501368677 (epub) | ISBN 9781501368660 (pdf) | ISBN 9781501368653
Subjects: LCSH: Bowie, David–Criticism and interpretation. | Rock musicians–England–Biography. | Actors–Great Britain–Biography.
Classification: LCC ML420.B754 I456 2022 (print) | LCC ML420.B754 (ebook) | DDC 782.42166092–dc23/eng/20220309
LC record available at https://lccn.loc.gov/2022006049
LC ebook record available at https://lccn.loc.gov/2022006050

ISBN: HB: 978-1-5013-6868-4
PB: 978-1-5013-7048-9
ePDF: 978-1-5013-6866-0
eBook: 978-1-5013-6867-7

Typeset by Deanta Global Publishing Services, Chennai, India

To find out more about our authors and books visit www.bloomsbury.com and
sign up for our newsletters.

I'm Not a Film Star

David Bowie as Actor

Edited by
Ian Dixon and Brendan Black

BLOOMSBURY ACADEMIC
NEW YORK · LONDON · OXFORD · NEW DELHI · SYDNEY

BLOOMSBURY ACADEMIC
Bloomsbury Publishing Inc
1385 Broadway, New York, NY 10018, USA
50 Bedford Square, London, WC1B 3DP, UK
29 Earlsfort Terrace, Dublin 2, Ireland

BLOOMSBURY, BLOOMSBURY ACADEMIC and the Diana logo are trademarks of
Bloomsbury Publishing Plc

First published in the United States of America 2022
Paperback edition published 2024

Volume Editor's Part of the Work © Ian Dixon and Brendan Black
Each chapter © of Contributors

For legal purposes the Acknowledgements on pp. xxiii-xxvi constitute an extension
of this copyright page.

Cover design: Eleanor Rose
Cover image: David Bowie in *The Man Who Fell to Earth*, 1976, Dir. Nicolas Roeg
© Ronald Grant Archive / ArenaPAL

All rights reserved. No part of this publication may be reproduced or transmitted in any
form or by any means, electronic or mechanical, including photocopying, recording, or any
information storage or retrieval system, without prior permission in writing from
the publishers.

Bloomsbury Publishing Inc does not have any control over, or responsibility for, any
third-party websites referred to or in this book. All internet addresses given in this
book were correct at the time of going to press. The author and publisher regret any
inconvenience caused if addresses have changed or sites have ceased to exist, but
can accept no responsibility for any such changes.

Library of Congress Cataloging-in-Publication Data
Names: Dixon, Ian (College teacher), editor. | Black, Brendan, editor.
Title: I'm not a film star: David Bowie as actor / edited by Ian Dixon and Brendan Black.
Description: New York : Bloomsbury Academic, 2022. | Includes bibliographical references
and index. | Summary: "A critical exploration of David Bowie's varied works as
an actor, revealing who 'Bowie' is while affording the reader keen insights into
the nuances of performance studies"-- Provided by publisher.
Identifiers: LCCN 2022006049 (print) | LCCN 2022006050 (ebook) | ISBN 9781501368684
(hardback) | ISBN 9781501370489 (paperback) | ISBN 9781501368677 (epub) |
ISBN 9781501368660 (pdf) | ISBN 9781501368653
Subjects: LCSH: Bowie, David–Criticism and interpretation. | Rock musicians–
England–Biography. | Actors–Great Britain–Biography.
Classification: LCC ML420.B754 I456 2022 (print) | LCC ML420.B754 (ebook)
| DDC 782.42166092–dc23/eng/20220309
LC record available at https://lccn.loc.gov/2022006049
LC ebook record available at https://lccn.loc.gov/2022006050

ISBN: HB: 978-1-5013-6868-4
PB: 978-1-5013-7048-9
ePDF: 978-1-5013-6866-0
eBook: 978-1-5013-6867-7

Typeset by Deanta Global Publishing Services, Chennai, India

To find out more about our authors and books visit www.bloomsbury.com and
sign up for our newsletters.

For Iman, Lexi, Duncan and David
And for Rodney, friend and mentor

CONTENTS

List of figures ix
List of editors xii
List of contributors xiii
Foreword: Acting as medium xvi
Acknowledgements xxiii

Introduction *Ian Dixon and Brendan Black* 1

1 Ziggy Stardust, Direct Cinema and the multimodal performance of *Gesamtkunstwerk* *Lisa Perrott* 25

2 David Bowie is ... actor, star and character: Entangled agencies in *The Man Who Fell to Earth* *Dene October* 53

3 The posed and the unposed: Inhabited clowns and grotesques in Bowie's *Scary Monsters* and *The Elephant Man* *Amedeo D'Adamo* 73

4 Consuming Bowie: *Christiane F.* and the transgressive allure of Anglo-American pop culture in Cold War West Berlin *Susanne Hillman* 97

5 Gesturing Dust: Sensing David Bowie's performance in *Merry Christmas, Mr. Lawrence* *Sean Redmond* 115

6   *The Hunger*'s deathly shadow: The sweet annihilation of David Bowie, NYC, c. 1980–3   *Mitch Goodwin*   131

7   'Who can I be now?': Codpieces, carnival and the blurring of identity in *Labyrinth*   *Brendan Black*   151

8   Bowie as actor/Bowie as icon: Authenticity versus iconography in Martin Scorsese's *The Last Temptation of Christ*   *Ian Dixon*   173

9   The surveillant power of the (a)temporal cameo in *Twin Peaks: Fire Walk with Me* (1992)   *Tyne Daile Sumner*   199

10   Loving the alienation: Bowie, *Basquiat*, Brecht   *Glenn D'Cruz*   219

11   Performative emotional symbolism and stylistic gesture in Christopher Nolan's *The Prestige*   *Toija Cinque*   237

12   'Just like the films': *Lazarus* and cinematic melancholia   *Denis Flannery*   253

Filmography 273
Discography 275
Bibliography 276
Index 295

FIGURES

1.1	Bowie performatively adopted a repertoire of feminized self-touching gestures and poses	30
1.2	Close-up shots of fans showed their emotional response	34
1.3	Bowie and three assistants collectively squeeze his skeletal frame into thigh-gripping striped pants	36
1.4	Bowie enhances his starlet pose with a feminine hair flick	37
1.5	For a split second, Bowie's eyes make contact with his film audience	38
1.6	A full-body shot displaying the spectacle of Bowie's costume	39
1.7	A silhouette shot displaying Bowie's figure in an ambiguously sexualized pose	40
1.8	A low-angle close-up shot emphasizing emotion during Bowie's performance of 'My Death'	40
1.9.1	Bowie's Kabuki mask-like face is fixed, staring into the distance	42
1.9.2	With overt 'sign language' like gestures, Bowie returns to the stage to sing 'Width of a Circle'	43
1.9.3	The Followspot accompanies Bowie's every move as he explores the 'wall' with the palms of his hands	43
1.9.4	The light from the Followspot grows and shrinks in empathy with the widening and narrowing of the crack between the doors	44

1.9.5	The spotlight expands in concert with the expanding guitars 45
1.9.6	Bowie waves his arms akin to the wings of an elegant eagle 45
3.1–3.2	Period photograph of the actual John Merrick and publicity bill from *The Elephant Man* (1980) 74
3.3–3.4	Bowie's bend – *Scary Monsters* (1980) album cover and Bowie onstage as Merrick in *The Elephant Man* (1980) 75
3.5–3.6	The parade of posed Bowies on stage in the 1970s 77
3.7–3.8	Bowie in the short mimed film *The Mask* (1969) and onstage performing in the Diamond Dogs tour (1974) 79
3.9–3.10	Stills from the music videos 'Look Back in Anger' (1979) and 'Fashion' (1980) 80
3.11–3.12	Manufacturing the posed: the inspiration of Roquairol by Erich Heckel (German, Dublin 1883–1970) and the proof sheet of photographer Masayoshi Sukita for the 'Heroes' (1977) album cover shoot 81
3.13–3.14	The posed versus the unposed: Bowie's posed 'Heroes' album cover (1977) versus Bruce Springsteen's unposed album cover for *The Wild, the Innocent & the E Street Shuffle* (1973) 82
3.15–3.16	The backstage inhabited clown: inner sleeve for the *Scary Monsters* album (1980) and contact sheet 84
3.17–3.18	A publicity still and Bowie in the black-box video of *The Elephant Man* (1980) 87
4.1	Screenshot of David Bowie performing 'Station to Station' in Christiane F 98

FIGURES

1.1 Bowie performatively adopted a repertoire of feminized self-touching gestures and poses 30

1.2 Close-up shots of fans showed their emotional response 34

1.3 Bowie and three assistants collectively squeeze his skeletal frame into thigh-gripping striped pants 36

1.4 Bowie enhances his starlet pose with a feminine hair flick 37

1.5 For a split second, Bowie's eyes make contact with his film audience 38

1.6 A full-body shot displaying the spectacle of Bowie's costume 39

1.7 A silhouette shot displaying Bowie's figure in an ambiguously sexualized pose 40

1.8 A low-angle close-up shot emphasizing emotion during Bowie's performance of 'My Death' 40

1.9.1 Bowie's Kabuki mask-like face is fixed, staring into the distance 42

1.9.2 With overt 'sign language' like gestures, Bowie returns to the stage to sing 'Width of a Circle' 43

1.9.3 The Followspot accompanies Bowie's every move as he explores the 'wall' with the palms of his hands 43

1.9.4 The light from the Followspot grows and shrinks in empathy with the widening and narrowing of the crack between the doors 44

FIGURES

1.9.5	The spotlight expands in concert with the expanding guitars 45
1.9.6	Bowie waves his arms akin to the wings of an elegant eagle 45
3.1–3.2	Period photograph of the actual John Merrick and publicity bill from *The Elephant Man* (1980) 74
3.3–3.4	Bowie's bend – *Scary Monsters* (1980) album cover and Bowie onstage as Merrick in *The Elephant Man* (1980) 75
3.5–3.6	The parade of posed Bowies on stage in the 1970s 77
3.7–3.8	Bowie in the short mimed film *The Mask* (1969) and onstage performing in the Diamond Dogs tour (1974) 79
3.9–3.10	Stills from the music videos 'Look Back in Anger' (1979) and 'Fashion' (1980) 80
3.11–3.12	Manufacturing the posed: the inspiration of Roquairol by Erich Heckel (German, Dublin 1883–1970) and the proof sheet of photographer Masayoshi Sukita for the 'Heroes' (1977) album cover shoot 81
3.13–3.14	The posed versus the unposed: Bowie's posed 'Heroes' album cover (1977) versus Bruce Springsteen's unposed album cover for *The Wild, the Innocent & the E Street Shuffle* (1973) 82
3.15–3.16	The backstage inhabited clown: inner sleeve for the *Scary Monsters* album (1980) and contact sheet 84
3.17–3.18	A publicity still and Bowie in the black-box video of *The Elephant Man* (1980) 87
4.1	Screenshot of David Bowie performing 'Station to Station' in Christiane F 98

FIGURES   xi

7.1   Promotional poster for 'Labyrinth' 153

7.2   What kind of magic spell to use? 161

7.3   The finger point through the fourth wall 161

7.4   The 'aggressive phallus' 162

7.5   Bowie the father? 163

7.6   The mock crowning of the carnival king 166

7.7   The disarming Jareth 167

7.8   The subsequent decrowning of the carnival king 168

8.1–8.6   Bowie's derivations in 'Heroes': *Close Encounters*, Brando and Hindu Goddess Parvati 182

8.7–8.8   Bowie's Baudelairean Marcus Aurelius, like Charlie Chaplin, he 'never simply stands, he *poses*' 183

8.9–8.10 Bowie's comb-down fringe as Barthes's 'self-righteousness, virtue and conquest'; his robes referencing Nikolai Ge's *What Is Truth?* (1831–91) 185

8.11   Bowie/Pilate's gest: 'Roman prefects stand like this' 186

8.12   Bowie politely explains: his anisocoric eyes denoting evil/madness in juxtaposition to his gentleness 190

8.13   Hristo Shopov's melodramatic Pilate in Mel Gibson's *The Passion of the Christ* (2004) 191

9.1   Agent Dale Cooper and Phillip Jeffries in the office hallway 200

11.1   Bowie-as-Tesla on stage 247

EDITORS

Ian Dixon completed his PhD on John Cassavetes at the University of Melbourne, Australia, in 2011 and currently lectures at NTU in Singapore. Ian publishes on Bowie, celebrity studies, cultural studies and film theory and delivers academic papers internationally including a plenary speech for CEA in the United States (2013) and a keynote in India (2016), recently winning best paper at CMCS conference, University of Southern California. He also acts and directs for film and television (including *Neighbours* and *Blue Heelers*), writes funded screenplays and novels and recently appeared in *Underbelly: Squizzy* on Channel 9 in Australia. His acting work can also be viewed in *City Homicide*, *Blue Heelers*, *Martial Law*, *Guinevere Jones*, *Heartbreak High*, *Struck by Lightning*, *Shadows of the Heart* and *Rush*.

Brendan Black is a Melbourne-based filmmaker, playwright and wine writer, with a master's in applied linguistics. He has written widely on wine, food, travel and film for titles such as *Gourmet Traveller Wine*, *Royalauto* and *Senses of Cinema*, and he is currently working on a book on independent wineries, breweries and distilleries of Victoria. He has premiered three plays through the Melbourne International Comedy Festival: *Trotsky and Friends* in 2016, *The Business of God* in 2021 and *Empathy Training* in 2022. He has also written, produced and directed eight short films, on topics such as clerical sexual abuse and asexuality. More information on his work can be found at his website: www.brendanblack.com.

Editorial assistant

Alexander Sun is a scholar and writer interested in aesthetics and urban spaces. With a background in sociology, Alex's current passion is his work with the BKAZ, a Singapore-based collective of like-minded scholars and creatives interested in making critical ideas from the humanities accessible and engaging to young people.

CONTRIBUTORS

Toija Cinque is Associate Professor in Media and Communication at Deakin University, Australia. Cinque's research encompasses celebrity, audience and reception studies, data cultures, studies in radical and participatory transparency/digital surveillance practices and dark social studies. As an aca-fan, Toija has written multiple research articles on David Bowie. Published and in press books include *The Fandom of David Bowie: Everyone Says 'Hi'* (co-written, 2019), *Enchanting David Bowie: Space, Time, Body, Memory* (co-edited, 2015; second edition, forthcoming) and *Materializing Digital Futures: Touch, Movement, Sound and Vision* (co-edited, 2022).

Amedeo D'Adamo currently teaches in the Directing and Producing tracks and is a creative mentor at the American Film Institute (AFI) in Los Angeles, United States. His published work includes essays on national anthems, TV sitcom music, music videos, David Bowie and Dante and reflects a fascination with how narrative encodes agency, empathy, nationalism, race and gender. His film and TV work focuses on how character and story are expressed through the crafts of production design, cinematography, editing, sound track and performance. Most recently he is the editor of *Producing for the Screen* (2020). He is also a filmmaker whose features have been to festivals such as Rome, Miami, Austin, Torino and others.

Glenn D'Cruz is an Associate Professor and Head of Art and Performance in the School of Communication and Creative Arts at Deakin University, Australia. He teaches theatre and cultural studies and dabbles in various artistic pursuits.

Denis Flannery is Associate Professor in English at the University of Leeds, UK. He is the author of *Henry James: A Certain Illusion* (2000) and *On Sibling Love: Queer Attachment and American Writing* (2007). In 2016 he co-edited *Alan Hollinghurst: Writing under the Influence*. Current projects include writing a book on the work of Ivo van Hove and editing *The Cambridge Companion to David Bowie*.

Mitch Goodwin is a media artist, curator and an academic with a research focus on digital aesthetics, media ecologies and cultures of automation. He has a diverse publication profile having outputs in the fields of cultural studies, critical media and digital anthropology. Mitch was the founding director of the Screengrab Media Arts Award and curator of the associated exhibition programme which interrogated the political and technical infrastructures of network culture. His creative works have screened internationally; however, his guitar strumming is barely heard beyond the bedroom door. Mitch currently holds an academic post at the University of Melbourne, Australia. #YNWA

Susanne Hillman earned her PhD in history from the University of California, San Diego, United States, with an emphasis on modern Germany. She is currently employed as a lecturer in the Department of History at San Diego State University. Her writing has been published in a wide variety of academic journals including *German Studies Review*, *Holocaust Studies*, the *Journal of the History of Ideas*, *Celebrity Studies*, *Soundings* and the *Journal of Women's History*. Hillman's eclectic research interests range from modern Germany and the Holocaust to popular culture including celebrity and fandom. She is a native of German-speaking Switzerland.

Dene October is a Senior Lecturer at the University of the Arts London, UK, teaching options like audiences, writing design and David Bowie studies. He studied fashion journalism at the London College of Fashion and won the London Fashion Week Graduate Journalism Award. He writes lifestyle features, academic articles, poetry and fiction – his recent horror story *Nippy* appears in the anthology *Folk Horror* (2021). He has contributed widely on David Bowie – including entries to *Bloomsbury Encyclopaedia of Film and Television Costume* (2023) – and British TV programme, *Doctor Who* – including the monogram *Marco Polo* and (as co-editor) the volume *Doctor Who and History*.

Lisa Perrott is Senior Lecturer and Programme Convener of Screen and Media Studies at the University of Waikato, New Zealand. She is co-editor, with Ana Cristina Mendes, of *Navigating with the Blackstar: The Mediality of David Bowie* (special issue of *Celebrity Studies*, 2019) and *David Bowie and Transmedia Stardom* (2019). Her publications include *Time Is Out of Joint: The Transmedial Hauntology of David Bowie* (2019) and *Music Video's Performing Bodies: Floria Sigismondi as Gestural Animator and Puppeteer* (2015). Her interests include animation, cultural studies and transmedia, with an emphasis on the relations between audio and visual media, popular music, music video and the avant-garde.

Sean Redmond is Professor of Screen and Design at Deakin University, Melbourne, Australia. He is the author of *Celebrity* (2019), *Liquid Space:*

Science Fiction Film and Television in the Digital Age (2017) and *The Cinema of Takeshi Kitano: Flowering Blood* (2013). He is the founding editor of *Celebrity Studies*, shortlisted for the best new academic journal in 2011.

Tyne Daile Sumner is a researcher and teacher at the University of Melbourne, Australia. Her work explores the relationship between literature and surveillance, with a focus on the ways that poetry is engaged with concepts such as privacy, identity, confession and subjectivity in the context of digital technology and the increasing datafication of everyday life.

FOREWORD

Acting as medium

The notion of acting is one that appears repeatedly in David Bowie's long career. The idea encompasses so much about him, his success and his personality, that it is difficult to know how to create a typology that matches his various changes and permutations. In general, we might say that Bowie emphasized at least two different approaches to acting: the kind of acting that he did on stage in concerts, in music videos and just generally as himself before the public (walking down the street, appearing on talk shows, etc.) and the acting he did in film and the occasional play (*The Elephant Man* (1979; performed by Bowie 1980–1), in particular). The former can be characterized as Brechtian, the gesture standing in for emotion and affect, the movements on stage or in the attenuated time frame of a video standing in place of character development or plot as we would normally have them. The music conveys the context, and Bowie, as an actor in these situations, has to complete the meaning visually with his body, props, set and, in the case of video, the surrealist style of compression and startling juxtapositions that he seems to have borrowed from Buñuel. In the more conventional film roles, Bowie comes closer to the Method style that we might associate with naturalistic acting, though even here, Bowie is rarely, if ever, one to blend into a scene. Far from being a chameleon, which adopts the colours of its environment, Bowie frequently contrasts with or stands out in almost any scene in which he appears – whether it is the bright red-orange hair of *The Man Who Fell to Earth* (1976) or the golden pompadour of *Merry Christmas, Mr. Lawrence* (1983), visually Bowie always hovers slightly above any filmic gestalt upon which he is placed, always at least slightly stylized and, thus, an actor who remains always a star, which raises the concomitant question, is he also, therefore, always an actor as well?

To an extent, yes. That is, he was always an actor in that he was comprised of at least two layers – the self (David Jones), the persona (David Bowie) and the persona's persona (Ziggy Stardust, et al.). Bowie said on numerous occasions that he could not have been a singer without a character, that going onstage was too terrifying without one. Eventually, the songs themselves explored the theatrical or cinematic aspects of these characters, which then leaked into the set designs, costumes and choreography that make Bowie's staged and filmed performances such multimedia affairs. In that sense, acting was essential to his interdisciplinary approach to the arts. While singing is the central text, the paratext is acting, which leads to the other strains of Bowie's aesthetics. The importance of acting is acknowledged at least by the time Bowie records *Hunky Dory* (1971), where he famously refers to himself on the album back cover as 'The Actor' and in the most famous song on the album, 'Changes', calls himself the 'faker'. By the next album, *Ziggy Stardust* (1972), the more specific influences on Bowie begin to emerge, ones that would guide him through the 1970s, at least – Andy Warhol, Japanese theatre and his earlier training in pantomime.[1] From this point on, Bowie's strengths as an actor were always to be in his control of the body, his ability to make meaning with his stance, his gestures and, in his manipulation of masks, his ability to suggest the artificiality of all acting, its inherent surface quality and alienation effect.

If acting was many things to Bowie, including, but not limited to, the model for everything he did, it could also be an excuse: that he wasn't a rock star but only plays one. Tied up in this claim is both the idea that he is above rock, or not limited to one modality or art form (he is a painter, for example, not just a musician), and that he sees the role of the rock star as always contingent. But as the 1970s rolled on, he seems to have often deferred acting except for the signature role in *The Man Who Fell to Earth*. In the 1980s he finally gave himself time to explore acting more thoroughly by starring in two films, *Merry Christmas, Mr. Lawrence* and *The Hunger* (1983), back to back. His imposed tax exile in Switzerland may have allowed acting to come to the foreground, maybe as songwriting seemed to have momentarily escaped him.

Acting was always central to his desire not only to be the one performing but also to see himself as a director. The film planned for the Diamond Dogs tour, or the live rock opera based on *Ziggy Stardust*, were ideas he continued to reference in interviews throughout his career. Only at the very end of his life did Bowie finally check this item off his bucket list in the form of *Lazarus* (2015) which, though he neither directed nor wrote it, he arranged for it to happen and found a form with which to create both a new play and a new setting for much of his own music. It is also a comment on and extension of his role in Nicolas Roeg's film and an attempt to write new music as well. That one of his best tracks on *Blackstar* (2016) has the same title shows the extent to which Bowie was inspired by this project. Other songs in the play were written for a possible follow-up to *Blackstar*. Though recorded, the album remains incomplete.

Over the span of his career, Bowie's acting fit a number of different subtypes: cameo appearances based on his fame from the 1980s (of which *The Linguini Incident* (1991) might consist of one long cameo); minor roles

(*The Last Temptation of Christ* (1988), *The Prestige* (2006) and others); and starring roles. While at his best in choreographing his characters' movements, such as the alienness and passivity of Jerome Newton in *The Man Who Fell to Earth* or Warhol's posture and walk in *Basquiat* (1996), he was not technically trained in acting. Towards the end of his acting career he seemed to embrace the sort of performances that relied on an internalization of character more in line with a Stanislavsky approach to naturalistic acting. But prior to this late phase, Bowie's acting in film seemed to rely much more on what he had learnt from the rock arena – the psychology of gesture and the Brechtian fusing of the character and the role that allows the viewer to see both the character and the creation of it by the performer so that the audience can examine both.[2] Brecht saw the alienation effect of his epic theatre as a way to teach the audience about the social forces that were at work on them, to avoid mystifying or mythologizing them through the use of psychology or subjectivity. While Bowie is perhaps never so openly political in his performance, he does refuse to get lost within his characters, to internalize them, and in that sense always invites his audience to see that a performance is about more than words. Bowie reconnected film or theatrical performance to the body, away from the interior life of realism, which is itself an invention of the nineteenth century, towards the expressionism of silent cinema, the face as a mask.[3]

While we might think of *The Man Who Fell to Earth* as his most enduring role, it may not be his best performance. If one compares a scene from this film to one in *The Hunger*, one can see how much his acting changed over time. In the first, Newton visits the home of Oliver Farnsworth (Buck Henry), a patent lawyer, to show him the technical innovations from his futuristic home planet, ones that will allow him the money to amass a fortune to launch a private space programme to bring water back to his dying world. Bowie waits all night for Henry to read the material. Bowie plays with his glasses and calls attention to his eyes, which will later be shown to be elaborate contact lenses covering a distinctly alien visage. Henry himself wears thick glasses and isn't allowed to drive a car. His alienness resides in his being gay and he becomes, after reading the technical specs, a partner in Newton's plans.

Roughly ten years later, Bowie plays another cold, determined, even cruel figure in John Blaylock in Tony Scott's *The Hunger*. While a horror film with its own high-art pretensions, it shows how much more comfortable Bowie has become with acting. Though never one to play a warm character, he manages to bring a determined sense of anguish to an equally mysterious character. Blaylock is the lover of a vampire (Catherine Deneuve) who dates back to ancient Egypt. She alternates lovers between men and women keeping them around for roughly 200 years, after which they suddenly begin to age quickly. They never die, however, and are instead entombed in the attic of her Manhattan townhouse. Bowie has another scene of waiting when he arrives at the office of a doctor, played by Susan Sarandon, who does geriatric research. Over the course of several intercut scenes, we see Blaylock ageing during the long time he is kept in the waiting room of the hospital, left to spend the latter half of his lifetime in a series of wasted hours. Bowie brings a poignancy to the performance, becoming, in front of us, an exasperated and angry old man who, when he finally meets the doctor, by accident, as he is leaving, excoriates her for her refusal to take him seriously. He rushes back to Deneuve, who ultimately carries him to his coffin in a scene that echoes one in *The Man Who Fell to Earth* when Candy Clark carries an equally supine Bowie to bed. Through tons of make-up and subtle movements of face, body and vocal changes, Bowie is able to make the transformation convincing. His time spent, especially, in the cast of *The Elephant Man* seems to have been time well spent when he was able to use his physical abilities as an actor, especially, to suggest John Merrick's own disabilities by adjusting his mouth, his stance and his voice to reflect the turned spine, fungoid skin and weight of enlarged body parts.[4] *The Hunger*, like much of Bowie's creativity in the 1980s, seems to reference his work in the 1970s, or at least to try to build upon it. Bowie was able to draw together his acting abilities to create seamless illusion in extreme characters: an alien from outer space, a vampire, a deformed man in Victorian London.

While we might see Bowie as a cinema actor who slowly evolved towards a more conventional player, his primary acting on the rock stage was always as an avant-gardist. He plays the part of Bowie as an artist. This approach is perhaps most clearly evident in his tour with Trent Reznor of Nine Inch Nails when Bowie debuted his new material from the album *Outside* (1995).[5] While superficially similar to Reznor's industrial rock, Bowie's music at that time owed more to experimental jazz and the cinematic sound experiments he had completed with Brain Eno in the Berlin era of his career. The long asymmetric pieces of music that Bowie performed from the album worked unexpectedly well performed live and Bowie doubled down in the concert to make the initial part of the tour, at least, as nakedly uncompromising as the album itself. Bowie sometimes sang with his back to the audience and performed songs in rapid succession, mostly from the album or songs from his back catalogue that seemed similar in spirit. The mood never changed and even songs that might have an ultimately uplifting message, such as 'Under Pressure', appear in this context to emphasize their serious side. The grim 'art-murders' of the album's narrative take precedence. And yet, amidst the gloom, Bowie performs a number from *Hunky Dory*, 'Andy Warhol', which is probably a tie-in at the time to his performance in *Basquiat*. The song is staged under a bright light that is lowered in place over a simple table and chair, which perhaps suggests an interrogation, but during the song's chorus, Bowie dances and the light flashes, though rather than a disco, Bowie looks like a puppet, his movements controlled, like a character in a flicker of film that is trying to come back into focus through a projector.⁶ His bare arms and skeletal make-up suggest the rotting flesh that is referenced in the songs on the new album. Yet, despite the severity of the spotlight that is shown on Bowie and the foregrounding of his body under harsh conditions, Bowie's swishy parody of Warhol's distinctive way of speaking, which we hear at the end, is comical. Bowie is doing his best ironic imitation of Warhol's voice, the same one he uses in the film. After all is said and done, we might think of Bowie not as an actor of either the Brechtian or the Method schools, or something in between, but as a comedian, perhaps in the French sense of *le comédien*, an actor with theatrical attributes who is adept at comedy. Anyone who has seen multiple interviews of Bowie knows him as someone who consistently cracks jokes, does funny voices and imitates various types. As he became more comfortable with himself and his life in the 1990s, especially, he seemed to revel in entertaining the people around him through a comic style of acting. In the closing credits to his promotional film for his *Black Tie, White Noise* album of 1993, he appears in costume as Buster Keaton doing a series of short sketches. Keaton's physicality, his blank mask-like face that rarely registers emotion and his association with silent film are, in a sense, the key to Bowie's own acting abilities. He is, finally, not a tragic figure, however serious his art often was, but a comic one – a clown who made us see life from an artificial perspective, but one that was only deceptively tragic. Perhaps Bowie's ultimate message was an upbeat one, even on his last album.⁷

Bowie exists for us now as absence. From 'Starman' to *Blackstar*, his gravitational pull remains strong. In David Lynch's *Twin Peaks: The Return* (2017), Bowie exists only as sound and vision. Lynch originally wanted Bowie to reprise his role of Jeffries from the original Twin Peaks film, but Bowie's health made that impossible. The character of Jeffries is replaced on the show first with the voice of actor Nathan Frizzell and then with a large mechanical vessel created by Lynch himself. Always a fan of Lynch's first film, *Eraserhead* (1977), it is fitting that his last major film appearance is as a device that would have been right at home in that film's surreal industrial design. It is clear from the plot of the third season that Jeffries is the link that ties much of it together, and that Bowie's absence forced Lynch to adapt in a creative way. Like *Blackstar*, *The Return* is, among other things, a show about dying and leaving. Many of the actors in the series, both series regulars, such as Catherine E. Coulson and Miguel Ferrer, and guest stars, such as Harry Dean Stanton, made posthumous appearances on the show. Here as on *Blackstar*, Bowie tugs at the space-time continuum. He lives on as influence and presence. Perhaps that was always his greatest gift – what he represented, what we made out of him as opposed to any one performance. While his best subject matter was always himself – from 'Ashes to Ashes' to *Blackstar* – the latter allowed him finally to return to the greatness of *Scary Monsters* (1980), arguably his last masterpiece before the final album.

One of the threads that runs through this collection is the notion of Bowie's performances fusing with his life – that the referentiality is always self-referential. Or, perhaps, that it is not possible, after a point in his career, to separate him, or his iconicity, from the performance of a character on the screen. All performances by Bowie are, at some level, about the performance of David Bowie, or of the life of the man who 'plays' him. That Bowie stepped out of this role after his heart attack to become, finally, or again, David Jones adds yet another level to how we might now reflect on his cinematic roles.

Acting is underappreciated in Bowie's biography and undertheorized in academic studies of Bowie where it is not looked at thoroughly enough. With the recent advent of Bowie studies, this situation is beginning to change. This volume fills a need as we begin a more systemic analysis of his many contributions. The writing here mirrors the multiplicity of approaches that Bowie brought to the arena of acting – Eastern influences, queer aesthetics, the notion of personality that comes from rock music, to name only a few that he highlights. This book argues that the new approaches to acting and performance that Bowie himself embodied be taken seriously as a singular influence not only on musical performance but on stage and screen as well. The variety of films, clips and performances discussed here are seen through a wide variety of theoretical lenses and approaches, some of which contradict each other just as Bowie's many permutations themselves require a great deal of erudition on the part of scholars of Bowie. But it is a testament to the richness of Bowie's legacy that we can mine it for so much in terms of performance, which is the central hub of everything that is, and was, David Bowie.

Shelton Waldrep

Notes

1 Note James Naremore's discussion of shaving: if this real-life activity is done on stage or film, within a narrative, it becomes acting. If it is mimed without a razor, it is '"pure" imitation' or '*mimetic gesturality*' (*Acting in the Cinema* (Berkeley: University of California Press, 1988), 27). This idea can be applied to Bowie's miming of a shave, cigarette and final cup of tea before he goes to his execution in *Merry Christmas, Mr. Lawrence*.

2 For more on the differences between externalized and internalized acting, and the fact that the distinction itself might be a false dichotomy, see Counsell, chapter three, and Naremore, chapters two and three. While Brecht championed mime as another alienation technique, as Counsell notes, Brecht differentiated between 'mime' and 'gesture': 'We shall term this separation of the character into actor and role the *gestic split*, and, after signs of social relations, it is the second essential feature of Gestus' (Colin Counsell, *Signs of Performance:*

An Introduction to Twentieth-Century Theatre (New York: Routledge, 1996), 96). The tradition of 'heteroglossia' created by Brecht blends bits of artifice from several cultures and time periods and 'draws other elements of a production into the same fractured reading' (ibid., 104). The attitude of the actor cannot be divorced from the 'signs' that make up the role. The meaning has to be completed by the audience, especially as the performance pertains to the world. The actor merely offers an 'opinion' for the audience to examine (quoted in ibid., 105). '[T]he spectator must take a position outside of all the performance's discourses' (ibid., 106). This description of the actor's centrality to what is actually a three-part structure is a useful way of understanding Bowie's performances both in film and elsewhere. Naremore, referencing Brecht, notes that 'an actor should always behave as if he were quoting' (*Acting in the Cinema*, 18).

3   Naremore, *Acting in the Cinema*, 50.
4   Merrick's first name was actually Joseph, but John is used in the play.
5   Bowie's performance on this tour might well be thought of as nihilistic and closer in feel to Beckett than to Brecht. Bowie suggests that all performance is metaperformance and that life itself is a form of theatre. Reality is formed from signs which are themselves empty signifiers that suggest an endless loop of self-referentiality. See Counsell, *Signs of Performance*, 138.
6   For more on the cinematic aspects of gesture, see Giorgio Agamben, 'Notes on Gesture', in *Means Without End: Notes on Politics*, trans. Vincenzo Binetti and Cesare Casarino (Minneapolis: University of Minnesota Press, 2000), 49–62; and Andrew Burke, 'The Perfect Kiss: New Order and the Music Video', in *Music/Video: Histories, Aesthetics, Media*, ed. Gina Arnold, Daniel Cookney, Kirsty Fairclough and Michael Goddard (New York: Bloomsbury, 2017), 79–90.
7   Agamben and Naremore also discuss the importance of the notion of the comical to the idea of gesture, as can be seen in the gag (Agamben, 'Notes on Gesture', 59–60) and the performances of Chaplin. In terms of the latter, Naremore notes that '[a]t every level his costuming is built on a set of formal contrasts that signify he is an art object, a figure who says, "I am an actor"' (*Acting in the Cinema*, 16). Indeed, 'He never stands, he *poses*' (ibid., 17). 'Chaplin . . . was . . . so intent on exhibiting the virtuosity of theatrical movement that he is nearly always more stylized and poetically unnatural than the people he plays alongside' (ibid.).

ACKNOWLEDGEMENTS

This book germinated as an idea after the *Bowie Symposium: The Stardom and Celebrity of David Bowie* at the Australian Centre for the Moving Image in July 2015.[1] The event was the brainchild of Toija Cinque, Sean Redmond and Angela Ndalianis representing Deakin University and the University of Melbourne as an attachment to the Victoria and Albert Museum's *David Bowie Is* exhibition, which found its Australian home in Melbourne. At the symposium, this several-hundred-strong collection of aca-fans, artists and scholars celebrated what was then an under-researched arena of Bowie studies – not knowing we were just six months away from Bowie's unexpected demise.

The symposium organizers welcomed us with a stirring rendition of Bowie's 'Heroes' by operatic tenor Marco Cinque and composer David Kram, before Will Brooker of Kingston University – then midway through his legendary year posing as the poseur himself – gave the keynote address in his hybrid Thin White Duke/Thomas Jerome Newton blonde/Hot Red Schwarzkopf hairdo,[2] fuelled by Bowie's infamous mid-1970s diet of chillies and milk. It was my honour to then present the first paper of the symposium on David Bowie's performance and performativity as a screen actor in *The Man Who Fell to Earth* (1976) – a subject which later became a central focus for this book.

Each night of the *Bowie Symposium*, we discussed, we revelled and we danced to Bowie songs performed live by Geraldine Quinn, Jeff Duff, *The Thin White Ukes* and others. Scholars and fans bonded and celebrated what it meant to be inspired by this twentieth- and twenty-first-century icon whose career spanned fifty years in the public eye. During that time, a spark was ignited: an invitation to delve into increasingly complex analyses of Bowie. After many conversations with academics who eventually became close friends as well as contributors to this present volume – notably, Amedeo D'Adamo, Toija Cinque, Denis Flannery, Mitch Goodwin, Lisa Perrott, Sean Redmond and Tyne Daile Sumner – I returned to lecturing and realized that no one had dedicated a volume to the analysis of Bowie as a film actor. This book subsequently manifested with editorial by linguist Brendan Black and I, including the invaluable editorial assistance of Alexander Sun, attracted contributors and now augments the growing corpus of film performance and celebrity scholarship on David Bowie. The volume soon found its title: in true Bowie style 'borrowing' a lyric, as Ana Mendes and Lisa Perrott reiterate, from the song 'Blackstar', in which Bowie 'set the record straight about which type of star he is: [i.e. Bowie is] . . . not a film star'.[3]

The long process of bringing this book to print could not have been done without my long-suffering and inexhaustible colleague and co-editor Brendan Black, who credits the loving support of Clare, Gabriel and Pascal for getting him through the arduous journey. We both pay full credence to Alexander Sun whose dedication to editorial on the book went far beyond his job description as assistant to the editors. Especial thanks to Alex's significant other, Tessa Kaur, and to his mother. Further, the book would not have been completed without the assistance of the Wee Kim Wee School of Information and Communication at Nanyang Technological University and the Workforce Singapore's (WSG) SGUnited Traineeship Programme fund which paid Alex's wage.

Without a doubt, the guidance and support of our publisher Katie Gallof of Film and Media Studies at Bloomsbury Academic, along with her assistant editor Erin Duffy, was exemplary – we wish all editorials could be so amenable and personable. Katie and Erin's professionality and vision made this a smooth process indeed.

We owe a great deal to the collegiality and friendship of our colleagues at Wee Kim Wee, especially the compassion and scholarship of our chair, May O. Lwin and her predecessor Charles 'Chuck' Salmon and the associate chairs Lee Chei Sian, Jung Younbo, Edson Tandoc and Dion Goh, along with Ang Peng Hwa and Alton Chua Yeow Kuan. I would especially like to thank Lee Sangjoon – the man is a veritable river of knowledge and encouragement. To the good humour of Andrew Duffy and his family, Harry, Barnaby, Sam and Caroline. Gerard Goggin and Jacqueline Clark along with Liam and Bianca. Especial thanks to the Wee Kim Wee film department: Liew Kai Khiun, Ella Raidel, Nikki Draper, Kym Campbell and Stephen Teo along with Teo Hee Kwang Vincent, Allan Ooi Cheong, Joseph Yee and all those wonderful techies. Also thanks to Lee Kwan Min, Chris Khoo, Andy Prahl, Sonny Rosenthall, Jessica Tan and our colleagues in other schools and departments: Saritha Samudrala and Aravind Dasari, Lisa Winstanley, Bilal Saddik, Janelle Thompson, Eric Hill, Ella Thompson, Jessie Thompson, Sunny Low, Quek Yee Ser Sharon, Yanti Bte Aris, Nur'Aisyah Bte Ahamad Mukthar, Goy Yi Ru, Ang Sey Min, Tan Sian Ting and the NTU Medical Humanities Cluster, especially Melvin Chen and Graham John Matthews. Especial thanks to the tireless academic staff at WKWSCI: Karin Loh May Ling, Tan Hanjie Alvin, Nithiyah d/o Muthukrishnan, Shireen Lai, Karen Boh and Sim Sor Hui and Jacqueline Goi Way Ling. To the tireless library staff at NTU and all the amazing 'Wee Kid' students who inspire us daily – especially my friends Jing Tong Lau, Sheryl Chua and Choy Mei Yen.

ACKNOWLEDGEMENTS

A special thanks to all our supporters, Andrea Baker, Victoria Broackes, Will Brooker, Sophia L. Deboick, Ian Chapman, Shannon Finck, Hans Peter Frühauf, Lisa Gotto, Grady Hancock, Alexandra Heller-Nicholas, Glenn Hendler, John Hipwell, Leah Kardos, Gillian Leslie, Geoffrey Marsh, Angela Ndalianis, Tanja Stark, Adam Rudegeair, Inga Walton, Julie Lobalzo Wright and the mellifluous scholarship of Shelton Waldrep. Thanks also to Frank, Allison and everyone at Kumbada for tolerating my endless references to Bowie and to Nigel and Imogen Hall for her ongoing comparisons with her friend Iggy Pop.

We also take this opportunity to praise the inspiration of the theatre and filmmakers whose privilege was to work with David Bowie including Alan Clarke, Uli Edel, Christiane Felscherinow, Ricky Gervais, Jack Hofsiss, Lindsay Kemp, Nicholas Kendall, David Lynch, Stephen Merchant, Christopher Nolan, Nagisa Ōshima, D. A. Pennebaker, Nicolas Roeg, Martin Scorsese, Tony Scott, Richard Shepard, Ben Stiller and Ivo Van Hove. While on the subject of inspiration, especially thanks to my wonderful lecturers back at Flinders and Adelaide University, in particular George Anderson, Julie Holledge, Michael Morley, Noel Purdon and Michael Fuller. My peers at SAE Institute: Adrian Bruch, Tim Dalton, Sian Mitchell, Adam Parker, Stella Tan, Justine Wallace, Phil Wilkinson, Nick Wilson, Darcy Yuille as well as Darren, Dave, Jen, Lance, Robbie and Trinski. Thanks to the ever-changing Victorian College of the Arts, University of Melbourne – especially Chris Magill and Jenny Sabine. On that note, I must acknowledge the passion and level-headed guidance of my mentors: Toija Cinque, Lisa Dethridge, Rodney Hall, Leon Marvell, Neil Murphy, Colin Perry and Sean Redmond. Thanks also to Stephen Mitchell – the man who made me a hardcore Bowie fan by playing *Moonage Daydream* full bore while I was blindfolded. Robbie Ratan and (Jean-)Jeanne Loh, Thelo, Atticus, Fibonacci and Pascal – thanks from the 'funniest adult in Singapore' and especially for the Bowie doll. Priya Mendis and Oliver Perera, Ged Cogley and the Asian Film Archives, Singapore.

To the incredible inspiration of my Mum and Dad, Elaine and Les Dixon, and my atypical siblings, Brier, Michael and Glenda – I thank you. With great respect, the ongoing influence and parasocial relationships with David Bowie, Iman Abdulmajid, Alexandria and Duncan Jones. Further thanks to the dedication of Tony Visconti, Brian Eno, Mike Garson, Iggy Pop and Claudette Corbet. All the young dudes and gender benders we have crossed paths with: the artists, the fans and aca-fans including the inimitable Bowie-ites in the *Bowie Downunder* Fanclub, especially its convener Adam Robert Jones-Dean and his associates: Bruce Butler, Louise Coulter, Cass Moore and Harry Williams. Div Collins, Bec Johnston, Nick Peters, Sarah Tarr and *The Thin White Ukes* also deserve a mention.

Finally, to Topaz and to the love, the *Sound and Vision* of Sheersha Perera and Ranishka Autumn Perera Dixon who champions *The Laughing Gnome* and sang *Space Oddity* for my fiftieth birthday when she was just three. You are my deepest colleagues. Thank you.

Notes

1. acmi.net.au/bowie-symposium; #bowiesymposium.
2. D. October, 'The Man Who Fell to Earth', in *Bloomsbury Encyclopaedia of Film and Television Costume Design*, ed. D. Landis (New York: Bloomsbury, 2021).
3. David Bowie, Blackstar, Sony Music 88875173871, 2016; Ana Cristina Mendes and Lisa Perrott, 'Introduction: Navigating with the Blackstar: The Mediality of David Bowie', *Celebrity Studies* 10, no. 1 (2019): 4–13.

Introduction

Ian Dixon and Brendan Black

Bowie's influence is the stuff of legend. While acknowledging that Bowie's performance acumen spans rock shows, performance art, video clips and interviews, the nucleus of this book remains with his canon of narrative feature films. Bowie's beginnings as an experimenter par excellence in the 1960s, drawing on other art forms and genres with relevance to cinematic performance, are also noted. Rock 'n' roll, literature, fine arts and theatre became fertile ground for the Bowie-performer, still seeking his burgeoning identity and his famous stage personae. As such, the acquired skills Bowie brings to screen performance incorporate his development through theatre, mime and television series to exploit his megastar iconicity. Despite Bowie's personal misgivings about his acting (and notwithstanding his capricious delight in confounding his interviewers on the subject), Bowie draws on pantomime, persona and mime compellingly within and beyond both naturalistic and expressionistic texts/images.

This book contextualizes Bowie as a figure whose notoriety precedes him – a cultural figure signifying a self-constructed aesthetic and performative Otherness. As Bowie, the artist, notably shed the skin of David Jones, established himself as a maverick of gender transformation and eventually exploited his own megastar status for countless cultural affects, clever directors of stage and screen such as Jack Hofsiss, Christopher Nolan and Martin Scorsese exploited the iconic/ironic space alien's self-invention in their creation of meaning on screen; Bowie was never simply Bowie or the personae he established on stage (*Ziggy Stardust*, *Halloween Jack*, *The Thin White Duke*, *Screaming Lord Byron*, etc.). Nor was he just the characters he played on film or the personal shell of Jones he had publicly discarded. He was a culturally relevant floating signifier, an amalgam, a formidable presence, an absence and an unrivalled legacy. Despite his notable artistic eclecticism, on film he never quite disappeared into the role as would be befitting of a Method actor nor simply drew attention to his self-as-signifier like a Brechtian actor might, nor did he appear only 'as himself' as some scholars claim.[1] Indeed, Bowie formed a synthesis of performance and performativity, actor and role, star image, personae and assumed person: always liminal, always fresh, never formulaic, never a stock character, even in jaded archetypes such as the ironically colourless singing of Jack Sikora in *Il mio West/Gunslinger's Revenge* (1998). Bowie remained, in screen performance, a slippery fusion of all the above and more.

Bowie's film performances may have diverse effects and stem from contrasting opportunities linked to directors with varied talent, but all his screen performances generate an ocular phenomenon of particular note and, as this volume attests, are worthy of deeper analysis. Bowie's screen performance acumen began with his mime training with Lindsay Kemp and spilled over into his own intellectual appreciation of film as an artform beyond the craft of acting, having penned screenplays himself and taught his son, filmmaker Duncan Jones, about cinema.[2] According to Waldrep, creations such as the unwieldy *Diamond Dogs* stage show borrowed from the 'dark dystopianism' of German expressionist cinema, especially Robert Wiene's *Das Cabinet des Dr. Caligari* (1920) and Fritz Lang's *Metropolis* (1927).[3] With a rare respect for film form, Bowie moved into filmic performance.

Review of literature

I'm Not a Film Star: David Bowie as Actor has consulted the growing corpus of academic literature dedicated to Bowie as a cultural icon, yet also locates a gap in the field, specifically regarding Bowie as a film actor. The following books contemplate related ideas but do not engage the specific texts or analytical processes of *I'm Not a Film Star*. These source texts provide a vital scholarly launching pad for the arguments embedded within the upcoming pages. From the perspective of interdisciplinary scholars, this volume objectively assesses most of Bowie's noteworthy feature films while avoiding the often-myopic field of 'professional' cinema and acknowledging the fluidity of Bowie's talent.

At the time of the *Bowie Symposium: The Stardom and Celebrity of David Bowie* at the Australian Centre for the Moving Image in July 2015,[4] there had been only a handful of scholarly texts on Bowie, notably: Shelton Waldrep's 2004 book *The Aesthetics of Self-Invention: Oscar Wilde to David Bowie*; *David Bowie Is*, edited by Victoria Broackes and Geoffrey Marsh in 2013; Eoin Devereaux, Aileen Dillane and Martin J. Power's 2015 collection *David Bowie: Critical Perspectives*; and Toija Cinque, Christopher Moore and Sean Redmond's *Enchanting David Bowie: Space/Time/Body/Memory*, also published in 2015. With the *Bowie Symposium* an exciting field within celebrity studies emerged: the art, stardom and cultural influence of the future legend – David Bowie.

Despite rising critical attention on Bowie as rock musician and performer, aesthetic and cultural icon, specific scholarly attention to Bowie as a film actor is still limited to Cinque, Ndalianis and Redmond's 'In Focus: David Bowie On-Screen'.[5] However, there are scholarly precedents to our book worth mentioning also. *I'm Not a Film Star* owes much to the work of Philip Auslander in his book on Bowie and theatrical performance, *Performing Glam Rock*. Auslander's research in cultural and media studies concentrates on authenticity in rock music, a position determined by the 'counterculture's antitheatricalism' and rock music's 'antiocular bias'.[6] Auslander's reference to the high priest of performance theory, Richard Schechner, illustrates that performance is 'always a matter of the performers not being themselves',[7] which precipitates Auslander's comment that 'David Bowie is not David Jones, yet he also is not not David Jones, as suggested by the fact that the name David Bowie belongs now to both the real person and the performance persona'.[8] Auslander opines that glam rock's 'overt and self-conscious theatricality presents clear and dramatic cases of the creation and presentation of performance personae by popular musicians'.[9] The author thereby exposes Bowie (along with Marc Bolan) as a theatrical presence and instigator of a unique rock movement and traces resistance to glam rock's inauthenticity back to the hippie movement and psychedelic rock of the late 1960s. Auslander opines:

> The ideology of authenticity mandated that musicians appear on stage as themselves, not as any other persona or character, and discouraged forms of overtly theatrical performance that would emphasize the differences between performers and spectators.[10]

These are rock conventions Bowie flagrantly ignored.

As is often quoted by Bowie scholars, Ziggy is the invention of Bowie and Bowie is the invention of David Jones, but this inventory of masks is problematic for reading Bowie as a film actor. To his credit, Auslander cites Colin Counsell as a successful semiotician whose analysis becomes pivotal for reading Bowie. Auslander points out that *commedia dell'arte* informed Bowie's inclusion of improvisatory mime acts in performances (including his short film *The Mask* (Malcolm J. Thomson, 1969)), which further alienates his countercultural critics (especially in *Merry Christmas, Mr. Lawrence* where, according to Mark Kermode, Bowie's shaving scene is simply 'pompous, pretentious and boring').[11]

Other authors describe glam rock as necessarily flamboyant. Accordingly, *I'm Not a Film Star* draws upon Peter Doggett and Barney Hoskyns, key authors on Bowie, glam and performance. The genius of glam rock, opines Barney Hoskyns, is that it is 'all about stardom'.[12] Targeting glam's camp edge, Hoskyns cites Susan Sontag's *Notes on Camp* as celebrating the Bowie-esque 'swooning, slim, sinuous figures of

Pre-Raphaelite painting and poetry'.[13] Further to the problem is Bowie's inclusion of mime skills from his association with the sexually provocative Kemp (who considered the young artist as both a joy and a 'load of shit').[14] Bowie as a film actor clearly transcends his *kabuki*-inspired mime and glam rock, yet his cultural value cannot be disentangled from the glitz of stage make-up.

Paul Morley's unique impressionistic biography *The Age of Bowie* and Brooker's ongoing interrogation of Bowie's performances also apply to the film readings in this book. Brooker's autoethnographic studies, particularly *Why Bowie Matters*, interrogate the *Bowie that is* and the *Bowie he might have been* as a cultural icon and meaning maker – even posthumously. From the megastar's beginnings, Brooker traces the places and spaces of Bowie's youth like a fan pilgrimage,[15] particularizing the megastar's early struggles while speculating whether premature success might have hampered the ambitious vision that constitutes David Bowie's remarkable oeuvre. Besides some exacting analyses of Bowie's songs, however, Brooker makes only passing reference to Bowie as a film actor.

Other recent publications such as Mendes and Perrott's 2019 collection *Navigating with the Blackstar: The Mediality of David Bowie* assert that, in associated art forms, and despite his death, Jones/Bowie 'continues to shine with a distinctive luminosity and navigational function'.[16] While resisting glib definitions of mediality (loosely speaking, a shift in focus from media as technology to the exigencies of mediation), Mendes and Perrott draw upon Marshall McLuhan's approach including Norm Friesen's (2013) reference to media as a 'constellation'. Mendes and Perrott encourage their contributors to dream large on the 'kaleidoscopic aspect of Bowie's approach to stardom' in powerful and surprising manner to explode the Bowie universe. As such, 'Bowie is examined; as a medium, becoming a medium, transiting across media platforms, inciting processes of remediation, and mediating his audience's engagement with time, space, celebrity, stardom, spectrality and death'.[17] Film is just one of the artforms Mendes and Perrott celebrate to trace the mediality of the star.

Most significantly, Toija Cinque, Christopher Moore and Sean Redmond's *Enchanting David Bowie: Space/Time/Body/Memory* provides excellent analysis of Bowie as a cultural phenomenon. Although deconstructing the iconography of Bowie in such video clips as 'Let's Dance' and evaluating the meaning behind films like *The Man Who Fell to Earth*, *Enchanting David Bowie* does not engage with performance methodology in the manner of this current volume. The formidable academic team behind *Enchanting David Bowie* also edited a volume of *Continuum: Journal of Media & Cultural Studies* for Routledge entitled *Intersecting David Bowie*, which utilizes Paul du Gay's (1997) 'circuit of culture model' to examine Bowie's role in 'how cultural forms are established, maintained, circulated and circumnavigated'.[18] Joined by Ndalianis, the team features Bowie as a film actor for 'In Focus',[19] but their attention to film acting is not dedicated to Bowie's entire oeuvre as this current volume is.[20] *In Focus* also concentrates on Bowie's cultural meaning rather than investigations of the actor's interior choices.

On its own terms, Devereux, Dillane and Power's *Critical Perspectives* is an exploration of Bowie as an independent social, historical, political and cultural event. In the editors' declaration, the analysis is neither exhaustive nor referential to acting theory. Instead, *Critical Perspectives* concentrates on psychoanalytic, Jungian, cultural and critical readings of mostly musical texts featuring fandom, Otherness, Japonism and Nihilism. The volume visits just three Bowie film texts: Mehdi Derfoufi's analysis of stardom in *Merry Christmas, Mr. Lawrence*; Julie Lobalzo Wright's influential reification of Richard Dyer's theories in *The Extraordinary Rock Star as Film Star*; and Dene October's Deleuzean analysis in *The (becoming-wo) Man Who Fell to Earth*, a work which underpins his exceptional chapter in this present volume. In that same volume, Usher and Fremaux emphasize that authenticity is 'not a property *of*, but something we ascribe *to* a performance' and that authenticity cannot be 'fixed'.[21] They establish a vital premise for *I'm Not a Film Star*: the 'hyperreal simulations of "David Bowie"' actually present '*who* he really is. Performing "the other" *is* his authentic self'.[22]

The nature of authenticity haunts Bowie through his space alien/glam rock past and into film performances that appear to be fixated on post-Method procedures. Qualifying such notions of authenticity, Shelton Waldrep's *The Aesthetics of Self-Invention* offers a phenomenological study of Bowie's performativity at the nexus of art and life. In *Future Nostalgia: Performing David Bowie* Waldrep focuses on the personae at the core of David Bowie's performances on stage. Waldrep focuses on Bowie's musical and aural output with some reference to films, including an excellent analysis of queerness and imperialism in *Merry Christmas, Mr. Lawrence*. This is the point where *I'm Not a Film Star: David Bowie as Actor* begins.

The scholars and aca-fans in this volume use varying methodological techniques to objectively critique the 'cracked actor' on film. As such, Bowie's uncanny ability to enmesh various performance modalities within and alongside the iconicity of stardom, rather than limiting his approach to a singular naturalistic acting 'talent', is viewed from a cinematic performance stance. Both the star's personal acting protocols and his capacity for controlling the meaning generation of his filmed image are acknowledged. Beyond scholarly insight into Bowie as performer, such as Usher and Fremaux, debate still highlights performative 'authenticity' rather than looking at how Bowie mimes, mimics, implicates and engages his unique screen and stage presence within a modern context. Indeed, the effects of mimicry and iconicity combined are almost totally ignored in contemporary naturalistic acting theory. This book uses Bowie as a vehicle to implicate meaning through embedded signage, Stanislavskian performance signs and Chekhovian 'language of gesture' rather than outmoded modernist claims to inherent emotional understanding of filmic text or, as Cinque cites of Plato in *Parmenides*, 'everything has a class and an absolute essence'.[23] In this way, *I'm Not a Film Star* takes a critical stance on these phenomena to expose the hypocrisies of modern acting modalities in the manner of Counsell's account and cross-examines the on-screen significance of a meaning-making entity like Bowie.

The scope of this book therefore begins with David Bowie as practical performer in feature films and ends with the actor/character/person interface. While the various chapters involve differing foci, all are embedded in Bowie's on-screen performances. Further to scholarly texts, the plethora of commercial biographical material on Bowie tends to underrepresent the importance of the star's filmic output. Charles Sandford's *Bowie: Loving the Alien* and George Tremlett's 1997 book *David Bowie: Living on the Brink* sporadically consider Bowie as actor but do not consider deeper theoretical notions beyond a casual appreciation and avoid any finessed understanding of the craft of performance. Indeed, Wendy Leigh's estimation of Bowie as 'Method' actor is simply incorrect. Paul Trynka's (2011) *Starman: David Bowie – The Definitive Biography* discusses Bowie as an actor from the point of view of professional peers in theatre, yet still appeals to aggrandizing notions of fandom.

By considering all of Bowie's keynote feature film texts, therefore, our scholars deconstruct, reconstruct and analyse the methodologies and filmic conventions behind Bowie's performances and critique his appearance on screen as semiotic, sensual, even seductive. The celebrated academics in this volume analyse these Bowie films from a philosophical, phenomenological, performative, historical, celebrity studies, theatrical and cinematic perspective with expressed focus on contributing to contemporary film and performance theory. The volume traces Bowie's evolving art and popularity from performer to the (meta-discursive) alter ego in the service of stardom and on to megastar as contemporary cultural icon. The book's chronological treatment of his performances allows equal emphasis on celebrated films such as *The Prestige*, *Merry Christmas, Mr. Lawrence* as well as his cult hits *Labyrinth* (which inspired a new wave of fandom in younger generations) and *The Man Who Fell to Earth*.

Modalities and disciplinary fields

I'm Not a Film Star draws upon a multitude of interdisciplinary theories consulting performance experts from Bertolt Brecht to Constantin Stanislavski. A danger for Bowie scholarship is that it slips through a crack in the sky and falls between theories without providing due respect to their academic sources. On this note, Auslander points out that performance studies can be unconstructively divisive. Noting the breadth of Bowie scholarship, then, Auslander opines:

> Although performance analysis is a semiotic enterprise at heart, theater scholars' flirtation with the technical vocabulary of semiotics, popular during the 1970s, has largely dissipated in favor of a less 'scientific', more eclectic set of approaches drawn from reception theory, phenomenology, cultural anthropology, sociology, feminist theory, cultural and literary theory, and other theoretical orientations.[24]

While the field of reference for this book may seem broad, so are the cultural references of the megastar we investigate. As Waldrep suggests, only an interdisciplinary study can do justice to 'someone who has not only come from the "low" art form of rock n roll but who has affected so many forms of art simultaneously',[25] including acting and film. With an emphasis on Bowie's 'role-playing and use of character voices',[26] for example, Waldrep consults five separate disciplines in his art-historical take on performance studies.[27] Following this, it is necessary to briefly define and cover the various disciplines that intertwine within this book, notably: film acting; semiotic analysis as film theory; performance and acting theory; celebrity studies; sensorial readings of cinema; critical historicity; philosophy; and psychoanalysis and include terminologies such as acting persona mask mimicry and performance.

Most importantly, in relating Bowie directly to the specific craft of film acting, *I'm Not a Film Star* responds to the seminal text *Acting in the Cinema* by James Naremore and considers Counsell's argument on the hypocrisies of modern performance theory in his book *Signs of Performance: An Introduction to Twentieth-Century Theatre*.[28] Naremore locates cinematic acting within the greater body of theatrical tradition, pointing out the specifics of film performance. He suggests that formal acting places human behaviour into a theatrical context. Based on Erving Goffman's analysis, Naremore categorizes people appearing on film in three ways: performers projecting a theatrical persona, celebrities inhabiting theatrical representations of themselves and 'documentary evidence'.[29] Whether a person is aware of the camera or not, they nevertheless present evidence of role play.

For Naremore, twentieth-century acting convention tends towards psychological interests. In transposing the interests of acting into the cinema, Naremore describes how the film experience creates a hitherto unprecedented illusion whereby the 'existential bond' between audience and actor is permanently destroyed.[30] Naremore defines such performance in two categories, 'presentational' and 'representational', pointing out cinema's preference for representational conventions.³¹ *I'm Not a Film Star* adopts Naremore's definitions of representational as filled with the inner life of the actor and presentational (or indicative) as either theatrical artifice or rhetorical device. Presentational acting is particularly inappropriate to film in that the camera amplifies any lack of psychological authenticity making it unpalatable to the modern spectator.

In *Signs of Performance*, Counsell outlines key acting methodologies – notably, Brecht, Strasberg and Stanislavski. Counsell also highlights the shortfalls of these acting theories using their own claims as investigative tools. For Counsell, there is nothing innate about our understanding of performed emotion. Whereas Stanislavski contends that emotions are instantly recognizable and transcend all cultural boundaries, Counsell asserts that we learn to speak performance codes like language. This implies that emotions are indeed read, not merely recognized. Gestures adopted by Lee Strasberg's Method actors are an attempt to avoid symbolism of any kind. The psychotherapeutic nature of Strasberg's approach to performance takes precedence over communicability and renders its practitioners victims of an 'iconography of neurosis' which, far from being naturally understood, presents a 'rich mist of generalised signs of the psyche'.³² Other actors worldwide who are not Method school still copy the gestures and signs in deference, sometimes with a complete absence of inner process. The conventions suggested and critiqued by Counsell and Naremore are crucial to an understanding of Bowie as performer, which brings us to celebrity scholarship.

Most importantly, *I'm Not a Film Star* consults celebrity theory, which P. David Marshall sees as deriving, in turn, from cultural theory, psychoanalysis and sociology, making this a truly interdisciplinary study with experts in specific fields congregating under the banner of David Bowie's film performances. Without question, the discipline of celebrity studies establishes a strong presence behind the work of *I'm Not a Film Star*, partly deriving from notions of the charismatic authority of Max Weber. Stars also function according to Francesco Alberoni's critique of neoliberalist celebrities as forming a 'Powerless Elite' and, as Barry King reasserts, the film industry is built around stars as 'commodity production'.³³ As such, celebrity studies suggest the cultural omnipresence of stars as polysemic and complex beings, concepts largely deriving from Richard Dyer's influential theories on star constructions as a confluence of persona, actor and real person. Emphasizing Dyer's insistence on the affective power of the cinematic close-up and the condensation of ideological opposites as a facet of impossible ideology, celebrity scholars question stars as constructed social phenomena with an emphasis on the difference between sociological and semiotic analysis.³⁴ For Su Holmes and Sean Redmond, this examination reaches back to Barthes's analysis of Greta Garbo's non-ageing face.³⁵ Further, celebrity studies consider the film star's centrality to meaning making and specifically how their star images function within their screen constructions.[36] The discipline of celebrity studies also notes the influence of religion and sexuality condensed into the star image and consults Christine Geraghty's tripartite division of stars into celebrities, professionals and performers or combinations of the above.[37]

With stars comes affective/sensual readings of cinema and, as such, this book consults corporeal readings of cinema, notably Redmond's *Sensing Film Performance* published in *Performance Phenomenology: To the Thing Itself*.[38] Drawing upon the writing of V. F. Perkins (1990) and Andrew Kleven (2016), Redmond illustrates how the personal is brought to bear on our reading of filmic texts, which in the case of Bowie involves the viewer's complex parasocial relationship to the megastar.

Following Cinque, Moore and Redmond's claim that *Enchanting David Bowie* is the first interdisciplinary edited work on Bowie, our collection of Bowie-related reflections stems entirely from the megastar's acting on film, which then ramifies into associated art forms. Like *Enchanting David Bowie*, our book finds significance in gender, race, sexuality and performance,[39] but we also consult acting theory in that same vein.

As Brooker surmises, for the Bowie scholar, critical theory and philosophy serve primarily as tools to manifest 'new understanding and a valuable perspective'.[40] As with this present volume, Brooker consults theorists from Michail Bakhtin, Roland Barthes, Jacques Derrida, Gilles Deleuze and Pierre-Félix Guattari to 'elevate Bowie's popular work to some loftier academic plane',[41] providing new ways of perceiving Bowie and his craft. As such, *I'm Not a Film Star* employs critical theory within the author's individual chapter approaches.

Finally, as Auslander opines, critical theory, semiotics and performance theory can be divisive, yet our book's contributors variously refer to all three and we emphasize that the star's eclecticism is here reflected in theory, so performance theory remains relevant. As the primary proponent of this theory, Richard Schechner points out that performance may be an innate part of the human condition. In this matter, Schechner collides with the Cambridge scholars who bring all theatrical events back to an ancient Greek origin. Schechner, on the other hand, questions the existence of any 'primal ritual' in favour of innate human performativity.[42] Drawing on Goffman's work, Schechner – along with Ray Birdwhistell and Paul Ekman – highlights the difference between Goffman's everyday performers and professional actors as being more problematic than Goffman assumes. Emphasizing reflexivity as this point of difference – one that Bowie exploits well – performance theory illustrates that 'professional actors are aware that they are acting',[43] which immediately condenses the gap between performance purists and perceived 'interlopers' like Bowie.

Filmography

It is clear from the contributors in this book that respect should be afforded Bowie for his performance acumen – he is not merely a crossover artist but an actor with considerable talent brought liberally to the big screen. In Paul Morley's impressionistic analysis of Bowie's early artistic and cinematic influences, purportedly written in a single weekend at the Victoria and Albert Museum's *David Bowie Is* exhibition in London, the author details only a few aspects of Bowie's screen performances. Morley suggests of Bowie's juvenile appearance in the Ken Pitt-financed filmed pantomime *The Mask* (1969) that 'the mime might be the central performer that David Bowie is'.[44] This runs contrary to Waldrep's intriguing claim that Bowie is essentially a comedic figure. In any case, such divisive opinions only emphasize how intriguing and expansive Bowie's performances can be. Bowie's acting development runs parallel to his phenomenal musical output and warrants a chronological enquiry to orientate the reader and demonstrate that, in film performance, Bowie is indeed the quintessential 'chameleon, comedian, Corinthian and caricature'.[45]

This volume covers mostly Bowie's groundbreaking feature film acts, starting with the über-controlling artist behind his eponymous final performance of *Ziggy Stardust* (1973) at London's Hammersmith Odeon. The unutterable transferability of stage performance to screen in D. A. Pennebaker's film of the event synchronizes Bowie's personal interests with the cultural zeitgeist of the 1970s.[46] Bowie then evolves with 1980s *The Elephant Man* to learn lessons of performance 'internality' and emerge as a fine naturalistic actor as witnessed through the remaining eleven minutes of the videoed stage version.[47] As his iconicity grows, Bowie offers some haunting renditions of real-life entities such as Andy Warhol, Pontious Pilate, Nikola Tesla and a host of other fictional screen characters. Finally, having achieved a synthesis of actor and role, upon his death, Bowie exits stage left with a performance to remember, even in his physical absence, in his play *Lazarus* (2016). In this way, *I'm Not a Film Star* traces Bowie's evolving film art from performer to alter ego in the service of stardom, to megastar and on to contemporary cultural icon. Yet, just as Waldrep argues regarding Bowie biographers, the Bowie story we collude in telling cannot be historically accurate. It can only be a concoction through which we imagine a life in just one element: Bowie's film acting.

Although this chronological treatment elides the lesser-known texts, it is necessary to mention them in context as, apart from *The Elephant Man*, short films or filmed theatre performances have not been included. Regrettably, this omits texts such as *Theatre 625* (1968) and *Pierrot in Turquoise* (1969), snippets of which can be located on YouTube and various other websites. The following constitutes a filmographic 'story' with an emphasis on Bowie's films not included in our book and, except for a short mention for the sake of chronology, we leave our main texts to the subsequent chapter outline.

In *Pierrot in Turquoise* or *The Looking Glass Murders*, the self-conscious Bowie appears as the character Cloud, having been 'discovered' by Kemp – who had previously fallen in love with the song 'When I Live my Dream' and apparently also with the composer who penned it. *Pierrot in Turquoise* is a poorly videoed theatre production in which the burlesque Kemp apparently dramatizes his reverse Oedipal terror of discovering his paramour Bowie in bed with the costume designer, Natasha Korniloff. The surviving pantomime fragment happens to the accompaniment of an adaptation of Bowie's juvenile song 'London Bye Ta-Ta' – sung unconvincingly by Bowie from the show's centrepiece prop: the bed – a befitting fantasy with which to record Bowie's first significant theatrical performance (curiously just one year after James Broughton's experimental film *The Bed* (1968)). *Pierrot* reveals more of Kemp's pansexual fantasies than the not-so-charismatic appearance of Bowie can accommodate.[48]

These filmed theatrical events contrast and compliment Bowie's juvenile performances on film, particularly in *The Virgin Soldiers* (John Dexter, 1969, filmed in November 1968), which features a singularly unimpressed Bowie sweeping through the background frame in the arms of another recruit. Bowie's first significant screen performance, however, was in Michael Armstrong's befittingly titled silent horror film *The Image* (1969), a short film receiving little accolade from the megastar himself. Alexandra Heller-Nicholas – notable for her horror research – scrutinizes the megastar's performance in this film as a pre-celebrity Bowie.[49] Heller-Nicholas opines that Bowie's signification remains that of his face, body and movement rather than the extra-textual readings subsequently bestowed upon him as a crossover rock 'n' roll star.

After the meteoric rise of Bowie's next half decade as a recording and musical stage artist, the mid-1970s saw Bowie's screen performances proper emerge. After Nicolas Roeg famously cast Bowie from a smuggled copy of Alan Yentob's BBC/Imagine documentary *Cracked Actor* (1975), Bowie starred in *The Man Who Fell to Earth* (1976).[50] By contrast, in *Just a Gigolo* (David Hemmings, 1978), Bowie provides an understated but self-conscious performance where he famously failed to meet his idol Marlene Dietrich (under a heavy mask of concealer) even though cast in the same scenes with her.[51] Dietrich shot her scenes from her Paris flat showing no desire to meet the real-life Bowie on the actual set in reverse shot.[52] The film shows the two icons balanced across the screen with repeated renditions of the theme song announcing a celebrity's greatest horror: that 'Life goes on without me'. Hemmings's indulgent direction prevents any effective empathy for the stars, which is not helped by Bowie's mannered, externalized presentational performance. Constricted in this part though he may be, Bowie's performance reeks of the Thin White Duke persona underpinned by the Germanic overtones of his scenes with Dietrich. Such constriction was overturned with his next two film performances.

Bowie reinvented himself not just musically in the 1980s, a period painstakingly defended by Waldrep in *Future Nostalgia*, but also as a film performer. The 1980s was the decade that Bowie dedicated himself to megastardom, part of which was his reinvigorated focus on his acting career beginning with *The Elephant Man* (1980).[53] Bowie's cameo in the West German cult film *Christiane F.* (1981) followed, and in 1982 Bowie played the lead in Alan Clarke's BBC adaptation of Brecht's first play, *Baal*.[54] The occasion promised to blend Bowie's notable expressionistic musical oeuvre with this juvenile piece of Brecht's dramaturgy prior to the playwright's development of epic theatre. However, while the character's hedonistic epicureanism drew on Ziggy's outrageous performativity it promised a greater result than Bowie and Clarke might have achieved with the benefits of time and funding; television, however, always unfolds in a pressure-cooker environment and can impede performance excellence. According to his director, Bowie was exceptional in the part, providing a complimentary album of Brecht/Weill songs in tandem, but it appears that Bowie's acting cannot find the appropriate tone for a Brechtian production and, as Wendy Leigh indicates, 'critics were underwhelmed' by Bowie's *Baal*.[55]

Following *Baal*, Bowie ventures upon some delightfully silly screen renditions from overzealous sharks to schmaltzy children's animation voice-overs. In *The Snowman* (1982), apart from a tastelessly beige woolly jumper clashing with his platinum blonde hair, Bowie risks changing his 'imaginary audience', that is, his direct camera address appears only slightly conscious of an adult audience as it is directed to children. We can only speculate that he may have been drawing from his relationship with his son Duncan Jones, but there is a warmth and a counterproductive static quality to the performance which renders the work paradoxical. Enter Bowie's shark, screen right, in Pythonesque comedy *Yellowbeard* (1983): Bowie's vaguely Irish accent juxtaposes the repeated gesture of constantly fingering his nose – a curiously external habit, perhaps a nod to cocaine use passed off as diegetic seawater. In any case, what this part proves more than anything is that a megastar can easily be cast from a coincidental meeting with the director, can command the screen with sheer joy and include a cheeky nod to homosexuality re meeting Eric Idle in the 'pump room'. The year 1983 also brought Bowie's casting as John Blaylock in *The Hunger* and Major Jack Celliers in *Merry Christmas, Mr. Lawrence*. Subsequently, *Into the Night* (1985) shows Bowie sporting a ludicrous Freddie Mercury-like moustache and indulging in an equally ludicrous quadruple knife thrusting dance of violence for comic affect.

Two months before the release of *Labyrinth* in June 1986 came Julien Temple's *Absolute Beginners*, a musical about life in 1950s London, based on the book by Colin MacInnes. *Absolute Beginners* (1986) saw Bowie ham it up on a typewriter and lends his songwriting genius to an otherwise genre-confused pastiche of teen films and *West Side Story*. While the title song from *Absolute Beginners* reached number two on the UK Singles Chart,[56] the film itself was a flop, barely making back one-quarter of its budget. Bowie plays the role of Vendice Partners, an avaricious advertising executive and property developer, and he contributed three songs to the film. *Absolute Beginners* was beset by a range of problems, including a blown budget, which led many in the press to denigrate it before they'd even seen it. Due to British studio Goldcrest's recent and immense box office failure with the Al Pacino film *Revolution* (Hugh Hudson, 1985), *Absolute Beginners* was portrayed as British film's last chance for success[57] – and it failed dismally to live up to the hype.

A key component of the marketing strategy, Bowie, with a fake tan and even faker accent, looks uncomfortable in the film and is given little opportunity to be anything more than a thinly drawn caricature, barely rising above his superficial characterization. The efforts to emulate the elaborate Busby Berkeley set pieces of the 1930s in the song 'That's Motivation', with an oversized typewriter, globe and Mount Everest, are accompanied by awkward choreography and vapid lyrics. These are definitely not Bowie's finest moments committed to celluloid, and *Absolute Beginners* ends up being a confused and confusing film, despite the best intentions of the director. Bowie's presence does not help the film at all, and the mask hides not only his persona but also, seemingly, his skills as an actor.

Bowie and Temple's first collaboration, *Jazzin' for Blue Jean* (1984), however, was far more successful on many fronts. The short film was used to promote Bowie's single 'Blue Jean' and features him in two roles: Vic, a hapless odd-jobs man desperately trying to win the affections of a girl, and Screamin' Lord Byron, a flamboyant, drug-addicted and paranoid rocker with whom the girl is besotted. While *Absolute Beginners* couldn't decide whether to take itself seriously or not, *Jazzin'* has a sense of fun right from the beginning, with Bowie mainly parodying himself and his 1970s personae, such as when Vic screams to Byron: 'You conniving, randy, bogus Oriental old queen! Your record sleeves are better than your songs.'[58] Bowie's acting, although comedic, is also more naturalistic, less forced, than in *Absolute Beginners*, even giving him the chance to utilize his training in mime, and his comic timing is excellent; Temple had proclaimed that 'Bowie is just getting better and better as an actor'.[59]

At the end, when Bowie (no longer in character as Vic/Byron but still acting) argues with Temple about their narrative differences and how they've run out of darkness in which to shoot the night-time scenes, the camera pulls back to reveal the crew, and the film gives a sly nod and a wink to the audience. This demonstrates Brecht's *verfremdungseffekt* by 'representing real-life incidents on the stage in such a way that their causal interconnection is highlighted and engages the spectator';[60] the actors give up their charade and cease being in character but continue to perform, blurring the lines between the realms of pure fiction, parody and mockumentary. In other words, *Bowie as character* and *Bowie as character satirizing Bowie* become simply *Bowie satirizing/performing Bowie*, essentially the entire raison d'être of *Jazzin'*. For a Bowie then stripped of Vic and Byron, the decade concluded with Bowie playing Pontius Pilate in *The Last Temptation of Christ* (1988).

By the 1990s, as Bowie struggled to regain his artistic integrity (or so the story goes), it was not so productive a period cinematically: a decade in which Bowie's cameo roles mostly descended into parodic pastiche, such as the obnoxious Sir Ronald Moorecock in HBO's *Dream On* (1991). *The Linguini Incident* (1991) represents Bowie's foray into the romcom genre where his postmodern tryst with Rozanne Arquette conveys their capricious joy in each other's company, not quite saved from their hammy antics, to disguise a basically sadomasochistic plot – not just in its fetishism but also in its deeply dishonest attitude to love. Although it would have been rewarding to analyse the subversion and polymorphous perversion that Bowie brings to this otherwise conservative romantic comedy, sadly this volume could not afford the space. David Lynch's *Twin Peaks: Fire Walk with Me* follows in 1992, then Bowie plays Andy Warhol in *Basquiat* (1996). Shortly after, Bowie's foray into Tony Scott's *The Hunger* television series in 1997 – not so much a spinoff from the previous film as an attempt to cash in on its belated cult status – juxtaposes ordinary naturalism against the megastar's extraordinary persona.[61] In episode one, Bowie celebrates the virtues of artificiality as an antagonistic postmodern artist with an extra-diegetic twist. His performance is natural, conversational and charming to initiate this underrated series in episode one.

Similarly, the intelligence Bowie brings to the otherwise turgid gangster clichés of B.U.S.T.E.D. (1998) sees him emerge from behind the well-worn British trope of the crooked intellectual behind the horn-rimmed glasses (which nevertheless still fail to obfuscate his deliciously mismatched eyes). In this film, Bowie, an artist renowned for looking down the barrel of death,[62] gets to deliver the self-reflexive line of dialogue 'Look at my eyes. Look at my eyes. Just stay with me, alright?' to a dying gangster – a transcendent moment in an otherwise perfunctory film.

In *Il mio West* or *Gunslinger's Revenge* (1998), Bowie adds to his canon of extra-diegetic comment by playing the ironically flat-twanging Jack Sikora in this Italian comedy-western starring Harvey Keitel. The film forms a third tongue-in-cheek reference to a character who cannot sing, the joke repeated in *Mr Lawrence* and *Man Who Fell*, but in *Il mio West* it clearly takes considerable vocal control to 'twang' so consistently in such a menacing antagonistic presence. In this classic bad guy role, Bowie remains a slippery fusion of performance, filmic artefact, singer, non-singer and megastar. Ushering in the end of the millennium, *Omikron: The Nomad*

Soul (1999) includes an animated version of himself as a digital projection. Bowie's iconic voice compels the inhabitants of Omikron to 'wake up' and win back their freedom – an uncanny simulacrum, complete with overly gesticulating head and understated mismatched eyes.

In the year 2000, *Mr. Rice's Secret* sees Bowie in a performance as reliant on his charismatic personae as on the screenplay's shallow dialogue. In this part as a delightfully unextraordinary middle-ager-next-door (foreshadowing the self-righteous parody of himself in 'The Stars (are Out Tonight)' (2013) opposite Tilda Swinton),[63] Bowie mentions that 'Every man needs to have a good blue suit' – not an overly obvious reference but enough to charm any diehard fan of *Life on Mars*. The real question is: How does he say these cheesy lines without laughing?

In *Zoolander* (2001), answering the invitation 'Alright, who's gonna call this sucker?', Bowie steps into freeze frame as the arbiter of cool to offer his service, 'If nobody has any objections . . .'. Despite the unfailing mask of 'Bowie' in his early 2000s honest-but-still-cool phase, in *Zoolander*, Bowie's comedic mask slips to one side by comparison to the seasoned funnymen Ben Stiller and Owen Wilson. Yet Bowie's mask upon mask helps maintain his status as a megastar and arguably shows up the self-loving performances of the two would-be models. Similarly, in a blink-and-you'll-miss-it still cameo, Bowie lives the on-screen micturition fantasy befitting of his perverse yet naughty reputation in TV mini-series *Nathan Barley* (2005).[64]

In 2006, in Luc Besson's impressive animation film *Arthur and the Invisibles*, Bowie performs the voice-over for Malthazar, the suitably megalomaniacal antagonist. Along with seasoned Bowie fan Madonna, the part allows Bowie to postmodernize this otherwise grand narrative. This self-parody is similar to his double-standard, much-loved comedic performance in the television production *Extras*, also in 2006 – obviously a year to ham it up lovingly (without the dourness of *Absolute Beginners*). Christopher Nolan's 2006 masterpiece *The Prestige* follows, with Bowie playing the maligned icon Nikola Tesla,[65] just before his memorable cameo in 2007's *SpongeBob SquarePants* as the Lord Royal Highness.

As Cyrus Ogilvie in *August* (2008), Bowie underplays the cranky British business mogul despite his icon-exploiting screen introduction with a walking cane held at erectile angle. The part understandably leads some critics to repeat that he only ever plays himself on screen, but as will be seen in this book, this is a naïve claim. In *August*, glowing with anisocoric (apparently) blue and hazel irises opposite Josh Hartnett's characteristically narrow eyes, Bowie cuts a charismatic presence: his postcardiac, once Elvin face, a sad advertisement to his stagnated musical output.

In *Bandslam* (2009), the editor directs Bowie's gaze towards the computer image of rock chick Vanessa Hudgens – just in case the audience misinterprets any transgressive pansexuality or ageing androgyny as queer masculinity – but Bowie is faking it all the way through this cameo – even as he legitimately plays himself on screen, almost for the last time. Then again, fans will always have his final dextrous performance in the astounding video clip of *Blackstar* (2016), where Bowie plays an enigmatic charismatic cult leader, oscillating between funky jazz and macabre communication with an absent god – a final testament to his extraordinary talent.

Chapter outline

The story behind this book lies within its chapters, a collection of apparently disparate elements, which constitute a narrative thread for just one aspect of Bowie's phenomenal skillset: his journey through film acting and its associated ghosts in theatre. The book organizes Bowie's acting milieu into his feature films chronologically – one film per chapter – from D. A. Pennebaker's *Ziggy Stardust and the Spiders from Mars* (1973) to Christopher Nolan's *The Prestige* (2006). This includes a vital diversion into *The Elephant Man* (1980) and beyond the star's physical life to the filmic representations inherent within Bowie's play *Lazarus* (2015). Each chapter debates the changing significance of Bowie throughout his film career with attention to the interior/exterior binary based on Bowie's lucid performances and star image.

Launching the book in Chapter 1, Lisa Perrott draws upon various disciplinary approaches to examine Bowie's stage/screen performance in D. A. Pennebaker's 1973 motion picture *Ziggy Stardust and the Spiders from Mars*. Perrott unravels Bowie's first major feature film performance as an example of Direct Cinema and the Wagnerian *Gesamtkunstwerk* or 'total work of art'.[66] Returning to the year that Bowie killed Ziggy, Perrott studies Bowie's desire to achieve *Gesamtkunstwerk* while seeking a 'multisensory synthesis of artforms' within Pennebaker's performative-filmic assemblage involving a plethora of differing art forms. Perrott interrogates the slippage between Bowie's theatrical performance and his playing to camera for an implied cinema audience – an act which becomes digitized decades later, but in 1973 serves to demonstrate Bowie's capacity to play with simultaneous performance modes.

In Chapter 2, Dene October draws on his own and other scholars' work to assess Bowie's 'naïve and polysemic' performance as Thomas Jerome Newton in Nicholas Roeg's *The Man Who Fell to Earth*. October's argument involves Bowie's contemporary interviews, considers perspectives from Jacques Derrida to Gilles Deleuze and problematizes the concept of Bowie as a matrix of texts and intertexts within the Bowie-Newton universe. By honing his performance craft, Bowie on screen, opines October, triangulates the relationship between actor, megastar and public persona. October asks how Bowie inflects Roeg's film by reference to his other performances and the spectator/star relationship to interrogate quotidian performance boundaries and identity as *performative*.[67]

In Chapter 3, film producer Amedeo D'Adamo illuminates *The Elephant Man* (1980) via the remaining eleven-minute video of the play, emphasizing Bowie's vocality and exploitation of 'raw' emotion in parallel to the performativity of *It's No Game (Part 1)* (1979). D'Adamo identifies the specific creative moment in 1980 when Bowie shifted from figurative representations that were obviously 'posed' towards an 'unposed' naturalism in performance. As D'Adamo illustrates, Bowie created his anxious clown character for *Scary Monsters*, then played the hideously afflicted John Merrick in Jack Hofsiss's stage version of *The Elephant Man* – which gained him high praise as an independent actor. Bowie's prior performances involving clowning, grotesquery, automatons and alien consciousness – creatures without consistent internal lives – graduated from performative caricatures to three-dimensional characters. While D'Adamo's chapter traces the megastar's theatrical and aural recordings, he nevertheless involves the cinematic angle via filmed snippets of the original Broadway production.

Susanne Hillman's Chapter 4 examines the ideological inclusion of Bowie in West Germany's high-grossing motion picture *Zoo Station/Christiane F.* (Uli Edel, 1981) from a cultural, performative and historical perspective to provide an alternative reading. According to Hillman, this film – dramatizing the drug addiction of a teenage prostitute during the Cold War – implies that the image of David Bowie seduced the protagonist (and the eponymous author Christiane Felscherinow) into her devastating lifestyle. As a star performer returning to a theatrical version of himself/Thin White Duke for this film, Bowie resolves two irreconcilable positions: celebrating Anglo-American pop culture and lamenting West Germany's surrender to capitalist consumerism. As such, Bowie's embrace of performative 'externality' contributed to the film's meaning making: cashing in on the Americanized *Konsumgesellschaft* (consumer society) while simultaneously denouncing it. By drawing on historiography, Americanization and Naremore's theory of film acting, Hillman critiques the Anglo-American pop culture introduced into the Federal Republic of Germany after 1949 with Bowie as its primary metaphor.

Sean Redmond's Chapter 5 reads Nagisa Ōshima's *Merry Christmas, Mr. Lawrence* (1983) sensorially to examine how Bowie *affectively acts* on screen as Major Jack Celliers through movement, body language, gesture, speech pattern and 'silences'. Observing the rich tradition of close textual readings, Redmond scrutinizes the restrained Bowie/Ryuichi Sakamoto seduction scene based on the writings of V. F. Perkins, Andrew Kleven and the author's own sensorial analyses of cinema.[68] For Redmond, Bowie's uncanny, even alienating, performance in this scene becomes 'ulterior and unnameable',[69] enunciating queer desire through longing and liminality while allowing its meanings and impressions to emerge shot by shot – a sophisticated confluence of performative and cinematic tropes.

A notable favourite with cult film fans is Tony Scott's *The Hunger* (1983) covered in Chapter 6. Following the death of John Lennon and the consequent impermanence of New York City, Mitch Goodwin traces the metamorphosis of Bowie from the methodical annihilation of *Ashes to Ashes* to John Blaylock, the ill-fated vampire. In *The Hunger*, Bowie encapsulates decay as a catalyst for change while embodying the grotesquery and entrapment the role demanded. This is a film part Bowie plays from both interior and exterior positions with himself at the epicentre providing a stream of images iconic to himself and to vampire lore, which in Scott's hands becomes an exercise in style over substance.

Subsequently, Brendan Black guides the reader down into the *Labyrinth* (1986) as Bowie's performance forms the celebrity fulcrum of the dark, yet capricious, underworld of Jim Henson's underrated cult film in Chapter 7. Both a critical and box office failure, *Labyrinth* arguably represents Bowie's most iconic, enigmatic screen performance ever as Jareth the Goblin King – androgynous and challenging the demarcation between role and actor – a character which earned Bowie a new coterie of younger fans. By applying theories of the carnivalesque and theatrical mask from Mikhail Bakhtin, Black asks the impossible question 'who is Bowie?' By crowning and then decrowning the carnival king himself, through free and familiar contact among people, eccentricity, carnivalistic mésalliances and profanation, Black interrogates Bowie's Goblin King through the lens of Bakhtin's *carnivalesque* and asks why *Labyrinth* became such a pivotal role.

In Chapter 8, Ian Dixon investigates how Bowie fuses iconicity and naturalistic performance within the finessed film direction in Martin Scorsese's *The Last Temptation of Christ* (1988). Playing the equally iconic Pontius Pilate, Bowie creates character and scene by synthesizing contrasting acting methodologies. Through sign and performance analysis and by applying acting terminology to Bowie's portrayal of Pilate, this chapter considers Bowie as both consciously signing and 'internally' generating the performative meaning of his cameo scene from opposing ends of the Brechtian/Stanislavskian spectrum. Consulting Goffman's everyday performance, Naremore on film acting and Counsell's semiotic analysis of performance conventions, Dixon breaks down Scorsese/Paul Schrader's screenplay as a vehicle for Bowie's effective fusion of acting styles – another high point in the Bowie as actor story.

Steering the argument in a surrealist direction, Tyne Daile Sumner propels Chapter 9 into Bowie's peculiar (a)temporal cameo in *Twin Peaks: Fire Walk with Me* (1992). Balancing Michel Foucault and Deleuze against Mary Ann Doane's cinematic temporality and Thomas Mathiesen's 'The Viewer Society',[70] Sumner observes how Bowie's casting in this film creates a unique panopticon for Lynch's vision. Chapter 9 considers time and absence as functional aspects of director David Lynch's vision, in which Bowie – ever the Othered outsider – fashions a performance out of the 'constitutive tension between insider and outsider' – a liminality well suited to the star. As Sumner elucidates, Bowie deflects any logical or fixed subjectivity through the disruption of cinematic time to attain a surveillant distortion within the text. Simple though Bowie's performance may appear, it nonetheless embodies the 'technological, temporal and psychological dislocation' of Lynch's film: both panoptic and synoptic simultaneously.[71]

In Chapter 10, Bowie's acting story further complexifies with Julian Schnabel's film *Basquiat* (1996). Glenn D'Cruz consults David E. R. George's triadic model of acting to illustrate the differences between the *fusion model* (inside-out) and *fission model* (outside-in). D'Cruz also references Brecht's concept of *Gestus* to show how Bowie adopts an 'attitude' towards Andy Warhol in *Basquiat*, rather than representing Warhol as the historical figure with naturalistic accuracy. Contrary to claims that Bowie merely plays himself on screen, D'Cruz illustrates how Bowie unsettles and effectively triangulates the relationship between 'authentic' self and 'inauthentic' persona, thus analysing Bowie's presentational approach to the role as sublime cinema.

By 2006, Bowie's star image becomes culturally ingrained and Toija Cinque elucidates Christopher Nolan's *The Prestige* (2006) where Bowie plays Nikola Tesla through the iconicity of both character formations: pop star and historical figure. Chapter 11 experiments with the tension between Plato's notion of the artist's 'absolute essence'[72] and John Locke's thesis that only direct experience, not innate nature or identity, forms the basis for an individual's understanding. Cinque examines Bowie as icon and actor as being fundamental to the film's narrative, which demands attention to the star playing the genius and their performative linkage. In this way, Cinque considers Bowie's 'stylistic gesture' as *performative emotional symbolism*,[73] pitting Brecht's *gest* and dialectical circumstance against Michael Chekhov's 'Psychological Gesture' to enunciate the unassailable contradictions within the Bowie star image.[74] According to Cinque, as Catherine Soussloff explains, the 'mythic aura' of Bowie as artist cannot be separated from the role of Tesla.

In the final chapter, Denis Flannery illustrates Bowie's posthumous significance in his and Enda Walsh's 2015 musical dream play *Lazarus* as an example of cinematic melancholia – a term Flannery defines as mournful, ambivalent and mimicking attachment to missing desires and forms as represented on film. Drawing on Freud's 1917 writing on mourning and melancholia and Judith Butler's subsequent qualification of the former theory, Flannery brings genuine feeling to the analysis of Bowie's absent performance. Returning the reader to Roeg's *The Man Who Fell to Earth*, the author shows how the 1976 film remains a haunting presence within *Lazarus* the play, and the post-Bowie world alike, as he explores Bowie's final work and the nature of melancholia. As we collectively bid Bowie *adieu*, we see it is the memory of Bowie that sustains us into the future. In consort, the twelve chapters of *I'm Not a Film Star* argue strongly for the multifaceted inclusion of Bowie as a notable twenty-first-century icon and film actor – not just a pop star, not just a *Blackstar*, but a canonical film star.

Notes

1. Will Brooker, *Why Bowie Matters* (Great Britain: William Collins, 2019).
2. Christopher Sandford, *Loving the Alien* (Boston: Da Capo Press, 2009).
3. Shelton Waldrep, *Future Nostalgia: Performing David Bowie* (New York: Bloomsbury Academic, 2015), 150.
4. acmi.net.au/bowie-symposium; #bowiesymposium.
5. Toija Cinque, Angela Ndalianis and Sean Redmond, eds, 'In Focus: David Bowie On-Screen', *Cinema Journal* 57, no. 3 (Spring 2018): 126–75. doi:10.1353/cj.2018.0034.
6. Philip Auslander, *Performing Glam Rock: Gender and Theatricality in Popular Music* (Ann Arbor: The University of Michigan Press, 2006), 13.
7. Ibid., 5.
8. Ibid.
9. Ibid., 6.
10. Ibid., 13–14.
11. Mark Kermode, 'David Bowie Then . . . David Bowie Now', in *David Bowie Is*, ed. Victoria Broackes and Geoffrey Marsh (London: V&A Publishing, 2013), 292.
12. Barney Hoskyns, *Glam!: Bowie, Bolan and the Glitter Rock Revolution* (USA: Faber and Faber, 1998), 6.
13. Susan Sontag, 'Notes on Camp', in *Camp: Queer Aesthetics and the Performing Subject-A Reader*, ed. Fabio Cleto (USA, University of Michigan Press, 1999), 53–65, quoted in Hoskyns, *Glam!*, 11.
14. Brooker, *Why Bowie Matters*, 59.
15. C. Rojek, 'Celebrity and Religion', in *Stardom and Celebrity: A Reader*, ed. Sue Holmes and Sean Redmond (Los Angeles: SAGE, 2007), 171–80.
16. Ana Cristina Mendes and Lisa Perrott, eds, *David Bowie and Transmedia Stardom* (London: Routledge, 2020).
17. Ibid., 7–8.
18. Toija Cinque and Sean Redmond, 'Intersecting David Bowie', *Continuum* 31, no. 4 (2017): 495; Paul du Gay, Stuart Hall, Linda Janes, Hugh Mackay and Keith Negus, *Doing Cultural Studies: The Story of the Sony Walkman* (London: Sage, 1997).
19. Cinque, Redmond and Ndalianis, *In Focus*, 3/57.
20. Although there were no such sites at the inception of *I'm Not a Film Star*, there are currently websites offering Bowie's entire acting oeuvre.

21 Sarah Rubridge, 'Does Authenticity Matter? The Case for and against Authenticity in the Performing Arts', in *Analysing Performance*, ed. Patrick Campbell (London: Reaktion, 2001), 219–33.

22 Sarah Rubridge cited in Bethany Usher and Stephanie Fremaux, 'Turn Myself to Face Me: David Bowie in the 1990s and Discovery of Authentic Self', in *David Bowie: Critical Perspectives*, ed. Eoin Devereux, Aileen Dillane and Martin J. Power (New York: Routledge, 2015), 75.

23 Plato, *Parmenides* (South Bend: Infomotions, Inc., 2000), 9.

24 Auslander, *Performing Glam Rock*, 3–4.

25 Waldrep, *Future Nostalgia*, 1.

26 Ibid., 4.

27 Ibid., 2–4.

28 Colin Counsell, *Signs of Performance: An Introduction to Twentieth-Century Theatre* (London and New York: Routledge, 1996).

29 James Naremore, *Acting in the Cinema* (Berkeley, CA: University of California Press, 1988), 15; Goffman as cited in Naremore, *Acting in the Cinema*.

30 Ibid., 29.

31 Ibid., 28.

32 Counsell, *Signs of Performance*, 70–1.

33 Anthony Elliott, *Routledge Handbook of Celebrity Studies* (London: Routledge, 2018).

34 Sean Redmond and Su Holmes, *Stardom and Celebrity: A Reader* (Los Angeles: SAGE, 2007).

35 See Ian Dixon, 'Always Crashing on the Same Synth: Voice/Synth Counterpoise in David Bowie's *Low*', in *Interpreting the Synthesizer: Meaning Through Sonics*, ed. Nick Wilson (Newcastle upon Tyne: Cambridge Scholars Publishing, 2020), 21–35.

36 Redmond and Holmes, *Stardom and Celebrity*, 2.

37 Christine Geraghty, 'Re-examining Stardom: Questions of Texts, Bodies and Performance', in *Stardom and Celebrity: A Reader*, ed. Sean Redmond and Su Holmes (Los Angeles: SAGE, 2007), 98–110.

38 Sean Redmond, 'Sensing Film Performance', in *Performance Phenomenology: To the Thing Itself*, ed. Stuart Grant, Judy McNeilly-Renaudie and Matthew Wagner (Switzerland: Palgrave Macmillan, 2019), 165–83.

39 Toija Cinque, Christopher Moore and Sean Redmond, eds, *Enchanting David Bowie: Space, Time, Body, Memory* (New York: Bloomsbury Academic, 2015), 2–3.

40 Brooker, *Why Bowie Matters*, 13.

41 Ibid.

42 Richard Schechner, *Performance Theory* (London: Routledge, 2003), 3–7; Counsell, *Signs of Performance*.

43 Schechner, *Performance Theory*, 303.

44 Paul Morley, *The Age of Bowie: How David Bowie Made a World of Difference* (New York: Gallery Books, 2014).
45 Alexandra Heller-Nicholas, 'The Art of Immortality: David Bowie and *The Image*', Kill Your Darlings, published 13 January 2016, https://www.killyourdarlings.com.au/2016/01/the-art-of-immortality/.
46 Waldrep, *Future Nostalgia*, 7.
47 See Amedeo D'Adamo in this volume.
48 Chris Ford, 'David Bowie, Actor: A Complete Look Back at His Film and TV Career', VCR Classic Rock and Culture, published 15 January 2016, https://ultimateclassicrock.com/david-bowie-acting-career/.
49 Heller-Nicholas, 'Art of Immortality'.
50 See Paul Trynka, *David Bowie: Starman* (New York: Little, Brown and Company, 2011).
51 Ibid.
52 Ibid.
53 See Ian Dixon, '"So, Where's the Moral?": David Bowie becomes *The Elephant Man* (1980) in The Theatre of Disability', in *Cambridge Companion to David Bowie*, ed. Denis Flannery (United Kingdom: Cambridge Scholars Publishing, 2022); Amedeo D'Adamo in this volume.
54 *Baal*, directed by Alan Clarke, aired 9 March 1982 on BBC TV.
55 Wendy Leigh, *Bowie: The Biography* (New York: Gallery Books, 2014), 216.
56 https://www.thinwhiteduke.net/1236-david-bowie-songs/absolute-beginners/ (accessed 23 December 2020).
57 Nicholas Pegg, *The Complete David Bowie, New Edition* (London: Titan Books, 2016), 671.
58 *Jazzin' for Blue Jean* (1984), [Music video] Dir. Julien Temple.
59 Pegg, *Complete David Bowie*, 642.
60 Tom Kuhn, Steve Giles and Marc Silberman, eds, *Brecht on Performance: Messingkauf and Modelbooks* (London: Bloomsbury Academic, 2014), 130.
61 Richard Dyer, *Stars* (London: British Film Institute, 1998).
62 Tanja Stark, 'Confronting Bowie's Mysterious Corpses', in *Enchanting David Bowie: Space/Time/Body/Memory*, ed. Toija Cinque, Christopher Moore and Sean Redmond (New York: Bloomsbury Academic, 2015), 61–77.
63 See Ian Dixon, 'The Return of the Thin White Repressed: Uses of Narcissism in The Stars (Are Out Tonight)', *Celebrity Studies* 4, no. 3 (October 2013): 397–400.
64 Ford, 'David Bowie: Actor'.
65 See Toija Cinque in this volume.
66 Counsell, *Signs of Performance*; Auslander, *Performing Glam Rock*.
67 D. October, 'The Man Who Fell to Earth', in *Bloomsbury Encyclopedia of Film and Television Costume Design*, ed. D. Landis (New York: Bloomsbury, 2021).

68 See Sean Redmond in this volume.
69 Redmond, 'Sensing Film Performance'.
70 Thomas Mathiesen, 'The Viewer Society: Foucault's 'Panopticon' Revisited', *Theoretical Criminology: An International Journal* 1, no. 2 (1997): 219.
71 See Tyne Daile Sumner in this volume.
72 Plato, *Parmenides*.
73 Joe Gore, 'Changes 2.1: New Digital Stimulation from David Bowie and Reeves Gabrels', *Guitar Player*, June 1997, 46–7.
74 Michael Chekhov, *Lessons for the Professional Actor*, from a collection of notes transcribed and arranged by Deirdre Hurst du Prey; introduction by Mel Gordon (New York: Performing Arts Journal Publications, 1985).

1

Ziggy Stardust, Direct Cinema and the multimodal performance of *Gesamtkunstwerk*

Lisa Perrott

I'm going to play a character called Ziggy Stardust. We're going to do it as a stage show. We may even do it in the West End. When I'm tired of playing Ziggy I can step out and someone else can take over for me.

(DAVID BOWIE, AUGUST 1971)[1]

With my laptop perched on my knees, I conceived this chapter from the comfort of my bed. I'm watching a digitized version of Donn Pennebaker's film *Ziggy Stardust and the Spiders from Mars* (henceforth *Ziggy Stardust*), which was shot in 1973.[2] Somewhere between nostalgia and déjà vu, I recall my excitement as a sixteen-year-old Bowie fan, experiencing this film on a cinema screen upon its theatrical release in 1983. Jaunt to 2020, and I'm transported from the haven of my New Zealand bedroom back to a warm and relaxed gathering in London on 3 July 1973. The grainy handheld footage is momentarily punctuated with golden lens flares presciently sent from the late afternoon sun. Anticipation builds among colourful youths and perplexed police officers; I chuckle at the culture clash. The street outside London's Hammersmith Odeon teems with fans adorned with platform boots, space-age copper mullets and faces painted with lightning bolts and forehead patches. David Bowie is nowhere to be seen, yet Ziggy Stardust is everywhere: performed by fans, in anticipation for the onstage performance of Bowie.

As we shall see, this instance of collective mimicry serves as a colourful illustration of Judith Butler's concept of performativity, in which gender is 'an identity instituted through a stylised repetition of acts', and in particular 'the stylization of the body'.[3] However, these acts of fan performativity go beyond the notion of gendered performance and are best understood by first examining the layers of performance synthesized by Bowie at this terminal event. To this idolatrous audience, David Bowie 'played a character called Ziggy Stardust' onstage, *and* backstage for a promotional film that was considered by RCA as an experiment.

Through Pennebaker's cinematic vision and the Ziggy Stardust persona, Bowie and his collaborators synthesized the kinetic art form of mime together with glam rock, theatrical stage lighting, Leni Riefenstahl-esque branding and *kabuki* theatre. This spectacle is complicated by the alien figure of Ziggy, whose performance is characterized by the *Noh* mask tradition, make-up and costumes inspired by glam and sci-fi aesthetics and the elaborate costume designs of Kansai Yamamoto. This multimodal cultural canvas is further hybridized by the performativity of ambiguously gendered gestural signifiers. While this conglomerate of intertextual references, art forms and mediums achieved Bowie's long-held desire to synthesize multiple art forms as a 'total work of art', the different modes of performance were filmed under Pennebaker's direction, thus contributing his distinctively raw cinematic aesthetic to document Bowie's traverse of stage and screen. With its intimate depiction of Ziggy's onstage sexual ambiguity, backstage dressing room performance, fan adulation and emulation, the resulting film serves not only as a historic record of Ziggy Stardust's demise but also as an exemplar of Direct Cinema,[4] and a cultural and ethnographic record of the role of persona in the performativity of gender, sexuality and identity. While the term 'persona' can be understood as a perceived or expressed aspect of a person's character, it is used here to refer to a character that has been adopted and performed, onstage and in daily life. I draw upon Philip Auslander's theorization of 'musical persona and physical performance',[5] which emphasizes the gestural and performative dimensions of persona and builds upon the idea that personae are 'negotiated between musicians and their audiences within the constraints of genre framing'.[6] Following this vein, the framing devices established by the genres of rock stage performance and rockumentary play an important role in establishing the codes, conventions and boundaries of musical personae, all of which Bowie transcended via the Ziggy Stardust persona. By documenting this transcendence through multiple and intersecting layers of performance, *Ziggy Stardust* became a cinematic and cultural relic. As in archaeology, this relic is performatively stratified and thus imbued with revelations about Bowie as a transmedia actor.

To understand Bowie as a film actor we must examine his acting across media, a task that requires consideration of different approaches towards performance. How do we interpret his multimodal performance in this film? I argue that we experience a cleverly constructed cinematic record of *Gesamtkunstwerk*,[7] in which Bowie has written the script, provided the cast and pulled together a raft of collaborators to produce an intermedial performance comprising mime, pose, gesture, mask and 'frontality' for the camera.[8] An important antecedent to contemporary intermedia practice, *Gesamtkunstwerk* has been translated as 'total work of art' or 'synthesis of arts'.[9] In her article on Richard Wagner's theories on *Gesamtkunstwerk*, Krisztina Lajosi suggests the concept 'might also be rendered as "communal or collective artwork of the future"'.[10] Contemporary proponents of *Gesamtkunstwerk* strive for a multisensory synthesis of art forms, often involving the communal and integrated performance of music, literature, theatre, dance, film, photography, painting and sculpture.[11] As a performative-filmic assemblage, *Ziggy Stardust* raises questions about the slippage between Bowie simultaneously acting for a theatrical audience, for the film camera, for a cinema audience and eventually for a digital screen audience. Tracing this intermedial and performative slippage across stage, analogue film and digital screen, this chapter examines *Ziggy Stardust* as a performative vessel for Bowie to act through multiple mediums. While probing the depth and versatility of Bowie's acting skill, my analysis explicates the material capacity of this film to document a performative synthesis of art forms, thus serving as a performance itself.

By drawing together different disciplinary approaches towards performance, this chapter dissects the performative stratification and multimodality that result from Bowie's collaborative impulse and the synthesis of media documented and performed by Pennebaker's film. Taking up Wagner's notion of *Gesamtkunstwerk*,[12] I weave this together with theories of performance that have developed through the study of popular music, theatre, mime, acting for film, documentary, gender identity and the performance inherent in everyday interactions, as theorized in 1959 by Erving Goffman.[13] This polyphony of voices provides a dialogic framework for examining the fluidity of performance as it traverses stage, screen and mundane daily communication – which is essential for understanding Bowie as a film actor. Before delving into this theoretical quagmire, it is important to consider how Bowie perceived himself as a performer.

'Crossing over': From stage to screen

I thought, 'Well, here I am, I'm a bit mixed up creatively, I've got all these things I like doing at once on stage . . . I'm not quite sure if I'm a mime or a songwriter or a singer, or do I want to go back to painting again. Why am I doing any of these things anyway . . .' and I realised it was because I wanted to be well known [. . .] I wanted to be the instigator of new ideas, I wanted to turn people on to new things and new perspectives . . . I always wanted to be that sort of catalytic kind of thing.[14]

Although expressing some uncertainty about his role on stage, this extract from a 1976 interview reveals Bowie's early awareness of how artistic agency might be leveraged from his natural capacity for 'crossing over'.[15] Never comfortable with fixed notions of artistry or identity, Bowie manifested a restless drive to work across many different platforms, mediums and modes of performance. Elsewhere I have discussed Bowie's work across mediums in relation to the ideas of 'transmedia surrealism' and 'loose continuity', ideas related to Bowie's long-held desire to achieve *Gesamtkunstwerk*.[16] While the show at Hammersmith Odeon has become eternally memorable for Bowie having publicly killed off Ziggy Stardust, its documentation on film enabled it to be recognized as Bowie's first historic record of *Gesamtkunstwerk*, which Bowie had been edging towards achieving through his numerous stage performances as Ziggy Stardust. Bowie and his collaborators (including Lindsay Kemp and Mick Rock) came very close to achieving this during the *Rainbow Theatre* show in August 1972, an intermedial performance that included live music, dance, mime, costume, stage lighting and projected still photographs. But without being accompanied by a purposeful and coherent film with synchronized sound, the intermedial innovation of the *Rainbow Theatre* show was eclipsed by *Ziggy Stardust*.

Pennebaker's film is significant because it documents a historic moment in which traversing stage and screen enabled Bowie to achieve *Gesamtkunstwerk*. The filming process purposefully instigated an expanded choreography and a multiplicity of performance, occurring simultaneously across different mediums, and via extensive collaboration with an array of designers and musicians.[17] Bowie performed on stage to a live audience while also acting for the camera. Bowie's performance in this film cannot be studied in isolation from all the components comprising this 'total work of art'; his performance must be understood as intertwined with the multiplicity of performative elements, including mime, mask, make-up, costume, set design, lighting and the characterization of other stage performers. When examining further layers of this 'total work of art', we must take into account the presence of the film crew and cinematic elements such as framing, camera movement, film stock and editing decisions, which work in concert with all of the performative stage elements to achieve a multifaceted 'total' performance.

Stage performance and collaboration

For the Ziggy Stardust show, Bowie relied extensively on collaborations with his band members and sessional musicians, along with artists specializing in lighting, costume and make-up. His collaborative spirit extended to 'cultural borrowing' from artists such as Jacques Brel, Mick Jagger, Lou Reed and others, including his synthesis of coded signifiers, which he gleaned from literature, subcultures, popular culture and more. On stage, the Ziggy persona presented a synthesis of gestural traits derived from cabaret, avant-garde, popular music, science fiction, *kabuki* theatre and mime; Bowie and his band reworked the sounds and performance traits of particular star performers, genres and times. Through gesture, pose and vocal intonation, Bowie conjured the vocal and gestural traits of Jacques Brel and Anthony Newley. Although not physically present as a performer on stage, Lindsay Kemp's aesthetic presence as stage director is significant. The *Ziggy Stardust* film depicts avant-garde stage theatricality merging with Kubrick-inspired science-fiction aesthetics and expressionist elements, such as the lightning bolt iconography. As a reiterated element of the set design, this motif recalls the repeated iconography in Leni Riefenstahl's documentary representation of the Nuremberg rally, *Triumph of the Will* (1935). According to Frederic Spotts, this film inspired Bowie to exclaim to Mick Jagger: 'Hitler was one of the first great rock stars . . . he was no politician, he was a great media artist. How he worked his audience . . . he made an entire country a stage show.'[18] The idea of choreographing a stage show for a documentary film was not lost on Bowie, as was the reiteration of iconography to construct an enduring brand.

The Ziggy Stardust brand involved a complex array of signifiers. Bolan-esque platform-booted glam costumes alternate with the costume designs of Kansai Yamamoto, which Bowie described as 'heavily inspired in equal parts by *Kabuki* and *Samurai*'.[19] Reinforcing the strong Japanese aesthetic of Bowie's costume, make-up artist Pierre La Roche used the *Noh* mask as a base, from which he added layers of shimmer to produce a fusion of Japanese *geisha* with glam alien. Beautifully ornate earrings, oversized bangles and a feather boa add touches of femininity and camp to Ziggy's onstage costume. These aesthetic codes merge syncretically with cabaret and Hollywood starlet aesthetics, all working together to reinforce Ziggy's gender ambiguity. Acting as Ziggy, Bowie performatively adopted a repertoire of feminized self-touching gestures and poses that had been performed by Hollywood starlets such as Dietrich and Greta Garbo, a strategy of mimicry he had utilized for the *Hunky Dory* album (1971) cover art.[20] This melding of a starlet's gestural traits is a distinctive feature of Bowie's performance as Ziggy Stardust, on and offstage (Figure 1.1). Perceiving himself as a type of 'transmedia navigator', Bowie migrated

FIGURE 1.1 *Bowie performatively adopted a repertoire of feminized self-touching gestures and poses*. Ziggy Stardust and the Spiders from Mars *(Donn Pennebaker, 1979) (01:05:13)*.

gestural traits across media platforms, from stage to promotional film to magazine photographs and album cover art.[21] Hollywood starlets, fashion designers, make-up artists and musical performers such as Brel, Newley, Jagger and Reed were implicated as performative collaborators during the final Ziggy Stardust show, since Bowie reiterated their visual and sonic gestures. Given the significance Bowie placed on this collaborative aspect of performance, it is important to turn our attention to those who taught him the skills to act for stage and screen.

Learning to act for stage and screen

In the years leading up to his notorious last gasp as Ziggy Stardust, Bowie had developed skills in theatrical performance prior to mastering the art of performing for the camera. He underwent at least four years of tuition with Lindsay Kemp, an avant-garde dancer, theatre actor and mime artist who taught Bowie the stagecraft elements of mime, mask and make-up.[22] This 'internship' segued into Bowie's development of the Ziggy Stardust persona, a period of several months that coincided with the beginnings of his creative relationship with photographer Mick Rock. This collaboration produced numerous iconic photographs and a handful of distinctive music videos, all of which contain vital information about Bowie's developing adroitness in front of the camera. If we compare the videos directed by Rock with

Bowie's earlier promotional film *Love You till Tuesday* (1969),[23] it would seem that Rock helped develop Bowie as a film actor. Bowie's prowess in front of the camera became more sophisticated with each photo session and video directed by Rock. From a performer who was skilled onstage, but uncomfortably self-conscious in front of the camera, within three to four years he developed into a versatile performer who had learnt to use the camera as a tool for activating a direct, intimate and powerful connection with his audience. For 'John, I'm Only Dancing' (1972),[24] Bowie practised the art of directly addressing the camera, using gesture and pose to play with gender codes, integrating sexual ambiguity with fledgling punk mannerisms. By the time Rock directed the video for 'Life on Mars' (1973),[25] Bowie had learnt to skilfully alternate direct address to camera with indirect address, another strategy he'd borrowed from the cinematic and gestural codes of Hollywood starlets. This video's sequence of extreme close-ups compels his viewers into a powerful engagement with his anisocoric eyes. Not relinquishing control over this gaze, Bowie lowers his eyelids, seductively enticing his audience to gaze upon his artfully made-up face, performing as an object of beauty and desire. His performance is honed for maximum impact in front of Rock's camera; facial and bodily gesture, pose and mime are skilfully performed to work in tandem with alternating framing, camera movements and abrupt transitions.

Having sharpened his screen performance skills for Rock's videos and photo shoots, Bowie was primed to integrate these skills with multiple elements of stagecraft. He achieved this on 3 July 1973 with the help of Donn Pennebaker, a pioneer of Direct Cinema. Emerging alongside *Cinéma Verité* during the late 1960s, Direct Cinema is a subgenre of documentary that advocated an observational approach towards documenting reality, stipulating non-intervention of the filmmaker. Often this meant filming from a distance with a long lens so as to create the impression of unfettered access to people and events. This attempt to minimize the presence of the camera and create the impression of an unobtrusive filmmaker obscures the mediating presence of the camera, director and film crew, creating an audience akin to being a 'fly on the wall', thus being witness to the daily (sometimes mundane) lives of famous and 'ordinary' people.[26] Being a proponent of Direct Cinema, Pennebaker required Bowie to perform in a manner that was diametric to what he had achieved for Rock's camera in 'Life on Mars'. In contrast to the extreme close-ups and intense direct address of Rock's promos, Bowie was now being expected to act as though he was unaware of the presence of the film crew, their large cameras and audio-recording equipment. Even a momentary accidental look directly into the camera would transgress Direct Cinema's contract with the audience, which hinged upon *indirect* address, non-participation of the film director and the subject's ability to feign non-awareness of the presence of the camera, all of which was intended to construct an audience experience of being like a 'fly-on-the-wall'.[27] Having only recently mastered the strategy of engaging his audience with playfully stylized transitions between direct and indirect address to camera, Bowie had to rapidly adjust to Direct Cinema's requirement to perform in a way that appeared as though he was oblivious to the presence of the large film cameras aimed at him. In order to understand the significance of these restrictions, it is helpful to consider how Direct Cinema might be considered in relation to theories of documentary performance.

Documentary performance

Extending upon his pragmatic schema of documentary modes,[28] Bill Nichols added the 'performative mode' to describe films that 'stress subjective aspects of a classically objective discourse'.[29] Portraying a somewhat cynical view, Nichols indicated that by drawing attention to themselves, these films move away from their realist representational function. Departing from this view, Stella Bruzzi expresses a positive approach towards performative documentary, defining it as 'a mode which emphasizes – and indeed constructs a film around – the often hidden aspect of performance, whether on the part of the documentary subjects or the filmmakers'.[30] Since Direct Cinema films are 'predicated upon the realist assumption that the production process must be disguised', these films tend to focus on individuals who are well versed in acting or are comfortable with performing on film.[31] With its adherence to the principles of Direct Cinema, *Ziggy Stardust*'s performance elements reflect the principle that the 'naked truth' inherent in observational film will only be accessible if the performance is uninhibited by anything that might draw attention to the production process.

Bruzzi argues that all 'documentaries are a negotiation between filmmaker and reality and, at heart, a performance' and that 'whether built around the intrusive presence of the filmmaker or self-conscious performances by its subjects', documentary performance exemplifies 'the enactment of the notion that a documentary only comes into being as it is performed, that although its factual basis (or document) can pre-date any recording or representation of it, the film itself is necessarily performative because it is given meaning by the interaction between performance and reality'.[32] This idea is also reiterated in Auslander's remark that 'the act of documenting an event as a performance is what constitutes it as such. Documentation does not simply generate image/statements that describe an autonomous performance and state that it occurred: it produces an event as a performance and ... the performer as "artist"'.[33] Bruzzi and Auslander's comments about documenting performance also parallel Butler's argument that gender only comes into being via performative acts; in other words, that our sense of gender is only given meaning by our actualized experiences of reiterated performative acts, which often involve stylization of the body.[34] As we shall see, both concepts of performativity theorized by Butler and Bruzzi are activated by Bowie in *Ziggy Stardust*. While stylized acts are documented by Pennebaker in an unobtrusive manner, it is Bowie (performing as Ziggy) who catalyses the interaction between performance and reality, and it is his stylized acts that produce an alternate sense of gender, one that is performatively mimicked by his fans.

Donn Pennebaker: Directing screen performance

For this final Ziggy Stardust show, Bowie and his collaborators were mindful that all the elements of stage performance were on this occasion also elements of screen performance. While each collaborator contributed to this 'total work of art', the cinematic representation of these elements was in the hands of Pennebaker. RCA flew Pennebaker to London to film the last Ziggy Stardust show, initially with the intention of using the footage to test their new 'SelectaVision VideoDisc' technology.[35] Pennebaker recalled that 'it was only supposed to be a half-hour but that concert was so amazing that I said "this is a feature film, I don't know why I know that, but I know it"'.[36] Together, Pennebaker and Bowie eventually achieved this vision.

Bowie's first meeting with Pennebaker occurred only a day before the filming of the Hammersmith Odeon concert. As this was Bowie's first encounter with a vanguard of Direct Cinema, it is likely that Pennebaker introduced Bowie to an entirely new approach to performance, one that was possibly at odds with his leanings towards affectation. Pennebaker arrived in London a day before the final Ziggy Stardust show, allowing him only hours to take test footage of the prior night's performance and consider potential technical challenges.[37] In addition to devising a method for recording quality sound from performers and the recording desk, he needed to develop strategies for adequate film exposure. The lighting design for the stage show required minimal, low-key stage lighting, with the primary light source provided by a series of directional Followspot lights. Responding to these challenges, Pennebaker used film stock suited for low lighting situations, resulting in a distinctively 'grainy' film look. With only three camera operators available, each needed to focus on capturing certain types of shots.[38] This enabled an abundance of tightly cropped footage of Bowie performing onstage, shot from multiple angles and vantage points. This approach also provided a plethora of close-up shots of fans, which were usefully intercut with key moments of the performance to accentuate the emotional response of fans (Figure 1.2). Pennebaker also situated a camera in the dressing room, ensuring plenty of well-lit, behind-the-scenes

FIGURE 1.2 *Close-up shots of fans showed their emotional response.* Ziggy Stardust and the Spiders from Mars *(Donn Pennebaker, 1979) (00:37:13)*.

close-ups, thus achieving the intimacy necessary to attain the 'direct truth' of Direct Cinema. Compensating for the lack of available light, the audience were asked to take as many flash photographs as possible. This audience interaction added to the spacey strobe effect, momentarily illuminating elements of the stage and audience and rendering them only fleetingly visible during parts of the film.

Zones of performance

As an analytical framing device, I have demarcated *Ziggy Stardust* into four distinct zones, differentiated by different modes of performance, distinct approaches to filming and site-specific lighting situations:

Zone 1 is the external location, distinguished by handheld footage of fans mingling and 'performing' as they wait for the show to open. This zone includes the different types of performance of fans, police and Angie Bowie arriving on the scene.

Zone 2 includes the behind-the-scenes shots within the dressing room, ranging from mid shots to extreme close-ups illuminated by bright film lights. Feigning oblivion of the presence of camera and crew, Bowie's performance can usefully be examined in relation to theories of performance in documentary film posited by Nichols, Bruzzi and Jane Roscoe.

In contrast to the brightness of zone 2, **zone 3** is marked by predominantly dark onstage footage of Bowie and his band, who are lit primarily by coloured theatre light projected from large Followspots. These are designed to place a salient spotlight on the most prominent actors and follow their action as they move across the stage. Bowie's onstage performance combines theatrical acting techniques with mime and the anticipated codes of rock performance, all of which are punctuated with strategies more akin to film acting.

Also minimally lit, **zone 4** is distinguished by shots of audience members as they respond emotionally to the stage performance. Their tragically devoted faces are illuminated by the theatrical light reflecting off a large mirror ball. These close-ups and mid shots are intercut with stage footage to evoke a sense of drama and to trigger affective engagement from the film audience.

Zone 2: The dressing room as haven of authenticity – or voyeuristic space shuttle?

Interviewer: What about Bowie in the dressing room?

Pennebaker: There was a lot of kinetic energy around Bowie. He was like an orchestra leader.[39]

Drawing to the conclusion of 'Moonage Daydream', Bowie subtly disappears into the background, leaving Ronson to command the audience's attention with an extended guitar solo. Enthralled by Ronson's virtuoso one-act, the audience are oblivious to Bowie's vanishing act and speedy costume change backstage. The film audience, on the other hand, has the privilege of being transported from the guitar solo, back in time and backstage to see Bowie's semi-naked figure in the dressing room. We see him changing his costume while the sound of Ronson's guitar retrospectively plays from the stage. Flanked by attentive costume assistants, Bowie's lithe, snow-white body commands salience within this mid shot. He appears hyperfocused and unaware of the camera as he and three assistants collectively squeeze his skeletal frame into thigh-gripping striped pants (Figure 1.3). Zipping up his matching sci-fi jacket, the assistants adorn Ziggy with bracelets and earrings. Hearing the guitar solo winding towards its close, we can empathize with Bowie's time pressure. With no time to be self-conscious about the presence of the camera aimed at intimate body parts, Bowie appears unconcerned about his physique being the object of this roaming lens. The camera creeps down to reveal his waist, hips, crotch and thighs, tightly clad in gloriously stripy space pants – a visual spectacle ironized by the overheard words of the costume assistant exclaiming: 'it's going well David. The audience are lovely . . . beautiful audience!' Coming to rest at floor level to give us an eyeful of Ziggy's red space boots, the camera quickly tilts back up to

FIGURE 1.3 *Bowie and three assistants collectively squeeze his skeletal frame into thigh-gripping striped pants.* Ziggy Stardust and the Spiders from Mars *(Donn Pennebaker, 1979) (00:29:48).*

reveal the completed package. Hearing the guitar solo concluding from the stage, Bowie leaves just in time to emerge on stage for Ronson's concluding glissando. One can't help feeling the live audience has missed out on the film audience's privileged access to this intimate costume change.

After a stirring rendition of Brel's song 'My Death', Bowie beams at the adoring audience as they collectively complete his words 'there is . . . me'! The camera follows him as he disappears into the dark backstage area for his second costume change. Juxtaposed to the darkness of the stage, we then see a brightly lit extreme close-up of Bowie's eyes in the mirror as a make-up brush glides across his nose. Dragging on a cigarette, he asks, 'how long have we got?' The camera pulls back to reveal his naked flesh in the foreground and Ringo Starr sitting in the background. The two stars share a nervous glance and chuckle. Although careful not to show his consciousness of the camera's presence, his acute awareness of being the object under observation is portrayed by his pose and gestures. Bowie is seated in a semi-posed position, forming an elegant naked triangle with his wrist resting upon up-tilted knee – the sort of pose one would expect of a Hollywood starlet. He enhances this starlet look with a bit of self-touching, giving the top of his spiky mullet a pronounced feminine flick (Figure 1.4). He chats excitedly with off-screen dressing room inhabitants, expressing glee at the audience answering his call-and-response moment at the end of the song 'there is . . . me!' By imposing obstructions around acknowledging the presence of the camera, Pennebaker enabled Bowie to extend upon what

FIGURE 1.4 *Bowie enhances his starlet pose with a feminine hair flick*. Ziggy Stardust and the Spiders from Mars *(Donn Pennebaker, 1979) (00:45:30)*.

he had learnt about acting for the camera as an object to be gazed upon. Without looking directly into the camera lens, he could use gesture and pose to work the camera and maintain control of a sexualized gaze. This use of indirect address was an important development to Bowie's masterful skillset in front of the camera.

A few cuts later and Bowie is dressed in an asymmetrical knitted jumpsuit designed by Kansai Yamamoto. With a focused jiggle to the background music, he probes his ear with his thumb, possibly a deliberate use of a normally unconscious gesture to feign a lack of awareness of being filmed. The camera captures him in the mirror as his costume assistant wraps him in an elaborate Yamamoto cape. Then, just for a fleeting moment, we see Bowie looking into the mirror, straight through the camera lens at us. Just for a split second, his eyes make contact with his film audience (Figure 1.5). Whether accidental or purposeful, this momentary look into the lens breaches Direct Cinema's prohibition of direct address to camera. As a result, the film audience becomes instantly aware of Bowie's knowledge of the camera's presence, possibly even jolted out of the 'fly-on-the-wall' viewing stance.[40] This creates a momentary rupture in the overall continuity in which a documentary subject performs indirectly, as though they are not performing. Could this moment represent a 'flicker of authenticity' within a documentary performance based on feigning non-performance?[41] Roscoe first developed this idea to describe a moment in reality TV shows, in which participants unexpectedly let down their guard to show rare moments of emotional authenticity. This momentary 'flicker' breaks

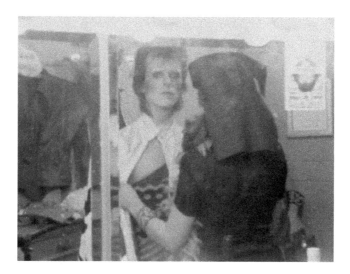

FIGURE 1.5 *For a split second, Bowie's eyes make contact with his film audience.* Ziggy Stardust and the Spiders from Mars *(Donn Pennebaker, 1979) (00:46:08).*

with coded performance, which often involves acting as though unaware of the presence of the camera. In this sense, 'flickers of authenticity' are moments in which 'the mask of performance falls away from the Reality TV contestant/participant'. By deliberately recalling 'Barthes' notion of the 'punctum' and Brecht's 'alienation effect',[42] these 'flickers' can be used as strategies of performative defamiliarization by actors and directors of both stage and screen. In the context of *Ziggy Stardust*, Bowie's fleeting flicker of authenticity may cause an abrupt breach of the conventions of Direct Cinema. However, the directness of address to camera is complicated by the mediating presence of the mirror. Interestingly, Bowie has repeatedly played with the motif of the mirror as mediator in many of his performances to camera.[43]

Zone 3: Performing for different audiences

While performing primarily as stage actor and live musician, Bowie's awareness of the location of lights and cameras ensures that he achieves spotlight salience *and* 'frontality' for the camera. Developed by David Bordwell and James Naremore, the concept of 'frontality' is useful for examining Bowie's film acting technique.[44] Naremore describes 'frontality' in terms of the film actors' practice of maintaining an acute awareness of the spatial parameters within which they can extend their performance. In other words, this spatial awareness is necessary in order to remain within the borders of the cinematic frame. He explains:

Movie actors therefore learn to control and modulate behaviour to fit a variety of situations, suiting their actions to a medium that might view them at any distance, height or angle and that sometimes changes the vantage point within a single shot . . . In all films, however, the behaviour of players is designed to make significant faces and gestures visible, important dialogue audible. Hence the average two- or three-figure composition will involve a 'shared' position, with the actors in three-quarter profile to the camera . . . their faces turned slightly toward the lens, leaving an open space for the sightline of a hypothetical viewer.[45]

This modulated behaviour by film actors was described by Bordwell as a 'classical use of frontality',[46] a strategic approach to film acting that was apparently not lost on Bowie. Since he was primarily performing for a live audience, his movement across stage appears unconstrained by the presence of cameras. However, it is possible to observe specific moments of intensity where Bowie seems to position his body strategically so as to allow the camera lens to capture a slightly indirect frontal perspective, or a full-body shot to display the spectacle of his costume (Figure 1.6), or a silhouette shot to display his posed figure (Figure 1.7), or a low-angle close-up shot to emphasize emotion and position Bowie as powerful, such as during the song 'My Death' (Figure 1.8). Bowie's use of frontality for the camera, and Pennebaker's cinematic response to this, demonstrates the collaborative spirit in which this film was created. While Bowie is attentive to and skilled at the art of posing for the camera, Pennebaker is attentive to and skilled

FIGURE 1.6 *A full-body shot displaying the spectacle of Bowie's costume.* Ziggy Stardust and the Spiders from Mars *(Donn Pennebaker, 1979) (00:48:43)*.

FIGURE 1.7 *A silhouette shot displaying Bowie's figure in an ambiguously sexualized pose.* Ziggy Stardust and the Spiders from Mars *(Donn Pennebaker, 1979) (00:49:02).*

FIGURE 1.8 *A low-angle close-up shot emphasizing emotion during Bowie's performance of 'My Death'.* Ziggy Stardust and the Spiders from Mars *(Donn Pennebaker, 1979) (00:44:12).*

at the art of filming the posed and stylized body. This mutual attentiveness was put to the test during the sequences of mime and metaphorical stage theatrics.

Mime

As stage director for the Ziggy Stardust shows, Kemp's contribution is most evident through Bowie's use of mime. Kemp studied with Marcel Marceau, a twentieth-century French mime master who also influenced Bowie, particularly with regard to his use of the mask and masking more generally as a stage and screen performance tool.[47] Given Bowie's interest in the filming of mime performance, it is significant to mention the parallels between Étienne Decroux and Marshall McLuhan, both inspirations for Bowie. Observing their 'parallel worlds', Wayne Constantineau writes: 'While Marshall McLuhan (1911-1980) was fond of repeating that we could understand media through mime, Étienne Decroux (1898-1992), the founder of corporeal mime, spent sixty years investigating McLuhan's world of media.'[48] Decroux developed an approach he termed corporeal mime, which he described as 'making visible the invisible', an approach that would require a performer to explicitly use their body as a tool to communicate internal states.[49] Theatre actor and director Nicola Baylis explains Decroux's definition of the corporeal mime performer as 'one who possessed the body of a gymnast, the mind of an actor, but also the heart of a poet' – an approach to mime that may have resonated with Bowie.[50] Decroux's ideas 'were intrinsically bound in life, its passions, and its dreams. Ways of expressing thought, love, reverie, work, struggle, social relationships, and the divine are central to the practice of corporeal mime.'[51] Baylis observes that in the teaching of corporeal mime, 'movement concepts are expounded with references to the work of sculptors, painters, musicians, playwrights, philosophers, and poets, as well as to a diverse range of stories and legends'.[52] Given the intermedial and philosophical centrality of this approach, it's easy to see why Bowie was inspired by Decroux's version of corporeal mime, particularly given Bowie's fascination with combining philosophical and literary elements with intermedial performance. Decroux's approach to mime provides a useful context for considering Bowie's mime and gesture-infused performance of 'The Width of a Circle'.

'The Width of a Circle'

A shaky camera slowly zooms in to a bust shot of Bowie. As the guitar opens the song, Bowie's *kabuki* mask-like face holds a fixed, entranced stare into

FIGURE 1.9.1 *Bowie's Kabuki mask-like face is fixed, staring into the distance. Ziggy Stardust and the Spiders from Mars (Donn Pennebaker, 1979).*

the distance (Figure 1.9.1). After several seconds, a musical change jerks him suddenly out of this frozen pose. Singing 'I looked and frowned, cos the monster was me . . . me!', he prods his finger at his chest. He then retreats into the darkness, leaving Ronson under the spotlight doing a one-handed guitar solo. The camera zooms in to a blurry close-up of Ronson's fingers flourishing across his fretboard. In the darkness we can barely see Ronson and Trevor Bolder engage in a guitar players' duel, intercut with strobe-lit shots of tortured, tear-stained faces of audience members. When Bowie returns, donning a skimpy bunny-print playsuit and a pretty chandelier earring, he slips straight back into the song, again accompanied by overt sign-language-like gestures (Figure 1.9.2). Turning his back on the audience, he saunters away from them, only to turn and run towards the front stage where he is bounced back by an invisible 'wall'. With a small spot of orange glow from the Followspot accompanying his every move, he explores the wall with the flattened palms of his hands (Figure 1.9.3). Following from the anticipated rock guitar duel, many audience members would not be expecting a mime performance by an androgynous glam-rocker wearing a bunny-print playsuit. If the wall routine was starting to feel clichéd for some, this thought would disintegrate with what follows: in sync with a shift in the rhythm and pace of the music, finding an opening in the top of the 'wall', Bowie runs his fingers down the meeting point between two 'doors', which he prizes open with his hands. At this epiphanous moment, we hear the spiritually awakening science-fiction tone of a stylophone, just as we see the light from the Followspot growing and shrinking in empathy

FIGURE 1.9.2 *With overt 'sign language' like gestures, Bowie returns to the stage to sing 'Width of a Circle'.* Ziggy Stardust and the Spiders from Mars *(Donn Pennebaker, 1979) (01:03:23).*

FIGURE 1.9.3 *The Followspot accompanies Bowie's every move as he explores the 'wall' with the palms of his hands.* Ziggy Stardust and the Spiders from Mars *(Donn Pennebaker, 1979) (01:03:56).*

FIGURE 1.9.4 *The light from the Followspot grows and shrinks in empathy with the widening and narrowing of the crack between the doors.* Ziggy Stardust and the Spiders from Mars *(Donn Pennebaker, 1979) (01:04:23)*.

with the widening and narrowing of the crack between the doors (Figure 1.9.4). When Ziggy finally pushes the doors wide open, the light expands in concert with the expanding guitars (Figure 1.9.5). Bowie tilts his torso forward, spreads his arms and waves them elegantly like the wings of an eagle (Figure 1.9.6). The significance of this mime sequence was later described by Bowie:

> The eagle mime was a throwback to a dramatic piece that I performed as an opener for Tyrannosaurus Rex at the festival hall in 1968. Called 'Yet San and the Eagle' it told the story of how the Chinese had invaded Tibet and though the Tibetans may be struck down their spirit would fly for eternity.[53]

While Bowie underplays this as a 'throwback' piece, I experience this as a masterful audio-visual-kinetic mime sequence that perfectly illustrates the artistic-literary dialogue, intermedial transit and collective assemblage of *Gesamtkunstwerk*. It also exemplifies the multimodal and collaborative aspect of performance, as well as Decroux's theories about the capacity of mime to communicate mythical stories. This sequence also illustrates mime's shared kinship with persona as an artistic strategy.

FIGURE 1.9.5 *The spotlight expands in concert with the expanding guitars.* Ziggy Stardust and the Spiders from Mars *(Donn Pennebaker, 1979) (01:04.27).*

FIGURE 1.9.6 *Bowie waves his arms akin to the wings of an elegant eagle.* Ziggy Stardust and the Spiders from Mars *(Donn Pennebaker, 1979) (01:04.46).*

Persona, performing identity and the artificiality of rock

Given the significance Bowie placed on persona as an artistic strategy, it is important to stress the role of the Ziggy Stardust persona in the performance of identity. This topic has already been covered exceptionally well by Auslander and Shelton Waldrep, among others, so I aim to show how their contributions to the topic shed further light on understanding Bowie's approach to multimodal performance. Waldrep observed that 'Bowie's theatrical approach to rock music, especially in its visual form, is dependent upon a mixture of Brechtian minimalism and Asian theatre gesture'. Supporting this argument, he adds that 'Bowie's gestures are matched, at times with the purposeful inexpressiveness of his face'.[54] As we have seen from my examination of Bowie's performance of 'Width of a Circle', Waldrep's observations help to explain the artistic strategy behind Ziggy's mask-like facial quiescence at the start of the song. In his book *Future Nostalgia*, Waldrep argues that 'Bowie gives us a way to understand the vicissitudes of performance, aestheticizing the link between rock music and everyday life by calling attention to the artificiality of both'.[55] By dissecting the multiple threads of Bowie's multimodal approach to performance, Waldrep shows how Bowie articulated several different performance strategies together with mime, gesture, mask and persona. Bowie's calling attention to the artificiality of rock music is also explored by Auslander.

Writing from the disciplinary perspective of popular music studies, Auslander contributes an astute assessment of Bowie's use of persona and the performance of gay sexuality in *Ziggy Stardust*, as a subversive strategy to undermine the normativity of heterosexuality in rock culture. Viewing Bowie's performance of sexuality in *Ziggy Stardust* as 'multiply subversive', Auslander asserts that 'it flew in the face of rock culture's traditional heterosexual imperative . . . without simply asserting Gay Rock as an equal alternative'.[56] Bowie utilized rock performance via *Gesamtkunstwerk* as a form of 'theatrical role playing' to challenge the ideological construction of authenticity that had become a naturalized facet of the rock genre.[57] But rather than performing '"authentic" homosexuality' Bowie used the persona of Ziggy to throw 'the sexuality of rock into question not only by performing a sexual identity previously excluded from rock but also by performing that identity in such a way that it was clearly revealed as a performance for which there was no underlying referent'.[58] These observations are accompanied by Auslander's discussion of a particular part of the stage performance in the Ziggy Stardust show: the feigned fellatio act between Ziggy and Ronson's guitar had stirred extensive media gossip about Bowie's sexuality, so he chose to exploit the media attention by elaborating the act as a routine part of the stage show.

Conclusion

I opened this chapter by evoking the sense of time travel and remediated performance I experienced while researching for this chapter. From my portable computer screen I viewed a digital record of a cinematic performance, which documented the phenomenon of identity performativity as fans waited in anticipation for the stage performance of Ziggy Stardust. Fascinating as they are, the internal and external zones of fan performativity depicted so intimately by Pennebaker for *Ziggy Stardust* have necessarily taken a back seat in order to shine the spotlight on the object of their adoration. In order to draw out the complexity of Bowie as a performer, and to consider the significance he placed on the multimodality of performance as artistic practice and subversive strategy, it is necessary to transit across vast interdisciplinary terrain.

Considering Bowie's early perception of himself as a performer across media, I reflected on his formative tutelage vis-à-vis collaboration with Kemp and Rock, a period in which he developed the skills for acting across stage and screen. Moving across media, synthesizing art forms and collaborating were not only fundamental to Bowie's modus operandi, these processes were the key ingredients of *Gesamtkunstwerk*. Edging towards this total work of art, Bowie's stage performance was characterized by a holistic merging of art forms, brought about by the collective efforts of his collaborators. Working in concert with them, Bowie understood that all aspects of stage performance were also aspects of screen performance.

As director of *Ziggy Stardust*, Pennebaker understood the multimodal complexities of performance that Bowie was orchestrating. Within the context of documentary performance, Direct Cinema required Bowie to act as though he was not acting, a potential challenge for someone who had just mastered the art of direct address to camera. Taking up the challenge, Bowie exploited all he had learnt from Hollywood starlets about gesture and pose as strategies to perform for the camera as a feminized object to be gazed upon. These strategies are fully on display in the dressing room sequences, where Bowie feigns oblivion of the camera, only momentarily rupturing the 'fly-on-the-wall' pretence of the Direct Cinema contract with a 'flicker of authenticity'. Perhaps this 'flicker' achieves a similar type of subversion alluded to by Auslander and Waldrep, by 'calling attention to the artificiality' of concert films about rock performers. Bowie casts light on this through many aspects of his stage performance, as is famously exemplified by the elaborately choreographed fellatio act. However, the most significant exemplar of multimodal performance in *Ziggy Stardust* has to be the 'Yet San and the Eagle' mime sequence, in which so many performance modes work collectively towards an artistically unified moment of *Gesamtkunstwerk*. It is a beautiful moment of intermedial synthesis and dialogue between performance artists.

As I shut down my laptop and pull up the bed covers, I'm left with an image: *Ziggy Stardust* is like an elaborately painted *matryoshka* doll. If we crack open and peel back the glitter-embellished layers, we find a performance within a performance, within a performance, within a performance. At the centre of it all, we find the 'naked truth' of David Bowie.

Notes

1. Bowie quoted in Philip Auslander, 'Watch That Man David Bowie: Hammersmith Odeon, London, 3 July 1973', in *Performance and Popular Music: History, Place and Time*, ed. Ian Inglis (London: Routledge, 2006), 70–80.
2. *Ziggy Stardust and the Spiders from Mars*, [film], Dir. Donn Pennebaker. Filmed: July 1973, first released at Edinburgh Film Festival: 1979, subsequently released on film, VHS and DVD on various dates.
3. Judith Butler, 'Performative Acts and Gender Constitution: An Essay in Phenomenology and Feminist Theory', *Theatre Journal* 40, no. 4 (1988): 519.
4. Direct Cinema is a documentary genre that emerged between 1958 and 1962 in Quebec and the United States. Donn A. Pennebaker was a pioneer of this genre.
5. Philip Auslander, 'Musical Persona: The Physical Performance of Popular Music', in *The Ashgate Research Companion to Popular Musicology*, ed. Derek B Scott (Farnham, Surrey; Burlington, VT: Ashgate, 2009), 303.
6. Phillip Auslander, 'Musical Personae', *TDR, The MIT Press* 50, no. 1 (Spring, 2006): 114.
7. For more on *Gesamtkunstwerk* ('Total Work of Art'), see also: Richard Wagner, *Das Kunstwerk der Zukunft* (*The Artwork of the Future*), trans. Emma Warner (London: *The Wagner Journal*, 2013).
8. 'Frontality' is defined later in the chapter. It is also defined by James Naremore, *Acting in the Cinema* (Berkeley: University of California Press, 1988), 41.
9. Krisztina Lajosi, 'Wagner and the (Re)mediation of Art: *Gesamtkunstwerk* and 19th Century theories of Media', *Frame* 23, no. 2 (2010): 43.
10. Ibid., 46.
11. Michael Goddard, 'Audiovision and Gesamtkunstwerk: The Aesthetics of First and Second Generation Industrial Music Video', in *Music/Video: Histories, Aesthetics, Media*, ed. Gina Arnold, Daniel Cookney, Kirsty Faircough and Michael Goddard (London: Bloomsbury Academic, 2017), 163–80.
12. Wagner, *Das Kunstwerk der Zukunft*.
13. Erving Goffman, *The Presentation of Self in Everyday Life* (New York: Anchor Books, 1959).
14. David Bowie, interview extract from 'Changes' (1976), quoted in Kathryn Johnson, 'David Bowie is', in *David Bowie: Critical Perspectives*, ed. Eoin Devereux, Aileen Dillane and Martin Power (New York: Routledge, 2015), 1–18.

15 'Crossing over' is a phrase used by Tony Oursler to describe Bowie in the context of his generation of artist's 'stary-eyed belief' in 'leaving the elitism of the white cube for other media and venues'. Tony Oursler, 'David Bowie', Artforum, accessed 1 March 2020, https://www.artforum.com/print/201603/David-bowie-58102.
16 Lisa Perrott, 'The Alchemical Union of David Bowie and Floria Sigismondi: Dialogic World-building, "Transmedia Surrealism", and "Loose Continuity"', in *Transmedia Directors: Artistry, Industry and New Audiovisual Aesthetics*, ed. Carol Vernallis, Holly Rogers, and Lisa Perrott (New York: Bloomsbury, 2019), 194–7.
17 Collaborators include set design and choreography by Lindsay Kemp, costume design by Kansai Yamamoto and Natasha Korniloff, make-up by Pierre La Roche, lighting by theatrical designers and instrumentals by band members and sessional musicians.
18 Frederic Spotts, *Hitler and the Power of Aesthetics* (New York: Overlook Press), 56.
19 David Bowie and Mick Rock, *Moonage Daydream: The Life and Times of Ziggy Stardust* (Bath, UK: Doppelganger, 2002), 192.
20 Camille Paglia explores this in 'Theatre of Gender: David Bowie at the Climax of the Sexual Revolution', in *David Bowie Is*, ed. Victoria Broackes and Geoffrey Marsh (London, V&A Publishing, 2013), 69–92.
21 Perrott, 'The Alchemical Union of David Bowie and Floria Sigismondi', 197.
22 For more on Lindsay Kemp, see the official Lindsay Kemp website at: https://www.lindsaykemp.eu/.
23 'Love You till Tuesday'. Promotional film, directed by Malcolm J. Thomson, 1969.
24 'John, I'm Only Dancing'. Promotional film, directed by Mick Rock, 1972.
25 'Life on Mars'. Promotional film, directed by Mick Rock, 1973.
26 For more on Pennebaker's approach towards Direct Cinema, see: Frank Verano, 'D.A. Pennebaker and the Politics and Aesthetics of Mature Period Direct Cinema', PhD diss., (University of Sussex, 2015).
27 Keith Beattie, 'Reworking Direct Cinema: Performative Display in Rockumentary', in *Populäre Musikkulturen im Film. Film und Bewegtbild in Kultur und Gesellschaft*, ed. Carsten Heinze and Laura Neibling (Wiesbaden: Springer VS, 2016), 11–152; Keith Beattie, 'It's not Only Rock n Roll: "Rockumentary", Direct Cinema and Performative Display', *Australasian Journal of American Studies* 24, no. 2 (2005): 21–41.
28 Bill Nichols, 'How Can We Describe the Observational, Participatory and Performative Modes of Documentary Film?' in *Introduction to Documentary*, ed. Bill Nichols (Bloomington, IN: Indiana University Press, 2017), 132–58.
29 Bill Nichols, *Blurred Boundaries: Questions of Meaning in Contemporary Culture* (Bloomington: Indiana University Press, 1995), 95.
30 Stella Bruzzi, *New Documentary* (London and New York: Routledge, 2006), 185.

31 Ibid., 190.
32 Ibid., 186.
33 Philip Auslander, 'The Performativity of Performance Documentation', *PAJ: A Journal of Performance Art* 28, no. 3 (2006): 5.
34 Butler, *Performative Acts and Gender Constitution*, 519; Judith Butler, *Gender Trouble* (London and New York: Routledge, 1990).
35 Keith Beattie, *D.A. Pennebaker* (Bloomington, IN: University of Illinois Press, 2011), 136.
36 Ibid.
37 Donn Pennebaker, quoted in Harvey Kubernik, 'D.A. Pennebaker on David Bowie', Cave Hollywood, published 12 January 2016, http://cavehollywood.com/d-a-pennebaker-on-david-bowie/.
38 Ibid.
39 Ibid.
40 This moment shares some similarities with a similar mirror shot in which one of the Maysles Brothers accidently films himself through a mirror during a very intense moment in the film. Both moments could be regarded as 'flickers of authenticity'.
41 Jane Roscoe, 'Real Entertainment: Real factual Hybrid Television', *Media International Australia* 100, no. 1 (2001): 9–20.
42 Derek Paget and Jane Roscoe, 'Giving Voice: Performance and Authenticity in the Documentary Musical', *Jump Cut: A Review of Contemporary Media*, no. 48 (Winter 2006): [online] https://www.ejumpcut.org/archive/jc48.2006/MusicalDocy/.
43 See, for instance, Mick Rock's iconic photograph of Bowie gazing into a mirror at Haddon Hall. Shot in 1972, this photo was reproduced in Club International and later in Playboy magazine. See Bowie and Rock, *Moonage Daydream*, 42; Bowie also created a photo collage of manipulated film stills from *The Man Who Fell to Earth*, in which his reflection in the mirror is at odds with his gesture in front of the mirror (1975–6). See Victoria Broackes and Geoffrey Marsh, eds, *David Bowie Is* (London: V&A Publishing, 2013), 85; mediated mirror shots are also a reiterated feature in his music videos (e.g. 'Thursday's Child', 'Love is Lost').
44 Naremore, *Acting in the Cinema*, 41; David Bordwell, Janet Steiger and Kristin Thompson, 'The Classical Hollywood Cinema – Cap 5', Leyendocine, published 1 May 2007, http://leyendocine.blogspot.com/2007/05/classical-hollywood-cinema.html.
45 Naremore, *Acting in the Cinema*, 41.
46 Bordwell, Steiger and Thomson, 'The Classical Hollywood Cinema'.
47 The influence of Marceau's mime performance 'The Mask Maker' (1959) is perhaps most apparent in Bowie's short film *The Mask*, in which he adopts similar methods for miming the donning and removal of a mask, where his

painted face undergoes an instant change each time the mask is applied or removed. https://www.youtube.com/watch?v=naXMPbd2pJ4.
48 Wayne Constantineau, 'Mime and Media: The Parallel Worlds of Étienne Decroux and Marshall McLuhan', *Dalhousie French Studies* 71 (Summer 2005): 115–34.
49 Nicola Baylis, 'Making Visible the Invisible: Corporeal Mime in the Twenty-first Century', *Theatre Quarterly: NTQ, Cambridge* 25, no.3 (August 2009): 274.
50 Ibid., 275.
51 Ibid.
52 Ibid.
53 Bowie and Rock, *Moonage Daydream*, 233.
54 Shelton Waldrep, *Future Nostalgia: Performing David Bowie* (New York: Bloomsbury, 2015), 17.
55 Ibid., 3.
56 Auslander, 'Watch That Man David Bowie', 74.
57 Ibid.
58 Ibid.

2

David Bowie is ... actor, star and character

Entangled agencies in *The Man Who Fell to Earth*

Dene October

I got lost at one point. I couldn't decide whether I was writing the characters or whether the characters were writing me.
(BOWIE, CRACKED ACTOR, 1975)

Introduction

In 1977, David Bowie rang up Herb Caen of the *San Francisco Chronicle*, agitated. Someone had stolen his identity and was acting as him, a lookalike fooling fans into parting with cash and living it up at expensive restaurants. 'I have not been in San Francisco since April', Bowie complained, 'and I am highly irritated by this imposter.'[1] This odd story about a *doppelganger* is an uncanny mirror to scenes in *The Man Who Fell to Earth*, *Cracked Actor* and 1970s interviews in which Bowie is a most slippery subject. 'Don't ask me any questions', he warns Dick Cavett, 'cos I'll say something different every time.'[2] 'I'm sort of inventing me at the moment', he tells Russell Harty.[3] Bowie's serial construction of character, across multiple media,[4] challenges the notion of a stable, coherent identity, as well as established theories about acting.

In this chapter, I consider Bowie's performance as Thomas Jerome Newton in *The Man Who* as the product of untimely and entangled agencies – of actor, star and character – rather than solely on acting ability. Newton seems to exert a particular agency including stepping from the celluloid screen into the star interview, thus ensuring the continuation of the character's story.[5] Although Bowie later claims his interviews were often acted 'as the character',[6] even he doubts the extent of his own agency, claiming to be haunted by characters. In stating this, I am contributing to a debate on the general orientation of the actor never fully resolved within performance theory (and its dovetail with *performativity*), regarding the sameness and unity of actor and character. Indeed, Bowie's performances in general might be understood through the concept of matrixed identity, something I explore in previous analyses of Bowie and the film,[7] applying strategic frameworks such as Deleuzian concepts of becoming;[8] seriality and actor network theory;[9] the composer, performer and listener as artistic figures;[10] and the agency of costume in character construction.[11] This reading of Bowie as actor, star and character is indebted to the seminal work of James Naremore and Richard Schechner on acting,[12] Richard Dyer on stardom[13] and Shelton Waldrep on the management of public personae.[14] My argument is also obliged to Erving Goffman for his conceptualizing of 'self', 'personality' and 'character' as outgrowths of everyday performance.[15]

According to Judith Butler, identity is *performatively* constituted by those 'expressions' which are claimed to be its results[16] – an assertion that takes up Goffman's observation that all social life involves acting – and J. L. Austin's 'speech act' theory insisting language constructs rather than merely describes the world.[17] For Butler, the scene of construction is also a scene of agency – a 'frame', to use Goffman's term – here performance is a regulated and repeated practice, yet equally involves reflexivity. The performance of Newton invites us to consider how identity congeals through everyday acting and speculate on David Bowie as an acted identity par excellence. 'I'm Pierrot. I'm Everyman. What I'm doing is theatre, and only theatre',[18] he claims, presenting himself as a puzzle of performer and role, for who is this ascendant 'I'? 'I'm using myself as a canvas and trying to paint the truth of our time on it', he continues, acknowledging his immanence in an untimely matrix of social and psychic contexts.

The Man Who can itself be read as a rejection of identity essentialism, one addressing the fallacy at the heart of Method approaches to acting, by substituting the film's central metaphor of Newtonian gravity with Entanglement Theory. The latter posits the instantaneous interaction between distantly separated agents – a quantum handshake[19] – since once entangled, they behave as part of the same system.[20] Thus, Newton is never alone in acting himself. His alien Otherness is an unstratified desire, a schizoid *becoming* force, free to congress with other agencies such as the polycentric television waves in space he picks up, learning what it is to be human,[21] or Bowie's own agency as actor and performer. These agencies frequently actualize Newton as a discreet identity, a (human) being, a spirit Bowie claims was evoked from within. Yet, Newton's becoming challenges ascendance since,[22] as Butler says, there is no one behind the act: the acting is everything.[23]

Unmasking the actor

When jaded professor Nathan Bryce (Rip Torn) attempts to unmask his employer as an alien imposter, Newton is highly aware of the betrayal yet distracted by his simulacrum appearing on a television commercial. The ad begins with the camera positioned behind the *doppelganger*, so audiences share Newton's immanence in the puzzle of who is acting as whom. 'Why does the guy in the W. E. television commercial look like you?' Bryce asks. Newton's response maintains the polysemy. 'Does he?' he says, indifferent to questions of provenance and the boundaries separating actor, character and spectator.

The connection between actor and audience is a theme in James Naremore's book *Acting in the Cinema*. Tracking the history of acting under the disappearance of the viewer and proscenium arch, the author attempts to develop a method for analysing performance in the era of mechanical reproduction. Walter Benjamin has argued that 'the technique of reproduction detaches the reproduced object from the domain of tradition' substituting 'a plurality of copies for a unique existence ... permitting the reproduction to meet the beholder'.[24] For Benjamin, the most powerful agent of this is film, for which *The Man Who* seems a perfect study, with its repeated scenes of television gazing, suggesting the screen as a scene of identity construction and blurring any distinction between original and copy.

In tracing its history, Naremore reminds us that acting is an extension of social performance. Reviewing *Kid Auto Races at Venice* (aka *The Pest*, 1914), the earliest film featuring Charlie Chaplin's famous character Little Tramp, Naremore calls attention to Chaplin's ambiguous performance as an annoying and drunk spectator who repeatedly steps in front of director Henry Lehrman's camera, dissolving the distinctions between actor and audience by 'exaggerating the role-playing that was already happening on the street, turning it into theatre'.[25] Naremore argues that

> people in a film can be regarded in at least three different senses: as actors playing theatrical personages, as public figures playing theatrical versions of themselves, and as documentary evidence.[26]

Like Chaplin, David Bowie was publicly known through his persona (Ziggy Stardust), a role incorporated into his first major film which capitalizes on themes associated with him (e.g. alienation and masks such as the death mask Alan Yentob got him to model for his documentary *Cracked Actor*).[27] Newton, like the tramp, can be regarded as a drunken imposter fascinated by visual media and narcissistically inserting himself into the frame.

Like Chaplin, Bowie was provided a general steer by his director and repeatedly pulled away from 'ostensive' acting. Nicolas Roeg hadn't sought an established actor, preferring 'someone uninfluenced by previous roles, or by fear',[28] drawing parallels between actor and character in the perception of new experience:

> With an actor's performance you must just let it happen. Newton had never encountered human beings before. He had been taught and set up as to what to expect but it was completely new to him. He hadn't built up any experience.[29]

Roeg's comments note the tension between what Newton has 'been taught' and his experience, thus drawing a distinction between an actor's schooling and praxis. Bowie came to the role with expectations about acting and was considerably troubled when Roeg urged him to 'float through the film, with a vacant stare'.[30] Roeg's strategy of relying on Bowie's 'natural' mannerisms, way of speaking and meticulous self-crafting – indulging, for example, the actor's *own* stage wardrobe and hairstylist – recognizes how acting is matrixed.

Theoretically, the concepts of performance and performativity are related ones drawing from theatre and wider studies of human interaction within anthropology and psychology. Each theoretical area addresses performance as an event or ritual, taking place within a social context that governs the production of meanings. Goffman uses the term 'frame' as the convergence point for actor and observer, yet permits the possibility for an identity behind the act, whereas Butler is unequivocal in stating identity is about *doing* rather than *being*. Her theory is a critique of common-sense claims to authentic identity, insisting the 'repeated stylization of the body' takes place within the regulatory social contexts where we pick up the tools that make identity intelligible: one does not transcend these contexts as an actor, instead one is already the expression of identity since the 'I' is constituted through repeated assertions that come to feel natural and inarguable.[31]

Although Butler's and Goffman's ideas might seem too broadly theoretical when applied to acting theory, they can be seen to dovetail with it. The performance studies theorist, Richard Schechner, in his book *Between Theater and Anthropology*, argues that acting is not restricted to the discreet boundaries of stage space, but crosses into the everyday, a liminality 'suspended between "my" behaviour and that which I am citing or imitating', which may include transitions into acts that 'actors' are not simply 'playing', such as laughter and crying.[32] In the scene where Mary-Lou (Candy Clark) persuades Newton to accompany her to church, the latter's voice falters as he joins her in singing a hymn. Clearly when Newton sings, Bowie does, the act a transition through the materiality of the body. The act is also a pose where original and copy are visible at once.[33] The constructed artificiality of the performance is a reminder of how Bowie's singing is often contrived as 'a self-conscious performance of character and emotion'.[34] This is of course a joke the film plays on its knowing audience, but one that nonetheless challenges the notion of stable subjectivity.[35]

Naremore draws critical attention to the instability of the figure of actor in his survey of the history of acting, particularly noting the dominant tension between the approaches of Konstantin Stanislavsky and Bertolt Brecht. Stanislavsky's 'System' of spiritual realism draws on 'emotional memories' and experiential truth, with Lee Strasberg's Method school bringing a naturalness to expression that falls 'back upon the behavioural regimes of ordinary life'.[36] This style of internalized acting had overturned the mannered conventions of the theatre and proved suitable for cinema where the audience is removed. Brecht, on the other hand, in developing *epic theatre* and *verfremdungseffekt* (V-effekt, or 'alienation effect'), sought to *estrange* the audience and empower them as intellectual agents: 'The audience can no longer have the illusion of being the unseen spectator at an event which is really taking place.'[37] This tension is evident in its influence across Bowie's acting portfolio: his mime training; inhabiting of character as an 'integrated performance' through to the spectacle of awkward 'autonomous performance';[38] his use of 'stylistic gesture' in drawing 'audience into the emotional content';[39] and his unglamorous performance in the BBC's version of Brecht's *Baal* (1982). Bowie argued, 'A lot of what is perceived as mannered performance or writing is a distancing from the subject matter to allow an audience to have their own association with what I'm writing about. That comes straight from Brecht.'[40]

Bowie's acting in *The Man Who* can be seen as collapsing these schools of thought together through a naïve and polysemic performance, reflecting not only the strategy of the director and sincere intentions of the star but also the alienation of the character Newton and how the relationship between observer and observed is embodied in an apprehensive self-reflexivity. Afraid of letting Roeg down, Bowie pressed the director for meetings, feeling 'pushed out' when co-star Candy Clark – in a relationship with Roeg – was the one granted support. Still, Bowie's acting was recognized by winning the Saturn award.[41] According to cinematographer Tony Richmond, he was always punctual and prepared, spending hours alone rehearsing and practising scenes so that he was word-perfect.[42] Offset photos show him absorbed in a biography of acting hero Buster Keaton upon whom Bowie modelled his stone face – 'on which you could read anything'.[43] He rehearsed one scene so diligently, when it came for Mary-Lou (Candy Clark) to clumsily knock over a bottle of gin, he – as Newton – caught it in the same practised way, not once but on every single take.[44]

All the same, his 'one snapshot memory of that film is not having to act', and of putting in 'a pretty naturalistic performance'.[45] He took so many drugs that, at one point, filming was delayed by two days when – having seen an alien in his milk – he was convinced he'd been poisoned; many on the crew considered it part of his 'Method approach'.[46] Despite a poor memory of the shoot, Bowie notes his performance was 'a good exhibition of someone literally falling apart in front of you. . . . I was totally insecure with about 10 grams a day in me.'[47] The comment might speak equally to Newton succumbing to unhealthy human habits as to a general philosophy for performance: 'People go to concerts to gain information, and the information they go to get is that of seeing an artist reconcile himself with his own failings, gradually, over a period of years.'[48]

As Keir Elam points out, the theatrical exchange between actor and audience is a moment of transformation which grants 'a symbolic or signifying role' whereby roles are acknowledged.[49] The BBC documentary *Cracked Actor*,[50] in mixing Bowie's stage performances with candid backstage filming, dissolves the boundaries of this exchange. Its crowd scenes, as with *Kids Races*, celebrate liminality and show the theatre-going fans, some in costume and make-up, performing codified gestures while taking their cue from the camera. 'I'm just a space cadet. He's the commander', one fan says, indicating their role in the performance. These observers act in one of two ways: either ostensibly aware of the camera and self-consciously breaching the well-known conventions of the fourth wall or posing, as though the camera isn't there.[51] In *The Man Who*, Bowie seems to extend this combination of the ostensive (onstage) and apparently 'candid' (backstage) – or, as Richard Dyer puts it, ordinary and extraordinary, presence and absence, in constructing himself as a star.[52]

Snapshot of the star

Roeg encouraged his team to pursue the slippage between his star and Newton, delighted when Bowie insisted Martin Samuel, the film's hairstylist, source Ziggy's original Schwarzkopf Hot Red colour from the UK, while the director provided precise instructions on the maintenance of the look.[53] After watching *Cracked Actor*, he was also convinced Bowie embodied Newton, waiting eight hours at the star's house on West 20th Street, New York, to sign him up. Bowie eventually turned up wearing the olive duffle coat that later appeared in the film.[54] The eerie entanglement continued on set with Roeg pampering his star, feeding him martinis,[55] mirroring scenes where the abducted Newton is subdued with alcohol. In both films Bowie plays an unsettled passenger in a limousine chauffeur-driven by Tony Mascia (whom Roeg cast as Arthur), paranoid about being discovered by the authorities and complaining about going too fast.

Newton's association with Bowie's Otherness is established early with a backlit, low-angle medium close-up exaggerating his awkward, yet studied, body movements in descending the New Mexico mine slag heap. A formal shot-reverse-shot displays Newton's pasty and fragile look, then jumps to his distorted perspective of the drunk on the child's swing. In the pawn shop, where Newton must show his British passport, anamorphic lenses and dizzying camera mobility suggest the imposter's paranoia. In another scene, the camera is positioned behind Newton just as he removes the hood to his duffle coat, at which point we recognize the iconic flame hair of late Ziggy Stardust. This mixture of identification and spectacle is enabled by techniques of focalization commonly employed in film when shifting between internal and external gazes, rendering subjective point of view as readable as objective 'reality'. Occurring simultaneously, it is experienced here as schizophrenic, an opportunity to hop from Newton's altered point of view into an eerie spectatorship of the alien, and the star playing him.

In recalling Bowie as an ethereal subject to shoot, cinematographer Tony Richmond acknowledges, 'I can't imagine any other actor in that role.'[56] Critics were equally convinced. Jonathan Rosenbaum was 'particularly transfixed by [the] extra-terrestrial persona', considering the performance 'genuinely uncanny with his sexual ambivalence, surreal red hair, chiseled features, and underplayed reactions [and] one of the eeriest screen presences since Katharine Hepburn in *Sylvia Scarlett*'.[57] Tom Milne, of *Sight & Sound*, felt everyone would be 'unanimous . . . in finding David Bowie entirely convincing as a visitor from another planet'.[58] Even the author of the original novel, Walter Tevis, upon visiting the set, 'was stunned to see what I had years before imagined become flesh – or something like flesh . . . [Bowie] gave me the *déjà vu*'.[59] Thus Roeg and Richmond were hardly alone in considering Bowie 'absolutely perfect' as Newton, and simply acting himself.

The view that stars act as themselves permits the assumption that an actor is just 'being' while his characters are '*fictional extension*[s] of the *actors*' true personalities'.[60] The personification style of acting, which Barry King describes as a fusion of roles played by the actor with their own personalities in 'concerted cynosure',[61] has been associated with non-acting, even bad acting,[62] since the actor is visible behind the role, and is seen to compare poorly with schooled impersonation approaches, which require the sacrifice of the actor's personality. On the other hand, a simple commutation test highlights the value of imagining the quality another actor would bring to the role.[63] Peter O'Toole, Roeg's original casting for Newton, was an appropriate one for the novel's tall alien, while Bowie's stardom promotes an intriguing intertextuality as a visual spectacle, significantly enriching the semiotic thickness of Roeg's non-linear narrative through an extraordinary mirroring between star and character.

Stars come to embody different social types which accord with various fits between actor and character, ranging from problematic to perfect.[64] As Julie Lobalzo Wright says, some music stars are able to adapt stardoms constructed through music into a cinematic fit.[65] Bowie was a perfect fit for Newton, since he had already been constructed through his visual transformations, the performance focus to his songs and his alien image – all aspects that relate to his queer iconography, the very elements that make him a problematic fit for many later films.[66] Although it limits the lens through which Bowie's acting is viewed,[67] Dyer's notion of the 'perfect fit' is useful in demonstrating how a wide range of industry and consumer interests accord, meeting the expectations and desires of audiences in choosing constructions that help them 'feel secure . . . they had fallen in love with an image . . . very much like the real thing'.[68]

The Man Who operates as 'an ironic dramatization' of Bowie's 'desire to become a star' (as Naremore opines of Chaplin's first tramp film),[69] mirroring his early dogged pursuit of fame through to an encounter with its drug-fuelled effects. His song 'Fame' (1975), co-written with John Lennon, is inspired by the latter's cynicism about the star industry, and a reflection of Bowie's exhaustion and doubts.[70] Stardom did not arrive instantly; in the 1960s and early 1970s, Bowie moved swiftly between musical genres in its pursuit, astutely switching from penning character voices for songs to the construction of himself as a star persona. With the help of a coterie of close friends, like the designer Freddie Burretti, he posed as a star, dressing and behaving like one, while manager Tony Defries modelled his strategy to break into the United States after the Hollywood star system.[71]

In *Cracked Actor*, Bowie reflects on his rising stardom, using the limousine as a metaphor about agency:

> Do you know that feeling you get in a car when somebody's accelerating very fast and you're not driving? And you get that 'Uhhh' thing in your chest when you're being forced backwards [. . .] That's what success was like.[72]

In retrospect, the comment suggests *The Man Who* as an autobiographical continuum given how, in particular cases, 'all aspects of a star's image fit with the traits of a character'.[73] Dyer reminds us that while stars perform 'constructed representations of persons',[74] their image is also constructed through the promotions and interviews associated with the film and press coverage 'of the star's doings and "private" life'.[75] Yet by already posing as a star in the everyday, and in his management of a created persona, Bowie challenges the already slippery concept of star authenticity. Stars may not always offer fixed meanings or positions; they are, as Christine Gledhill notes, both signifying elements in the performing arts and 'products of mass culture . . . carrying cultural meanings and ideological values',[76] *structured polysemies* referring to a multiplicity of sometimes contradictory values and meanings some of which are 'foregrounded and others are masked or displaced'.[77] Stars may thus challenge analysis by crossing boundaries between disciplines. Indeed, as Sean Redmond suggests of Bowie's later films, which seem *always* to be in cameo, his performances range from modern to postmodern, self-reflexive registers, leaving his star image polysemic.[78]

Roeg seems to anticipate this, by inserting into the movie static black-and-white portraits posed by his two leads, images that would be more conventionally employed in the promotion of the movie. These images can be understood both as spectacular disruptions to the narrative and as intertextual augmentation of the semiotically thick, visual storytelling that is Roeg's forte.[79] Spectacle need not always be considered an interruption to film but can invite a deeper critical or reflexive contemplation normally associated with art.[80] As Newton himself discovers, the screen surface can avail itself to a surprising depth, encouraging spectatorial immersion alongside critical reflection on the media or cinematic construction.

Media constructions of stars, Dyer says, encourage us to ask 'really'?[81] What is Bowie really like? Which biography, and which moment in film, reveals him as he really is? The spectacular and uncanny doubling between Bowie and Newton adds to this by subverting the relationship between original and copy. Stars generate prototypes for behaviour, influencing our body shapes and fashions,[82] connecting us memetically through apparently trivial images,[83] even perhaps providing the flesh and blood for Jungian archetypes onto which are mapped dominant cultural discourses.[84] Through the character Newton, Bowie is arguably at his most accessible as a star, offering a fan connection far in excess of his stage characters. This is something I discussed in conversation with Nick Knight, Tim Blanks, Dylan Jones and Victoria Broackes, at the V&A's *Ooh Fashion!* event, arguing the intensity of Newton's fashion influence on fans, including my own teenage wardrobe choices and poses as Newton. Was this because Newton brought Bowie more vividly alive, as both extraordinary and equally down to earth, through film's capacity to promote stars as authentic?[85]

Psychoanalytical approaches foreground stars 'as mechanisms of identification' involving complex subjective processes and acting as an inducement to watch films as part of the 'completion of star image and self image'.[86] Stars thus operate at a threshold between screen and social space, a scene of construction and agency, where the struggle to make sense of social identity is played out with consequences for observer and observed, positions collapsed in the posed figure of Newton as watcher. Bowie's self-conscious stardom serves to deconstruct the star-making process that he himself falls victim to. This is perhaps what Newton reflects on during the commercial in which he is shown watching his *doppelganger* posing before the camera, who in turn is holding yet another camera and slowly turning to watch him back. According to Judith Peraino, posing 'insists on self-awareness, image, and surface and keeps in place the temporal and material positions of "original" and "copy"', pausing 'to allow the viewer to become absorbed in visual pleasure and desire, and also to allow the poser the pleasure of inhabiting the object position'.[87] Posing and self-construction are 'not opposed to agency' but are 'the necessary scene' of it.[88]

Character construction

Cracked Actor begins with a close-up on a television set upon which is playing a broadcast interview between Bowie and bewildered reporter Wayne Satz of *Eyewitness News*. 'If you didn't understand that [interview] don't feel too badly', Satz tells the viewer, 'because I certainly didn't.' A sequence of edits shows Bowie sitting in a darkened room watching the footage. 'David, I know you're watching tonight', Satz continues, as we continue to watch Bowie watching.

Yentob's documentary makes for an untimely reflection of the cracked actor caught in a hall of mirrors, one that foreshadows Newton's television watching in *The Man Who* and presents an uncertain account of Bowie's agency in marshalling his promotional interviews as a stage on which to act (as it were) his characters. The *Radio Times*, in previewing *Cracked Actor*, makes it sound easy: 'In the beginning there was no David Bowie, so he had to invent himself',[89] yet Bowie's talent for character construction is a reminder of how the media has been used by certain artists in wrestling control of their 'star presence' from industry manipulation in the creation and management of a public persona.[90] Shelton Waldrep notes of Oscar Wilde how the study of the writer begins with self-invention.[91] Wilde, who desired to transform his life into art, influenced the queer pose of Truman Capote (a writer whose appearances on *The Tonight Show* made him a celebrity) while Andy Warhol's star obsession with Capote is uncannily mirrored by Bowie's fascination with Warhol. Like Wilde, Capote and Warhol, Bowie set about overturning the 'tyranny' of the media and inserting himself into art by using an alarming star persona, mixing gossip, 'autobiography . . . doctored fact, stardom and the quotidian' in what Capote labelled the 'conversational portrait' (even noting how being a chameleon 'is a way to survive').[92] 'You can't let it use you', Bowie told *Rolling Stone*,[93] quoting Marshall McLuhan's argument 'the medium is the message'[94] and claiming himself as 'the medium for a conglomerate of statements and illusions'.[95] Bowie's *talk as performance* echoes Austin's observation that certain speech acts have a performative power and underlines Dyer's query: who is the star *really*?

Bowie's 'autobiography', which he started during filming of *The Man Who*, is certainly in the mode of written works by Warhol and Capote in blurring the lines between conversation and construction. *The Return of the Thin White Duke* is a documentation of his life and ideas, with fiction and 'a deal of magic in it',[96] using themes and images that crystalize in the icy figure of the Duke character from the album *Station to Station* (1976). 'I've still not read an autobiography by a rock person that had the same degree of presumptuousness and arrogance that a rock & roll record used to have', Bowie says, in explaining his ambition for the work.[97] It may also be considered an assertion of his agency in taking control of his star image, in the same way Newton compiles an album of Anthean poetry called 'The Visitor', countering any media construction of him his wife may eventually receive, broadcast through waves in space. Mary Desjardins has argued the conventional biography is a cultural battleground for the star body, while the experimental biography exposes the 'interpellative/hegemonic functions of the "star"'.[98] *Rolling Stone*, however, considered *The Return* merely 'a series of sketchy self-portraits and isolated incidents . . . more telling of Bowie's "fragmented mind" than of his life story'.[99]

Asked in interview whether his bisexuality was real or a stunt, Bowie teased, 'We'll talk all about it.' When it is pointed out that former publicist, Cherry Vanilla, claims he only lets people think he likes guys, Bowie is delighted: 'Oh, I'd love to meet this impostor she's talking about', adding, 'Cherry's almost as good as I am at using the media'.[100] This ambiguity is echoed in *The Man Who* when Newton tells Mary-Lou, 'I see things . . . Bodies.' 'Women?' she asks. 'And men', he responds enigmatically, the scene then dissolving into the alien's fisheye perspective of his dying family. Bowie's words create a puzzle of identity, candid yet slippery, confessional yet staged, claiming to be haunted by characters and the spectre of (his family's) mental illness, while also asserting authorship. 'You strip down all the things you don't like about yourself', he tells Lisa Robinson of *New Musical Express*. Robinson nevertheless alerts her reader to the trickster whose laugh is itself a performance – '[t]he eyes flash, the head is artfully tossed back' – suspecting the 'entire production' is little more than 'a film David's directed himself'.[101]

In his broadcast interviews, the slippage between actor and character suggests a less than clear account of Bowie's agency. On *The Dick Cavett Show* (1974), he sniffs (from coke use) through an interview in which Cavett tellingly refers to him as 'a working actor', then *glits* – a word, he explains, is 'like flit, but it's the '70s version' – from persona to persona, seemingly out of control of his self-presentation. At points haughty, he warns Cavett not to ask certain questions, drawing images on the studio floor with his cane (as if suffering stage fright) and switching from formal received pronunciation to relaxed cockney. When prompted by the host, Bowie insists, intriguingly, 'I don't want to know whether I'm nervous.'

Bowie's *glitting* is also a feature of his appearance on the *Russell Harty Show* (1975), a live interview made to promote his performance in *The Man Who*. The international time delay adds to the sense of the pair being out of kilter, with Bowie grumpily refusing to give direct answers and spurning attempts by Harty to lighten things up. The strange studio set-up has Harty sitting in a chair in front of a television, watching Bowie from the perspective of the audience. When asked about his plans for 1976, Bowie replies, 'I'm coming back to England in May to . . . play shows and . . . look at you . . . and look at England . . . and be English'; the 'look at you' is of course something he is already doing from a shifted perspective.

Like Cavett, Harty seems to be onto 'Bowie's act', ironically suggesting Bowie hasn't changed since they last met two years ago: 'You know you haven't . . . your accent, your voice, your method of speech has not changed.' The phrase 'method of speech' is a particularly odd and technical one, seemingly an attempt to unmask an intruder. There follows an icy exchange of words and an escalation of Bowie's body tics, his double eyebrow wriggle used as visual quote marks in asserting himself over Harty. But when Harty introduces a clip from the film, the eyebrow wriggle is equally evident in Bowie's performance as Newton. He particularly uses it to emphasize his request that Mary-Lou bring him a television. The clip suggests a *mise en abyme*, a mirror in each text, but without definitive origin.

When asked what he contributed to the movie, Bowie's answer is his acting 'and persona in general'. It is a slippery response, inviting the viewer to speculate on his agency in character construction, one undermined somewhat by the order of events. In *The Man Who* press pack, he claims he centred in Newton in a way that differs from previous characters: 'stage performances are more ceremonial. . . . In a film you are evoking a spirit within yourself.'[102] He thus echoes Gerald Mast's comparison of film and stage actors: 'Movie stars do not so much play characters; they are the characters. The movie star capitalizes on an essential paradox of the movies – that they are fictional truths.'[103]

As many actors find, costume played a role in the formulation of character. But outfits sourced for *The Man Who* found previous use in the *Diamond Dogs* tour, and then appear in *Cracked Actor*, largely due to Bowie's relationship with costume designer, Ola Hudson. They were also used in subsequent performances, since 'I literally walked off with the clothes'.[104] While Bowie filmed *The Man Who* between 2 June and 25 August 1975, he had earlier ambitions to play the role of an alien, the Martian-raised Valentine Michael Smith, in a mooted film adaptation of Robert Heinlein's *Stranger in a Strange Land* (1961) from a novel which also influenced Tevis and Roeg. Later, he realized he'd found something in Newton 'I wanted desperately . . . not to finish'.[105] 'It rang so true', he told *Melody Maker*.[106]

Disagreeing with Roeg's interpretation of the alien as *fallen*, Bowie preferred to believe the character acquired a previously muted emotional drive to connect with people[107] and, shortly before his death, resurrected Newton for his Broadway play *Lazarus*. These apparently discreet biographical events indicate something less local or causal than a Newtonian analogy for identity suggests, something more along the lines of an untimely and entangled handshake. As Bowie himself recalls, on location, he isolated himself from the film crew, returning alone to his rented ranch every night, crossing the 'hauntingly beautiful desert' as if he was 'skimming along through some kind of parallel interpretation of the film itself'.[108]

While Bowie appears to use the media as a sandpit for identity construction, he may nevertheless have presented the opportunity for his characters to make their voices heard. As his list of 100 favourite books attests, Bowie was well versed in the controversial theories of R. D. Laing and Julian Jaynes.[109] Jaynes's book claims to identify the beginnings of consciousness, arguing inner thoughts were perceived as outer presences, destabilizing the boundary (and sequential ordering) of inner and outer. Bowie pursued an interest in decentring his voice through various character experiments: the cut-up techniques popularized by William S. Burroughs; the pencil sketches of characters in early songs; the multitracking of his own vocals as backing voices; and songs with a dialectical dimension, such as 'Space Oddity' (1969), performed on the *Diamond Dogs* tour (1974) with a telephone prop as the medium through which Bowie separates Major Tom and Ground Control. In the song's performance shown on *Cracked Actor*, the two voices are revisited through Halloween Jack, a character haunted by the ghost of Ziggy.

Bowie professed he lost control of the persona: 'he tried to take me over',[110] denying the author's in-built death drive,[111] evident in the *Ziggy Stardust* song where 'the kids killed the man'. On the contrary, it was the kids who kept Ziggy alive, rejecting Bowie's retirement of the character at London's Hammersmith Odeon on 3 July 1973, while the press continued to hail Bowie as Ziggy.[112] Rikke Schubart, writing about *Rocky* (Avildsen, 1976), notes how an entanglement may occur between actor and fictional role collapsing them into a single star persona in the public consciousness.[113] In *The Man Who* Newton's posing as a human decentres him, smudging away the alien's Otherness, into an identity actualized through human observation, thus providing identity's alibi as being stable and coherent. Newton, like Ziggy, can be considered a serial character, reprised through public popularity, into a continuation of story exceeding any authorial agency. It is their reciprocal agency that leads me to speculate, in 'Transition Transmission',[114] that Bowie might just as easily be the invention of Newton, a switch that makes sense of the untimely way identity is exhorted through performance.

Bowie's press and media performances illustrate the conundrum in whether to take him at his word – indeed whether that word originates with Bowie or one of his characters. His mid-1970s broadcast and print interviews can be understood equally as Bowie acting out his public persona and, as with cases of stage fright, opportunities for nervy, liminal entanglements between person and persona. Speech acts, regardless of their truth or fiction, construct a believable world, a scene where the agency of the actor may be usurped by 'his' act.

Conclusion

Bowie's acting in *The Man Who* can be considered a study in self-conscious (perhaps highly managed) stardom and equally the chance to observe something slippery in an actor's performance – a mindfulness – or hint of a challenge to the notion that behind any character construction, or acting performance, is an authentic self. The scene I have made central to this chapter, that of the watcher watching, assembles actor, star and character, an entanglement of agencies which resist preferred hierarchies and find expression as a chaos of signs and spectacular affects, where original may be usurped by imposter copy. Where do we draw the line between Bowie the actor and the character created by David Jones in 1965, upon which other characters are premised? Where on this line is that San Francisco imposter? Bowie's talking-as-performance suggests he was always acting. Yet, whether in the feature film, documentary or 'candid' media performances discussed above, there is also a suspicion that he was merely the medium for other agencies.

Notes

1 'People' column, *The Daily Register*, 18 October 1977.
2 *The Dick Cavett Show*. Aired 5 December 1974, on ABC.
3 *The Russell Harty Show*. Aired 28 November 1975, on ITV.
4 Dene October, 'Transition Transmission: Media, Seriality and the Bowie-Newton Matrix', in *David Bowie and Transmedia Stardom*, ed. Ana Cristina Mendes and Lisa Perrott (London and New York: Routledge, 2019), 104–18.
5 Ibid.
6 *Afternoon Plus*. Aired 16 February 1979, on Thames Television.
7 The matrix has been a model I have worked on since presenting a paper at the New Myths conference, Buckinghamshire, 2003, through to 'Transition Transmission' in 2020.
8 Dene October, 'The [becoming-wo]Man Who Fell to Earth', in *David Bowie: Critical Perspectives*, ed. Eoin Devereux, Aileen Dillane and Martin J. Power (London and New York: Routledge, 2015), 245–62.

9   October, 'Transition Transmission', 104–18.

10 Dene October, 'Sound and Vision: Low and Sense', in *Enchanting David Bowie: Space/Time/Body/Memory*, ed. Toija Cinque, Christopher Moore and Sean Redmond (New York: Bloomsbury Academic, 2015), 275–304.

11 Dene October, 'The Man Who Fell to Earth', in *Bloomsbury Encyclopedia of Film and Television Costume Design,* ed. Deborah Nadoolman Landis (New York: Bloomsbury, 2022).

12 James Naremore, *Acting in the Cinema* (Berkeley, CA: University of California Press, 1988); Richard Schechner, *Environmental Theatre* (New York: Hawthorn Books, 1973) and *Between Theatre and Anthropology* (Philadelphia: Pennsylvania University Press, 1985).

13 Richard Dyer, *Heavenly Bodies: Film Stars and Society* (New York: St. Martin's Press, 1986) and *Stars* (London: BFI Publishing, 1979).

14 Shelton Waldrep, *The Aesthetics of Self-Invention* (Minneapolis: University of Minnesota Press, 2004).

15 Erving Goffman, *The Presentation of the Self in Everyday Life* (London: Allen Lane, 1969) and *Frame Analysis: An Essay on the Organization of Experience* (Cambridge, MA: Harvard University Press, 1974).

16 Judith Butler, *Gender Trouble: Feminism and the Subversion of Identity* (New York and London: Routledge, 1990), 33.

17 J. L. Austin, *How to Do Things with Words,* ed. J. O. Urmson and Marina Sbisà (Cambridge, MA: Harvard University Press, 1975).

18 Jean Rook, 'Waiting for Bowie and Finding a Genius Who Insists He's Really a Clown', *Daily Express*, 5 May 1976.

19 See my discussion of John Cramer's quantum handshake in October, 'The [becoming-wo]Man Who Fell to Earth', 256.

20 John Gribbin, *Schrodinger's Kittens and the Search for Reality: Solving the Quantum Mysteries* (London: Weidenfeld and Nicolson, 1995), 223.

21 October, 'The [becoming-wo]Man Who Fell to Earth,' 245–62.

22 Gilles Deleuze and Felix Guattari, *Anti-Oedipus: Capitalism and Schizophrenia* (Minneapolis: University of Minnesota Press, 1983) and *A Thousand Plateaus Capitalism and Schizophrenia* (Minneapolis: University of Minnesota Press, 1987).

23 Butler, *Gender Trouble*, 33.

24 Walter Benjamin, *Illuminations*, ed. Hannah Arendt, trans. Harry Zohn (New York: Schocken Books, 1969.), 4.

25 Naremore, *Acting in the Cinema*, 15.

26 Ibid.

27 Alan Yentob, 'Alan Yentob: *Cracked Actor*', Evening Talk, *David Bowie Is* Exhibition, (presentation, Victoria and Albert Museum, 5 April 2013).

28 Mel Gussow, 'Roeg: The Man Behind The Man Who Fell to Earth', *New York Times*, 22 August 1976.

29 Jay Glennie and Darryl Webber, *The Man Who Fell to Earth* (London: Unstoppable Editions, 2016), 56.
30 George Perry quoted in Glennie and Webber, *The Man Who Fell to Earth*, 67.
31 Butler, *Gender Trouble*, 33 and 43.
32 Schechner (1988) quoted in James Loxley, *Performativity: The New Critical Idiom* (London: Routledge, 2007), 149.
33 Judith A. Peraino, 'Plumbing the Surface of Sound and Vision: David Bowie, Andy Warhol, and the Art of Posing', *Qui Parle* 21, no.1 (2012): 142.
34 Waldrep, *The Aesthetics of Self-Invention*, 116.
35 Schechner quoted in Loxley, *Performativity*, 149.
36 Colin Counsell, *Signs of Performance: An Introduction to Twentieth-Century Theatre* (London and New York: Routledge, 1996), 54.
37 Bertolt Brecht, *Brecht on Theatre: The Development of an Aesthetic*, ed. and trans. by John Willett (New York: Hill and Wang, 1964), 91.
38 Richard Maltby, *Hollywood Cinema,* 2nd ed. (Malden: Blackwell, 2003), 389.
39 Joe Gore, 'Changes 2.1: New Digital Stimulation from David Bowie and Reeves Gabrels', *Guitar Player*, June 1997, 46–7.
40 Ibid.
41 Awarded by the Academy of Science Fiction, Fantasy and Horror Films since 1973.
42 Glennie and Webber, *The Man Who Fell to Earth*, x.
43 Chris Hodenfield, 'Bad Boys in Berlin: David Bowie, Iggy Pop and the Terrible Things an Audience Can Make You Do', *Rolling Stone*, 4 October 1979, 42.
44 Nicholas Pegg, *The Complete David Bowie: Revised and Updated 2016 Edition* (London: Titan, 2016), 657.
45 Ibid.
46 Susan Compo, *Earth Bound: David Bowie and The Man Who Fell to Earth* (London: Jawbone, 2017), 138.
47 Kurt Loder, 'Straight Time', *Rolling Stone*, 12 May 1983, 24.
48 Ben Edmonds, 'Bowie Meets the Press: Plastic Man or Godhead of the Seventies?' *Circus*, 27 April 1976, 24.
49 Keir Elam, *The Semiotics of Theatre and Drama* (London: Methuen, 1980), 8.
50 The documentary includes excerpts from D. A. Pennebaker's concert footage shot in 1973 and made into the film *Ziggy Stardust and the Spiders from Mars* (1979, with worldwide release in 1983).
51 See previous point about the three ways people *act* on screen. Naremore, *Acting in the Cinema*, 15.
52 Dyer, *Stars* and *Heavenly Bodies*.
53 October, 'The Man Who Fell to Earth'.

54 Ibid., 9.
55 Steve Shroyer and John Lifflander, 'Spaced Out in the Desert', *Creem*, December 1975, 41.
56 Alex Ritman, '"The Man Who Fell to Earth" Cinematographer on David Bowie's "Defining Role"', Hollywood Reporter, 19 September 2016. https://www.hollywoodreporter.com/news/man-who-fell-earth-cinematographer-930640.
57 Jonathan Rosenbaum, 'The Man Who Fell to Earth', review of *The Man Who Fell to Earth*, directed by Nicolas Roeg. *Monthly Film Bulletin*, April 1976.
58 Tom Milne, 'The Man Who Fell to Earth', review of *The Man Who Fell to Earth*, directed by Nicolas Roeg. *Sight & Sound*, Summer 1976.
59 Walter Tevis, 'Letter', *Circus*, 30 December 1975, 8.
60 Maltby, *Hollywood Cinema*, 384.
61 Barry King, 'Articulating Stardom', in *Star Texts: Image and Performance in Film and Television*, ed. Jeremy G. Butler (Detroit: Wayne State University Press, 1991), 125–53.
62 Karen Hollinger, *The Actress: Hollywood Acting and the Female Star* (London: Routledge, 2006), 47.
63 Robert B. Ray, *The ABCs of Classic Hollywood* (Oxford: Oxford University Press, 2008), 37.
64 Dyer, *Stars*, 142–6.
65 Julie Lobalzo Wright, 'The Extraordinary Rock Star as Film Star', in *David Bowie: Critical Perspectives*, ed. Eoin Devereux, Aileen Dillane and Martin J. Power (London and New York: Routledge, 2015), 230–44.
66 Ibid., 231 and 241.
67 Toija Cinque, Angela Ndalianis and Sean Redmond, eds, 'In Focus: David Bowie On-Screen', *Cinema Journal* 57, no. 3 (Spring 2018): 128.
68 Samantha Barbas, *Movie Crazy: Stars, Fans, and the Cult of Celebrity* (New York: Palgrave, 2001), 11.
69 Naremore, *Acting in the Cinema*, 12.
70 Dene October, 'Is it Any Wonder I Reject You First?' David Bowie Studies, published 2018, https://davidbowiestudies.wordpress.com/is-it-any-wonder-i-reject-you-first/.
71 Michael Watts, 'Bowie's Mainman', *Melody Maker*, 18 May 1974, 40–1.
72 *Cracked Actor*, directed by Alan Yentob (BBC, 1975).
73 Dyer, *Stars*, 129.
74 Ibid., 109.
75 Dyer, *Heavenly Bodies*, 86.
76 Christine Gledhill, 'Introduction', in *Stardom: Industry of Desire*, ed. Christine Gledhill (London and New York: Routledge, 1991), xiii–xiv.
77 Dyer, *Stars*, 3.

78 Sean Redmond, 'David Bowie: In Cameo', *In Focus* 57, no. 3 (Spring 2018): 150.
79 Neil Sinyard, *The Films of Nicolas Roeg* (London: Charles Letts, 1991), 2–5.
80 Helen Wheatley, *Spectacular Television: Exploring Televisual Pleasure* (London: I. B. Tauris, 2016) and Dene October, 'Shooting Stars: Filming the Jodie Whittaker era of *Doctor Who*', in *Doctor Who: New Dawn*, ed. Brigid Cherry, Matthew Hills and Andrew O'Day (Manchester: Manchester University Press, 2021).
81 Dyer, *Heavenly Bodies*, 2.
82 Angela Ndalianis and Charlotte Henry, *Stars in Our Eyes: The Star Phenomenon in the Contemporary Era* (Westport: Praeger, 2002).
83 Louise Krasniewicz and Michael Blitz, 'The Replicator: Starring Arnold Schwarzenegger as the Great Meme-Machine', in *Stars in Our Eyes: The Star Phenomenon in the Contemporary Era*, ed. Angela Ndalianis and Charlotte Henry (Westport: Praeger, 2002), 22–43.
84 Josephine Dolan, 'Crumbling Rejuvenation: Archetype, Embodiment and the Aging Body Myth', in *The Happiness Illusion: How the Media Sold us a Fairytale*, ed. Luke Hockley and Nadi Fadina (London and New York: Routledge, 2015), 74–88.
85 Dene October, 'David Bowie: Ooh Fashion!' (panel discussion, Victoria and Albert Museum, 22 March 2016).
86 Gledhill, 'Introduction', xiv–xv.
87 Peraino, *Plumbing the Surface of Sound and Vision*, 156.
88 Butler, *Gender Trouble*, 147.
89 Anthony Haden-Guest, 'Bowie: The Wild Side', *Radio Times*, 25–31 January 1975, 6.
90 On the studio star system, see Brian Gallagher, 'Some Historical Reflections on the Paradoxes of Stardom in the American Film Industry, 1910–1960', *Images: Journal of Film and Popular Culture*, published 3 March 1997, http://www.imagesjournal.com/issue03/infocus/stars1.htm.
91 Waldrep, *The Aesthetics of Self-Invention*, xi–xii.
92 Ibid., 78–85.
93 Cameron Crowe, 'Ground Control to Davy Jones', *Rolling Stone*, 12 February 1976, 83.
94 Marshall McLuhan, *Understanding Media*, 2nd ed. (London: Routledge, 2001).
95 Fred Hauptfuhrer, 'Rock's Space Oddity, David Bowie Falls to Earth and Finds His Feet in Film', *People*, 6 September 1976.
96 Pegg, *The Complete David Bowie*, 658.
97 Crowe, 'Ground Control to Davy Jones', 83.

98 Mary Desjardins, 'The Incredible Shrinking Star', *Camera Obscura* 19, no. 3 (2004): 25 and Helen Darby, 'I'm Glad I'm Not Me: Subjective Dissolution, Schizoanalysis and Post-Structuralist Ethics in the Films of Todd Haynes', *Film-Philosophy* 17, no. 1 (2013): 335.

99 Crowe, 'Ground Control to Davy Jones', 81.

100 Cameron Crowe, 'Candid Conversation: An Outrageous Conversation with the Actor, Rock Singer and Sexual Switch-Hitter', *Playboy*, September 1976, 33.

101 Lisa Robinson, 'The First Synthetic Rock Star. There Is No Other', *New Musical Express*, 7 March 1976.

102 Anon, *Long Star Biographies*, Davidson Dalling Associates Information Folder (London: Davidson Dalling Associates, 1975), 19.

103 Gerald Mast, *A Short History of the Movies*, 5th ed. (New York: Macmillan, 1992), 96.

104 Pegg, *The Complete David Bowie*, 658–9.

105 Glennie and Webber, *The Man Who Fell to Earth*, 11.

106 Robert Hilburn, 'Bowie: Now I'm a Businessman', *Melody Maker*, 28 February 1976.

107 Angus MacKinnon, 'The Future Isn't What it Used to Be', *NME*, 13 September 1980, 34.

108 Glennie and Webber, *The Man Who Fell to Earth*, 11.

109 R. D. Laing, *The Divided Self: An Existential Study in Sanity and Madness* (London: Penguin Books, 1965) and Julian Jaynes, *The Origin of Consciousness in the Breakdown of the Bicameral Mind* (Boston: Houghton Mifflin, 1976).

110 Tina Brown, 'The Bowie Odyssey', *The Sunday Times Magazine*, 20 July 1975, 11.

111 For more on this, see Ana Leorne, 'Dear Dr. Freud – David Bowie Hits the Couch: A Psychoanalytical Approach to Some of his Personae', in *David Bowie: Critical Perspectives*, ed. Eoin Devereux, Aileen Dillane and Martin J. Power (London and New York: Routledge, 2015), 111–27.

112 October, 'Is it Any Wonder I Reject You First?'.

113 Rikke Schubart, 'Birth of a Hero: Rocky, Stallone, and Mythical Creation', in *Stars in Our Eyes: The Star Phenomenon in the Contemporary Era*, ed. Angela Ndalianis and Charlotte Henry (Westport: Praeger, 2002), 149–64.

114 October, 'Transition Transmission', 104–18.

3

The posed and the unposed

Inhabited clowns and grotesques in Bowie's *Scary Monsters* and *The Elephant Man*

Amedeo D'Adamo

Introduction: Bending into *The Elephant Man*

It was a dramatic opening. As the lights rose on the Broadway stage in September 1980, they revealed large photographs of the grotesque body of John Merrick (Figure 3.1). Merrick is based on a real person from the Victorian era, a terrible victim of body disfigurement who'd been saved from a life of abuse by a well-intentioned Victorian doctor only to then become his ward and quasi-prisoner. On the stage next to the photos stood a silent, still 33-year-old David Bowie dressed only in a loincloth (Figures 3.2 and 3.4), contrasting the most famous grotesque in modern history with an actor described by the play's reviewers as very handsome. But then in a staging of performative inhabitation, Bowie began to move. He slowly twisted his body until it stooped like Merrick's, bending it into the contortions that he adopted for the rest of the play, creating a deliberate visual frisson by collapsing the distance between the misshapen and the normative body.

In this first moment, the play makes clear it will bring a new sense of life and inhabitation to the figure of the grotesque, a figure commonly deployed

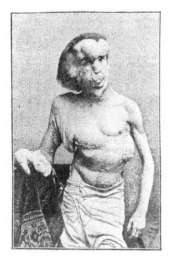 

FIGURES 3.1 AND 3.2 *Period photograph of the actual John Merrick and publicity bill from* The Elephant Man *(1980)*.

as a simple emblem of ugliness and excess. But this play is a study of a person struggling against his grotesque physical afflictions: Bowie would inhabit Merrick, a character written with a rich interior life, by layering this twisted Merrick with a panoply of remarkably unusual physical choices that dramatized Merrick's struggles with his tortured body, traumatic past and anxious emotional present.

While the role would mark perhaps the high point of Bowie's acting career, there are more wide-ranging reasons for dissecting Bowie's turn as Merrick. By requiring Bowie to play a grotesque with a rich backstory, inner conflicts, complex antagonistic struggles and a slow arc of revelation about the true nature of his final confinement, this play became more than just another chance for Bowie to explore the liminal figures, weirdness and fascinations that lay at the edge of the culture. Unlike the characters he had sketched out or played in his previous work, this character would force him to bend into an Aristotelian character arc and a rich backstory that demanded he almost continually perform vulnerability, empathy and anxious interior reflection.[1] I will argue that though Bowie lacks the conventional training for achieving this, he instead repurposed some of the tactics he had created for his recently completed album *Scary Monsters and Super Creeps* (1980) (Figure 3.3), which he finished just before taking on the role of Merrick.

To make this argument I first define how this role and this album mark a real break with Bowie's previous performative tactics, a change that Bowie himself has remarked on a number of times. Bowie's aesthetic approach until the late 1970s specialized in the creation of otherworldly characters

 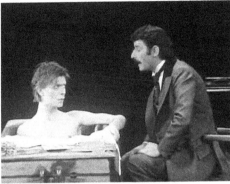

FIGURES 3.3 AND 3.4 *Bowie's bend* – Scary Monsters *(1980) album cover and Bowie onstage as Merrick in* The Elephant Man *(1980)*.

and imagining events or lives that were at the very most only tangentially connected to his lived experiences. This eventually produced a real creative crisis for him and, looking back on the 1980s in two late-career interviews, Bowie noted that he changed in those years because this approach was 'getting in the way of myself as a writer'.[2]

I will suggest in this essay that this crisis can be understood, at least in part, as a break from the performance tradition which dominates classical musicals, mime and other forms of performance and which I will label the 'posed', to make a leap into another tradition, which I will label the 'unposed'.

The posed and unposed

First, it is necessary to justify the use of these labels in this chapter's methodology – an approach I have called Media Craft studies.[3] With decades of experience as a professional filmmaker, director and actor,[4] I find it striking that the language of acting and affect studies seems to have had little influence on actual performance practices. Possibly this is because these theorists capture more of the effect of the performance on viewers and less of the performance's actual craft machinery. For instance, Naremore's powerful distinction between presentational and representational performance has been personally influential, but this vocabulary has failed to enter craft practices due to its focus on narratological analysis.[5] It is also important to note that while interiority, another term that's central to this analysis, is a contested phenomenon in critical theory, it is a crucial concept in unposed dramatic construction; while concepts like 'inner' and 'outer' life raise rich questions about the construction and reinforcement of the bourgeois self or some imagined Cartesian space, in acting and directing craft this is a necessary distinction that carries great pragmatic weight.

The typical tools of performance theory also fall short when thinking about a performer like Bowie who cannot be easily situated in a specific acting tradition. First, Bowie is singular in taking innovations from modelling, clowning and mime into his acting. Second, he also repurposed physicality techniques drawn from the painting and graphic art figurative traditions that, generally speaking, are not taken advantage of by actors working on stage and screen, and he then refined this bricolage of techniques in his many album cover sessions, music videos, photo shoots, staged concert performances and even his personal figurative art practice. Third, to inflect or adjust his performances Bowie often worked alone without reference to any other actors, directors, producers or even audiences to craft character voices and narratives.

For these reasons, I instead deploy the terms posed and unposed which I argue are much closer to the physical basis, language and aesthetics of the two main traditions found in Western performance. I then argue that there is a bend in Bowie's career: before 1980 Bowie's work is largely posed, but his work in this year on *Scary Monsters* and on *The Elephant Man* began his own unique forays into the unposed tradition of performance. I then argue that these terms not only help tease apart Bowie's innovations but also help us define and delineate other common dramatic concepts such as caricature, clown, grotesque, character and empathy. Taken together these categories help reveal the great performative bend in Bowie's career, but they can also help us trace the migration of aesthetic techniques from crafts outside mainstream performance training into our performative tradition.

Acting training in the posed

The rich history, deployment and uses of the posed and the unposed traditions have divided acting training in the West. In fact, most audiences today have become acclimated into this dichotomy: in general, audiences would not judge a performance by Joel Grey or William H. Macy, actors who excel at the posed, on the same terms as an unposed performance by Meryl Streep or Robert De Niro where they 'disappear' into the role. Though an audience may not have the words to describe these two traditions, most sense that posed performances are not intending to achieve the effects of the unposed but have their own separate aesthetic framing, goals and standards of success.

It is worthwhile to trace this background knowledge. For centuries, there have been posed schools which focus on creating the most eye-catching performative styles, charismatic poise and physical carriage; Lindsay Kemp, Bowie's principal trainer in mime and performance, is solidly in

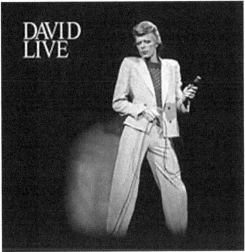

FIGURES 3.5 AND 3.6 *The parade of posed Bowies on stage in the 1970s.*

this tradition. Here a performer often strives to create a somewhat stable, identifiable and unique persona that might then be carried over to larger or lesser degree from role to role. This generalizing, gestural style is found, for example, in circus performances; in most silent cinema; in theatre training before Stanislavski's methods came to dominate the field; in Vaudeville and its comedy-skit descendants; in certain (but not all) Hollywood star performers of the 1930s; in the schools of Jacques Lecoq and others; in most classical animation and in the training of most fashion models. As noted earlier, Bowie has said that from his earliest work until the late 1970s he conceived of himself as a creator of musicals (see Figures 3.5 and 3.6), which is important since the classic musical genre is largely strikingly posed.[6]

Though sometimes labelled as bad performance, the posed might more accurately be described as opening a gap between the performer and the character, thus making the performance self-conscious as opposed to mimetic or simply general as opposed to specific (a goal we see in most modelling training). Though often simply enjoyable as entertainment or used as a technique of advertising, posed styles have also often been deployed by Bertolt Brecht and others as an alienation tactic intended to break the fourth wall and interrupt psychic distance.

Acting training in the unposed

In contrast to these posed traditions are the craft techniques of the unposed, an authentically grounded, anti-indicating performance style in which the actor enters into and subsumes herself inside a character, living within that character on a moment-by-moment basis in the drama and learning to focus not directly on the audience but on other actors. For stage and cinema, this unposed craft begins with Stanislavski and is found today in many forms of acting training from Stella Adler's acolytes down through Uta Hagen and others.[7]

In this discipline, a performer hones their trained mental focus (or by way of a director's delicate ministrations) to remain inside the specific circumstances and emotional memories of a character's life and to stay connected to the lived moments of other characters in the scene. Performers in this style practice techniques designed to remove false feeling and indicative gestures by creating spontaneity, discovery and authenticity – thus eliminating the signature aspects of the posed.

In fact, different approaches to creating interiority and personae mark the line between these two traditions of acting and directing craft. When setting out to direct the unposed actor, for example, an action or gesture must not come across as an 'indication'; this criticism implies that it was not a result of the proper inner-life work by the actor but rather an explicit gestural communication to the audience of what the character is feeling. However, in posed performance the very explicitness of this communication is often celebrated. Anyone who mistakenly casts well-trained, high-level models, clowns or comics who excel at the posed into an unposed drama, or who does the reverse, runs immediately into the radical difference in training and goals of these two performative traditions.

Monsters with interiority: Inhabited clowns and grotesques

Outside of acting training, the posed and unposed dichotomy can also help us define the gamut between *caricatures* and *characters*, two concepts in narrative performance that roughly map onto the same distinctions discussed above.

A *caricature* is a form of highly posed figure which possesses little backstory usually because it stands in for a type rather than an individual. By contrast, a *character* is defined by the specificity and depth of personal history and social role crafted by a writer, director and/or actor. In fact, it is largely because a well-drawn character has been gifted with a complex specific backstory of the kind that is lacking in simple caricatures that a very different training is required to play the two types of figures.

This divergence between caricatures and characters runs through the Western narrative tradition; consider, for example, the history of clowns and grotesques.[8] Classically, both clowns and grotesques were usually simple, posed caricatures with little interior life or backstory. In the West, the clown has ancient roots but is codified certainly by the time of the *commedia dell'arte* tradition as a simple figure of pure posed performativity, and so they are, generally speaking, played by those trained in posed work. Think, for example, of the highly posed clowns Bowie himself played in the 1960s and 1970s (Figures 3.7 and 3.8).

However, thanks to the work of Grimaldi,[9] Pagliacci and others, in the nineteenth century the clown gained a complex interior life and an offstage existence. As the mask dropped and the clown's emotional range and depth of character grew radically, the stage became just a small part of a character's larger and more specific emotional life and world. Now the role changes into what I would call the 'inhabited clown', that is, a character with a real life outside of their posed simple clown role; this character then wrestles with the difference between their staged, posed role and their unposed, offstage, lived life with its intimate conflicts, anxieties and doubts. Playing an inhabited clown with its interiorities requires very different skills and training than those needed to play the simple clowns of the posed tradition.

A similar shift can be found with the grotesque figure, a related role that also began as a simple and largely posed character. The classical simple grotesque (a role which was often mined by clowns) is a shallow character with little backstory, a liminal figure defined largely or entirely by their ugliness and body horror. Throughout his career, Bowie himself performed simple grotesques: consider, for example, the eerie, caricatured figures that feature prominently in his 1979 video for 'Look Back in Anger' (Figure 3.9) and his 1980 video for 'Fashion' (Figure 3.10). Here he stages typical, simple grotesque figures, which are usually marked by deformity and scarring but can include putrefaction and other forms of normativity distortion. In

FIGURES 3.7 AND 3.8 *Bowie in the short mimed film* The Mask *(1969) and onstage performing in the Diamond Dogs tour (1974).*

FIGURES 3.9 AND 3.10 *Stills from the music videos 'Look Back in Anger' (1979) and 'Fashion' (1980).*

general, the simple grotesque is deployed to trigger the viewer's conflicted fascination, to define and possibly threaten the beautiful and the ordinary, to heighten fear, to inscribe difference and/or to enter the dark forces of the unconscious by bridging reality and nightmare.

However, in early modernism a new kind of grotesque appeared which I would call the *inhabited* grotesque, with the exemplary being pioneered by Mary Shelly in her novel *Frankenstein*. Much like the Merrick of *The Elephant Man*, Shelly's unnamed monster is an intelligent, inhabited character gifted with a rich interiority and agency who struggles to speak and act from the margins against the normal-bodied, the conventional, the commonsensical and those in power.[10]

Like most, if not all, deployments of the ugly,[11] both forms of the grotesque express the constructed social nature of disgust and the culture's exotic oppositions of liminality and non-liminality.[12] But while the *simple* grotesque was a simple liminal figure reinforcing social control, instead the *inhabited* grotesque offers a new, dramatic point of view for audiences: because we are given an interior window on their struggles to overcome their shame and desperately join the normative culture that excludes them, we empathetically experience a culture's cruel surplus necessities through their point of view.[13] To paraphrase Bowie, now the shame is on the other side; this new window of anxiety can show how the grotesque's powers of liminality lie largely in the prejudiced minds of others.

In fact, the late 1970s was rife with inhabited grotesques such as Merrick being used as empathetic lenses for social critique.[14] And these examples also reveal how the posed craft needed to play simple grotesque caricatures is simply inadequate to play an inhabited role like Merrick with its complex interiority and depth of character history. But in 1980 as he took on the role of Merrick, Bowie strikingly lacked such unposed training.

The posed and the unposed in Bowie's work

Instead, by 1980 Bowie had become an acknowledged master of the posed. Its roots lay in his own formal aesthetic training in graphic design at the Croydon School of Art and also his training in mime by Kemp, his own love for certain highly posed painters, artists and 1950s performers like Little Richard and Vince Taylor. It had been expressed in his operatic sets; his stage performance style in the 1970s; his many iconic album cover poses, which depend on so many modelling techniques; his heavy use of studio techniques to craft non-realistic soundscapes; his focus on creating escapist, science-fiction characters and storytelling vignettes; his glam rock innovations and spectacular costumes; his continual display of gestural couture; and nearly all of his acting performances prior to 1980. His concert films and his music videos for 'Heroes' and other songs show him striking remarkable and fascinating poses from shot to shot but lack any grounded specificity of character.

One specific way to see how deeply immersed Bowie is in the posed aesthetic before 1980 is to look at the creation of the iconic, highly posed cover of Bowie's 'Heroes' album (1977, Figure 3.13). Below is the proof sheet of the photographer Masayoshi Sukita (Figure 3.11). Note that the final shot was inspired by the highly posed painting *Roquairol* by German artist Erich Heckel (Figure 3.12).

A glance at the session's contact sheets suggests it was selected because it possesses many of the core defining elements of posed figures: performative surprise; fascinating mask-like visage; and a purposefully broadcast, defamiliarized display of musculature taken to an extravagantly exaggerated

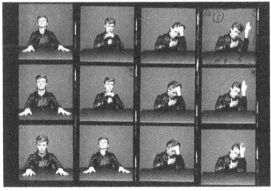

FIGURES 3.11 AND 3.12 *Manufacturing the posed: the inspiration of Roquairol by Erich Heckel (German, Dublin 1883–1970) and the proof sheet of photographer Masayoshi Sukita for the 'Heroes' (1977) album cover shoot.*

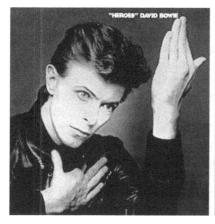 

FIGURES 3.13 AND 3.14 *The posed versus the unposed: Bowie's posed 'Heroes' album cover (1977) versus Bruce Springsteen's unposed album cover for* The Wild, the Innocent & the E Street Shuffle *(1973).*

degree that announces itself as purposefully unmoored from any underlying interiority – all emblematic of the posed aesthetic.

Now contrast the final posed cover (Figure 3.13) with that of Bruce Springsteen (Figure 3.14), a contemporaneous musical performer whom Bowie admired but who is noted for quite different songs, those of brooding authenticity, high interiority and moments of grim Romantic poetics. As Springsteen's cover photo for his 1974 album *The Wild, the Innocent & the E Street Shuffle* shows, the deployment of the unposed means the character is revealed as if by accident and as if caught up in a spontaneous emotional flow. Springsteen's brooding moment, like his songs, also purports to allow us empathetic access to the star himself.

Bowie's highly posed cover celebrates its mannered gestural artificiality and stretched-out reactions – a virtuosic, practised gestural craft is on display. By contrast, Springsteen's unposed cover hints at some underlying anxious choice or meditation. The two cover-art photos overtly announce their respective fields of judgement about figuration, character depth, performativity and level of access to a character's interiority. The posed strengths of the 'Heroes' cover photo all mitigate against the unposed immediacy and interiority of Springsteen's photo. Bowie's posed album cover also tells the cognoscenti what line of posed artists and narratives Bowie sees himself being linked to. By contrast, Springsteen is well served by his strikingly unposed album cover, which deepens his own very different celebrity role as a Romantic poet who tells emotional tales of lived working-class love and loss, often from an internal point of view.

These covers hint at another phenomenon: the posed is singularly unsuited for playing empathetic roles because an empathetic reaction by viewers actually *requires* the projection of interiority. Because only the unposed can create interiority, inviting us into an inner life of emotional immediacy and subjective experiences, this style allows for the use of the machinery of empathy. We can cry for unposed characters like Merrick or Springsteen, who are wrestling with situations of social or psychic damage or repair, but we do not and cannot cry for the posed performer because their characters project little or no interiority for us to participate in or mirror.[15]

For our purposes, this phenomenon is useful because it aligns with Bowie's departure from the posed realm. Just as much of 1980s pop began to adopt his posed methods, Bowie instead dove in the other direction, away from posed caricatures into the realm of unposed characters with interiority. First, he created the anxious, inhabited clown figure of the *Scary Monsters* album, recasting Major Tom as a thoughtful victim, screaming and torturing his body in his singing. Then, carrying over some of the same performative tactics, he went on to play an inhabited grotesque in his interpretation of Merrick as a thoughtful victim in *The Elephant Man*. These changes brought a new empathy and immediacy into Bowie's acting oeuvre, beginning his turn towards the unposed and interiority that would mark his later performances in films like *Merry Christmas, Mr. Lawrence*, *Baal*, *The Hunger* and *Basquiat*.

Scary interiority

The first clue that in 1980 Bowie was shifting his focus from simple posed figures to more inhabited and unposed ones can be found on the album cover and album sleeve of *Scary Monsters* (Figures 3.3 and 3.15). The sleeve contrasts Bowie's older posed versions of himself from the earlier covers for *Low*, *'Heroes'* and *Lodger* with a new figure, an offstage clown caught in unposed moments smoking casually in his harlequin dress as if caught backstage while in pensive reflection between performances. This time the careful selection from the contact sheets (Figure 3.16) reveals the reverse of the *'Heroes'* contact sheet: now Bowie's *least*-posed performance, featuring a pensive quotidian expression, was selected.

Bowie's new bend towards interiority was also unfolding in the songs, stories and personae inside the album's sleeve; nearly every song on the album is sung from the first-person point of view of some peculiar, regret-filled, self-reflective and often uncertain subjectivity, which taken together might or might not all be the same figure. There is the screaming anxious character of 'It's No Game (No.1)'; the guilt-ridden character of 'Scary Monsters' who regrets destroying the mind of a woman he loves; the anguished Major Tom of 'Ashes to Ashes' struggling to escape addictions from the future;

FIGURES 3.15 AND 3.16 *The backstage inhabited clown: inner sleeve for the* Scary Monsters *album (1980) and contact sheet.*

the disenchanted David of 'Teenage Wildlife' pronouncing on celebrity; the mourning friend of Sam who was made to 'Scream Like A Baby' and was then killed by a fascist homophobic culture; the toiling purgatorial character of 'Kingdom Come'; the knowing figure warning us against social pressure in 'Fashion'; the knowing older figure of 'Teenage Wildlife' who is observing a doomed younger relationship between two 'war-torn and resigned' lovers; and, finally, the narcotized character reprising a Muzak version of the anxious vivid tensions of 'It's No Game (No.2)'. Previously, I have suggested that this concluding posed, narcotized voice is there as a contrast to all the unposed, anxious voices that have come before, inserted here for the same reasons a painter might apply a dull underpaint behind figures painted in saturated colours to help them stand out with greater vividness.[16]

The songs share a frame of interior struggles ranging from disenchantment, alarm, dismay, warning and doubt to attempts to confront past experiences, goals, idols, passions and addictions with a clear eye. The point of view unifying the album is of someone observing other people being destroyed and oppressed all around him and regretting that he led a celebrity life that never accomplished anything good or bad. Whether these meditations are all by one figure or many is unclear; possibly they are all the clown of the cover, the album's ad campaign and the video for 'Ashes to Ashes', this resigned, unnamed panicked and drugged offstage narrator who is injured when someone takes a photograph of him. This clown who never does anything clown-like is inhabited by a pensive interiority, engaged in reluctant reminiscences full of 'sordid details' as if trying to make some life decisions, all of which suggests that he might be our guide through this purgatorial realm.[17]

The awkward interiority of inhabited grotesques and Scary Monsters

Just as Bowie released this album of strange interiorities, he jumped boldly straight into the role of Merrick in the Broadway production of *The Elephant Man*. In fact, the previous lead who had anchored the play had steered it to a Tony Award, which dramatically raised the stakes of Bowie's surprising venture onto the legit stage. Which brings us to the question: how did Bowie, who lacked any real theatrical training, now create this empathetic, anxious character?

As many reviewers noted, Bowie's work on Broadway was remarkable and impressive because of how he used both his voice and body.[18] Bowie's delivery manages to emphasize Merrick's outsider status and childlike naivete while constantly conveying his tortured frame; both ground his voice and physicality in Merrick's actual human circumstances and also markedly deepen our empathy for his tragic situation. I will argue that though Bowie lacked all the traditional actor's training in creating an unposed performance, he actually transitioned from *Scary Monsters*'s inhabited clown to Merrick by using the same toolkit of interiority, utilizing certain unique vocal and physical tactics of that weird inhabited clown who wrestles internally with celebrity and cultural oppressions, to become Merrick, an inhabited grotesque who also wrestles internally with his celebrity and cultural oppressions.

The first clue that the two performances are connected comes from a contemporaneous interview on the television show *Videodrome Discotheque* where Bowie himself links Merrick to his singing work on the recently released *Scary Monsters* album.[19] At one point Bowie shifts from discussing his performance in a play about Victorian times to then describe how his peculiar musical phrasing on *Scary Monsters* was also drawn from Victorian times. Bowie notes that in 'Ashes to Ashes', while taking on the first-person position of the old Major Tom character, and in order to 'bring him up to date a bit ... I put him in a sort of Victorian nursery rhyme kind of atmosphere. Even though it's not Victorian it has that sort of queasiness that some of those "ring-a-ring-a-rosies", "this is about the plague and we're all gonna drop down dead – bump" kind of thing about it'.[20]

In fact, this weird, Victorian rhyming work seems directly carried over into Merrick's oddly bouncing intonations. Take for instance Bowie's sung falsetto line 'I'll stay clean tonight' in the song to the similar melodic falsetto he brings to Merrick's line in the play 'For as long as I like?' (1:16 in the Broadway recording). In fact, there is also a melodic parallel: Merrick's vocal range in the Broadway recording seems to quaver around the key of high G just like the opening verses of 'Ashes to Ashes'. This parallel is most evident in the performance at 4:04 where Bowie's performed lines as Merrick are nearly identical to the peculiar high melodic range of his voice in the song's verses.

There are wider parallels than weird intonation, melodic line and musical phrasing. For example, like the narrator of 'Ashes to Ashes', Merrick's voice continually counterpoints between drugged calm and quavering panic. And just as the song's voice is shorn of any basso masculine range and peeps up into strange, often falsetto, fluting trills, on stage Bowie's voice also warbles rapidly in the upper registers, also buttressed by liquid melodic lines that usually end on a questioning note or in the vibrating panic similar to how Bowie sings the song's line, 'Time and again I tell myself'.

Note, too, how melisma – the process of adding more than one pitch to one syllable – which is used in 'Ashes to Ashes' with his descent on '. . . too-oo-oo', is also heard in Bowie's Merrick: for example, in the crucial word 'Rules' – the doctor's rules are arguably Merrick's fatal antagonist in the play – Merrick's panicked vowel ascent gains the soaring pitch range of a songbird.

All of these choices grant Bowie's Merrick the empathetic aura of a childlike innocent taking nervous flights into preadolescence; they embody what the play tells us, that Merrick has really had no real conversations since childhood but is now constantly, physically, yet shyly struggling to have one, using a throat traumatically trapped in his scarred childhood, quite unused to talking yet constantly, nervously hoping to reach out to others. On stage this high treble range also has a contrastive purpose: it takes Bowie's Merrick away from Dr Treves's profundo, overly confident male voice and aligns it closer to the vocal range of the only woman in the play, the female actress who visits and befriends Merrick.

Agentic Friction: The phenomenological presence of Bowie's awkward body in his voice

While Bowie's choices mark Merrick as an innocent, an adolescent and an outsider, other choices craft an awkward self-consciousness and bring Merrick's misaligned physicality (Figure 3.17) into presence in Bowie's animating, tortured and very unusual voice.

First, there is Bowie's pronounced, askew jaw (Figure 3.18), which seems to force an apparently involuntary swallowing and undulation of his tongue to roll consonants into vowels; note for instance how his Merrick says 'Romeo and Juliet'. Here the dancing labial articulations of his rolling jaw are reminiscent of *Scary Monsters*'s song 'Ashes to Ashes' with its similar peculiarly rolled, half-swallowed lines such as 'Oh no not again' and 'I've loved all I've needed, love'.

FIGURES 3.17 AND 3.18 *A publicity still and Bowie in the black-box video of* The Elephant Man *(1980).*

Note also when Bowie's Merrick grows nervous, his rictus-like tics grow even stronger and his consonants become unusually clipped: his *b*, *t* and *k* are often given an exaggerated, sharp percussive cut as if some small door is being slammed shut in his throat. All this grants Merrick's voice short, sudden gusts of force and amplification that, as if taking the character himself by surprise, must then be quickly shut off by the half-askew mouth. The effect is as if his voice grows from a body that just cannot find its sea legs. Here too the muscular work creating this strange and unique voice also resembles some of the remarkable physical contortions required to sing the *Scary Monsters* album's first song 'It's No Game (No.1)' where Bowie sets his body's muscle groups against each other to create a desperate yelling and screaming, often with anxious breathing, a technique that is not just technically but physically difficult. When Bowie first begins to scream his lines in the song, it sounds as though he is using tight constriction of the throat muscles to close down the air passage and then tight constriction of the stomach and lower muscles to force air past this constriction, risking damage to the vocal cords as his voice darts rapidly in wildly different melodic directions in bursts of panic. The same rapidly darting technique and these weird articulatory phonetics not only dramatize Merrick's own phenomenological interior struggles with his physically contorted body, but their very blurred nature heightens our commitment to hear and decipher him.

Similarly, Bowie's unusual bravura screaming on the album's opening cut 'It's No Game (No.1)' is arguably also feeding his work as Merrick in a very different way: this disturbing, ripping screaming brings an intense bodily immediacy to listeners of his performance. Recent scientific work in screaming reveals why:[21] unlike language, which filters through higher levels of the brain and is unpacked on many levels, panicked screaming operates a separate, older neural network to cut into the lower brain with far greater rapidity, seizing the listener's attention far more quickly than spoken language, overriding other forms of attention to bring the listener's body awake and ready to respond. In this jolting manner a sudden sense of the immediacy of another's pain is achieved.

The same panicked contortions of both body and voice box are central for his Broadway performance as Merrick; while there are unfortunately no publicly available recordings of the play's early scene where Merrick is desperately screaming for help, consider for example Bowie's brief but similarly panicked leap into a near scream on Merrick's line 'Like what?!' at 2:04.

The phenomenological presence of physical contortions

To help trace the special presence these choices grant his performance I want to introduce the idea of *agency friction*, defining it as that sense conveyed in a performance that a vocal or physical choice indicates some kind of difficult internal struggle or choice. It is the opposite of the phenomenologically habitual in Merleau-Ponty's sense:[22] in other words, agency friction is not present in the performances of effortless, practised virtuosity of the posed tradition.[23]

Note how agency friction is being pressed into service here to give dimension to Merrick's interiority. Against the phenomenological, polished fluidity of the ordinary physical life of his co-stars (much like the confident, stage-commanding polish Bowie had himself been bringing to his own stage performances for years – see Figures 3.5 and 3.6). Here as Merrick his own struggles to walk – like his struggles to speak – always risk disaster (Figure 3.17), a struggle which emphasizes both his presence and his active interiority. Consider for example Bowie's weak and helpless push off the bench in the video of the play and his weird swivelling of hips. Bowie's 'unnatural' struggles veer between him hanging his body with a scarecrow-like laxness to scrunching his face in an effort to consciously manipulate a limp body requiring great awkward focus to move.

Viewers experience the awkward effort of this body consciously being forced into lurching as if both hamstrung yet animated by consciously directed efforts to move, a body barely and continuously controlled by tenuous mental strings that threaten to break, rather like a Pinocchio struggling with some of the strings cut. Here, internal tension is broadcast because the mind's connection to the body seems so tortured that only desperate acts of willpower can move limbs. By making this interior psychological mechanism overt in its conscious manipulation and its constant risk of disaster, Merrick's body's movement is always cast forth from the usual unnoticed phenomenological background of our own effortless movements and into presence. He, his co-stars and we the audience are potentially all joined in our fear of him falling over, while his mental struggle to move offers another palpable window onto his active interiority.

All of this physical work – which Bowie admitted was itself rather painful[24] – leads him away from struck poses towards a continually surprising awkwardness, a purposeful lack of grace and fluidity that implies trapped subjectivity and a crippled agency. This Merrick must stay constantly careful as he struggles not just with his thoughts and with these new delicate situations, with his fear of frightening the actress or of overstepping the Doctor's many boundaries.

Meanwhile Merrick is fumbling and stumbling his way down the unfamiliar two-way street of human dialogue, and these verbal struggles remind viewers that the Doctor has only recently taught him to speak clearly enough to be understood by others. This effort of self-awareness in navigating the syllabic action of every line, often needing to manipulate his whole body in order to speak clearly, similarly informs us about his roiling interiority, a place where anxiety and the need to make decisions about exactly how to proceed are ever-present companions.

All of this work is opposed in every way to the performances of Bowie's co-stars. As the Doctor and the Actress move about with the smooth movements of arrogant aristocratic pose, he moves about uncertain, crippled and unposed. As they speak in practised easy-to-understand fluting tones, his voice constantly makes unexpected tonal choices. As they react predictably within social scripts, he considers every mental and physical step with some uncertainty. The contrasts all reveal the posed nature of their class and power and Merrick's lack of both.

Meanwhile, his unexpected intonations and an out-of-breath unevenness (itself reminiscent of Bowie's voicework in 'It's No Game (No.1)') are also opposed to their practised intonations, in contrast to his curious hesitant voice both declaim in confident, polished, well-breathed and well-projected phrases even as they find themselves growing lost in what Erving Goffman would describe as social scripts. The contrast doesn't simply highlight the weirdness of Merrick's voice: the way it steps cautiously or skitters without control also suggests that as a linguistic newcomer he does not have any of their civilized and typically theatrical vocal habits. What are the reasons for such contrasts in performance?

Empathy and empathy funnels: Precision versus moment-by-moment work

The opposition is to some degree structured in the play's dramatic writing; while Merrick's lines are deeply characterized by rich layers of meaning, his co-stars' dialogue lines are far less layered. This effect is worth noticing because it helps illustrate and define the gamut between caricature and character; while richly layered dialogue like Merrick's creates a character,[25] their bleached dialogue is a typical technique for creating a caricature.[26]

However, in a contemporaneous interview in *Rolling Stone* magazine, Concetta Tomei who played the actress opposite Bowie suggests the contrast reflects different levels of acting training. Tomei argued that 'David apparently has no acting background to speak of, and consequently, he really has no "technique", as we know Gielgud and Olivier as having'.[27] Tomei's concerns that Bowie had no 'technique' might be somewhat responsible for the fact that both she and Tom Fitzsimmons, the actor playing the Doctor, are continually indicating, meaning they are broadcasting their emotional beats to the audience with a bit of overemphasis rather than reacting moment-by-moment with and against Bowie. It is in fact not possible to work moment-to-moment opposite an actor who is not himself trained to play off your performance with true moment-by-moment spontaneity but can 'give back' little but repetitive precision. And for Bowie, working solo without real performance partners would not have been an unfamiliar task; in general, he crafted roles to be performed entirely by himself for studio mics and for concertgoers and was famous for his precision in repeated studio takes. Arguably, the ways Bowie's work on *Scary Monsters* seem to be directly imported into his performance as Merrick suggests that Bowie arrived at the unposed by a different route, one that does not require, include or perhaps even allow his co-stars to also be unposed.

Alternatively, this contrast might not be only a result of Bowie's lack of training. The fact that the co-stars are also rather posed in how they are staged by the play's director Jack Hofsiss suggests that perhaps Hofsiss is purposefully deploying Tomei and Fitzsimmons as posed characters around Bowie's unposed performance. This is a common tactic directors use to not only throw a main character like Merrick into a kind of contrastive relief but also to powerfully funnel our attention and our empathy away from them and towards Merrick, deepening our understanding of what it is like to inhabit the life of a lonely grotesque.

I would label such a tactic an *empathy funnel*. Empathy funnels are found in many narratives – consider for example films like Federico Fellini's *8 ½* (1963), Bob Fosse's *Cabaret* (1972) and Taika Waititi's *Jojo Rabbit* (2019). All three feature unposed characters similarly foregrounded against a posed cast of simple clowns, grotesques and caricatures in order to focus and intensify an audience's empathy for the main characters.

Whatever the reasons for the play's opposition of unposed and posed performances, the effect at its dramatic best is to heighten Merrick's longing to join a society that is fundamentally hollow, while at its worst the Doctor and the Actress turn into little more than human props feeding Bowie lines so that he can perform with such precise, fascinating weirdness.

Conclusion: Defining the posed and unposed

In this chapter, I have suggested a topography of concepts – of caricature versus character, simple versus inhabited and posed versus unposed – to propose that Bowie's work up until 1980 was largely of simple caricatures performed in the posed tradition, but that there is a bend in David Bowie's work in 1980 away from simple posed caricatures towards inhabited, unposed characters with rich interiority.

To summarize the methodology here,[78] the posed dramatic character's tradition, practice and nature – which I suggest makes up the great majority of Bowie's work prior to 1980 – are marked by the following characteristics:

(1) Playing emotions in exaggerated ways that lack specificity and thus often feel melodramatic.

(2) Gestures and physicality that 'indicate': that is, that convey emotions directly to the audience.

(3) Exhibiting an unspontaneous quality to actions.

Over time these tropes became harnessed to other aesthetic goals:

(4) A non-naturalistic fluidity or rigidity of style. Often the posed performance seems to have been carefully practised, as if tried out in front of a mirror many times.

(5) Deploying this artificiality as a strength, the style explores irony, parody, a knowing self-awareness and overtly playing to the audience. This can grant a performance more than one communicative plane at a time.

(6) Because their work is so gestural and, unlike unposed performances, can warp time by sliding between movement and stasis, using unnaturally frozen or slowed musculature and peculiar vogueing postures, posed performers are more likely to be inspired by and borrow from static figuration than are unposed performers. This more closely links the posed style to figurative painting, graphic design, caricatured drawing, cartoons and graphic design than the unposed style.

(7) Many posed characters are partly or entirely constructed by the actor playing them while most unposed roles have been constructed by a novelist, playwright or screenwriter. Often this performer's path of creation lays stress on performative experiments and investigations rather than on the lengthy backstory creations that novelists, playwrights and screenwriters bring to create unposed characters.

I would suggest that these seven points tend to be markers of Bowie's work before 1980.

I argue that in 1980 Bowie dove away from this performative frame and tradition and into the unposed tradition of dramatic figures and characters, which differ from their posed contemporaries in many ways.

(1) The unposed is praised for its rejection of overdetermined, simple, emotional portraits such as caricature or simple clowning in favour of much more subtle and ambivalent emotional portraits involving more than one emotional state.

(2) The style is concerned with conveying a character's interiority, that roiling struggle of anxiety and choice that I have labelled agency friction to denote the moments when an audience glimpses the character's moment-by-moment, spontaneous-seeming inner struggles. This allows in turn for empathetic relationships with an audience.

(3) In this pursuit, unposed characters illustrate fleeting and transitional emotional states and/or apparently spontaneous emotions and reactions to events inside the drama. By moving through instances of action, this style avoids the physicality of indication, that posed method of communication between an actor and an audience that as a method of conveying emotions and objectives in an *un*posed frame tends to come across as 'theatrical', overprepared, false and 'too big'.

(4) Unposed actors usually avoid this by bringing an uninterrupted attention and focus on another character in the scene, and often a full-blown emotional interaction with another figure in their story, contrasting the posed actor's tactic of putting their focus on how their own body and voice are communicating or conveying emotional information to the viewer.

(5) Such characters require an extensive creation in writing rich backstory which takes training, skill and time to accomplish well. In theatre and film, this is usually (though not always) a writer's job, separate from the actor or director.

Most of these points about the unposed distinguish Bowie's work in 1980 from his earlier craft choices. However, I would argue that Bowie was not trained to focus on other actors – point 4 above of the unposed tradition. Instead, to create Merrick's striking interiority I suggest he compensated by focusing on point 2: by bringing vocal craft he'd used on his *Scary Monsters* album, joining that to a constant fight against awkwardness and falling over, in nearly every line Bowie is constantly fighting vocally and physically against his own grotesque shape, bringing both his agency and its great physical barrier into our phenomenological presence. I have called this phenomenon agency friction. This gave the role not only a sense of spontaneous agency but also conveyed an interiority and a history of struggles, aspects of the unposed performance which helped connote Merrick's agency and interiority and trigger viewers' empathy.

Perhaps this investigation of Bowie also helps us understand how in general posed performances, with their irony, self-announced physical virtuosity and distancing devices, function so differently from unposed performances with their backstory work and their claims to spontaneity, interiority and empathetic machinery. Hopefully, this foray also helps reveal how an actor's manipulation of the phenomenology of vocal craft and physical movement can shape how we, audience members, construct the interiorities of characters.

Finally, I have suggested how an empathy funnel is constructed in this play (as well as in many other narratives), that the contrastive deployment of all of these categories funnels our attention and our empathy towards the unposed character of Merrick. *The Elephant Man* illustrates how certain powerful, dramatic effects can be achieved by surrounding a character rich in interiority with much more posed figures who have less or no interiority.

In the end this analysis leads to some related questions. While the posed and the unposed are performative frames that extend over many genres, forms of narrative and even extend into social life to distinguish social power structures and forms of identity, nevertheless I think each form has its own rough psychographic attractions. And if I am drawn to and immerse myself specifically in posed forms of culture, how does that reflect and influence how I construct my own agency and the agency of the other? Alternatively, does immersing myself in unposed culture make me more or less of an agent in my own life? And does it make me more or less exposed to empathy, choice, agency friction and the class- and race-based empathy funnels that make up the myriad hegemonies that are narratively embedded in the culture all around me? And in the end are there benefits to striving, as Bowie did from 1980 onwards, to explore and even combine both sides of this dichotomy in new ways?[29]

Notes

1 Amedeo D'Adamo, *Empathetic Space on Screen: Constructing Powerful Place and Setting* (London: Palgrave Macmillan Press, 2018).

2 'David Bowie speaks to Jeremy Paxman on BBC Newsnight (1999)', *BBC Newsnight*, 12 January 2016, video, 16:06, https://www.youtube.com/watch?v=FiK7s_0tGsg. Bowie makes a similar point in a 1977 interview: see 8:36 of 'David Bowie - Interview - Hotel de L'Europe - Amsterdam, Holland - 14 October 1977', 7 July 2019, video, 31:08, https://www.youtube.com/watch?v=VudyGkGWDlc, accessed December 2020.

3 Amedeo D'Adamo, 'Dantean Space in the Cities of Cinema', in *Media and the City: Urbanism, Technology and Communication*, ed. Simone Tosoni, Matteo Tarantino, and Chiara Giaccardi (Newcastle upon Tyne: Cambridge Scholars Press, 2013), 244–58.

4 This chapter is dedicated to my teachers in performance, especially to Lenore DeKoven, Howard Fine, David Coury, Marylin Macintyre, the China National Beijing Opera Ensemble, Peter Steadman and the New York Greek Drama Company, Augusto Boal, Bread and Puppet Theatre and the Italian Theater of the Affections. I want also to thank Ian Dixon, Brendan Black and Alexander Sun for their incredibly generous editing help on this chapter.

5 James Naremore, *An Invention without a Future: Essays on Cinema* (Oakland, CA: University of California Press, 2014).

6 The Musical remained an essentially posed form until Bob Fosse began threading unposed stories, actors and scenes into the form in the 1970s.

7 It can be found in the schools of well-established acting teachers like Lenore Dekoven, Marilyn McIntyre, Howard Fine and many others and is arguably the dominant style of acting training today.

8 Andrew McConnell Stott, 'Clowns on the Verge of a Nervous Breakdown: Dickens, Coulrophobia, and the Memoirs of Joseph Grimaldi', *Journal for Early Modern Cultural Studies* 12, no. 4 (1992): 3–25; Wolfgang Kayser, *The Grotesque in Art and Literature* (New York: Columbia University Press, 1981).

9 Stott, *Clowns on the Verge of a Nervous Breakdown*.

10 Unfortunately, the famous filmic representations of Frankenstein's monster reduce it to a simple grotesque, a now iconic shambling beast lacking any real inner life or agency that often even lacks a voice and can only grunt.

11 Andrei Pop and Mechtild Widrich, eds, *Ugliness* (London: I.B Tauris & Co., 2014).

12 Martha Nussbaum, *Hiding from Humanity: Disgust, Shame and the Law* (Princeton, NJ: Princeton University Press, 2006).

13 Amedeo D'Adamo, 'Is Bowie our Kierkegaard? – A Theory of Agency in Fandom', in *David Bowie and Transmedia Stardom,* ed. Ana Cristina Mendes and Lisa Perrott (London, New York: Routledge. 2019), 57–71.

14 Consider *Stroszek* (1977) and *One Flew Over The Cuckoo's Nest* (1975) which has many characters who have been institutionalized because of grotesque attributes and who now struggle to communicate their interiority. Then, there is the role of Billy Kwan in the film *The Year of Living Dangerously* (1982, from a novel published in 1978) who suffers from

dwarfism and physical ugliness but who like Merrick deeply grasps the cruelties of a conservative and torturing regime that eventually kills him.

15 D'Adamo, *Empathetic Space on Screen*.
16 Amedeo D'Adamo. 'Urgently Communicating the Unintelligible: Bowie's Screaming Techniques on It's No Game' (talk, Australian Centre for the Moving Image, 2015). Presented at *The Stardom and Celebrity of David Bowie* conference at the ACMI museum show *David Bowie Is* in Melbourne, Australia.
17 Notably, all this regretful interior meditation is not nearly as present in Bowie's other releases with the striking exception of his last two albums.
18 Kathryn Johnson, one of the curators of the David Bowie exhibition David Bowie Is, notes this as well. 'David Bowie Is: John Merrick and The Elephant Man', Absolute Radio, 17 October 2013, 1:25, https://www.youtube.com/watch?time_continue=39&v=Fbql8z96TDQ&feature=emb_logo, accessed 12 December 2020.
19 'DAVID BOWIE – The Elephant Man Interview Special (Hosted By Sir Tim Rice)', 18 July 2014, video, 18:23, https://www.youtube.com/watch?v=UVqs7rPvgow.
20 Ibid. The musical term 'lullaby' is thought to be drawn either from 'to lull' or from the disturbing concept of warding off the evil Lilith who might plague the child at night. In fact, Bowie plays on this contradiction in the lullaby tradition.
21 Herman Ackermann, Steffen R. Hage and Wolfram Ziegler, 'Brain Mechanisms of Acoustic Communication in Humans and Nonhuman Primates: An Evolutionary Perspective', *Behavioural and Brain Sciences* 37, no. 6 (2014): 529–46 and Luc H. Arnal et al., 'Human Screams Occupy a Privileged Niche in the Communication Soundscape', *Current Biology* 25 (2015): 2051–6.
22 Maurice Merleau-Ponty, *The Phenomenology of Perception*, trans. Donald Landes (London: Routledge Press, 2012).
23 Shogo Tanaka, 'The Notion of Embodied Knowledge and its Range', *Encyclopaedia: Journal of phenomenology and education* 37 (2013): 47–66.
24 'DAVID BOWIE – Radio One Interview 1980-12-07 Recorded in New York broadcast on BBC Radio One on 1981-01-05; interviewer Andy Peebles Bootleg', David Bowie forever (blog), https://paola1chi.blogspot.com/2020/09/david-bowie-radio-one-interview-1980-12.html, accessed 1 December 2020.
25 D'Adamo, *Empathetic Space on Screen*, 185.
26 As others have pointed out, narrative dialogue can be broken out into six layers of meaning which I have elsewhere (D'Adamo, *Empathetic Space on Screen*) called the manifold of dramatic meaning. Dialogue can (1) reveal the past, (2) convey objectives in the present, (3) foreshadow the future, (4) reveal character, (5) reveal relationships and (6) be entertaining and engaging in itself. By applying these levels to the play one sees how many meaningful layers exist in Merrick's lines, which defines him as a deeply drawn character, while the Doctor and the Actress often deliver lines with few to none of these

layers of meaning, a bleaching of dialogue that is a very common technique for creating a caricature in narrative. Note too how Merrick gradually draws the Actress into expressing more meaningful lines, thereby deepening their connection.

27 Kurt Loder, 'David Bowie: Scary Monster on Broadway', Rolling Stone, 13 November 1980, https://www.rollingstone.com/music/music-news/david-bowie-scary-monster-on-broadway-100929/.

28 I am currently writing a book expanding on the roles of the posed and the unposed.

29 Amedeo D'Adamo, 'Freedom vs. Possibility: Bowie, Kierkegaard, and Stages of Time', in *The Cambridge Companion to David Bowie*, ed. Denis Flannery (Cambridge: Cambridge University Press, forthcoming in 2023).

4

Consuming Bowie

Christiane F. and the transgressive allure of Anglo-American pop culture in Cold War West Berlin

Susanne Hillman

In her second memoir published in 2014, Christiane Felscherinow looks back at *Christiane F. Wir Kinder vom Bahnhof Zoo* (1981), the film that told the story of her experiences as a heroin addict and teenage prostitute in Cold War West Berlin, and asserts: 'For me Bowie was the star of my film.'[1] Whatever the basis of this rather extravagant claim, David Bowie's cameo appearance certainly added glamour to an otherwise sordid tale of addiction and degradation. 'Bowie is featured throughout as a kind of dream fix running parallel to the heroin', writes Paul Morley, 'the two ways of making a dismal, violent life more interesting or palatable'.[2] Beyond the brief but pivotal concert scene and the soundtrack composed of songs culled from Bowie's Berlin trilogy and the album *Stage*, paraphernalia such as a concert poster, tickets and Bowie albums strategically placed within the film serve to impress the viewer with Bowie's omnipresence in Christiane's life.

The girl from the Bahnhof Zoo emerged into the limelight in 1978, one year after she had overcome her addiction. Her dramatic story was covered in a series of reports in the West German weekly *Stern*, galvanizing its estimated 20 million readers. Produced by Bernd Eichinger, the film became one of the highest-grossing German films of all time, winning the *Goldene Leinwand* for the most commercially successful West German

FIGURE 4.1 *Screenshot of David Bowie performing 'Station to Station' in Christiane F.*

film in 1981.³ Not merely entertainment, the film was a genuine event that entered the consciousness of the German public.⁴ Surprisingly, Felscherinow later professed to be annoyed at the role the film played in popularizing its musical star: 'My film had made Bowie even more prominent, especially in Europe . . . What an outrage!'⁵ This sentiment needs to be understood in the context of her subsequent disillusionment with the singer – a handful of critics shared her indignation.

Depending on national context, film reviews ran the gamut of enthusiastic to lukewarm. West Germans like Hans C. Blumenberg in *Die Zeit* dismissed the film as 'pedagogically valuable' but 'commendably boring'; as for the concert sequence, he criticized it as bland and suffering from incompetent editing.⁶ British critics, meanwhile, commented positively on director Uli Edel's commitment to realism and unflinching directing while making little of Bowie's performance or soundtrack.⁷ American reviewers were the only ones to underscore the singer's contribution, and expectedly so: by the time of the film's release, Bowie had attained superstar status in the United States whereas he was not yet known widely in Germany. The indefatigable Roger Ebert, for example, took a generally positive view of the film but disapproved of the exploitation [*sic*] of Bowie's presence, a move that, to Ebert, suggested the producers' hope 'to cash in on Bowie fans'.⁸ He had a point, but there is more: cashing in on Bowie fans also meant exaggerating the star's role in Christiane's life. This exaggeration, in turn, warranted a trenchant appraisal of the impact of Americanization in post-war West Germany.

In this chapter, I argue that Bowie's performance in *Christiane F.* constitutes the core of a subtle but devastating critique of Anglo-American pop culture and, by extension, the broader capitalist *Konsumgesellschaft* (consumer society) the Americans had introduced into the Federal Republic of Germany (FRG) after 1949. Ironically, consumption plays a crucial role in the film's narrative and its attraction. Part of the pleasure of watching *Christiane F.* resides in the viewers' ability to vicariously consume the dangers and temptations associated with the protagonist's descent into full-blown addiction *and* to partake in her experience of watching David Bowie on stage. In agreeing to pose as the object of Christiane's adoration, the singer appropriates the expressions and poses of other characters including those of the music star David Bowie and one of his personae, the Thin White Duke. In so doing, his star image resolves two irreconcilables: he represents and seemingly celebrates Anglo-American pop culture while using the 'self', specifically his faux-aristocratic, authoritarian Duke, as a symbol of West Germany's domination by capitalist consumer culture.[9] As an 'externalizing' actor, Bowie crafts a performance that emphasizes the fact that he is *playing* rather than *living* a role. Put another way, his adherence to the alien, other and 'outer' exposes the illusion of an inner realm of authentic emotions.[10] Parodying one of his own creations, the Thin White Duke, as an American rebel with a noble (European) pedigree, his embrace of performance 'externality' made Bowie supremely useful for a producer and director seeking to capitalize on West Germany's Americanized *Konsumgesellschaft* while concurrently denouncing it.

Despite its popularity, *Christiane F.* has received scant scholarly attention to date, none of which deals with Bowie's performance.[11] This remarkable neglect, which extends to academics working on German popular culture, is partly due to the persisting 'duality between art and popular cinema' in Germany – a duality which explains the glaring disregard of producer Bernd Eichinger's entire oeuvre.[12] Indeed, despite being a commercially successful producer with films like *The Name of the Rose* (1986), *Smilla's Sense of Snow* (1996) and *Resident Evil* (2002) under his belt, Eichinger is routinely ignored in German film studies. Bowie scholars have likewise given his cameo in *Christiane F.* short shrift.[13] Yet, it is precisely in *this* role, I suggest, that Bowie's perennial play-acting, his penchant for artifice and his reliance on the technique of 'externality' – working from the 'outside' rather than from 'inner' emotional experience – invite scholarly scrutiny. My essay thus fills a crucial gap in our appreciation of Bowie the actor and contributes to our understanding of Germany's fraught relationship with Anglo-American pop culture.

There is little doubt that Bowie's presence, besides heightening the film's market appeal, was meant to lend the film a great deal of its vaunted realism.[14] Seeking to recreate the *Lebensgefühl* (lifestyle) of the young public, Eichinger hired a specialist in 'product placement' who was tasked with making the idea palatable to Bowie.[15] In the end, it was screenwriter Hermann Weigel who managed to convince Bowie to contribute, with little or no remuneration.[16] Apparently, the singer had no problem with the topic; 'Bowie understood that it was a question of authenticity', Weigel explained in an interview.¹⁷ Whether he was aware of Bowie's reputation for 'famed artificiality' is a different question.¹⁸

Questions of authenticity aside, Bowie's part in the film was certainly vital to its monumental success and cult status among young viewers. At the same time, it allowed the filmmakers to problematize Anglo-American pop culture; Eichinger was plainly less concerned with social criticism than with triumphing at the box office. His shrewd sense for mass appeal resulted in an ideological promiscuity that allowed 'viewers to indulge in the thrills offered by countercinema, alternative lifestyles, or leftist politics', Hester Baer maintains, 'while ultimately foreclosing on the critique they offer by incorporating them fully into consumer-driven market culture'.¹⁹ The filmmakers' concern with the transgressive allure and seemingly deleterious effects of Anglo-American pop culture needs to be situated in the context of West German Americanization and, more broadly, the massive impact of Anglo-American culture in the FRG. In this respect, Bowie was the ideal vehicle for a critique of both.

Although Bowie was British, his lengthy stay and musical productivity in the United States made him a virtual personification of Anglo-American pop culture, and West Germans viewed him as such rather than as the Brit pop star Asian fans adulated. Indeed, the European/American binary was crucial to his music star image in the 1970s.²⁰ A European living in the United States, he drew on such varied inspiration as the Velvet Underground, Andy Warhol and Black American music; not surprisingly, the press took note of this influence. In 1976, *Der Spiegel*, Germany's largest weekly, featured an article on the man it oddly identified as a 'Frankieboy of nightmares', apparently a reference to Frank Sinatra.²¹ Bowie's music was a fusion of beat, soul, Hollywood and Vaudeville, and the star himself a 'James Dean with a touch of Aubrey Beardsley'.²² With the *Station to Station* album – especially its eponymous track – Bowie had signalled his farewell to the United States and his return to Europe, but much of his musical success as well as his most important film to date, *The Man Who Fell to Earth*, tied him indelibly to America. His West German fans therefore saw him as straddling both worlds, old and new. As a result, Bowie lent himself particularly well to a broader critique of Anglo-American pop culture.

In the absence of a genuine social critique, the filmmakers' negative appraisal of this heterogeneous culture takes on an outsized significance. Besides brief references to the soul-destroying environment of the satellite city Gropiusstadt where Christiane spent her formative years, *Christiane F.* dispenses completely with social and political references. There is no indication that Berlin is a divided city, nor any sign of the 1970s severe economic recession and renewed build-up of the NATO nuclear arsenal. Problems such as child mistreatment, lack of quality education and truancy which all play a prominent role in the memoir are equally ignored. Most glaringly, the heroine's subjection to parental abuse and neglect – surely a major reason behind her descent into addiction – is virtually ignored. What is singled out instead is the treacherous temptation exerted by Anglo-American pop culture, in the film almost entirely attached to the figure of Bowie.

Before we turn to Bowie's performance, we need to consider West Germans' attitude towards Anglo-American pop culture. Since I approach my topic as a historian, context is key to my argument. The first thing to note is that the process of Americanization in the FRG, a unidirectional process of cultural transfer that functioned according to the 'sender-receiver' model, was anything but straightforward.[23] For the post-war generation American pop culture in particular 'played a liberating function . . . by undermining key elements of the authoritarian personality structure', in the words of Winfried Fluck. It did so as follows:

> by replacing the still lingering ideal of the military man with rock'n'roll heroes like Elvis Presley, by glorifying youthful rebellion through film stars like James Dean or Marlon Brando, and by opening up new spaces for self-fashioning and self-expression without a loss in respectability through the playful exhibitionism of female actors like Marilyn Monroe.[24]

This sanguine assessment notwithstanding, the liberating function of American pop culture should not be overstated, nor was its success ubiquitous. After the political and economic stabilization of the 1950s, the 1960s and 1970s witnessed a growing disillusionment with the post-war American order. This shift was the result of the Vietnam War and the dawning realization that what had once seemed like a breath of fresh air was little more than capitalism and materialism run amok.[25] Without a doubt, by the 1970s West Germans' enthusiasm for all things 'Ami' had weakened considerably as citizens had to grapple with various political, social and economic tensions that came to dominate the FRG. West Germany's cultural elite was outspoken in its denigration of the allegedly stifling effect of American culture. The writer Hermann Peter Piwitt decried the 'everyday colonialism' of 'Yankee culture'.[26] A character in a film by the émigré filmmaker Wim Wenders put it even more starkly when deploring that '[t]he Yanks have colonized our subconscious'.[27] The younger generation, by contrast, not only tolerated Anglo-American pop culture but also actively embraced 'self-Americanization', a global and globalizing process fusing art, commerce and pop cultural innovation.[28] Unfortunately, Edel and Eichinger direct their ire at the baleful impact of this development rather than seeking to expose the socio-economic and psychological roots of Christiane's tragedy.

The Anglo-American temptation comes most vividly to light in the concert sequence featuring Bowie's performance of 'Station to Station', which is accordingly at the core of my analysis. To some degree, Bowie's acting style, with its emphasis on artifice and the malleability of the self, was suited perfectly to a critical portrayal of Anglo-American pop culture. As I will demonstrate, his technique is strongly indebted to Brechtian aesthetic theory that privileges anti-realism over emotionalism. In contrast to Stanislavski who eschewed simulation, Brecht demanded the uncovering of performance *as* performance. In theatre this was to be achieved with the help of the *Gestus*, a fusion of gesture and gist.[29] Gestic acting draws attention to the role and thereby reveals its artificiality. On this theory, specific gests convey a variety of ideological positions.[30] They are therefore anything but natural or spontaneous. Bowie, who had studied mime with Lindsey Kemp, unambiguously favoured a 'performance technique that relies on conventionalized poses to help the actor indicate "fear", "sorrow", "hope", "confusion", and so forth', to quote James Naremore on film acting.[31] According to Naremore, actors perform emotions in keeping with social conditioning rather than drawing on a well of uncontaminated feeling.[32] The lens of externality shifts our focus from emotional sincerity to what specific poses *do*, emotionally speaking. Relying on the external, in *Christiane F.* Bowie brings the artificiality of *all* performance or self-presentation home to his audience.[33] To reveal Bowie's didactic aim, I will focus on his expressive techniques (posture, gesture and voice) and certain aspects of the sequence's mise en scène such as stage set, lighting, clothing, make-up and inanimate objects. Taken together, these elements constitute the actor's 'movement vocabulary' on stage and screen which needs to be subjected to a close reading.[34]

Fittingly, the concert sequence is a patchwork of film shot in America and Europe. Even before Bowie's approval had been secured, concert scenes were being filmed at an AC/DC concert in Frankfurt am Main, which explains the leather attire of many of the fans. The performance that made it into the final product was filmed in October 1980 at the Hurrah club in New York, with Bowie lip-syncing to the *Stage* version of 'Station to Station'.[35] It differed in astonishing ways from the historic concert Christiane had attended at the Deutschlandhalle in April 1976. The beginning of the sequence features the venue, a crowded parking lot and fans waiting in line or entering the building. Once inside, the camera pans over the packed arena in which the Bowie track 'Boys Keep Swinging' is playing. It then cuts to a group of young men who get into a fight. The fighting scene is interspersed with shots of Christiane and her friends smoking a joint. Significantly, Christiane wears her Bowie jacket, a masculine varsity-type purple garment with white stripes on the shoulders and the word Bowie in big white letters on the back. The pre-concert scene thus sets the stage for what is to come by combining violence, drugs and Bowie.

The direction of the Bowie performance proper underlines the suite-like structure of 'Station to Station'. The opening part features rumbling guitars that mimic the ominous sound of a train slowly gathering steam while light beams criss-cross the audience standing in the dark. Suddenly, Bowie appears on screen, clad in blue jeans, a blue dress shirt and a red jacket. A simple silver necklace with a small cross constitutes his only item of jewellery. Clouds of fog swirl over the stage, largely obscuring the singer and the band and lending his figure an aura of mystery. In the second part, beginning with the line 'once there were mountains' Bowie's performance is marked by a restrained intensity. For the first time, the singer is seen in full light. To loud cheering and clapping, he launches into an uninhibited celebration of mountains, sunbirds, drinking and not least, 'the joyous relief of cocaine'.[36] A change of tune signals the beginning of part three, the segment featuring the hypnotic repetition of the phrase 'it's too late'. The switch in harmony coincides with Christiane's push forward to the edge of the stage. For the remainder of the scene, she stands at Bowie's feet, gazing up at her hero with desperate longing. The camera then cuts to Christiane outside the concert hall, getting ready for her first heroin sniff. This is the sequence I will now seek to unpack, beginning with the set design and lighting.

To make sense of the filmmakers' decision regarding the mise en scène, let us consider the original concert first. The set of the *Isolar* tour was pared down to essentials, as David Buckley describes:

> The 1976 show was stripped of props and obvious theatrical conceits, working through the use of an almost Brechtian sense of estrangement and the appropriation of lighting techniques from German expressionist theatre of the twenties and thirties . . . Bowie took the stage dressed in white shirt and black waistcoat, hair slicked back and bathed in a dazzling wash of white light, the intensity of which unnerved the audience.[37]

The show opened with a tape of the German band Kraftwerk, followed by a Luis Buñuel/Salvador Dalí film sequence from *Le Chien Andalou*. The singer then entered in the character of the Thin White Duke, the one persona in Bowie's repertoire in whose name he wrote a rudimentary autobiography. Some commentators have seen the Duke as an embodiment of Hitler's vision of the Aryan superman.[38] Bowie himself described his creation as a 'very Aryan, fascist type – a would-be romantic with absolutely no emotion at all'.[39] Little of this features in *Christiane F.* In lieu of the Buñuel/Dalí images which may have been Bowie's nod to modernist authenticity, the viewer is presented with the dark mass of the fans, and when the star finally appears on stage, he performs a postmodern play with selves that has few equals in the history of pop culture. Gone too are the spectacular light banks that flooded the stage on the *Isolar* tour; instead, a few solitary light beams are seen to play over the audience. The stage is mostly empty, and there is little to distract the viewers' attention from the star.

These differences in set design and lighting are only the most immediately apparent changes from the 1976 performance. Bowie's apparel is another indicator of the film's representation of the star as a personification of Anglo-American pop culture. This is indeed a major aspect of the broader meaning of the sequence. 'The expressive dialectic between people and things extends to the clothing actors wear', Naremore reminds us. 'Costumes serve as indicators of gender and social status, but they also shape bodies and behaviour.'[40] For someone as adept in sartorial transformation as Bowie, deciding what to wear both on and offstage was always a serious issue. On the original *Isolar* tour, as we have seen, the Thin White Duke was dressed in black and white, his hair styled in the manner of a Weimar-era cabaret singer, a 'European superman persona' exemplifying 'fascist chic', in the words of Paul Trynka.[41] For obvious reasons, this was highly problematic for a German audience.

Consequently, in *Christiane F.* the filmmakers went out of their way to disassociate Bowie from his notorious quasi-fascist pronouncements and to strengthen his link with Anglo-American pop culture instead. If it is true that clothes 'bestow form, vitality, and traits of character on the actors' movements', as Naremore suggests, this marked departure from his previous (and later) stage personae is definitely noteworthy.[42] While the jeans the Duke wears in the sequence are probably the most iconic item of American clothing, signifying rugged individualism and the can-do spirit of the Gold Rush era, the red Harrington jacket is very similar to the one worn by James Dean in *Rebel without a Cause* (1955). Even the hairstyle and hair colour conjure the young American anti-hero. Rather than having his hair slicked back à la Joel Grey's master of ceremonies in the musical *Cabaret* (1972), here Bowie sports an immaculately styled quiff. The salute to James Dean is indisputable and not entirely surprising: as a teenager David Jones emulated the young American actor.[43]

The Duke's skin colour is also noteworthy: Unlike the ghostly white face Bowie displayed on the first *Isolar* tour, an undeniable indicator of the Duke's racial superiority, in *Christiane F.* his skin has a healthier tone. In other words, in the role of the Americanized Duke Bowie no longer performs Aryan superiority but instead pays tribute to what we might call normative whiteness. This is particularly interesting in view of Bowie's natural paleness and his penchant for *kabuki*-style white make-up at an earlier period of his career. Assuming a healthier skin tone in the film signalled a departure from the more extreme features of the Thin White Duke. In connection with Bowie's performance in *Christiane F.*, the meaning is fairly straightforward: the singer is the embodiment of 'natural' Anglo-American whiteness, divorced from the racist excesses of Aryanism but nonetheless complicit in the ideology of Anglo-American cultural pre-eminence.[44]

In short, Eichinger and Edel's Bowie is dramatically different from the Bowie Felscherinow would have seen on stage five years earlier. Not only is there nary a hint of the icy elegance and aloofness of the Thin White Duke persona, Bowie's well-known partiality for flamboyant androgynous attire is nowhere in evidence either. The only nod to the stylish sophistication of the original Duke is the blue dress shirt. As a result, it appears as if Bowie performs the Duke as 'one of the lads' – jeans and jacket with carelessly arranged collar suggesting an uncharacteristic sartorial nonchalance. This man, the viewer is meant to feel, is as ready to jump into a Cadillac as to go for a beer in the neighbourhood pub. This is in keeping with evolving models of masculinity in the 1970s in Britain and the United States. With the original Thin White Duke Bowie had departed from the camp sensibility of his Ziggy and Aladdin Zane personae. As the Duke, he projected a 'New Man model of masculinity' which may have contributed to Bowie's mainstream acceptance.[45]

Indeed, at first glance *this* Duke appears to be a fairly unvarnished representation of Anglo-American pop culture, closer to the American Duke (John Wayne) than to the original Weimar-era cabaret singer. At second glance, however, the irony of the performance becomes apparent. For one thing, Bowie's Americanized Duke wears dark-grey eyeshadow, black eyeliner and light red lipstick which, while unobtrusive, are clearly visible and jar oddly with his macho posturing later in the song. Seemingly anticipating British lad culture, his make-up offers a pointed challenge to the backlash against new models of masculinity that Bowie himself had championed in the early 1970s. The impression of a straightforward Americanized Duke is thus partially misleading.[46] It is noteworthy, moreover, that when Bowie appeared on *The Tonight Show with Johnny Carson* in September 1980, roughly a month before the *Christiane F.* shoot, he sported the very same red Herrington jacket and blue jeans but combined with a white T-shirt and white sneakers, the quintessential accessories of American casual. It is obvious, then, that while the Duke in the film is Americanized, this Americanization only goes so far. The dress shirt indexes his class status as superior, indeed noble – he plays a Duke after all. Put another way, this garment helps offset the American myth of the classless society while the make-up destabilizes the ambiguous masculinity James Dean enacted.[47]

Bowie's Americanized posturing is part of an expressive repertoire that includes a very small number of objects, the topic we explore next. To do justice to the performance of any performer but perhaps especially an externalizing performer, it is essential to pay attention to accessories such as props, objects and attire. Objects on screen are never just objects; rather, they function as transmitters of meaning, both symbolic and personal.[48] Their absence is equally meaningful, since it deprives the actor of a means to channel emotions and ideologies. In keeping with the Brechtian emphasis on barrenness as a means to reveal the 'artifice of the performance', the concert sequence in *Christiane F.* boasts very few objects.[49] Apart from the band members, their instruments and drapes concealing the back, the stage is bare. An unadorned white mask is incongruously placed on the keyboard, its dead eyes occasionally gazing through the fog. Conventionally understood, masks suggest opacity and, by extension, insincerity. Within the context of my analysis, the white mask may be read as a brief but evocative visual reference to the superficiality or, from the German perspective, foreignness of Anglo-American pop culture. Its fleeting appearance notwithstanding, it thus signals a key theme of the overall sequence. The only object that is actually part of the performance narrative is the microphone and the stand.

Bowie's use of the microphone is an astonishing exercise in seduction and domination. Like any skilled actor, he keeps the microphone 'under expressive control', to quote Naremore, and thereby lets it become a signifier of feeling.[50] As he approaches the edge of the stage, the Duke gently clasps the object at the words 'here are we'. He runs his fingers along the handle, then curls them around the head, his lips almost touching. The gesture resembles an intimate caress, the first move in a process of enticement; his mien enhances this impression. Eyes half closed, he assumes an exaggerated expression of yearning, an ironic commentary on the Duke's 'would-be romantic' nature. Then his grip strengthens, signalling a sudden, barely contained intensity. When singing 'here I am', he grabs the microphone stand forcefully. The shot widens, and for the first time we see the singer from the groin up but also farther removed. During the pivotal segment featuring the repetition of 'it's too late', he shifts his weight from one foot to the other, marking the tempo with aggressive thrusts of the body in the direction of the audience. At the line 'it's not the side-effects of the cocaine', he seizes the stand with both hands, for a brief time transforming it into a powerless partner to be manhandled at his pleasure. He then sets it down so violently that it sways back and forth.

Bowie's handling of the microphone strikingly illustrates the intimate connection between objects and expressive technique. To varying degrees, objects become an extension of the actor's body and repertoire in live concerts, plays and film, but it is arguably in film that they assume the greatest storytelling power due to camera angle, movement and close-ups. In *Christiane F.* the microphone's handling amplifies the meaning of the story 'narrated' by Bowie's attire and song lyrics. Performed by the original white-faced Aryan Duke, the singer's movements might have been read as an expression of his psychotic character, a superman intent on conquest with no regard for the feelings of others. In the guise of the Americanized Duke, however, the message is somewhat different. The Thin White Duke is of course still as nasty as ever, but dressed up as a slightly feminized latter-day James Dean minus the youthfulness, this Duke embodies a message perfectly tailored to a West German public that had, to some extent at least, become disillusioned by the cultural stranglehold Americanization exerted on its national 'soul'. The triumphant narrative of Allied success in transforming the FRG downplays Germans' simmering resentment at this cultural colonization. How do Bowie's gestures and facial expressions support this interpretation?

From the perspective of externality, Bowie qualifies as a masterful performer who exposes the contrived nature of acting; the artificiality and exaggeration adopted to do so are deliberate. Naremore puts it starkly: there is 'no such thing as an uncontrived face in the movies. The features of the typical film actor are a regulated, controlled variant of the features we encounter in society – a field of signs prepared for a viewer, so conventionalized as to become a "mythology" or an invisible ideology.'[51] From the very first shot, Bowie's facial features are highly regulated. The profile view in which he is introduced conjures an aura of inaccessibility and mystery, since his face is not immediately visible. Shot against a bright spotlight high above the stage, Bowie's face is shrouded in shadow, with occasional bursts of white light flashing at the contours of his head. A nimbus-like reddish light effect created by the contrast of Bowie's dark figure against the spotlight heightens the impression of a superhuman, quasi-divine persona – an Anglo-American seducer come to entice the Germans into cultural promiscuity.

When Bowie is finally in full light more than halfway through the song, his face is fully visible. By now all the mystery has vanished, and what remains is the Thin White Duke's complete lack of empathy, conveyed by his facial expressions and the aggressive tone of his voice. The callous, derisive countenance Bowie assumes befits the character of the Thin White Duke as he keeps singing 'it's too late' – a line that makes him sneer. As Shelton Waldrep contends, the Duke's perpetual sneer provided Bowie with a mask to hide behind or to express his disdain for emotions. As such, it compels the audience 'to look elsewhere for emotion, or the significance of emotion, and to read the surface in a counterintuitive way'.[52] The Americanized Thin White Duke evidently enjoys being the harbinger of bad tidings, interspersing his sneer with self-satisfied smirks. In *Christiane F.* his performance conjures the cocky and heartless seducer, the one who promises that the 'European cannon is here' but has brought this message from the United States and in Anglo-American guise in matters of language, music and dress.

This impression is strengthened through Bowie's adoption of a deliberately Brechtian 'movement vocabulary'. After the opening segment of the song, he accompanies his vocal delivery with stylized gestures. As mentioned above, gestic acting connotes artificiality, and specific gests convey ideological meaning. What does it suggest when the Thin White Duke, pronouncing the word *Kether*, points upward, at the word *Malkuth* downward? In Jewish Kabbalah, *Kether* and *Malkuth* are two of the ten *sefirot* or divine emanations. The phrase 'from *Kether* to *Malkuth*' indicates a descending level of power and purity, a possible reference to Bowie's physical and mental travails in the mid-1970s. Whatever their meaning, the Kabbalistic references manifestly clash with the silver cross Bowie had started wearing at the height of his drug-induced psychosis as a talisman against evil.[53] Is it a coincidence that in contrast to the *Isolar* tour where the buttoned-up shirt regularly concealed the cross, in *Christiane F.* it is clearly visible? When singing 'you drive like a demon from station to station', the Duke indicates the direction of the drive by pointing first to the right, then to the left, thereby outlining the stations of the cross. Are the Duke's gestures referring to Christiane's own stations on the cross, or is he providing a sarcastic commentary on Germany's own 'Passion' vis-à-vis the overpowering impact of Anglo-American pop culture? The answer depends on the viewer's familiarity with the vicissitudes of post-war Americanization. One thing seems certain: through skilful editing the filmmakers posit Christiane as the primary victim of the Duke's seductions.

The seducer and the seduced are first brought into contact in part three of the performance. At this point we see the back of Christiane's head. This frame establishes for the first time a direct link between the song, the singer and the user, the drug and the 'un-German' transgression. The repetition of 'it's too late', which made such a harrowing impression on the real Christiane, shows Christiane looking up with eyes that fix the singer with a mixture of yearning and desperation, and a blurred part of Bowie's head and hand to the left of the screen. Remarkably, this is the only time throughout the entire film that Christiane's cheeks are visibly flushed. Up until this point and subsequent to the concert sequence, her skin is either translucently pale or, due to the night-time setting in which most of the action takes place, carries a bluish tint. To be sure, Brunckhorst's character does not exactly embody the idealized whiteness that scholars have associated with Western film stars. According to Sean Redmond, '[i]dealized white stars are supposedly above and beyond their own (and everybody else's) sexual desires, greed, and vices. They are "holy" vessels, embodiments of all that is good and virtuous about (super) human kind.'[54] If whiteness is associated with orderliness, as Redmond asserts, the blushed face conjures unruliness.[55] It is significant, therefore, that Christiane's face turns red at the moment she makes contact with her idol.

Seemingly locking eyes with the Thin White Duke who has stepped to the edge of the stage, the young German girl is the lover looking up adoringly at the Anglo-American performer who declares with such mocking abandon that the situation is hopeless. Her blushed cheeks signal her willingness to surrender herself to his seduction and to challenge the bourgeois social mores of West German society. In the Duke's delivery, the mantra 'it's too late' becomes a heartless litany of defeat, celebrated in the face of the conquered with shocking emotional callousness. In her first memoir Felscherinow recalled that the refrain had made her feel miserable: 'I thought that the song described my situation exactly. Now this "It is too late" [*sic*] knocked me down.'[56] In the film, what might appear to be a moment of rebellion swiftly turns into an indication of surrender to the forces of an alien Anglo-American pop culture. Evaluated through the lens of Naremore's acting theory, Bowie's exaggerated facial expressions and spatial positioning vis-à-vis his fan (he literally occupies a higher plane) signify deliberate performative choices that illustrate Bowie's aptitude as an externalizing performer.

In the end, the concert sequence is made to carry the burden of Eichinger and Edel's critique of the supposedly deleterious impact of Anglo-American pop culture on West German society. However, Bowie's carefully calibrated movement vocabulary challenges simplistic readings of the performance. Whether the sequence really is 'the best-ever film scene about a concert' as Quentin Tarantino declared, its inclusion was a master stroke of marketing.[57] By the time of the movie's release, Bowie's international stardom was sufficiently established to be a draw to prospective audiences who might not otherwise have considered watching a film with unknown actors. Bowie's performance encapsulates the dangerous seductiveness of Christiane's alternative lifestyle and, by extension, the tremendous pull of Anglo-American pop culture – drugs are at the heart of this seductiveness. Recall that Christiane consumes heroin for the first time right after leaving the concert, with 'Station to Station' playing in the background. The message is inescapable: Bowie has led her directly to the edge of the abyss. Remarkably, after the pivotal concert sequence and Christiane's first heroin use, Bowie tracks become far more sparing. Structurally speaking, Bowie has fulfilled his function in the story, and there is no more need to reiterate what the movie's first half seeks to assert with obsessive frequency: that in Cold War West Berlin, as in the rest of the Federal Republic, Anglo-American pop culture is the great and dangerous *Verführer*.

Instead of mounting a genuine political critique by addressing the implications of West Germany's sociopolitical convulsions of the seventies or the angst and hopelessness crushing West German teenagers like Christiane, *Christiane F.* wavers uneasily between criticism and endorsement of consumption as a means to freedom from the constraints of late capitalist modernity. From the perspective of post-war history, this reading makes sense. The economic miracle of the 1950s had brought unprecedented material security and a measure of affluence to the vast majority of West Germans. As noted earlier, it was only with the counterculture that the voices deploring the 'Yankee colonization' of the FRG became more widespread. Such criticism was never uniform across the generations, however. By the late seventies and early eighties, those who protested Americanization most vociferously were in their early thirties or older; interestingly, the producer, screenwriter and director of *Christiane F.* all fit into this category. For the younger generation Anglo-American pop culture was less problematic. To the youthful audience of the film *Christiane F.*, watching the concert sequence may have conjured enjoyable feelings of rebellion and transgressiveness. The film's almost complete disregard of the lack of hope and prospects Christiane's 'no future' generation confronted made such a pleasurable viewing experience possible.

Building on Naremore's path-breaking insight into the contrived nature of film acting, I have examined Bowie in terms of a polysemic star text and image. A close reading of *Christiane F.*'s concert sequence reveals the complexity of his performance. Playing himself as the music star David Bowie, David Jones performs Bowie performing the Thin White Duke recently returned to Europe and in Americanized guise, a tongue-in-cheek parody of himself, a 'rebel with a cause' whose recklessness the real Christiane F. emulated in different ways. In Bowie's cameo, the nastiness of the emotionally sterile Duke, while part of the original Duke persona, is complicated through its association with the fraught process of Americanization, conjured by the props, gestures and facial expressions that constitute essential parts of this narrative. Not least, the imitation of James Dean invokes the movie heroine's own rebelliousness. Incidentally, Screenwriter Weigel likened Felscherinow herself to a 'feminine James Dean'.[58] In view of the filmmakers' concerns with the transgressive allure of Anglo-American pop culture, this comparison seems entirely fitting.

Remarkably, Felscherinow herself, who had declared Bowie to be the star of her film, later dismissed him for having sold out to commerce. When she finally met the man, she was disappointed by his unassuming appearance: with his short stature and his moustache, he reminded her of her father. The album *Let's Dance* dealt the final blow to her obsession. 'I had admired the artist, the exotic dog-man creature from the cover of Diamond Dog [*sic*]. The crazy one, the nonconformist', she wrote in her second memoir.[59] The 'financial genius' who dominated commerce, who was 'his own marketing product' and who made 'melodies for the masses', in her view, had little in common with the singer whom she had been able to cling to in her darkest days.[60]

Although there was some truth to this cynical assessment, Bowie's performance in *Christiane F.* should have reminded Felscherinow that despite the singer's undeniable business acumen, he was a genuinely talented actor. When performing the Thin White Duke on screen, Bowie drew on a persona whose political position he had come to despise. By 1980 he had emerged from the worst phase of his career to date, both in terms of health issues and ideological confusion. The fascist stigma and Aryan pretensions, however, still clung to his creation. Performing the Duke for a German audience, Bowie downplayed the character's fascist affinities but also subverted the notion of a pristine German culture that was in danger of being infected by toxic Anglo-American pop culture. Ultimately, his persona turned out to be as malleable as any identity. The message seems clear: there is no such thing as cultural purity. Edel and Eichinger may have included the 'laughing gnostic' in the film to draw on Bowie's star capital *and* to send a message of the transgressive allure of Anglo-American pop culture and excessive consumption, but it was the Americanized Thin White Duke with his lipstick and Kabbalistic references – neither Duke nor fully American – who had the last laugh.[61]

Notes

1. Christiane V. Felscherinow and Sonja Vukovic, *Christiane F. Mein Zweites Leben* (Berlin: Deutscher Levante Verlag, 2014), 100.
2. Paul Morley, *The Age of Bowie: How David Bowie Made a World of Difference* (New York: Gallery Books, 2016), 412.
3. Eric Rentschler, 'Film der Achtziger Jahre. Endzeitspiele und Zeitgeistszenarien', in *Geschichte des deutschen Films,* ed. Wolfgang Jacobsen, Anton Kaes and Hans Helmut Prinzler (Stuttgart: Verlag J. B. Metzler, 1993), 292.
4. Andreas M. Rauch with Bernhard Matt, *Bernd Eichinger und seine Filme* (Frankfurt am Main: Haag + Herchen, 2000), 136.
5. Felscherinow and Vukovich, *Christiane F. Mein Zweites Leben,* 101.
6. Hans C. Blumenberg, 'Besonders wertvoll', *Die Zeit,* 6 April 1981. https://www.zeit.de/1981/15/besonders-wertvoll.
7. See, e.g. Geoff Brown, 'Down a Drink and Drug Drain', *The Times Preview,* 11–17 December 1981, 11.
8. Roger Ebert, 'Christiane F.', 1 January 1982, https://www.rogerebert.com/reviews/christiane-f-1982.
9. Matthew Pateman, 'Structuring Stardom: Identity and the Transmigration of Image in the Work of David Bowie', in *TechKnowledgies: New Imaginaries in the Humanities, Arts, and TechnoSciences,* ed. Mary Valentis with Tara P. Monastero and Paula Yablonsky (New Castle: Cambridge Scholarly Publishing, 2007), 132.
10. Shomit Mitter, 'Inner and Outer: "Open Theatre" in Peter Brook and Joseph Chaikin', *Journal of Dramatic Theory and Criticism* (Fall 1988): 49.
11. Exceptions are Hester Baer, 'Producing Adaptations: Bernd Eichinger, Christiane F., and German Film History', in *Generic Histories of German Cinema: Genre and Its Deviations,* ed. Jaimey Fisher (Camden House: Boydell & Brewer, 2013), 173–96, https://www.jstor.org/stable/10.7722/j.ctt31nhth and Andrea Rinke, 'Liminal Bodies in Liminal Spaces: The Depiction of Drug Addicted Youth in the Films *Christiane F* and *Drifter', Global Media Journal: Australian Edition* 4, no. 1 (2010): 1–12. https://www.hca.westernsydney.edu.au/gmjau/archive/v4_2010_1/andrea_rinke_RA.html.
12. Jamiey Fisher, 'Introduction: Toward Generic Histories – Film Genre, Genre Theory, and German Film Studies', in *Generic Histories of German Cinema,* ed. Jaimey Fisher (Camden House: Boydell & Brewer, 2013), 2.
13. See Eoin Devereux, Aileen Dillane and Martin J. Power, eds, *David Bowie: Critical Perspectives* (New York: Routledge, 2015) and Toija Cinque, Angela Ndalianis and Sean Redmond, 'David Bowie On-Screen', *Cinema Journal* 57, no. 3 (2018): 126–30. doi:10.1353/cj.2018.0034.
14. Detlef Dresslein and Anne Lehwald, *Bernd Eichinger. Eine Biografie* (Munich: Wilhelm Heyne Verlag, 2011), 105.
15. Katja Eichinger, *BE* (Hamburg: Hoffmann und Campe, 2012), 166.

16 Dresslein and Lewald, *Bernd Eichinger*, 105.
17 Eichinger, *BE*, 154–5.
18 Shelton Waldrep, *The Aesthetics of Self-Invention: Oscar Wilde to David Bowie* (Minneapolis: University of Minnesota Press, 2004), 106.
19 Baer, 'Producing Adaptations', 188.
20 Julie Lobalzo Wright, 'David Bowie: The Extraordinary Rock Star as Film Star', in *David Bowie: Critical Perspectives,* ed. Eoin Devereux, Aileen Dillane and Martin J. Power (New York: Routledge, 2015), 237–8.
21 In response to rumours about a Sinatra biopic, Bowie expressed an interest in playing the star, but Sinatra was less than enthusiastic about the prospect and insisted that 'no English fag' would play him. Christopher Sandford, *Bowie: Loving the Alien* (Da Capo Press, 1996), 132.
22 Siegfried Schoeber, 'Idol des letzten Rock', *Der Spiegel* 15 (1976): 237.
23 Anselm Doering-Manteuffel, 'Amerikanisierung und Westernisierung Version: 2.0', Docupedia-Zeitgeschichte, published 19 August 2019, http://docupedia.de/zg/Doering-Manteuffel_amerikanisierung_v2_de_2019.
24 Winfried Fluck, 'The Americanization of German Culture? The Strange, Paradoxical Ways of Modernity', in *German Pop Culture: How 'American' Is It?,* ed. Agnes C. Mueller (Ann Arbor: University of Michigan Press, 2004), 20.
25 David Clay Large, *Berlin* (New York: Basic Books, 2000), 482.
26 Hermann Peter Piwitt quoted in Burns and van der Will, 'The Federal Republic', 311.
27 Quoted from *Im Lauf der Zeit* in Burns and van der Will, 'The Federal Republic', 315.
28 Alexander Stephan, 'A Special German Case of Cultural Americanization', in *The Americanization of Europe: Culture, Diplomacy, and Anti-Americanism after 1945,* ed. Alexander Stephan (New York: Berghahn Books, 2006), 78.
29 Colin Counsell, *Signs of Performance: An Introduction to Twentieth-Century Theatre* (London and New York: Routledge, 1996), 86.
30 Ibid.
31 James Naremore, *Acting in the Cinema* (Berkeley, CA: University of California Press, 1988), 51.
32 Ibid., 69.
33 Erving Goffman, *The Presentation of Self in Everyday Life* (New York: Anchor Books, 1959), 252–3.
34 Naremore, *Acting in the Cinema*, 51.
35 Nicholas Pegg, *The Complete David Bowie, Revised and Updated 2016 Edition* (London: Titan Books, 2016), 665.
36 Pete Doggett, *The Man Who Sold the World: David Bowie and the 1970s* (New York: Harper Perennial, 2013), 88.
37 David Buckley, 'Still Pop's Faker?' in *The Bowie Companion,* ed. Elizabeth Thomson and David Gutman (New York: Da Capo Press, 1996), 8.

38 Doggett, *The Man Who Sold the World*, 301.
39 Quoted in Nick Stevenson, *David Bowie: Fame, Sound and Vision* (Cambridge: Polity, 2006), 134.
40 Naremore, *Acting in the Cinema*, 88.
41 Paul Trynka, *David Bowie | Starman* (New York: Little, Brown and Company, 2011), 302 and 305.
42 Naremore, *Acting in the Cinema*, 93.
43 Sandford, *Bowie*, 24.
44 See Sean Redmond, 'The Whiteness of Stars: Looking at Kate Winslet's Unruly White Body', in *Stardom and Celebrity: A Reader* (London: Sage Publications, 2007).
45 Peri Bradley and James Page, 'David Bowie – The Trans Who Fell to Earth: Cultural Regulation, Bowie and Gender Fluidity', *Continuum: Journal of Media & Cultural Studies* 31, no. 4 (2017): 591.
46 Ibid., 592.
47 Stevenson, *David Bowie*, 12.
48 Naremore, *Acting in the Cinema*, 86.
49 Counsell, *Signs of Performance*, 95.
50 Naremore, *Acting in the Cinema*, 87.
51 Ibid., 96.
52 Shelton Waldrep, *Future Nostalgia: Performing David Bowie* (New York: Bloomsbury Academic, 2015), 17.
53 Buckley, *Strange Fascination: David Bowie: The Definitive Story* (London: Virgin Books, 2005), 232.
54 Redmond, 'The Whiteness of Stars', 267.
55 Ibid., 273.
56 Christiane F., written on the basis of tape recordings by Kai Hermann and Horst Rieck, *Wir Kinder vom Bahnhof Zoo* (Hamburg: Carlsen, 2009), 88.
57 Tobias Rüther, *Heroes: David Bowie and Berlin* (London: Reaktion Books, 2014), 92.
58 Wilhelm Bittorf, 'Irgendwas Irres muß laufen', *Der Spiegel*, 6 April 1981, 242.
59 Felscherinow and Vukovich, *Christiane F. Mein Zweites Leben*, 100.
60 Ibid., 101.
61 Peter Koenig, 'The Laughing Gnostic: David Bowie and the Occult', first published 1996, updated version 2020, https://www.parareligion.ch/bowie.htm.

5

Gesturing Dust

Sensing David Bowie's performance in *Merry Christmas, Mr. Lawrence*

Sean Redmond

Introduction

In this chapter I explore David Bowie's performance as Major Jack Celliers in *Merry Christmas, Mr. Lawrence* through a sense-based, close textual analysis of a single scene. This scene appears near the end of the film, where Captain Yonoi (Ryuichi Sakamoto) orders all of the prisoners, including the sick and injured, to gather outside their barracks. When Group Captain Hicksley (Jack Thompson) refuses to obey these orders, Yonoi demands that he and other prisoner officers answer a question about the level of military skills in their camp. Hicksley refuses to answer and an enraged Yonoi has him dragged to a position where he is knelt and forcibly held, and prepares to behead him. Other Japanese soldiers/guards train their rifles on the prisoners so that they do not break rank. At this point in the scene, Celliers suddenly, if nonchalantly, walks past the guards and stands between Yonoi and Hicksley. Yonoi pushes Celliers backwards and to the floor, and he responds by kissing him on each cheek. Yonoi raises his katana only to collapse and fall to his knees. Celliers is then attacked and beaten by a number of Japanese soldiers. The scene under analysis lasts for three minutes and forty seconds.

I am centrally concerned with how David Bowie *affectively acts* in this scene, responding not exclusively to his star apparatus or wider cultural signifiers – although these play a central role – but to his movement, body language, gestures and 'silences'. These gestures and silences – or linguistic gaps – allow his performance to register beyond representation, as an affective assemblage. There is an alienation to his performance in this scene that springs forth like a coil: affectively speaking, Bowie's performance as Celliers registers as ulterior and unnameable. Further, what is being affectively enunciated in this scene is queer desire: a longing on the part of Yonoi, a liminality on the part of Celliers and of the star playing him. In addition, the asemiotic, aesthetic qualities of Bowie's performance are analysed through the mise en scène, which is read as performative too. The textures and spaces of the screen, the costuming and the objects caressed, are seen as sensory forms, forming entangled connections with Celliers and the other characters.

My approach draws on both the traditions of close film textual analysis, as outlined by writers such V. F. Perkins[1] and Andrew Kleven,[2] and sensorial readings taken up in my own writing.[3] The analysis of singular scenes has a long tradition in film studies: it is an approach that demands we spend quality time with the fictional world, closely allowing its meanings and impressions to emerge, shot by shot.

I have chosen to analyse this scene for three reasons. First, the scene is literally and metaphorically the 'climax' of Yonoi and Celliers's homoerotically charged relationship and, as such, is wetted with affective qualities. Second, the scene teasingly delays its introduction of Celliers, of David Bowie, but constantly gestures towards his arrival. In a sense, Celliers/Bowie is there and not there in the scene. Finally, the scene centrally functions through non-verbal gestures, and it is these non-linguistic properties that 'speak' the unnameable that I think drive the impressions and sensations of the scene. Of course, as an actor, Bowie very often carries meaning in and through his non-normative body,[4] and in this chapter I read his liminal corporeality through fine-grain analysis, from the text outwards. I *feel* or *screen-sense* David Bowie's performance in what I will refer to as the *gesturing dust* scene from *Merry Christmas, Mr. Lawrence*.

Gesturing Dust

The scene begins with a three-second, low-angle profile shot of Yonoi. His face is taut, his eyes accusatory and his mouth begins to silently growl, opening up the scene to the way gesture – and in his case, animalistic gesture – will organize the events and interactions that will follow. Yonoi is captured against a verdant canopy of green trees, suggestive of the thick jungle that surrounds the camp, and that he too is a 'prisoner'. The foliage also registers as a blanket of carnal humidity which seems to be eating its way into or through him: it swamps his body. After one second of screen time, non-diegetic sound enters the shot: a haunting set of notes that raises alarm and mournfully anchors the next shot it bleeds into.

The scene cuts to a slow, 23-second panning shot of the assembled prisoners, the camera positioned as if it is Yonoi's point of view. Some of the prisoners stare directly back, returning the gaze, while others look at the ground or into dead space. A number of soldiers are holding up their sick or injured comrades who struggle to stand. There are also soldiers whose gait is strong and firm, their hands placed on their hips, resisting the gaze, rejecting the biopower imbalance that is being imposed upon them.

Many of the soldiers look emaciated: they bear cuts, bruises, wear bandages and their limbs are missing or crippled. Their clothes are caked in sweat and dirt, and bands of perspiration wet their chests, shoulders, faces and arms. We can feel the sun falling on them and the heat rising, transferring itself into dissipating chemical energy. This panning shot draws on non-linguistic signifiers – on decimated bodies and forlorn gestures – to register its meaning. This metonymic panning shot carries the full force of the horror and abjection of being a prisoner of war. These gestural bodies suggest psychic trauma, 'indexing the agency of the unconscious',[5] enabling interior meaning to emerge through affective textures. What makes the shot even more powerful is the way it references other trauma images, and from the Holocaust in particular.[6] Given we are positioned from Yonoi's point of view, there is the uncomfortable sensation of being complicit in their trauma, as well as being silent witnesses to this horror show.

At the conclusion of this panning shot, we momentarily pause on two of the main protagonists in the film: Lieutenant Colonel John Lawrence (Tom Conti) and Celliers. Lawrence is one of the soldiers captured with his hand on his hips, returning and resisting Yonoi's gaze. Celliers is positioned behind Lawrence, partially blocked by him, but he also stares back at Yonoi. Celliers wears a different uniform to everyone else, not only to authenticate his background as a South African British soldier but also, narratively speaking, to highlight his difference to everyone else, and to signify the star status of the actor, 'David Bowie'. Celliers's presence in this shot almost feels incidental, inconsequential, however. There is no attempt to foreground him; rather, he appears ghost-like, hauntological, there-but-not-there. Such interminability, of course, perfectly fits with Bowie's star image, as one who 'by permitting a fluid and playful encounter with gender and other facets of identity ... enables others to activate their own propensity toward performative action'.[7]

The next shot, an abrupt cut, finds Yonoi quickly moving away from the prisoners. The camera tracks Yonoi and the soldiers, who are in the foreground of the shot, advancing with speed and urgency. This tracking shot, lasting eight seconds, contains only diegetic sound: the urgent walking movements, swords clashing against legs and, at the end of the shot, some dialogue. Visually, the shot reveals more of the camp: where the Japanese soldiers are positioned; an army truck; and a tented structure. The camp is sparse and organized for maximum surveillance and social control.

The cut is immediately disorientating not only because of the shift in pace and the change in camera movement but also because there is seemingly no single act or action that precipitates it. Further, there is a simultaneous violence registered across these planes of movement: through Yonoi's sharp, short strides; the way the soldiers mechanically move and crouch; and through the clothing and objects that are themselves pointed, honed, including his bamboo whip/cane, the Sen-bou or field hat and the Guntō or military sword.

However, the real force of the shot comes from its illegibility and the question of why Yonoi retreats so violently. On one level, his action can be read as the product of disgust: he finds the abject bodies of the prisoners disgusting, dishonourable, and so he rapidly moves, looks away, to dispel this feeling of nausea. The film has already established that Yonoi believes in the philosophy of the noble death and patriotic sacrifice, one which he was denied because he was unable to join the 'Shining Young Officers' who attempted a military coup. When it failed, the young officers were executed and, as we have already learnt, Yonoi feels the shame of not being there with them. The shame he feels is being conferred on the prisoners before him. Shame is 'tied to perceived deficiencies of one's core self . . . and is associated with more global and enduring negative attributions about oneself'.[8]

On another level, however, his action can be read as another form of disgust: one that emanates from his repressed desire for Celliers, whose gaze, as I note above, he lands on as the previous shot concludes. Disgust is often met with 'vile' inner materials let out, or it transforms palettes: we vomit, let out gas, shit, piss or we just experience the sense or feeling of having contaminants on our lips, caking the insides of our mouths. Disgust is also cultural and ideological: it works off normative and moralistic assumptions about right and wrong and helps construct and secure power-saturated binary oppositions between insiders and outsiders.[9] In terms of dominant discourse, this is particularly the case around sexuality, where anything that questions heterosexuality is – culturally and psychically – felt to be repellent. When Yonoi retreats from staring at Celliers, then, it is because of his feelings for him, which he finds nauseating. His violent flight from the prisoners on parade is actually a flight from his own desire.

Nonetheless, disgust can be seen to bring into sensory existence the very unregulated essences that it seeks to deny or repress. Disgust can also be understood as an anti-democratic force that opens up the body to new experiences and sensations that are usually denied expression.[10] What is being set in motion in these two shots – the play between disgust and desire – takes a powerful hold of the scene a little later.

As this shot comes to a close, we hear Hicksley, out of view, call out Yonoi's name, which makes him stop, turn and again face the prisoners. His angular pose, bony cheeks and grimace transmit a feeling of contempt, of his quiet rage. However, Yonoi's cheeks are also toned, or gently blushed, and his pristine white gloves stand out against the dust and the sweat on his face and clothes. The white gloves seem 'matter out of place',[11] but they also confirm Yonoi's care for his self-appearance, for a purity of the self and, subtextually or subconsciously, for a longing for the Other. The gloves, his uniform, his cheek bones, all help to undermine the masculine, heterosexual script to which he is wedded. This contradiction between masculine and feminine, straight and gay, registers as the competing impulses that lie beneath the visible, the nameable. Yonoi is a gestural contradiction.

Of course, the white gloves also gesture towards David Bowie's 'Let's Dance' music video, released in the same year as the film. In that video, Bowie finds himself in the Australian outback, a messiah-like figure, who is able to produce music that liberates indigenous people from their settler oppression. In this scene from *Merry Christmas, Mr. Lawrence*, his idealized whiteness, his blonde beauty, marks itself on/through Yonoi's hands. Yonoi's desire for Celliers (Bowie) is carried on and through the immaculate whiteness of his gloved fingers.

The next shot, three seconds in duration, is of Hicksley, initially crouched over a dead prisoner, rising to say, 'He's dead.' Hicksley is captured in a medium shot, with three Japanese soldiers positioned behind and their rifles trained on him. Again, the green jungle acts as a stifling ecology, almost swallowing the Japanese soldiers, while acting as a penetrating visual relay. Hicksley looks towards Yonoi, side on, with the branches and palms leaning that way also. The oppressive mise en scène carries forward the very elements of the prisoner's death that has just occurred and foreshadows the violence that is to come.

In the next shot, just under five seconds in duration, Yonoi is captured in close-up, an affect image, his face again registering disgust. He struggles to form words, his mouth first pursing and then 'shaping' words before they are spoken. The first sound that emerges from Yonoi's mouth is guttural, as if what he wants to say is not possible to speak, a 'speechless dwelling in language'.[12] He is framed side-on: the sharp, forceful lines of his physique, face, cap and the collars of his uniform, almost granite in composition. As he raises his arm to gesture, he shouts 'get over here', almost speechless with rage. And yet again, Yonoi is also androgynous: a delicate beauty infuses these lines, this forced aggression, with a different set of gender codes. Shame bubbles beneath his skin: he can barely speak because of it. But he doesn't really want to because:

Speak and you can be named a pervert or normal (even if perversion is celebrated). Remain silent and you are no longer a subject but a molecular dissipative desiring affectivity and potentiality.[13]

The scene then cuts to a position behind Yonoi, to see again what he is observing. Yonoi stands centre frame, facing the prisoners, who are collectively captured in long shot. Hicksley is also framed centrally, and the dead prisoner's emaciated body is beside him. The line of men stretches across the entire film frame, repeating – albeit from a distance and in a still shot – the earlier composition. Death haunts the image, not only through what is represented but also because of the Holocaust allusions it draws upon.

Hicksley then walks towards Yonoi, the slowness of his movement in stark contrast to Yonoi's stride and gait earlier. His are tired, weary steps. When Hicksley gets to a position where he is standing right in front of Yonoi, the camera begins to pan at the same time as Yonoi approaches a group of prisoner officers, to the right of the frame. Yonoi again moves with speed, and as he pushes between the officers, he picks four of them out, each representing a different area of the military. Yonoi returns to his position in front of Hicksley, and the other prisoner officers follow, standing next to Hicksley. One of the officers fixes his cap and then all of them stand to attention, embodying the protocols of the officer.

These officers are being positioned as gentlemen, in contrast to Yonoi, who is being racially Othered as savage and cruel. The officer's civility empties them of violence, while Yonoi is filled up with it, echoing or reinforcing cultural stereotypes about the Japanese. The 'gap' between these two positions, however, emerges complexly, unevenly. This shot reveals that the prisoner officers are separated from the rest of the men: a hierarchy is in place, one cut across social class lines. However, what is most interesting about this shot is the way Celliers is again not at all focused upon: he is barely perceptible from the other officers. Yet he is *there*: his honey blonde hair 'colouring' the line-up, a figure symbolically foregrounded, then. He is *there* on Yonoi's fingers, a translation and transference that undermines the usual white mastery relationship.[14]

The scene then continues with a quick shot-reverse-shot between Yonoi and Hicksley, at close-up position, lasting five seconds in total. Yonoi's face is animated by gestures, by his tongue rolling behind his closed mouth. He remains disgusted with Hicksley, his mouth is caked with it. Hicksley, wetted with sweat, stares into the distance, refusing the gaze, and the blue sky behind him creates a limitless horizon. When we then return to Yonoi, again in close-up, he struggles to ask Hicksley this question: 'As a representative of the British Air Force, how many experts in weapons and guns do you have in your group?' What is collectively happening across these shots is the building of Yonoi's anger, rage and shame. However, this repression is, as noted above, doubly unconscious: his disgust for the men is also his disgust of self, of the latent desire that wells within him. He is also performing for and in front of Celliers, his actual intended 'audience' and love interest.

In the next two-second close-up shot, Hicksley responds with a firm, clipped, 'none, sir', and we return again to a close-up of Yonoi. In this shot, the attempt to form language, words, fails Yonoi again and he strikes the floor with his bamboo cane, its noise cracking open the silence. Yonoi eventually forms a guttural response, but this is accompanied by foreboding non-diegetic music, an electric hum that unsettles the scene and atonally translates the grunt. Such human gestures,

> as utterances, are not always the product of conscious intent. Some gesticulations emerge unbidden. . . . Gestures, chattering fingers in Christian's circumstance, betray repressed memories.[15]

The next shot is seventeen seconds long: Yonoi moves away from the prisoner officers and towards the camera, flanked by two soldiers. However, his speed and urgency mean that within two seconds he is positioned off-screen, leaving the camera to witness Hicksley being grabbed and marched forward. This action is captured in a wide shot: we see the assembled prisoners behind Hicksley, as well as the other officers who have been lined up with him. Their barracks, the row of palm trees and the blue sky fill the shot with impressionable context.

As Hicksley is grabbed by two soldiers, the movement in the shot is forceful and yet irregular. Hicksley is propelled forward, albeit in a fitful way; the prisoners and the officers also briefly move or lurch forward, wanting to protect him, to intervene. As they do so, other Japanese soldiers fluidly move towards them, raising their bayonets. At the same time, the camera smoothly tracks backwards, mirroring Yonoi's movements while keeping the advancing Hicksley central to the frame. Movement occurs, then, in two planes and with two levels of intensity and fluidity. The prisoner and officers' movement are almost immediately arrested, and the gestures they make are resigned: symbolic acts of momentary resistance, crushed by the violence that would await them if they were to protest further. Collectively, they are being reduced to bare life.[16] The shot is sonically anchored by the musical score, including a barely perceptible drum beat that accelerates as the shot unfolds; the diegetic sound of Hicksley's feet, of soldiers' feet; and the angry calls of the prisoners, one who shouts, 'you Japanese bastards'. The axis of action slices through the scene's movement image but also affectively foreshadows Celliers's ghostly movement, one that will be eroticized later in the scene.

At the end of the shot, Hicksley is forced to kneel by the Japanese soldiers. He remains silent, a gesture of stoicism, carrying forward the associations of being gentlemanly. However, Hicksley bares his teeth, as do the soldiers, so that the sense that words are futile, or cannot be formed, again impregnates the shot. There is an animalization taking place. Yonoi now strides back into the frame, facing Hicksley and away from the camera. His katana sword is vertical to his waist, and his white-gloved right hand is tightly clenched. His movement registers like a coil about to spring, but also as someone who is erect and yet in denial of such detonation. Yonoi is a mass of contradictory energies that will shortly explode when Celliers enters the scene. In fact, there is a latent longing here for this to happen. This is a masochistic or self-loathing performance that calls out for his love interest in the film. Of course, the same will be true for Bowie fans: they – we – long for the moment when Celliers will directly enter the scene.

The next five-second shot frames Yonoi, again flanked by two soldiers, standing in front of Hicksley. Hicksley remains positioned submissively, at an angle that places his head at the level of Yonoi's groin. The positioning looks like an act of fellatio is taking place. Yonoi grimaces, his face is contorted, as he again struggles to speak. The sense of disgust has now been fully transferred to the arena of unspeakable sexual desire. However, as the shot continues, Yonoi reaches for his katana and we watch him unsheathe it, drawing it vertically, sharply, across the screen, and we hear its lacerating sound as he does so. The action is precise, clean and becomes one of (un) intended sexual violence. As the shot ends, we see Hicksley shrink slightly, which is followed by a two-second close-up of his anguished face. One of the Japanese soldiers removes Hicksley's hat, and Hicksley closes his eyes and lets out a slow, strangulated scream. In the same way that Yonoi has been unable to form words out of the shame he projects, so Hicksley loses the ability to speak as he imagines his own death. The primitivism, animalism of Hicksley's screech shatters the narrative image. Of course, across this shot we see the flash of the katana cutting into the dead space between Yonoi and Hicksley: it is his head that is to be decapitated, the very organ that moments earlier was sucking Yonoi dry. This shot lays his/their perversity bare, and yet it is also a dramatic punctuation point in the scene, a device to allow the hero, the real love interest, to emerge from the wings. Celliers's/Bowie's arrival is surely only seconds away?

The scene then returns to a close-up of Yonoi, as he draws the katana to his face. In this seven-second shot, the blade is brought to rest against the peak of his cap, as we watch him silently incant the Bushido code. Graphically, the blade cuts the image down the middle, while it glistens with sunlight, igniting and animating its silver materiality. Yonoi is again surrounded by, and entangled with, the thick, fervent greenery, as if he is caught in its liana. The soundtrack's volume has been raised and it now sonically registers as a million gnats or flies humming their insatiable hunger. The insectile enters the composition at the same time the shot intends to purify Yonoi, through this double gesturing of honour and sacrifice. The relative stillness at the end of this shot acts as a gestural bridge to the long-desired, but delayed arrival of Celliers/Bowie. We wait no more.

In the next shot we cut to a close-up shot of Celliers, the camera slowly moving towards his face. Lasting three seconds, he is clearly looking towards Yonoi, with an expression of quiet anger. Sweat covers Celliers's neck and brow, and his slouch or bush hat allows his blonde hair to fall forwards. His skin is bronzed and soft, while facial stubble roughens his appearance. Compositionally, this framing recalls the opening shot of Yonoi, but here it is Celliers's disgust which now cakes the shot. Celliers is clearly also being identified as androgynous and strange: a homoerotic mirror to Yonoi. Of course, David Bowie and Ryuichi Sakamoto are star mirrors: a set of extra-textual impressions flood the scene, as they do the entire film.

In the background of this shot, a Japanese soldier is holding his rifle and the straw huts limit the depth of field. Celliers, it is being conveyed, also has nowhere he can go, no escape route: nowhere he can take or hide his own shame. We have learnt earlier in the film that he let his brother be badly bullied, refusing to intervene. Yonoi and Celliers, then, are also *psychologically* alike. The shot's soundtrack, 'Sowing the Seed', a melodic, rhythmic piece that recalls both classical Japanese instruments and orchestral piano, provides a harmonious beat for Celliers to move to and through. At the end of this shot he exits right. Celliers/ Bowie will now lead the scene.

In a remarkable 22-second tracking shot, Celliers walks through the line of soldiers who have been stationed in front of the men, to take up a position right in front of Yonoi. His measured, unrushed approach goes seemingly unnoticed by the watching guards, as if he is part ghost, part visitation. As he strides towards Yonoi, Celliers gestures dust away from his shirt sleeve, does up the button on his shirt pocket, adjusts his slouch hat and wipes sweat away from his face. His walk takes him across the same spaces and lines that Yonoi has previously trodden, but in contrast to his short, hard steps, Celliers seems to float over the ground, barely touching it. Mehdi Derfoufi argues:

> When Celliers (Bowie) steps confidently forward toward Yonoi, he's the only one in motion. All the other characters stay absolutely still as if petrified. Time and space are organised around Bowie as he 'naturally' subjugates the direction of the film to his will. Thus, the desire Yonoi (Sakamoto) has for Celliers (Bowie) joins our desire (as Westerners, that is) to see Bowie the star get into action and offer himself to our gaze. The desire for otherness is structured around the star's body, in a double movement of fascination and repulsion aimed at both Western and Japanese audiences.[17]

Celliers's walk across the prison grounds doesn't entirely happen without the rest of characters also moving: two of the prisoners in the back of the frame, one of the guards and the officers present in the shot either see his movement and gesture towards it or move their positions slightly. Rather than time being frozen or petrified, it seems to be slowed down but not in slow motion. In this shot, time seems haunted, no longer chronormative but full of echo, delay and trace. Celliers is walking in or over Yonoi's footsteps, *presenting* him in the shot. Celliers's gestures also domesticate time: when he should be rushing to save the life of a comrade, he adjusts his clothes as if he is attending an officers' dinner. His attention to detail, to the way he appears, again mirrors Yonoi's sense of the perfected self. Of course, getting rid of dust, of sweat, is a beautification ritual, made for and because of Yonoi's interest in him.

However, these are not overtly eroticized gestures, and neither does Celliers's movement clearly suggest heroic action or intervention. As Celliers strides across the yard and towards Yonoi, the real power of his movement is in its illegibility and liminality. It gestures towards the unnameable, to the queer and to Bowie's star image which acts as a set of affective impressions and 'makes plain the centrality of perversity both to Bowie's performance and to the landscape of the film'.[18] The shot, then, not only calls upon the ectoplasm of what has happened previously in the scene but on the non-binary, sexually fluid star image of David Bowie, which functions as an

> open mesh of possibilities, gaps, overlaps, dissonances and resonances, lapses and excesses of meaning when the constituent elements of anyone's gender, of anyone's sexuality aren't made (or can't be made) to signify monolithically.[19]

The shot concludes in long shot, with Yonoi lowering his katana and pushing Celliers away, backwards, muttering for him to 'go back'. Celliers has his hands behind his back, a gesture of passivity, but also one that recognizes this is a queer space he has entered into and, in fact, has helped shape. A streak of sweat runs its way down Celliers's shirt. We cannot see his face or rather it is only through Yonoi's reaction, a look of abject horror mixed with unspeakable desire, that Celliers's ghostly visage is presented. Two of the soldiers reach for their swords but falter, while Hicksley and his Japanese guards look passively on: they are all bewitched by the violent tango that is now taking place before them.

What next follows is two rapidly edited shots: the first, a medium shot, lasting two seconds, involves Yonoi putting his white-handed glove on Celliers chest, and then his face, pushing him backwards as he does so. The second shot, in close-up, lasting one second, continues this movement, but from behind Celliers, so what we see is his desiring rage lighting up Yonoi's face. In the first shot, Celliers stares back and into Yonoi's eyes, with an expression that is neutral or unfathomable, taking on the gaze of the 'oriental'.[20] In the second shot, Yonoi scrunches up his face, while his white-gloved hand begins to propel Celliers backwards. Yonoi begs Celliers to 'go back', the ambiguity in the expression opening up queer lines of (in) sight. The gloved hand carries forward the marker of purity but here it mixes with, or rather touches, 'danger', the desiring Other that Celliers represents. More complexly, in a perverse switching of symbolism, as noted above, Yonoi wears the white gloves and the imagined mastery with it. But these white gloves belong to the 'David Bowie' found in *Let's Dance*. The film gestures to beyond its own fiction and to the power that Bowie's star image transmits.

The next shot is nine seconds long and is a match on action: Celliers falls into the space that Yonoi pushes him to. Shot in a low-angle, medium shot, from behind and to the side of Yonoi, Celliers struggles back to his feet, taking up his position in front of Yonoi. Celliers begins to kiss him on his cheek. His slouch hat has come off in the struggle and his blonde hair is matted but uncovered. They are together shot against the vast expanse of the blue sky: usually a 'perfect' setting for a charged kiss like this. Of course, without the hat on, with less of the clothing of the role present, more of the star iconography of David Bowie emerges. So much, in fact, that this act registers, for Bowie fans at least, as *David Bowie kissing Yonoi*. As Derfoufi suggests:

> We share Yonoi's desire of being touched by Celliers (Bowie). When Celliers (Bowie) crosses the invisible barrier that both separates and protects Yonoi's Oriental body from the body of the star, not only does Yonoi's desire of having a physical experience with the Western Other get realised, but so does our own desire of being kissed by Bowie, if only by proxy.[21]

The kiss, though, is not soft and Yonoi is not fully compliant. Celliers pulls Yonoi's rigid body towards him, his hands forcefully clutching his shoulders, and he looks past him, not directly into his eyes. Celliers's kiss is sadistic and knowing, and it 'exposes exactly how sexual Yonoi's sadism has always been'.[22]

The scene then cuts to a remarkable two-second, close-up shot: the camera positioned behind Celliers. The shot occurs in slow motion, which leaves a 'trace' of movement on the image. Yonoi's face fills the frame, his eyes full of tears, his mouth open – he is unable to form words. Yonoi is both thrilled and horrified by the kiss: it is the exact thing he has always wanted and the touch that reveals that which he has wanted to keep hidden, repressed. In this shot all we can see of Celliers is the back of his shoulders and blonde head. In fact, there is no shot in this entire scene where we see their faces together: we have to imagine what the other's face is doing, gesturing. And yet, given the mirroring the scene is built on, we can *call up* these impressions: their faces register equally as corporeal traces even when not together present in the shot. This is even more the case in this shot because Yonoi stares directly back at the camera, at the viewer, so that the terror of his lust is directed at us. His tortured gaze wounds as much as it eroticizes and given it is Celliers's kiss producing or eliciting such a response, it again carries forth the qualities and intensities of David Bowie's own perverse star image, which suggests that he is

> human and flawed (visibly so with a damaged eye) as well as extraordinary in appearance, demeanour and projected self-belief. The ethereal aspect central to Bowie's star persona and epitomized in many of his characterizations – Major Tom, Ziggy Stardust, Aladdin Sane and so on – overtly embraces the 'otherness' of the outsider.[23]

The following shot is nine seconds in duration: it is a match or continuous cut, beginning with Celliers completing the kiss, in close-up, and moving to a medium close-up, where he withdraws from Yonoi and stares back at him. Yonoi is positioned off-screen, so we are left only with Celliers's gestures to comprehend. At the beginning of the shot, Celliers's teeth are exposed and there is a degree of disgust on his face. Again, this relay of 'mouths' which do not speak but which registers as distaste washes the shot with, so to speak, the scene's dirty linen. As Celliers pulls back from Yonoi, he first looks into dead space and then directly into Yonoi's eyes. The stare is intense and is meant to penetrate Yonoi's shell. Celliers is surrounded by the thick, jungle canopy, in the same way Yonoi was in the opening shot to the scene. The raw animalism now attaches itself to both characters. There is a shared perversity that moves between and through them. Of course, Celliers's pupils are differently coloured and bring an ulterior form of difference to the scene. These are David Bowie's 'mismatched pupils . . . which have become a positive identifier of his individuality and his alternate, creative, way of seeing'.[24]

In the next shot, eight seconds long, Celliers and Yonoi are framed together. Yonoi faces Celliers, whose back is wet with sweat. Yonoi's mouth is again captured trying to shape words: it is open but silent, as if speaking of this shame would confirm his own 'dark desires'. He is lost for words, unable to call upon language to name the unspeakable, the unnameable. Yonoi slowly raises his katana, his mouth continuing to register the terror, his teeth entering its orifice. A glob of saliva forms in his mouth and the moment the katana has been fully raised, ready to strike, he collapses, falling back into the arms of two of his soldiers. Although we cannot see Celliers's face, it is clear that he doesn't flinch but stands there as a figure beyond representation: the very kernel or source of the perversity that shakes Yonoi. As Yonoi falls silently back, it is one of his soldiers who screams and attacks Celliers – his sounding and movement like an animal attacking.

Michel Chion terms the moment when the scream replaces language as one in which speech, verbalization, does not suffice: where 'words' cannot comprehend the event that has been witnessed.[25] For Chion, the screaming point is the exit of being and an entry point into experiential chaos, where language has failed in the face (mouth) of the unassimilable and unnameable. This chora, 'anterior to naming',[26] has a profound effect on the viewer since all they have at that moment in time is a screaming mouth with which to comprehend the events that they have observed. Celliers is the figure, of course, who brings into existence this screaming point. However, the fact that Yonoi fails to scream suggests both a subjugation to his desire and a defeat to his perversity. Celliers has *returned* his repression: Yonoi has been outed.[27] Yet it is not Celliers but Bowie who truly carries forth this dread and desire since his star image is made from these forces and intensities.

At this point in the scene, *Bowie is now completely Celliers*, the liminal star who cannot be fixed, adequately described, whose image exists at the axis of perversion, of queerness, of disgust and desire. As Jacqueline Furby writes:

> he can be read as the active instigator in attracting sadistic violence toward himself, or at least toward aspects of his persona, and positioning himself in a liminal, marginal space between life and death: a space that should be familiar to fans of his music.[28]

The final shot of the scene is twenty-two seconds long. Celliers is carried by the soldiers to a point in front of Hicksley and is savagely attacked by a group of five guards. Hicksley tries to intervene, as does Lawrence, but both are beaten back, their intervention merely a symbolic 'gesture' to arrest the violence. The camera is positioned at a long shot as punches and kicks rain down on Celliers. Yonoi and two soldiers are momentarily caught staring at the attack. We hear the sound of these punches and kicks and also the grunts from the exertion it takes. All the while, 'Sowing the Seed' provides a sonic envelope of melancholy and pathos.

Near the end of the shot, Celliers is picked up and dragged backwards to where the prisoners are lined up. His face looks to the floor, he may well be unconscious, but his hands are stretched out in a near Christ-like pose – a position he had also taken up earlier in the film. As they dump Celliers's body on the ground, the scene slowly fades to black, and the musical score also fades out. The violence meted out in this shot is meant, in one coded sense, to act as a punishment for Celliers's perversity and to bring back the heterosexual, masculinist moral order. Of course, Yonoi used violence as a code for his repressed desires, and so these soldiers are also caught in this desiring loop. Their defence of Yonoi, their collective repulsion at the sight of Celliers kissing him, confirms their own latent, desiring perversity. As the scene ends, Celliers is covered in dust: it cloaks him. He can no longer brush it away and neither can he fix his clothes or hair. He has given up his (star) self to out Yonoi, as he outs himself in the process.

Conclusion

According to Peter Brooks, mute gesture is

> An expressionistic means – precisely the means of the melodrama – to render meanings which are ineffable, but none the less operative in the sphere of human ethical relationships. Gesture could perhaps then be typed as the nature of catachresis, the figure used when there is no 'proper' name for something. . . . Yet of course it is the fullness, the pregnancy of the blank that is significant: meaningful though unspeakable.[29]

In the *gesturing dust* scene, we can see how mute gesture shapes, drives and energizes the disgust and desire that Yonoi feels. Celliers, his love/hate object, performs a similar function, acting as a perverse mirror: full of shame himself, he loathes the way he is desired. Yet that desire propels him to act, to perform. Of course, Celliers is played by David Bowie, whose star image is composed out of these perverse, floating intensities. The scene teases his arrival, and yet even when he is not present his presence is materialized through Yonoi. The scene powerfully uses gesture because of the affective desires it seeks to reveal.

In the *gesturing dust* scene, we witness how the full materiality and immateriality of a film 'senses' into existence suppressed desires, the flavours of shame, the violence of longing. David Bowie's Celliers haunts the scene from first to last: he is ghost, white glove, mirror, projection, apparition, love interest and figure of perversity. The architecture of the scene is built on his slow reveal, like a shirt or dress is being peeled away, increasing one's expectations. Yet his (physical) arrival is itself an act of sadism and a death wish. He outs Yonoi, symbolically returns the violence he has metered out on the other prisoners and condemns himself to death. These are the gesturing senses of David Bowie.

Notes

1. Victor F. Perkins, 'Must We Say What They Mean? Film Criticism and Interpretation', *Movie* 34, no. 35 (1990): 1.

2. Andrew Klevan, 'What Is Evaluative Criticism?' *Film Criticism* 40, no. 1 (January 2016), https://quod.lib.umich.edu/f/fc/13761232.0040.118?view=text;rgn=main

3. Sean Redmond, 'Sensing Film Performance', in *Performance Phenomenology*, ed. Matthew Wagner (Palgrave Macmillan, 2019), 165.

4. Rosalind Galt, 'David Bowie's Perverse Cinematic Body', *Cinema Journal* 57, no. 3. (Spring 2018): 131.

5   Nicholas Chare and Liz Watkins, 'Introduction: Gesture in Film', *Journal for Cultural Research* 19, no. 1 (2015): 1.
6   Joshua Hirsch, *Afterimage: Film, Trauma and the Holocaust* (Philadelphia: Temple University Press, 2004).
7   Lisa Perrott, 'Bowie the cultural alchemist: Performing Gender, Synthesizing Gesture and Liberating Identity', *Continuum: Journal of Media & Cultural Studies* 31, no. 4 (June 2017): 10.
8   June Price Tangney, Rowland S. Miller, Laura Flicker and Deborah Hill Barlow, 'Are Shame, Guilt, and Embarrassment distinct Emotions?' *Journal of Personality and Social Psychology* 70, no. 6. (1996): 1258.
9   Winfried Menninghaus, *Disgust: Theory and History of a Strong Sensation* (Albany: Suny Press, 2003).
10 William Ian Miller, *The Anatomy of Disgust* (Cambridge, MA: Harvard University Press, 1998), 5.
11 Mary Douglas, *Purity and Danger: An Analysis of Concepts of Pollution and Taboo* (London: Routledge, 1966), 44.
12 Giorgio Agamben, *Homo Sacer: Sovereign Power and Bare Life* (California: Stanford University Press, 1998), 78.
13 Patricia MacCormack, 'Perversion: Transgressive Sexuality and Becoming-monster', *thirdspace* 3, no. 2 (2004). [online], http://www.thirdspace.ca/articles/3_2_maccormack.htm, accessed 17 September 2020.
14 Earl Jackson Jr., 'Desire at Cross (-Cultural) Purposes: *Hiroshima, Mon Amour* and *Merry Christmas, Mr. Lawrence*', *Positions* 2, no. 1. (1994): 136–7.
15 Chare and Watkins, *Introduction*, 1.
16 Agamben, *Homo Sacer*, 5.
17 Mchdi Derfoufi, 'Embodying Stardom, Representing Otherness: David Bowie in '*Merry Christmas, Mr. Lawrence*', in *David Bowie: Critical Perspectives*, ed. Eoin Devereux, Aileen Dillane and Martin J. Power (London: Routledge, 2015), 171.
18 Galt, 'David Bowie's Perverse Cinematic Body', 133.
19 Eve Kosofsky Sedgwick, *Tendencies* (Durham, NC and London; Duke University Press, 1993), 8.
20 Derfoufi, 'Embodying Stardom, Representing Otherness', 173.
21 Ibid., 171.
22 Galt, 'David Bowie's Perverse Cinematic Body', 135.
23 Kevin J. Hunt, 'The Eyes of David Bowie', in *Enchanting David Bowie: Space/Time/Body/Memory*, ed. Toija Cinque, Christopher Moore and Sean Redmond (London: Bloomsbury, 2015), 178.
24 Ibid., 177.
25 Michel Chion, *Audio-Vision: Sound on Screen* (New York: Columbia University Press, 1994), 78.

26 Kaja Silverman, *The Acoustic Mirror: The Female Voice in Psychoanalysis and Cinema* (Bloomington: Indiana University Press, 1998), 142.
27 Robin Wood, 'Return of the Repressed', *Film Comment* 14, no. 4 (1978): 25.
28 Jacqueline Furby, 'New Killer Star', *Cinema Journal* 57, no. 3 (Spring 2018): 169.
29 Peter Brooks, *The Melodramatic Imagination: Balzac, Henry James, Melodrama and the Mode of Excess* (New Haven, CT: Yale University Press, 1984), 72–3.

6

The Hunger's deathly shadow

The sweet annihilation of David Bowie, NYC, *c.* 1980–3

Mitch Goodwin

Exit strategy
LAX-BER-JFK, 1980

He's a broken man.[1]

There's a real melancholy about David Bowie's journey out of the 1970s: 'I suppose my depression and alienation were in keeping with the times.'[2] It was, after all, a period of disillusionment on many fronts. The rust of late industrialization was corroding middle America, the energy had been sapped from race and equality struggles and neo-liberalism was in the ascendency. Meanwhile, the first blossoming of the environmental movement had begun to fade with the folding of the Apollo programme and the retreat from the moon.

A gothic ferment permeated Bowie's professional and personal life upon his return to New York in 1980. As with such moves, for any itinerant internationalist there is always something left behind and even more to come back to. Yet a sense of decay was in the off. Recently divorced, he was also being dogged by a lingering contractual hangover from his mid-1970s deal with RCA Records and his management company MainMan, a persistent reminder of the dark arts of the music business. The fine print devised by his former manager – the 'intimidating and bullshitting' Tony Defries[3] – required Bowie to pay MainMan a chunk of his earnings from any musical output or touring receipts until the end of 1982. It was a despicable state of affairs.

And then on 8 December 1980, John Lennon was shot dead. Lennon was one of Bowie's pin-up icons, as well as a friend and a mentor. In 1975, Bowie and Lennon may have just been messing about with 'Fame' – a 'nasty, angry little song' that skewered the music industry and the likes of Tony Defries as an 'all-enveloping, artificial construction'[4] – but it was also a life lesson from the elder Beatle.[5] By 1980, Lennon had become a strong presence for Bowie, who was obviously channelling Lennon's *God* during *Scary Monsters*, an album imbued with Lennonesque social critique. Later that autumn, after his debut on Broadway as John Merrick in *The Elephant Man*, a gushing Lennon beat a path to the Starman's dressing room door to praise the actor's performance. Theirs had become an artistic kinship: two English lads making it in New York.

Inevitable, then, that the maddening depravity of Lennon's murder took a toll on Bowie. According to Chris O'Leary 'Bowie watched television coverage of Lennon's murder until dawn, screaming, "What the fuck is happening in the world!"'[6] It is hard to ignore this event in the context of Bowie's own contemporary retreat from public life. 'A whole piece of my life seemed to have been taken away; a whole reason for being a singer and a songwriter seemed to be removed from me.'[7] Following him everywhere was the unnerving permanence of his own words that were on high rotation on the airwaves that winter: 'put a bullet in my brain, and it makes all the papers.'[8]

The confluence of these two events – the contractual vice of his business affairs and the death of his friend John Lennon – forced Bowie to make a calculated artistic move. It would be a self-imposed exile from the recording studio and a pause on live music performance. He now had space for other pursuits, a lust for a new sort of darkness – it was time to shift gears. Bowie's act of self-preservation by withdrawing from the music industry and doggedly pursuing an acting career – and in particular the decision to take on the role of John Blaylock – is the subject of this chapter. Richard Fitch speaks to the possibilities afforded by 'allusion' in Bowie's art and in our interaction with his output as a dynamic text.[9] It is important then that we ask 'why?' and examine his presence in the film in the context of Bowie's own active and ongoing construction of the image of 'David Bowie' the artist, but also in his process as an actor inhabiting dark spaces. The role of Blaylock came at a time of personal and professional chaos for the star which is reflected in his nuanced performance of death and maddening decay.

Our reading of Bowie in *The Hunger* is therefore full of monstrous allusions, reflecting upon Michel Foucault's understanding of madness, mortality and morbidity as well as Mark Fisher's philosophical take on *Gothic Materialism*, which examines Antonin Artaud's confrontation with darkness, 'the Inside confronting the Outside and recoiling'.[10] The challenge then is to understand how these sources interlock as discursive tools for examining Bowie in *The Hunger*. In this way, cogitating and surmising upon the remnants of Bowie's contemporary state of mind provides a meditation upon what would seem in retrospect a contradictory career choice, a choice that placed him with all his attendant allusions in the artificial excess of Tony Scott's film *The Hunger*.

On the page

Long Island Expressway, NYC, spring 1981

> An aspect of writing I've always admired in a lot of authors and pop writers is the ability to keep things on a surreal and real level, so they have feet on earth and heads in heaven. It's a twilight state.[11]
>
> – David Bowie, TVNZ, 1981

The character of John Blaylock in *The Hunger*, a doomed vampire in contemporary New York City (*c.* 1981), is an exploration of broken promises, of social isolation and ultimately of eternal confinement and decay. It must have felt like an attractive proposition for Bowie, the musician in exile, to explore a tortured Lazarus-type role at a distinctly dark interlude in his own creative and personal journey. Whitley Strieber's novel, upon which the film is based, details the cursed romantic contract between two undead lovers, a wicked entanglement centuries in the making but only hours from its ghoulish end.

In the opening scene of Strieber's text, we are cruising through Queens in a stately Volvo sedan with John and Miriam Blaylock, vampire lovers in a hasty retreat after a night out on the hunt. John, a 200-year-old Victorian dandy, has just gorged himself on the blood sack that was his prey only moments earlier, and he is content and dreamlike. His lover – his 3,000-year-old seductress – Miriam, is a true immortal of ancient stock, Egyptian royalty perhaps. Wary of the dangers of the human world outside, she, as always, sits steadfastly behind the wheel. She slips her cool hand into John's, fondly recalling their frenzied seduction of an unwitting couple at the 1939 World's Fair, amidst 'the cheerful beauty of its yellow and white walls and svelte stainless-steel furniture'.[12] For Bowie, Strieber's dark vision of surface capitalism encapsulated an uncomfortable junction for the megastar's personal alienation in the role of John Blaylock.

For John, America was a place of bold invention and excitement – 200 years had seen electrification, trips to the moon, Elvis – not to mention the promise of immortality via their weekly hunt in the outer boroughs, each strike an adventure anew. Yet his vampiric genes were on the clock. The promise of forever and the metaphysics of eternity, he would soon discover, are two very different things. What John Blaylock didn't know was that in the hours that would follow, the 'deathly shadow' would soon be upon him. The end would be unedifying and quick; a rapid decay would commence, and a perpetual hunger would set in. John's human DNA and his poisoned blood imposed a sentence from which he would never recover – eternal twilight. There awaits an empty coffin in the musty attic of the Blaylock's Upper East Side parlour house, among the other entombed souls. A bespoke design, it was made to order by Miriam in anticipation of this moment, for the inevitable eternal damnation of her lover.

And so, David Bowie takes on the role of the doomed vampire John Blaylock. A part that would enable him to disappear once again – like Bel Air, like Berlin, like Lausanne. This time, however, it would be on celluloid. For Bowie the actor, *The Hunger* would be a timely study of performance both in shadow and retreat. As we shall see, it is the darkest of roles not only in terms of Blaylock's character arc and the film's noirish production design but also its symbolic continuation of Bowie's process of erasure.

The actor prepares

JFK-LSGL-LHR, 1979-82

By the 1980s, Bowie had kicked Captain America to a ditch on the side of the road. For Ziggy, Halloween Jack and the Duke, the ride was over.

On 31 December 1979, he demonstrated that this process of annihilation would reach back deep into the Bowie songbook. With the help of director David Mallet, he spectacularly blew up Major Tom with an elaborately constructed set piece for a mournful acoustic version of 'Space Oddity' on the *Will Kenny Everett Make It To 1980? Show*.[13] The performance and staging of this one-off event underlined once again that there is an ephemeral temporality to Bowie's performance mystique. Each iteration serves a purpose in the moment and via the medium of his choosing, much as Major Tom had done once before and would do so again.

Revisiting 'Space Oddity', a ten-year-old novelty song on a novelty TV programme at ten minutes to midnight was itself an instruction: we were viewing the Bowie canon being wilfully scrapped. This echoes Mark Fisher's gothic materialist reading of Antonin Artaud, in which the genius in retreat (or is it decline?) performs a ceremonial act of absurdist electromagnetic erasure. Bowie, like Artaud, assumes the role of 'neuro/mancer – an electro-nerve sorcerer, an abstract engineer who left behind diagrams, plans and maps for escaping the meat'.[14] In retrospect, like 'Ashes to Ashes', like 'Blackstar' and very much like the trace lines of *The Hunger*, we are left to cross-check the errant data points.

Looking back at the broadcast we can now see not only the literal end of the seventies but also the beginning of something new. Perhaps hinted at but never fully dealt with, Bowie was on a path of wilful deconstruction, impatiently scattering his past lives and the characters he created to navigate them.[15] As Bowie would later recall, the *Scary Monsters* period had 'always been some kind of purge. It was me eradicating the feelings within myself that I was uncomfortable with.'[16] The act of dethronement in 'Ashes to Ashes' – and consequently his decay and annihilation in *The Hunger* – was a measured de-frocking of his stage personae of the seventies and their signifying husks and regalia – Bowie the chrysalid in reverse. 'Arranged artfully these rags can suggest a sad grandeur expectant of a better future', and as such recognize the precariousness of the moment. 'They connect the world of the songs to the dying world that is our world.'[17] Pressing ahead relentlessly, Bowie's skins are encoded with a persistent theatrical genealogy, from Pierrot to Yorick to Lazarus and beyond. The vampire John Blaylock was a new skin for an old game.

Perhaps he was aware too, watching the playback through the years, that his choice of roles could not help but tell their own story, and thereby exemplify the fraught struggle of the multidisciplinary artist working across mediums:

> I have to work hard at acting. But the reason for that, I think is that it's so hard for somebody in music to jump over and do movies. The idea of them being a rock musician is always at the front of the audience's mind.[18]

In reality, it's an inescapable conundrum, as the performance shapeshifting of Bowie the musician is an audience expectation; however, it is a far more complex lived experience for Bowie the musician-actor-artist-icon. He may have moved between these skins fluidly, but there is also a sense that Bowie the exterior is a curatorial exercise in wilful ambiguity while the interior constructions are far more fragile, enduring character explorations.

Bowie has always been a cultural assemblage on a dark performative journey across formats – 'I am the future / I'm tomorrow / I am the end'.[19] In the case of *The Hunger*, the format just happened to be the Hollywood vision machine. It's what Bowie does with Strieber's text internally and what director Tony Scott does with Bowie's body aesthetically that positions Bowie the actor in oddly duplicitous set pieces.

On the screen

Sutton Park, Upper East Side NYC, fall 1982

Strieber's novel is a carefully crafted reimagining of the typical vampire narrative. Strieber was a Texas native who – like the film's director Tony

Scott – was himself an adman; Scott in London directing commercials with his older brother Ridley (he of *Blade Runner* and *Alien* fame), Strieber in New York where he rose to the senior ranks of agency vice president. Both Strieber and Scott, we could say, knew a thing or two about dressing up an idea with smoke machines and soft boxes.

The Hunger continues the tradition popularized by Anne Rice in the mid-1970s with her *Interview with a Vampire* series, updating the isolated Dracula motif by deviating away from classic vampire tropes. In this modernist reading, wooden stakes hold up roses in Miriam's garden rather than turning the undead to dust, while hanging garlic is just a harmless decoration, a kitsch feature of the Nolita delis up on Mulberry Street. The parable, however, is no less tragic, as it plays to both the darkness of contemporary times and the interior turmoil of those who live outside of its atemporality.

This is the 'new vampyre', a communal rather than solitary figure, 'not simply the ultimately evil, soulless, undead, blood-feast-driven psychopath of yesteryear, but as a multi-dimensional, humanistic, cultured, and even pitiful creature'.[20] This is certainly the disposition of the Blaylocks, particularly the rapid and somewhat pathetic decline of John Blaylock who is Miriam's soon-to-be doomed and entombed companion. We also recognize this in Bowie the artist at various now infamous media engagements. 'Some people said you would bite my neck!' suggested Dick Cavett on live television in 1974 as an emancipated Bowie screwed his walking cane manically into the carpet, clearing his sinuses and flashing those rotting incisors.

For Tony Scott, *The Hunger* is a brash first step into high-concept American cinema, fusing the visual aesthetics of music video melodrama, high-gloss TV advertorials and the occasional art school indulgence. It is part Helmut Newton and part Irving Penn, what Scott has described as his 'surrealist opera'[21] – a cinema-graphic clash of 1980s futurism, glamour photography and Upper East Side opulence. An erotic vampire techno-noir for the New York crowd.

Scott intuitively places two beautiful creatures at its centre, archetypes of their own versions of Euro-cool magnificence. He knows Bowie is 'otherworldly' and that Deneuve has a shimmering cinematic pedigree; they are the perfect homoerotic creatures at which to point one's lens. As Scott has noted of their characters, John and Miriam Blaylock, 'they could be aliens',[22] conspicuously refined as they are: the hair, the clothes, the cultivated poise are in sharp contrast with the hive-like hustle and the weary grind of the metropolis outside. They are the hunters surrounded by the hunted.

Scott is not afraid of mining Bowie lore; he knows he is working with a cross-media icon and therefore has no problem hustling Bowie wares and mining the artist's catalogue of misfits. He brings Hunger City to Central

Park during a sequence filmed at Bethesda Terrace in which a ravenous, yet rapidly ageing, John Blaylock stalks a lone youth expressively roller skating to the tune of Iggy Pop's Bowie-produced 'Funtime' – 'Fun / Last night I was down in the lab / Fun / Talkin' to Dracula and his crew / All aboard for funtime'.[23] In this sequence, Bowie the musician becomes an existential signifier for Bowie the screen actor as his previous stage personae and dystopian connotations and illusions become props for the adman's mise en scène.

Scott also pinches from contemporary Bowie iconography too, in the opening minutes of the film, as the female mark of the Blaylock's nightclub hunt fashions a cigarette languidly from her slender hand and sways seductively in front of the blue light of a projector. The shadow play is clearly a riff on the cover of his most recent album *Scary Monsters* – or is she a super creep? It is a double image: like Bowie in his crumpled Pierrot outfit, she casts an elongated shadow. It's an ominous signalling of the vampires' imminent demise; for her it will be permanent, for Scott a double entendre of Bowies past. During her last fateful moments straddling a lascivious Bowie, she peels off his black wig; Bowie's head is arched back, his hypnotic vampiric stare a nod to the erotic glamour of Edward Bell's sketch of Bowie on *Scary Monsters*'s inner sleeve. A little while later, with the evidence disposed, Scott blocks a scene that recalls Bowie's graceful physicality as a performance mime: the requisite steamy shower scene between Bowie and Deneuve – post-kill, pre-coital. John extends his hand – it is a thin skeletal branch – fingertips barely touching the underside of Miriam's perfect chin, a precious moment of intimacy between near-perfect immortals. 'Forever? Forever and ever.' Indeed.

Bowie the artist lurks here too, appearing most clearly in a polaroid photograph taken by the Blaylock's young neighbour, Alice Cavender. It is Bowie the actor who holds it in his hand, staring down at the man he once knew, Bowie the young artist. The polaroid photograph is eerily evocative of a time before. It could have slipped out of a promo copy of *The Lodger* or been discarded on the warehouse floor by Warhol. Here, however, preserved on celluloid is the shadow play of distant reflections of actor and artist in collision.

As the film progresses, however, Scott and cinematographer Stephen Goldblatt rarely permit a clean frame of Bowie. As Jacqueline Furby has noted:

> The camera's view of his face is generally obscured: by fast cutting, by voile curtains (of which there are a great many in their home), by raindrops on a window, by the expressionistic shadows, by the chiaroscuro mist of remembrance, by the dim light of a nightclub, and by dark glasses.[24]

There are many allusions to the haunting of David Bowie and the eeriness of the 1980s in *The Hunger*'s more intimate framing of John Blaylock. Again, this is mostly played in shadow, and he is glimpsed best in profile: at first on the Heaven nightclub's mezzanine level scouting his prey on the dance floor below and later in the Blaylock's parlour house after their dawn escape from their Long Island hunt, when sleep – the necessary rest for the post-hunger-quenching feed – evades him. He edges out of bed, a hint of distress – could that be panic? Not yet. We catch Bowie looking out from behind the curtains, the rain-dappled bedroom window melting his features as he smokes – there is a lot of smoking in *The Hunger* – and Scott expertly captures its curling dance as it licks the sharp stubble of Bowie's hard black silhouette. John Blaylock is languid; he feels older now. The deathly shadow is upon him, such a wretched thing.

The opening scene

London, Heaven nightclub, 22 March 1982

> Silhouettes and shadows
> Watch the revolution.[25]

Bowie was never much of a club man, preferring band rooms and bookstores. Clubs for Bowie were feeding grounds as much as exercises in cultural sampling, 'He wasn't rowdy or raucous. He wasn't even flamboyant. . . . David was more taking it all in and always studying everybody.'[26] This description of course is also synergetic with the notion of the vampire, the shadow-dancing night hunter out on the prowl – both seducer and archetypal consumer.

So, to place David Bowie in London's Heaven club for the opening scene of *The Hunger*, soundtracked by Bauhaus's signature goth anthem 'Bela Lugosi's Dead', is a satisfyingly Bowie-esque cinematic moment. Nu-wave meets neon gothic, perhaps? For director Tony Scott, it was a mere practicality and an aesthetic choice – it made for 'an interesting title sequence', he said blandly.[27] In fact, this is the moment we are most aware of Scott's loaded use of the Bowie image. Akin perhaps to Virilio's notion of the 'iconoclasm of presentation',[28] this is not representation of artefact or mural; this is the presentation of David Bowie as image icon, designed for repetition and repeated viewing. It is both the exploitation of Bowie Inc. and, for what is to follow, the manufacturing of desire for that which we the audience crave but cannot have.

For the actors themselves, Bowie and his vampire queen, Catherine Deneuve, are as exotic a pairing one could hope for in a 1980s Hollywood vampire movie. London's Heaven, doubling as a New York dance club, is a wholly appropriate setting in which to orchestrate their glamorous reveal: two vampire lovers stalking their next meal, their strobic presence moving elegantly among the shadows and sniffing the reticulated smoke-scorched air. John and Miriam mark their prey: a young leather-clad couple throwing shapes and caressing the air on the densely packed flesh on the dance floor below, their warm hipster blood pumping, their bodies like white blotches on a Predator drone's infrared targeting computer.

For Bowie the actor, it is the only moment in the film in which we might recognize Bowie playing Bowie in situ. In fact, of all his performances of this period, at this moment in Heaven we are intimately engaged with Bowie's stardom – the red lips, the high cheeks, the iridescent foundation, the dark shock of hair and of course as he conspires with his lady Miriam, those infamous teeth are quite possibly vampiric.

Tony Scott described Bauhaus's lead singer Peter Murphy as having an 'ethereal, vampire quality about him'.[29] The characterization is evident from the opening image when we are confronted by Murphy's pale, junkie visage and his teased-up crow's nest of black hair, like Nick Cave in a soap commercial. Scott leverages his mannered performance and gothic iconography to signify the predatory violence that is to shortly unfold. As his band thunders through 'Bela Lugosi's Dead':

> The bats have left the bell tower
> The victims have been bled
> Red velvet lines the black box . . .[30]

John and Miriam set about seducing and blooding their victims, not with fangs but a gold blade in the shape of an ancient Egyptian ankh symbol, a matching pair they keep on chains around their necks. The sequence is intercut with a lab monkey eviscerating its caged companion while a terrified lab attendant bathed in a bloody red light attempts to beat it back. Murphy snarls, Bowie sucks and the monkey bites. It is an early glimpse of the kitsch pseudoscience world of *The Hunger* that is to follow – think *The Andromeda Strain* meets *Dynasty*.

For all of Deneuve's screen allure, it is the iconic pairing of Murphy and Bowie that defines this opening sequence. Their calculated placement is what gives the film its cult credibility and goth DNA. Murphy performing 'Bela Lugosi's Dead' in a film featuring David Bowie as a Manhattan vampire is like catnip to a Love Cat.

> The timeless beauty of Catherine Deneuve.
> The cool elegance of David Bowie.
> The open sensuality of Susan Sarandon.
> Combine to create a modern classic of perverse fear.

Haunting, mysterious, sensual, strange, perverse, riveting.
The Hunger.

– *The Hunger* Theatrical Trailer, MGM, 1983

It's not a stretch to say we are seeing the extravagant eighties and its consumerist indulgences coming to the fore in *The Hunger*. Amidst this excess, Scott turns his lens on the European cool of Deneuve and the internationalist charm of Bowie as a contrivance rather than character development. Dressed for success and a spot of bloodletting no matter the hour, Scott was doing *Miami Vice* well before Michael Mann had punched up the contrast on the pink and blue neon chic of the Florida underworld. Scott has described the film as his *Barry Lyndon* moment, 'very classical and very beautiful',[31] and as such, many of the staged sequences in the Blaylock home are ponderous compositions. Scott and Goldblatt use available light and deep shadows with abrupt edits or post-produced speed bumps, at times making for what feels like a filmic delirium. The effect is intensely cinematic yet with a music video impatience, more akin to a commercial magazine spread: *Chanel* meets *Norsca Fresh* with smoky *Body Heat* hues; high-end cinematography and production design for the Reagan era.

At the time of *The Hunger* shoot, Bowie's video clip for the single 'Fashion' was on high rotation on MTV. Filmed at the Hurrah nightclub in Manhattan, it was a lament on caged individualism, posturing New Romantics and media intoxicants. As such, it was an incongruous philosophical counterpoint to Scott's indulgent production ensemble that was very much about the language and surface texture of visual advertising. Surely, for an artist with such finely attuned situational awareness, such contradictions crossed the actor's mind as he sat in the wings chatting up Susan Sarandon, watching the background being finessed with smoke and mirrors – 'We're ready for your close-up, Mr Bowie'.

As O'Leary has pointed out on Bowie's vocal delivery on the song, it's hard not to associate the tone and the annunciation of the word *fashion* with 'fascism'. His intent would certainly seem to have a militant bent to it in an early draft of the lyrics he writes: '"hell up ahead, burn a flag/ shake a fist, start a fight/ if you're covered in blood, you're doing it right," while the goon squad threatens to "break every bone"'.[32] A similar venom laces his comments at the time about the evolution of disco and dancefloor culture, a scene that had morphed from a 'natural' flow of music and presence and style 'to be replaced by an insidious grim determination to be fashionable, as though it's actually a vocation'.[33]

The production techniques Bowie found himself immersed within for Tony Scott's *The Hunger* then are an ironic twist of fate – not only in the shadow of 'Fashion' but also for an artist in retreat from the stodgy business practices of an increasingly facile music industry.

Monstrous decay

And nothing can we call our own but death
And that small model of the barren earth
Which serves as paste and cover to our bones.

– Shakespeare, Richard III, Act 3 Scene 2

The winter of Lennon's slaying by gun violence saw a peak in crime across New York City, numbers that would not be seen again until the early 1990s.[34] It's fitting then that as John Blaylock hunts on the edges of Manhattan, greed is on the up and murder is a commonplace occurrence – so no surprises then that people were eating each other. As The Clash would have it in 1982, we were all 'starved in metropolis / hooked on necropolis / addict of metropolis'[35] – classic contemporary vampire territory for sure.

When we first come upon John Blaylock in *The Hunger*, the svelte pop star literally inhabits the monstrous body, as he ascends to the mezzanine level to select his prey for the evening. His character, though, is dying; having committed his soul to his vampire queen centuries earlier, the viral load is on the wane. Imminently, Blaylock would become a classical Foucauldian monster – albeit of the fictional undead – that 'not only refuses and escapes the law, it renders it unintelligible',[36] as he preposterously seeks respite from the deathly shadow. This abdication of responsibility is a necessary attribute of the urban vampire in crisis mode: evading detection at the edges of the teaming metropolis, hunting and feeding when it can, doing just enough to survive in the city – survivalist techniques in which Bowie himself was well versed. Death frames the narrative of Bowie's monstrous skins, whether it be on stage as Ziggy, in the alleyways of Hunger City or seared onto celluloid as John Blaylock.

As Shakespeare well knew, only death is something that we can truly call our own. For Foucault, death gives form to life, for 'it is in death that the individual becomes at one with himself, escaping from monotonous lives and their leveling effect',[37] and only in death may we see the definition of the monstrous shape, and 'the style of its truth' (2003). For Sharpe, Bowie might be a monster, but he is a noble one. In his lyrics he speaks back from the future, decoding the chaos, while on screen in *The Hunger* he reveals the anguish of approaching morbidity. The message back from the undead is plain and direct: *get on with it!* Within Sharpe's definition, which borrows from Foucault but also Canguilhem's monstrosity, the monster can give us hope. It approaches us from the outside, it is itself just as distinct from the other as we are; 'they prop us up through creating the fantasy of stable ground beneath our feet. They do this through providing an outside to our human outline.'[38]

What Bowie portrays in *The Hunger* is when that outline is broken, when the infection breaks the surface and the rot sets in. Bowie got *affect*; he understood its import. As Mark Fisher reminds us, 'Affect is a crash site, the trauma-event in itself. Trauma is a memory of the outside registered as rupture, but the trauma-event is raw contact with the Outside.'[39] For Bowie and for Blaylock, the trauma was irreversible decay – the body, the street, the social compact of 'the terrible eighties',[40] each in their own way trapped.

Bowie of course recognized decay when he saw it, he grew up amidst the craters and the crumbling edifices of post-war Britain, the ubiquitous greyness was translatable – the heavy sky, the crackle of the radio, the needle on the groove. He understood the limits of the analogue. In the time of Strieber's novel and the story world of Scott's film, it was still a quaint period in the history of technoculture; 8-bit gaming in the lounge room and 8-bit video effects in the edit suite, no mobile phones or internet for John and Miriam to stalk their prey, or CRISPR gene editing, retinol or coenzyme Q10 to put the brakes on John's rapid decline.

Human-bred chaos then is only ever just beyond the surveilled walls of the Blaylock's Sutton Park compound. John's desperate act is to engage with a hostile environment of not only rabid consumption and brutal capitalist logic but also of tribal fear. Miriam understands the threat humans pose: we are dangerous creatures, yet after three millennia of observation, we are, for the most part, sadly predictable. Never more so in the 1980s, in which humans are especially plague-like, our excesses and singular desires are clearly vulnerabilities to the immortal observer, to be both mocked and leveraged for sustenance.

This is the curse of the human infestation: reproducibility, destruction and then death, a perverse continuity amidst the unfurling chaos of each passing millennia. This also holds true of course for the more exotic and sublime vampiric creature who lurks and observes and feeds from the periphery. They are not immune from these consumerist tendencies, as William Burroughs caustically observes:

> They always take more than they leave by the basic nature of the vampiric process of inconspicuous but inexorable consumption. The vampire converts quality, live blood, vitality, youth, talent into quantity food and time, for himself. He perpetuates the most basic betrayal of the spirit, reducing all human dreams to his shit.[41]

Both Miriam and John venture out into that chaos to reconnoitre and to hunt, but also to make contact with the scientific world to keep one step ahead of the human tide. A key sequence of the film is John's pursuit of the young gerontologist, Dr Sarah Roberts, whose experimental medical treatment may stave off his inevitable demise. It is during these moments that the viewer's gaze most closely observes John's decaying visage. The camera lingers uncomfortably as we watch him endure the passing hours in the waiting room of Dr Roberts's West Side clinic. This is where everything begins to fall apart: Bowie is immaculate, and his waiting room demeanour is a study in polite desperation. We know Miriam is back at the Blaylock parlour house, attending to the formalities, prepping the coffin and hoovering up the cobwebs. Yet Scott chooses to stay with John – we experience his isolation, as the hunger takes hold, and the haunting begins. *This is not eternal love! This is not forever and ever! This is not divine!*

Bowie the actor, meanwhile, is disappearing beneath the creeping accumulation of latex, as John's plight becomes more acute, and clumps of his golden locks fall out by the fistful. It's hard to resist the presence of Bowie the star in this moment, the cornered musician enslaved by his personae – in the spotlight but on the edge, under close examination falling apart before our eyes. As John Blaylock, in his black coat and low-slung fedora, he is every bit the damaged, milk-slurping cocaine junkie of 1974 – Bowie the rock star seeking rehab at the sleep clinic to alleviate his paranoia, to smooth over the cracks, to give him what he needs: time, a commodity he once had in abundance, but now seems consumed by its finality. Lennon's dead, the music has stopped and the city is experiencing its own deathly shadow. 'All this will be destroyed. The world must be destroyed. It is corrupt and full of ugliness. It is full of mummies, I tell you. Roman decadence. Death.'[42]

On the Outside, the Inside

Foucault's notion of the plague is a familiar malaise for John Blaylock, warm and nostalgic against his cold, undead skin. It is a 'haunting of contagions' that were commonplace in his mortal adolescence as a manor house dandy in Victorian-era France, seduced by the mysterious lady on horseback. Miriam took his name, his loot and his loins and together they made the transatlantic vault to New York City. The hunger and the hunting would now be a shared enterprise, so would the layers of enclosure that fortified their otherness from the Outside. Blaylock is both wide-eyed and shallow of breath as he confronts Foucault's 'compact, swarming howling masses', representative as they are of 'the plague, of rebellion, vagabondage, desertions, people who appear and disappear and live and die in disorder'.[43]

With his demise imminent, Blaylock makes a hasty retreat from Dr Roberts's West Side clinic, and we feel the intoxicating warmth of the swarm. He is in an overcrowded elevator of young doctors and nurses, his back to the wall, his hunger barely tameable as he inhales the humid, sweat-laden air. In our contemporary experience of these plague years – these Covid-19 days – seeing an elevator stuffed with young medical types, cheek to jowl, seems alien to us now. But for a famished vampire in 1983, it is almost unbearably delightful; a tantalizing smorgasbord of warm pink cheeks, throats and cleavage, intimately if fleetingly exposed, surrounds him. Arteries ping on the way up and on the way down – *beep beep* – time stands still, but the blood keeps moving. Warm breath expelled deliciously and audibly, co-mingling with perfume, stale cigarettes, hair spray and cologne. The steel doors open – *beep beep* – John Blaylock exits.

As Fisher opines, 'count zero, get out',[44] the horror for John is that the Outside is very much now inside, the chaos of the human plague – wretched mortality – has now been awoken within him, the viral infection of vampiric lore is hitting peak load, his terminal passage assured – the myth of immortality and endless devotional love was just a heartless ruse. The deception comes tumbling down as we reach Fisher's 'zero intensity'[45]; the monstrosity is but a vague outline, and in Tony Scott's treatment, we recognize the iconography of the troubled Starman within.

As the desperate and unhinged John Blaylock staggers through the streets, dodging the ubiquitous yellow cabs, the harsh daylight reveals a sad truth: Bowie looks just as suspect in his trench coat and fedora as the next man cruising Sutton Park in the cool autumn twilight.

> The words which he uttered, very infrequently, were the plainest, most ordinary and necessary words, as deprived of depth and significance, as those sounds with which animals express pain and pleasure, thirst and hunger.[46]

'Kill me', John appeals to Miriam in the film's penultimate scene. 'Kill me. Release me, Miriam.' Spare me this pain, this indignity, that coffin. 'Stop it!' She snaps coldly – it is a well-rehearsed line. There will be no suicide, there will be no 'glorious exit'.[47] There is no right to die for the undead vampire, and there certainly would be no mercy killing – that is not the way. 'There is no release, my darling. No rest, no letting go', Miriam says as she cradles him, tears streaming down her perfect cheeks. 'Humankind die one way, we another. Their end is final, ours is not. In the earth, in the rotting wood, in the eternal darkness we will see and hear and feel.' Bowie is fully latex now, unrecognizable as his body takes on the jittery shape of the double-centurion, leaning into the horror with his voice. 'Kill me, Miriam.'

She is entombing him in a permanent dream state: John's new 'forever and ever'. He has seen the other coffins in the attic, he helped lug them across the Atlantic, he knows the endgame. He cannot be deceived into the false promise that he may rise again, Lazarus-like, to romp among the fields to see out his end days in blissful indulgence. Miriam's blood was a conditional contract, a gift of temporary respite from the ravages of time and the human infestation. Written within its code is the sad impermanence of eternal decay.

Richard Fitch sums up Søren Kierkegaard:

> True despair is not what prompts one to change oneself or to try to flee into another self. It is what arrives when you realize that, after all, you can't escape yourself.[48]

In retrospect, knowing the sequence of characters that have gone before and the torment of Bowie's private life and his business affairs, we can appreciate Bowie as Blaylock, monster *and* slave. He, too, was a victim of entrapment and deception and cruel ends. We can see the opportunity afforded the performer – a character study of isolation and melancholy – corrupted by his monstrosity, deceived by those he trusted, an old soul in a young man's body stuck between worlds. In *The Hunger*, there is no future for John Blaylock – he has been robbed by its opportunities and its promise. The 'forever and ever' is Miriam's alone – spare a dozen coffins in the attic that moan silently with the ebb and flow of the centuries and the deadly trysts and contrivances of their undead queen.

Bowie is substituted in his final moments in *The Hunger* by a floppy rubber mannequin, so Catherine Deneuve can be shown in full frame carrying his crippled 200-year-old body to the attic crypt. Bowie is now literally a mere latex skeleton physically incapable of any form of escape, completely and utterly erased. This plasticity is a false image then, like Defries and RCA's opportunistic imitations of the late seventies that milked the artist's otherwise carefully curated catalogue. All around, falsehoods and frustrations.

For Bowie the actor, his entombment in *The Hunger* becomes a metaphor for the artist forcibly in retreat, a study of both the enclosure of inhabited fictions and the sweet annihilation of the ghosts and the rags of characters past. From autumn in New York in 1980 at the Booth Theatre, twisted and contorted in the skeletal knot of John Merrick, to the tortured brutish artist in the black forest in *Baal*, left alone to rot amidst the truffles and the acid rain, to his role as Maj. Jack 'Strafer' Celliers in *Merry Christmas, Mr. Lawrence*,[49] buried up to his neck in sand, blistering in the sun, and then night falls and the jungle calls, darkness closing in.

John Blaylock is an exploration of the deathly shadow, an inquiry into the creeping mortality of the not-quite-undead, a haunting gothic interior. For Bowie, there are threads running everywhere across time, disciplines and geography, a persistent duality of death and decay on- and off-screen. Together, Bowie the actor and John Blaylock the doomed vampire inhabit a fragile twilight.

In Bowie's final minutes in *The Hunger*, he attempts to resist this perpetual torment, instead desiring finality, a respectable death. However, it is not forthcoming. Is Miriam denying John out of tradition and ceremonial order alone? Or is this, in the context of the supernatural order of things, just not possible? In 1983, John Blaylock is the one character Bowie could not kill off.

Finding David Bowie

Decoding Bowie's performance catalogue from this period is like playing a surrealist game of exquisite corpse or deciphering his cut-up lyric compositions in reverse. His characters are inevitably obscured to some extent by the glare of his stardom, yet concealment and obfuscation are often requirements of the characters he chooses to inhabit, either via physical or narrative necessity. As Fitch affirms:

> The point is not to embrace the strange for its own sake, or simply to play, or be, an exotic character in order to try to escape from oneself. It lies in what turning towards the strange does to one's relation to the world as we find it. The strange draws us out of that world for a moment, giving up a different perspective upon where we have found ourselves.[50]

Following Thomas Jerome Newton, Merrick and Baal, the role of John Blaylock in *The Hunger* required a disciplined performance technique within a physically constrained and damaged body. As director Tony Scott remarked, Bowie 'was flexing his muscles in terms of theatre acting . . . he gave you a lot of sadness, a lot of empathy, because he is a man who realizes that he's wasting away before his eyes'.[51] Post-BBC *Baal* and pre-Rarotonga *Lawrence*, we can assume time is stretched and procedural for Bowie, providing an opportunity for reflection and world building. Much like Kyoto, Sydney, Berlin, Lausanne and even Bel Air, the set of *The Hunger* functions as a refuge for the artist.

Paul Mayersberg, co-screen writer for *The Man Who Fell to Earth*[52] and *Merry Christmas, Mr. Lawrence*, has observed that the pace and mechanics of screen acting most likely provided the fragile artist with a level of functional support and collaborative energy needed to navigate the early eighties, both his enforced disappearance and the tumultuous societal atmospherics. 'David did films as a sort of relaxation, where he didn't have to take charge of anything. He didn't have to be responsible. At all. He could put his life in the hands of the director, and I think he liked that.'[53]

The concept of what it means to be David Bowie had always been a 'collaborative project with no real beginning and no real end'.[54] Now on screen, within the set parameters of the frame and chemical permanence of the final print, he gave himself over to the process. In the hands of directors and teams of creatives, he was giving over authorship of this mystique. His body was no longer the performative extension of his own literary constructions; he was now giving his body – and his image with all its iconic connotations – to the performance of a text.

Coda

By the time I got to New York . . .[55]

Bowie would finish the shoot for *The Hunger* in August of 1982 with some pick-ups and exteriors in New York. Then came the call from Nagisa Ōshima: in three weeks' time he would be required in Rarotonga in the Cook Islands to prep for *Merry Christmas, Mr. Lawrence*. He would leave almost immediately, taking a well-earned break in the South Pacific to settle into island life and dose up on some early jump blues and rock 'n' roll 45s.

For Tony Scott, *The Hunger* was a commercial failure, and he wouldn't make another Hollywood film for three years. Technically, it stands up, as Bowie reflected to *Rolling Stone*, 'there's nothing that looks like it on the market.'[56] Certainly, no other vampires would look so damn good until Coppola's sumptuous rendition of *Bram Stoker's Dracula* in 1992. Scott would go on to direct films such as *Top Gun* (1986) and *True Romance* (1993), developing a manic directorial style known as 'chaos cinema'.[57] Meanwhile, Whitney Strieber, the author of the original novel, would claim to have been visited and abducted by aliens in upstate New York in December of 1985. The recounting of this episode would become the hugely successful book *Communion*,[58] a core text for UFO enthusiasts.

Bowie in reverse is a frustrating subject for historical analysis, especially mid-metamorphosis. We can only tease out such allusions as to the motivations of the multidisciplinary artist in and around a project like Scott's *The Hunger*. Mark Fisher's essay, 'Gothic Materialism', points to the horror of writers like Edgar Allen Poe and Artaud, of the creeping internalization of the Outside. Was David Bowie the actor bringing the Outside to bear on his performance, the enslavement of the undead an articulation of his own torment? Was the deathly shadow that pursued the character of John Blaylock also hanging heavy over Bowie the actor? Was *The Hunger* the bad medicine the artist needed to confront not only the 'terrible eighties' but also his own gothic interior? How much of his own sadness – of things lost, of promises broken and of souls departed – are embedded in the dark lusty frames of Scott's surrealist opera?

We can certainly read Bowie's performance as a knowing extension of *Scary Monsters*'s themes, particularly Bowie's concerted attempts at dethronement and erasure. And as Richard Fitch might have us do, it is hard to resist the notion that Miriam's entombment of John Blaylock is a handy metaphor for MainMan's stranglehold on Bowie the artist. So too, Bowie inhabiting the role of an undead spook hunting at the edges of a decaying metropolis, a canny curatorial move by an artist refreshing his catalogue of aliens and misfits.

Tony Scott would revisit the film's gothic textures in a 1999 TV series of the same name, in which he cast David Bowie as the performance artist Julian Priest, a role which is brimming with Bowie lore and art-world symbolism. 'I push the boundaries of suicide art, even death itself', he says at one point. 'I paid the price for immortality in more ways than one.'[59]

Notes

1. 'Bowie's Elephant Man Debut 40 Years Ago Today', davidbowie.com, published 29 July 2020, https://www.davidbowie.com/blog/2020/7/29/bowies-elephant-man-debut-40-years-ago-today.
2. Dylan Jones, *David Bowie: A Life* (New York: Crown Archetype, 2017), 312.
3. David Buckley, *Strange Fascination: David Bowie: The Definitive Story* (London: Virgin Books, 1999), 226.
4. Peter Doggett, *The Man Who Sold the World: David Bowie and the 1970s* (New York: Harper, 2012), 277.
5. David Bowie, 'David Bowie Reflects on His Career', interview by Kerry O'Brien, *7.30 Report,* Australian Broadcasting Corporation, 2004.
6. Chris O'Leary, *Rebel Rebel* (Winchester, UK; Washington, USA: Zero Books, 2015), 142.
7. Paul Trynka, *Starman* (New York: Little, Brown and Company, 2011), 361.
8. David Bowie, 'It's No Game (No.1)', recorded 1980, track 1 on *Scary Monsters and Super Creeps*, Bewley Bros. Music, Warner Bros. Music Ltd., 1980.
9. Richard Fitch, 'In This Age of Grand Allusion: Bowie, Nihilism and Meaning', in *David Bowie: Critical Perspectives*, ed. Eoin Devereux, Aileen Dillane and Martin Power (London: Routledge, 2015), 21.
10. Mark Fisher, 'Gothic Materialism', *Pli: The Warwick Journal of Philosophy* 12 (2001): 239.
11. David Bowie, interview by Brett Hansen, *Radio with Pictures,* TVNZ, 1981.
12. Whitley Stieber, *The Hunger* (New York: William Morrow & Co, 1981), 13.
13. *Will Kenny Everett Make It To 1980? Show,* 'The Kenny Everett Video Show', directed by David Mallett, aired 31 December 1979 on Thames TV.
14. Fisher, 'Gothic Materialism', 239.
15. *Will Kenny Everett Make It To 1980? Show,* 'The Kenny Everett Video Show'.
16. Timothy White, 'David Bowie: Who Am I This Time?' *Musician*, July 1990.
17. Fitch, 'In This Age of Grand Allusion', 29.
18. David Bowie, interview by Cees van Ede, *Cinevisie*, Dutch Broadcasting Corporation, 1983.
19. David Bowie, 'Telling Lies', recorded 1996, Arista BMG, downloadable single.
20. Georges T. Dodds, 'Piercing the Darkness: Undercover with Vampires in America Today (Review)', SF Site, published 1998, https://www.sfsite.com/12b/pier47.htm.
21. DVD commentary. *The Hunger*, directed by Tony Scott (1983; USA: Warner Home Video, 2004), DVD.
22. Ibid.

23　Iggy Pop and David Bowie, 'Funtime', recorded 1976, track 3 on *The Idiot*, RCA, 1977.
24　Jacqueline Furby, 'New Killer Star', *Cinema Journal* 57, no. 3 (Spring 2018): 167–74.
25　Bowie, 'It's No Game (No.1)'.
26　Tony Zanetta, 'The Week David Bowie Met Lou Reed, Iggy Pop and Andy Warhol: An Inside Look', Bedford + Bowery, published 11 January 2016, https://bedfordandbowery.com/2016/01/an-inside-look-at-the-week-david-bowie-met-lou-reed-iggy-pop-and-andy-warhol-in-nyc/.
27　Jason Pettigrew, 'Goth Inventors Bauhaus Recall the Night They Met David Bowie', Alternative Press, published 23 January 2018, https://www.altpress.com/features/bauhaus_undead_met_david_bowie_the_hunger/.
28　Paul Virillo, *City of Panic* (Oxford; New York: Berg, 2005), 86.
29　Pettigrew, 'Goth Inventors Bauhaus Recall the Night They Met David Bowie'.
30　Peter Murphy, David Haskins, Kevin Haskins and Daniel Ash, 'Bela Lugosi's Dead', recorded January 1979, single, Small Wonder, 1979.
31　DVD commentary, *The Hunger*.
32　O'Leary, *Rebel Rebel*, 161.
33　David Bowie, *Scary Monsters Interview Promo Disc*, RCA, 1980, promotional CD.
34　'New York Crime Rates 1960–2019', Disaster Centre, published 2019, https://www.disastercenter.com/crime/nycrime.htm.
35　Joe Strummer and Allen Ginsberg, 'Ghetto Defendant', recorded 1981, track 4, side 2 on *Combat Rock*, CBS, 1982.
36　Alex Sharpe, 'Scary Monsters: The Hopeful Undecidability of David Bowie (1947–2016)', *Law and Humanities* 11, no. 2 (2017): 232.
37　Michel Foucault, *The Birth of the Clinic,* trans. A. M. Sheridan (London: Taylor & Francis, 2003), 171.
38　Sharpe, *Scary Monsters*, 231.
39　Fisher, 'Gothic Materialism', 241.
40　Bowie, *Scary Monsters Interview Promo Disc*.
41　William S. Burroughs, *The Adding Machine: Collected Essays* (London: John Calder, 1985).
42　Artaud, quoted in Martin Esslin, *Artaud* (London: J. Calder, 1976), 37.
43　Michel Foucault, *Discipline and Punish: The Birth of the Prison*, trans. Alan Sheridan (London: Peregrine, 1987), 198.
44　Fisher, 'Gothic Materialism', 242.
45　Ibid., 234.
46　Leonid Andreyev, 'Lazarus', in *Leonid Andreyev: Selected Stories*, trans. Dmitry Fadeyev (Boston: The Stratford Company, 1918), 10.

47 Katherine M. Ramsland, *Piercing the Darkness: Undercover with Vampires in American Today* (New York: Harper Prism, 1998), 318.
48 Fitch, 'In This Age of Grand Allusion', 24.
49 *Merry Christmas, Mr. Lawrence*, directed by Nagisa Ōshima (1983; Japan, New Zealand, United Kingdom: Palace Pictures).
50 Fitch, 'In This Age of Grand Allusion', 24.
51 DVD commentary, *The Hunger*.
52 *The Man Who Fell to Earth*, directed by Nicolas Roeg (1976; United Kingdom: British Lion Films).
53 Mayersberg, quoted in Jones, *David Bowie*, 295.
54 Elizabeth McCarthy, 'Telling Lies: The Interviews of David Bowie', *Celebrity Studies* 10, no.1 (2019): 89–103.
55 David Bowie, 'Lazarus', recorded 2015, track 3 on *Blackstar*, ISO Columbia, 2016.
56 Kurt Loder, 'Straight Time', *Rolling Stone*, 12 May 1983.
57 Steven Shaviro, 'Post-Continuity: An Introduction', in *Post-Cinema: Theorizing 21st Century Film*, ed. Shane Denson and Julie Leyza (Falmer: REFRAME Books, 2016).
58 Whitley Strieber, *Communion: A True Story* (New York: Beech Tree Books, 1987).
59 *The Hunger*, season 2, episode 1, 'Sanctuary', directed by Tony Scott, aired 10 September 1999, on Showtime.

7

'Who can I be now?'

Codpieces, carnival and the blurring of identity in *Labyrinth*

Brendan Black

Introduction

For David Bowie, the 1980s were a particularly fertile period in a cinematic acting career which, while it 'hardly qualifies as brilliant',[1] was certainly diverse. Among his catalogue is *Labyrinth* (Jim Henson, 1986), a film which failed on release but gained appreciation and fans later on, both for the film itself and for Bowie's role (and, as shall be discussed, his crotch). The creation of the enigmatic character Jareth the Goblin King became one of Bowie's most iconic roles, gaining the film a cult status and winning Bowie a new generation of fans.

As Peter Doggett states, Bowie was often self-conscious about his film roles, believing that audiences were always watching David Bowie rather than the characters he was portraying; music instead gave him a chance to 'un-become' himself and present various facets of his personality.[2] The first step in this process of 'un-becoming' was the adoption of a new identity and name in 1965 when David Jones joined the R&B-inspired band *The Lower Third* as 'Davy Jones'. After discovering that this name was already being used by two other singers – an American and a Brit – Jones instead took on the Bowie stage name.[3] Before he had even unveiled Ziggy Stardust in 1972, Jones was already concealing himself behind the performance persona of

David Bowie, playing against and even mocking the notion of authenticity, which is seen as a valuable quality for rock performers.[4] Part of the issue here also seemed to be that Bowie admitted to being a 'consummate faker' and that rock 'n' roll is 'so full of liars',[5] pulling back the curtain on apparently authentic rock musicians.

Despite the attitude regarding authenticity, many rock musicians have changed their names in an effort to adopt a new, perhaps more rock-oriented, persona, either before they found success or shortly afterwards: fellow glam-rocker Marc Bolan changed his name from Mark Feld, and former *The Rolling Stones* members Brian Jones and Bill Wyman were born Lewis Brian Hopkins-Jones and William George Perks Jr, respectively.[6] Bowie therefore is not alone among rock musicians in the use of different identities, although the lengths he went to in constructing new personae in the 1970s are likely unmatched.

Central to the thesis of this chapter will be the use and understanding of *persona* in regards to performance, as defined by Philip Auslander.[7] Helping to delineate the relationship between Bowie and identity, particularly in relation to his role in *Labyrinth*, is the work of Russian literary theorist Mikhail Bakhtin on *carnival* and *mask*, born from his analyses of the novels of Dostoevsky and Rabelais. Bakhtin's carnival has become an effective tool in research on art, theatre, film, music and even video games, which can likewise help to illuminate Bowie's acting and creation of character within *Labyrinth* through his use of persona and the *carnivalesque* nature of Bowie himself.

The motivations for using Bakhtin's notions of carnival and mask as theoretical anchors are many, as they assist in understanding Bowie and his works due to his use of metaphorical (and physical) masks in his creation of alternate personae such as Ziggy Stardust, Aladdin Sane and the Thin White Duke. Carnival has therefore been employed several times in discussions of his work. Two notable examples include Brad Erickson's 2016 exploration of space imagery in the works of George Clinton and Bowie, describing Bowie's modelling of 'white imaginations of evolutionary transcendence', contrasted against Clinton's 'black carnivalesque seeking liberation from lived inequality',[8] and Alison Blair's 2015 examination of the counter-hegemonic personae of Marc Bolan and Bowie, which questioned 'norms of identity, authenticity, gender and sexuality'.[9]

Equal parts suave and savage, androgynous yet overtly heterosexual, Jareth was a key film role where the boundary between actor, performer and character was blurred, as it is almost impossible to see Jareth without also seeing David Bowie. By *Labyrinth*'s release in 1986, Bowie had become a master of creating public personae, before tearing them down and creating new ones, layering these identities on top of David Bowie and David Jones, and always leaving open the question: 'Who is Bowie?' This process of disguising any notion of selfhood occurred not only in his guise as a singer but also in his many film roles, which also utilized and relied upon the construction of his star image – a strategy put to excellent use in the promotional poster for *Labyrinth* (Figure 7.1). As will be discussed, *Labyrinth* was one film where his acting, singing and song writing would work to obscure the boundaries between the mask of David Bowie and the mask of Jareth.

'You would be wonderful in this film'

After the financial and critical success of the puppetry fantasy film *The Dark Crystal* (1982), director Jim Henson was sharing a limo with Brian Froud, the British fantasy illustrator, and Brian's wife, Wendy Midener Froud, the sculptor and puppet maker, both of whom had worked on *The Dark Crystal*. Despite their exhaustion, the trio seemed keen to work together again on another film, and their discussion eventually settled on two important

FIGURE 7.1 *Promotional poster for 'Labyrinth'*. © *The Jim Henson Company*.

factors: this new film would feature goblins; and it would be set inside a labyrinth.[10]

Henson had originally envisaged the antagonist Jareth the Goblin King as a puppet but later realized that having a human play the role would 'change the film's whole musical style'.[11] His first choice was the musician Sting who had portrayed a villain in David Lynch's 1984 science-fiction epic *Dune*, and Henson had reportedly also been considering the likes of Michael Jackson, David Lee Roth, Rod Stewart, Mick Jagger, Roger Daltrey, Freddie Mercury, Prince, Ted Nugent and, of course, Bowie.[12]

What eventually swayed Henson to offer Jareth to Bowie, according to Henson's puppeteer son Brian, was that Bowie was clearly comfortable on stage and had no fear of being 'completely vulnerable';[13] Henson's other son, John, stated that while Sting was 'happening *now* . . . David Bowie is an artist, he's got longevity'.[14] In a personal note sent from Henson to Bowie, the director humbly expressed his feelings on the 'rough' nature of the script, on which he was looking forward to hearing Bowie's reactions, stating, 'you would be wonderful in this film.'[15] Bowie's 'audition' had already occurred several years before, when Jim and Brian Henson saw him play John Merrick in *The Elephant Man* on Broadway in 1980, causing Jim to remark: 'You know what, he really has got his chops.'[16]

The plot of *Labyrinth* centres on Sarah, a precocious and self-centred sixteen-year-old girl who spends her time daydreaming and pretending to be the heroine of fantasy tales. Tasked with once again minding her young half-brother Toby, who screams and remains inconsolable by her, she yearns to escape her predicament by naïvely imploring Jareth the Goblin King to take Toby away from her – which he does. Realizing she has made a terrible mistake, she pleads with Jareth to release Toby, and he states the only way she'll get him back is if she solves his labyrinth within thirteen hours. Along the way, Sarah meets an array of characters who either help or hinder her in her quest, and Jareth constantly complicates her task by subjecting her to puzzles and danger. Eventually, Sarah triumphs against Jareth and the labyrinth, rescuing Toby and making it back home unscathed.

The use of a labyrinth (as a device and the film itself) metaphorically frames Sarah's psychological journey towards adulthood. As Ilanah Shiloh states, a labyrinth

> presumes a double perspective: those imprisoned inside, whose vision ahead and behind is severely constricted, are disoriented and terrified, whereas those who view it from outside or from above – as a diagram – admire its structural sophistication and artistry. What you see depends on where you are.[17]

When Sarah views the labyrinth from above, she states that 'it doesn't look that far' to the castle beyond the goblin city where Toby is imprisoned, yet she can only truly judge the distance, complexity and inherent eccentricities of the labyrinth once she is inside it. Only after Sarah has successfully made her way into the centre of the labyrinth and overcome every obstacle that Jareth has placed in front of her can she see that he cannot win against her.

After a casting process that took almost nine months, the role of Sarah was finally awarded to fifteen-year-old Jennifer Connelly, who by that stage had already appeared in films by Sergio Leone and Dario Argento and had worked as a child model.[18] Bowie formally signed on to play Jareth on 15 February 1985, only two months before shooting was set to begin.[19] Bowie stated that he wanted Jareth to be a 'petulant rock star',[20] and in the film he gives the impression that Jareth is not the Goblin King by choice but has instead been tasked with overseeing the land. Bowie even stated as much: 'One feels that he's rather reluctantly inherited the position of Goblin King, as though he would really rather be – I don't know – down in Soho or something.'[21] This is a very apt suggestion given that Soho was, according to director Julien Temple (*Absolute Beginners*, 1986), a 'second home' for Bowie during the 1980s,[22] further strengthening the link between Jareth and Bowie.

Brian Froud recalled that Bowie was perfect for the role, given that he understood the world in which Jareth lives: 'There was so much you didn't have to say in dialogue when you had David Bowie as the Goblin King. He was almost a mythical presence in himself.'[23] In a sense, it can be said that Bowie was a carnival character beyond the film – with his regular embrace of mask and persona in the construction of new identities – illustrating why the actor and character were seen as so symbiotic and why Bakhtin's concepts are key to understanding Bowie and *Labyrinth*.

Bakhtin, carnival and mask

The creation of alternate personae and engaging layers of identity is akin to donning a mask during the celebration of carnival, in which people are free to forget the drudgery of their lives, at least for a short time, and pretend to be someone else, even a different gender – or, in regards to *Labyrinth*, for rock stars to become Goblin Kings. The notion of carnival (also sometimes referred to as *carnivalesque*) was explored in detail in the twentieth century by Mikhail Mikhailovich Bakhtin, the Russian philosopher and literary theorist, who developed the concept in his 1929 book *Problems of Dostoevsky's Creative Art* (republished in 1963 with many additions as *Problems of Dostoevsky's Poetics*). The book examines the work of Russian novelist Fyodor Dostoevsky (1821–81), in particular his use of polyphony, described as: 'A plurality of independent and unmerged voices and consciousnesses, a genuine polyphony of fully valid voices', which exist not in an objective world created by the author but in their own worlds and with their own consciousnesses.[24]

Poetics is perhaps best known for Bakhtin's notion of carnival in relation to Dostoevsky's works, which 'could not be adequately comprehended unless this ancient folk-carnival basis was fully acknowledged and appreciated'.[25] Bakhtin defined carnival as

> a pageant without footlights and without a division into performers and spectators. In carnival everyone is an active participant, everyone communes in the carnival act. Carnival is not contemplated and, strictly speaking, not even performed; its participants *live* in it, they live by its laws as long as those laws are in effect; that is, they live a *carnivalistic life*.[26] (emphasis in original)

Bakhtin delineated carnival into four main categories which describe the suspension of any laws, restrictions or social hierarchies that are in force at non-carnival times of year:[27] *free and familiar contact among people, eccentricity, carnivalistic mésalliances* and *profanation*. Framing the entire celebration of carnival is the *primary carnivalistic act*, referred to as *the mock crowning and subsequent decrowning of the carnival king*. The lack of division between performers and spectators, the embrace of carnival as a lived-in experience and the temporary nature of carnival permeate Bakhtin's categories, demonstrating how carnival came to represent life itself, with its beginning and end, and how participants could experience 'life turned inside out',[28] if only for a defined period.

The first category, free and familiar contact among people, refers to the cessation of hierarchical barriers between people, such as employers and employees or leaders and their subjects, so that people can address each other on friendly and intimate terms. Carnival is a celebration where participants are no longer separated due to barriers such as class, age or gender and masks obscure their identities and quell their inhibitions. They are able to interact and connect with each other on levels usually classed as taboo (physically and mentally), strengthening social bonds and reducing social isolation.[29] As shall be illustrated later, these elements come to the fore in *Labyrinth*, particularly during the 'Magic Dance' scene.

The second category, eccentricity, relates to carnival participants being allowed to express the latent aspects of their nature – even normally unacceptable ones – without fear of judgement. In fact, these behaviours are celebrated and encouraged, as the corporeality of mankind – eating, shitting, copulating – is to be extolled, not shied away from. Bakhtin defined this as *grotesque realism*, which came to a high point in the work of the French writer François Rabelais (*c.* 1483–1553), after which the 'official culture of seriousness' represented by mediaeval church culture won out against this grotesque realism and ushered in the Renaissance.[30] Each character in

Labyrinth (in particular, Sir Didymus the fox, Hoggle the goblin and Jareth) expresses eccentricity in certain ways, adding to the playful and subversive nature of the film.

The third category of carnivalistic mésalliances concerns the coming together of opposites: 'the sacred with the profane, the lofty with the low, the great with the insignificant, the wise with the stupid'.[31] Through removing the barriers between these opposites, carnival participants shine a light on the arbitrary nature of societal conventions that usually keep them separated and come together as equals.[32] *Labyrinth* is centred around a carnivalistic mésalliance between the two main characters of Sarah and Jareth, due to their sexes, ages, desires and goals.

Bakhtin's final carnival category, profanation, centres on enjoying and praising the blasphemous, the vulgar, the improper and the primitive – even the acts of reproduction and waste expulsion – to the point where the sacred can be ridiculed. Given the stranglehold that the church had over people in mediaeval Europe, carnival was a time of escape and resistance where this 'social safety valve' allowed the populace to 'let off steam, by adopting carnival masks'[33] in an officially sanctioned event where the church relinquished its power for a short time. Like eccentricity, profanation is a regular theme throughout *Labyrinth*, framing the relationship between Sarah and Jareth, as well as many of the other characters.

As a further facet of profanation, Bakhtin describes other important aspects of carnival, termed carnivalistic acts. The primary act is the mock crowning and subsequent decrowning of the carnival king, expressing the central theme of carnival, that of birth, death and subsequent renewal, and reflecting the temporary nature of this subversive festivity.[34] Like carnival itself, *Labyrinth* is focused around this primary carnivalistic act, its two stages occurring at the beginning and conclusion of the film, thus bringing an end to the film's carnival nature.

Bakhtin further explored and expanded upon carnival in his 1940 work *Rabelais in the History of Realism* (later titled *Rabelais and His World* for the 1968 English translation), where he examined the use of the mask during carnival times:

> The mask is connected with the joy of change and reincarnation ... with the merry negation of uniformity and similarity; it rejects conformity to oneself. The mask is related to transition, metamorphoses, the violation of natural boundaries, to mockery and familiar nicknames.[35]

Bakhtin's work on and interest in folk culture – 'that which pulls away from the centre'[36] – stemmed somewhat from his own marginalization by the Stalinist regime, which had its roots in a system which preached 'but also practiced openness, hybridization, and dehierarchization'[37] in text and culture during the 1920s, becoming one which was very much the opposite a short time later. Bakhtin's examination of Rabelais's work, in particular, mirrored his own desire to 'find gaps in the walls' in Stalinist Russia, where the static rules imposed from above conflicted with those below who desired for change, highlighting the disparity between old and new, official and unofficial.[38] The five novels which *Rabelais and His World* examines, the collected works known as *The Life of Gargantua and Pantagruel* (Rabelais, c. 1532–64), tell the story of two giants, father and son, and is full of bawdy, scatological humour which reconceives 'the human body in the face of Christian views and temporality'.[39] Through Bakhtin's own work, he uncovered in Rabelais's novel the subtext of carnival[40] – which 'is not limited to specific events but serves as an image of the will of the people apart from any social or political structure'[41] – thus opening up a new way of looking at identity, particularly when the need and urge to conform to society's rules has been pushed aside, either fully or temporarily.

Bakhtin and Bowie

The major reason it is complicated to discuss identity in relation to Bowie (or, more importantly, to Jones) is that there is no 'defined and stable position'[42] from which to assess this identity; as Shelton Waldrep states, Jones is regularly '[performing] himself performing an alter ego who himself frequently performs as someone else'.[43] Philip Auslander characterizes the performer in rock music as having three layers of identity: 'the real person (the performer as human being), the performance persona (the performer's self-presentation), and the character (a figure portrayed in a song text)',[44] a strategy regularly employed by Jones in both music and film.

Before taking on Jareth in *Labyrinth*, Bowie had appeared in films spanning a range of genres, with varying degrees of success, both in terms of their critical and public acceptance and his performance. Bowie's relationship to Bakhtin's concepts of carnival and mask in his on-screen characters stand out in two of his pre-*Labyrinth* roles. First, in *Yellowbeard* (Mel Damski, 1983), Bowie has a cameo in the role of a man who terrorizes a woman while dressed as a shark, in essence showing Jones playing Bowie playing a man playing a shark – probably the greatest number of masks ever worn by Jones. The scene draws on Bowie's transgressive status in his utterance of 'Shall I meet you in the pump room, sir?' inferring a homosexual encounter with his boss, imbuing the scene with eccentricity due to the sight of the rock star wearing a shark fin on his back, only two months after his album *Let's Dance* brought him immense commercial success.

Second, in *Jazzin' for Blue Jean* (Julien Temple, 1984), Bowie plays two roles: Vic, a loser who tries to impress a woman by telling her that he knows her favourite rock star, the vain and paranoid Screaming Lord Byron, also played by Bowie. The short film draws on his status as a rock star but also lampoons it, and in terms of the mask, different layers of identity are at play for each character, as Byron's singing and dancing align him closely with the performance persona of Bowie, while Vic's lack of success with women flies against the stereotype of the rock star. While Vic and Byron never converse within the same shot, such as with the aid of visual effects, there are images and dialogue which show these two contrasting characters coming together in a carnivalistic mésalliance, either diegetically through their direct interactions (and the use of a mirror and body double) or through their characters simultaneously occupying the cinema frame in various forms. Two examples are as follows: Vic, working as an odd-jobs man, erecting a poster of Byron, essentially showing Bowie in the mask of Vic promoting Bowie in the mask of Byron; and Byron crouching in a corner and Vic being reflected in a mirror next to him, the two masks of Jones seen simultaneously. The appeal of *Jazzin'* is that it is not only entertaining but also presents Bowie in conflicting roles/personae, never taking itself (or Bowie) too seriously and demonstrating his penchant for comedy.

After he first unveiled Ziggy Stardust in 1972, Bowie challenged dominant (heteronormative) cultures, institutions and power relations through his use of alternate and transgressive personae,[45] disrupting the masculine, heterosexual ideal of the rock star.[46] In doing so, Bowie influenced other musicians who grew up listening to his music by liberating them from sexual and gender norms and inspiring them to forge their own paths and identities.[47] Bakhtin's carnival and his notion of the mask are therefore useful tools to analyse Bowie's construction of personae and the deeper issues of defining his identity, as they perfectly illustrate the 'dissolving of the boundaries of self through the physical or spiritual commingling of self and other',[48] a prime function of the celebration of carnival. I contend and will illustrate that the world of *Labyrinth* – and even the utterances and gestures of Bowie within the film – is ideally suited for analysis using Bakhtin's concepts of carnival and mask, given the parallels that can be drawn 'between the putting on of the carnival mask, and . . . Bowie's adoption of a range of personae'.[49]

Labyrinth, Bowie and carnival

Within *Labyrinth* are a range of symbols, images and artefacts which give it depth and take it beyond the mere realms of a children's film. Adding to this depth is the inclusion of David Bowie, who for many decades of his career engaged in the adoption of personae and the physical and metaphorical wearing of masks, as well as revering the eccentric and the profane in his songs, making Bakhtin's concepts of carnival and mask – and their celebration of the mad, the unorthodox and the contrary – an effective tool for examination. While Bowie doesn't reach the nuanced or expressive heights of his character Jack Celliers in *Merry Christmas, Mr. Lawrence*, as will be discussed, Bowie at least adds a depth to Jareth above and beyond his status as a music icon.

In the 'Magic Dance' scene, Bowie's delivery, gestures and demeanour perfectly illustrate Bakhtin's first carnival category, namely free and familiar contact among people. 'Magic Dance' is perhaps the most well-known piece of music from *Labyrinth*, being the nineteenth most downloaded Bowie track in the UK.[50] The song is based around nursery rhyme lyrics, with its most famous lines lifted from an 'old playground nonsense-chant' featured in the Cary Grant/Shirley Temple film *The Bachelor and the Bobbysoxer*[51] (Irving Ries, 1947):

You remind me of the babe.
(What babe?)
The babe with the power.
(What power?)
The power of voodoo.
(Who do?)
You do.
(Do what?)
Remind me of the babe.

While the main contact is technically between a human and puppets – forty-eight puppets and twelve costumed humans, to be exact – it is the cheeriest and the least sinister of the songs sung by Bowie in *Labyrinth* and one in which Jareth appears to be enjoying himself, a rare occurrence in a film about turning babies into goblins and taking a young girl's innocence. It demonstrates free and familiar contact among people as every character within the song participates as Jareth sings and dances, and the usually unequal power relationship between Jareth and his goblins dissolves as king and servants come together as equals in the song. The goblins also provide devoted care to Toby, as does Jareth, who cradles the baby in his arms and throws him (or a doll) into the air.

Despite the contentious parenting advice ('slap that baby, set him free') and the ticking clock that will turn Toby into a goblin forever, it is a sweet scene where there is free and familiar contact between Jareth and the goblins, who come across as a little less frightening and appear to be motivated more by carnival than by adding Toby to the goblin horde. Bowie's body language and gestures within the number confirm this as he sways and swaggers around the set, staff in hand and his blonde mane swishing to and fro. At one point he looks just off camera as he bops and sings, and then breaks the fourth wall as he places his outstretched fingers on his face, feigning distress (Figure 7.2), and then punctuates the lyrics with a pointed finger and a

FIGURE 7.2 *What kind of magic spell to use?* © The Jim Henson Company.

FIGURE 7.3 *The finger point through the fourth wall.* © The Jim Henson Company.

wink towards the audience (Figure 7.3), a reminder of his performance of 'Starman' on *Top of the Pops* in 1972.[52]

In this moment, David Jones removes the outer mask of Jareth and reverts to the mask of David Bowie, collapsing the difference between music video and performance. He also stretches out his arms as a sign of enthusiasm, as well as despair, not knowing 'what kind of magic spell to use' for baby Toby. The innocence of the scene is lessened somewhat, however, when viewing Bowie's crotch bulge, reminding us once again of Bowie's status as rock icon and his transgressive, often eccentric, nature.

Bakhtin's category of eccentricity is at the heart of *Labyrinth*, as the land portrayed is one where nothing is at it seems, and the characters have no real fear of expressing forms of violence against each other. Another interpretation relates to the unconventional, strange and perverse personified by Bowie, and his sense of Otherness that he exploited in his many music personae. 'As Jareth, Bowie wears a series of spectacular New Romantic outfits, which combine foppish retro frills with more than a hint of the BDSM dungeon',[53] while his tight pants 'emphasize his genitals, a strategy that makes spectators highly aware both of their own eroticized gaze and of his nonchalant display'.[54]

This results in an antagonist who is equal parts frightening and powerful, but also camp and beautiful. There is very little that is hideous about his appearance, as only his actions and words indicate his sinister intents, and in the 'Magic Dance' scene he gives the impression of being a glammed-up horse-riding instructor (Figure 7.4). Rosalind Galt asserts that 'Bowie's Jareth is sexy regardless of the role he ultimately plays in the narrative',[55] which strips him of some of his physical danger while emphasizing that his main weapon is his 'aggressive phallus', the term used by Brian Henson to describe Bowie's codpiece in *Labyrinth*.[56] This again blurs the line between Bowie as rock performer and actor while also trading on his own sex appeal and iconicity, helping to create one of cinema's most erotic and eccentric villains.

Bowie demonstrates this eccentricity in myriad ways in *Labyrinth*, mainly due to his wearing of the mask, as 'such manifestations as parodies, caricatures, grimaces, eccentric postures, and comic gestures are per se derived from the mask'.[57] While Bowie turned down the role of a Bond villain for *A View to a Kill* (John Glen, 1985), saying he 'didn't want to spend five months watching my double fall off mountains',[58] he appears to channel them with his use of *grotesque laughter*, which is laughter filled with bitterness that takes on a mocking, cynical and 'satanic' form.[59] Jareth's laughs are usually at the expense of someone else's pain or misfortune (mostly Sarah's), often followed by stunned silence from the goblins, who (apart from in the 'Magic Dance' scene) must usually be prompted to laugh due to their slow-wittedness and fear of their king. While Sarah displays certain

FIGURE 7.4 *The 'aggressive phallus'. © The Jim Henson Company.*

aspects of eccentricity, such as her playing at being a character in a fantasy at the beginning of the film, it is Jareth's and the labyrinth's pronounced eccentricities which contrast him and them against the young Sarah.

For this reason, the main carnivalistic mésalliance centres on the characters of Sarah and Jareth, who inhabit two different worlds, are decades apart in age and have an unequal power relationship. Yet as the film progresses, the emotional distance between them lessens as Sarah appears to fall for Jareth's seductive charms but then realizes she can beat the labyrinth, rescue Toby and defeat Jareth, and Jareth comes to understand Sarah, her world and her motivations.

Further demonstrating an example of mésalliances is a shot near the beginning of the film showing an open scrapbook in Sarah's bedroom (Figure 7.5). Giving a glimpse of her backstory, newspaper clippings point to Sarah's mother, Linda Williams, being a theatre actress, helping to explain Sarah's fascination with the medium. On closer inspection, the unmistakeable visage of Bowie is noticeable, canoodling with Linda, under headlines 'WILLIAMS LOVE, IT'S ALL OVER' and 'LINDA WILLIAMS: "ON-OFF" ROMANCE! BACK TOGETHER?' In one of the photos, Bowie's hairstyle is somewhat reminiscent of Jareth's, although in the other two photos it is shorter and styled akin to that of Thomas Jerome Newton.

Given that Sarah, a sixteen-year-old girl, is being pursued by an older man who seems to represent her father and tempts her in not-too-subtle sexual ways, and that she has to fight back against him and her own feelings towards him, the film has clear references to Freudian psychoanalytic theory. Even though much of Freud's work has been questioned, the relationship between Sarah and Jareth involves obvious Freudian undertones, having at its core the female version of the Oedipus Complex, 'involving the daughter's love for her father, jealousy toward the mother, and blame of the mother for depriving her of a penis'.[60] While Sarah and Jareth's relationship

FIGURE 7.5 *Bowie the father?* © *The Jim Henson Company.*

may not perfectly fit this precise Freudian interpretation, reading it through Freud's theory adds further weight to this carnivalistic mésalliance and helps to illuminate their dynamic, even if the implications (a girl in love with her father; a father trying to bed his daughter) are quite salacious for a children's film. It also raises several questions prompted by the film: Is Jareth actually Sarah's real father? If so, does she know about it? Or is Jareth an imagined personification of the father she wishes she had?

The film itself does not definitively answer these questions, although the presence of Bowie/Jareth in the photos with Sarah's mother is likely an acknowledgement by Henson that Sarah does know who he is, which complicates her feelings towards him; after all, if the photos had not been included in the scene, then this Freudian interpretation would be far less obvious. Another possible reading, based on the work of Carl Jung, is that Jareth is a *father-imago*, a psychic residue of her experiences with her father or father figures,[61] and Sarah has essentially projected her feelings about her (real or wished-for) father onto Jareth. These opposites of Sarah and Jareth are actually more alike than Sarah may wish to admit – strengthening the mésalliance – as both are headstrong, expect the world to change for them and won't stop until they win.

The second main instance of carnivalistic mésalliance appears in the ballroom scene. Having been drugged by a tainted peach (itself an uncomfortable image given the age of Sarah and its allusions to the date-rape drug Rohypnol), she finds herself in a surreal ballroom populated by people dressed in opulent costumes and all concealing themselves behind masks (except for Sarah and Jareth), who engage in grotesque laughter and sneer at the pubescent girl; the whole scene is charged with erotic and phallic imagery – the adult world beckoning to Sarah. Bowie, wearing the mask of Jareth, brings to the character a 'transgressive sexuality' which is 'bold and textually excessive in a children's film',[62] heightening the contrast between the older Bowie and the adolescent Connelly.

Sarah searches for Jareth yet cannot find him, and he grins over his games and toying with the girl. Through them are seen the intense, sexualized stare of Jareth and the open-mouthed, doe-faced innocence of Sarah; even with little knowledge of Bowie and his history, the disparity between the characters and what they represent is obvious. Nothing is said between them in the scene – which is accompanied by the song 'As the World Falls Down' – apart from Bowie lip-syncing to the words, 'But I'll be there for you, as the world falls down', locating the sequence between film and music video. As Bowie expertly leads Connelly in a dance, the sexual symbology of the scene becomes even clearer, with Jareth/Bowie throwing his head back and examining Sarah closely, his breaking of the fourth wall doing likewise for the audience. This carnivalistic mésalliance reaches its zenith when it appears likely that Sarah will finally fall under Jareth's (sexual) spell.

Yet at the end of the scene, Sarah senses that she does not belong in this world and remembers her quest to save Toby, turning her back on this fantasy world; Galt states that it is possible to read this as Sarah affirming 'that looking after babies is her duty and that she must accept parental authority and a reproductive role'.[63] However, Galt acknowledges that other female-authored interpretations see it also as an emphasis on Sarah's agency and a pivotal emergence of her own feminism.[64] Interpreting Sarah's decision is therefore a matter for debate, as she comes to the realization that she is in control of her own destiny, and that doesn't necessarily mean she has accepted a future role as a mother, nor does it mean that she wishes to remain innocent and virginal forever – she is, after all, still a girl. It is because of her own eccentricity – calling upon the mythical Goblin King, for example – that her half-brother was taken away from her, but it is because of her intelligence, cunning and burgeoning maturity that she acknowledges she still needs to win him back, weakening this carnivalistic mésalliance through expressing ridicule of and having a profane disregard for Jareth's power.

In this way, profanation informs much of the behaviour of the inhabitants of the labyrinth, who live in a world where transgressions against their king can find them cast into 'the bog of eternal stench', a cesspool whose name negates the need for further explanation. Yet, as described above, the best example of profanation comes from the film's treatment of Sarah's progress towards womanhood, which is the main enticement offered by Jareth and represented by the glass balls he plays with (itself a fitting metaphor) and the floating bubbles he projects towards Sarah, offering her a glimpse of the future she could have if she accepts him.

Henson was reportedly quite concerned about the sexual connotations in the relationship between the main characters,[65] even though it adds a depth to the film over and above that of the surface plot and takes it beyond the realms of most children's films. It is difficult to view Jareth as the Goblin King without seeing the rock star beneath him, so while it is understandable if Sarah is repulsed by his actions yet is attracted to him sexually (after all, this is still David Bowie on the screen), Sarah as a character is still a construction of Jim Henson's, effectively making not a girl but a man's idea of a girl. Brian Henson stated that the famed codpiece – that 'aggressive phallus' – had to be reduced for the film as it was too large, although Jareth's representation of male sexuality (intertwined with Bowie's) certainly remained.[66]

Another example of profanation occurs at the beginning of the film, when the themes of sex and sexual maturation are discussed openly by Sarah's stepmother who states that 'you should have dates at your age', inferring that Sarah is not interested in boys or sex. Jareth's later attempts to woo Sarah come across almost as predatory, as is his overall treatment of and obsession with her, yet she resists all attempts by him to win her over. The relationship between Sarah and Jareth is unnerving when viewed through post-1980s eyes, as is his drugging of her with a tainted peach in order to defeat her, which highlights the power imbalance between the characters – though this soon shifts and wanes as the kingly crown slips.

The primary carnivalistic act of the mock crowning and subsequent decrowning of the carnival king occurs in two stages at opposite ends of the film. The crowning arises when Jareth first appears (see Figure 7.6): he stands resolutely with his clenched hands on his hips, dressed solely in a black leather outfit with oversized lapels and a thin, billowing cape blowing in the breeze; his hair is a teased and styled bouffant with two long manes flowing down the front; and his eyebrows are dark and pointed, and his eyelids are covered in blue eye shadow. There is no jarring sensation that the costume, hair and make-up seem out of place or caricature-like, primarily because it is David Bowie who exists under them, perhaps reigniting or reimagining one of his 1970s personae for a new age and audience.

Announcing Jareth in such a striking way instantly gives the audience a sense of his power and importance, highlighted by his stance and intense stare at Sarah. At her question 'You're him, aren't you? You're the Goblin King', he tilts his head to the left, exposing his neck, a sign that a person is listening and interested and which is also used as a disarming device (Figure 7.7).[67] Despite this gesture, there is no doubt that Jareth is in control of the situation; Sarah's plea for her brother to be returned is answered by Jareth folding his arms and dropping his chin in annoyance, the remark of 'what's said is said' delivered sulkily by Bowie, like a spoilt rock star denied his drugs. Jareth scowls and derides Sarah throughout the scene, his utterance of 'Go back to your room, play with your toys and costumes' said mockingly, the words punctuated by Bowie's sly smile, the same one that greeted audiences in the movie poster (Figure 7.1), declaring the arrival of a new, filmic Bowie persona.

FIGURE 7.6 *The mock crowning of the carnival king.* © *The Jim Henson Company.*

FIGURE 7.7 *The disarming Jareth.* © *The Jim Henson Company.*

The purpose of the scene is twofold: on the surface, it sets up Sarah with her quest to save her brother; while in the subtext, Jareth offers her the chance to become an adult, except that, 'this is not a gift for an ordinary girl who takes care of the screaming baby'. Bowie's coy smile on the statement of the last two words further cements the symbolism of the line, which mocks Sarah and assumes she will not give up the trappings of youth and innocence that fill her bedroom; she will not accept what Bowie the man and musician represent to his fans. From a Bakhtinian perspective, explicit in the crowning of the carnival king is not only his later decrowning but also the entirely mock nature of the event; the carnival king has no real power, something Sarah only discovers at the end of her quest. Sarah's life has teetered on the edge of carnival and all that it can offer her, yet she instead resists it.

Their final confrontation is marked by Jareth's attempts to exercise his power, underscored by Bowie's depiction of vulnerability and the 'petulant rock star'. His facial expressions and gestures, with head bent forward and body moving in and then back from Sarah, highlight his aggression and accusation, as he lists everything he has done for her and everything he can give to her – a futile plea for her to embrace her sexual awakening, perhaps sensing that his power is diminishing.

The decrowning of the Goblin King follows Sarah's realization of her own innate power, and Jareth throws the bubble in his hand (Figure 7.8) – a symbol of everything he can offer her – into the air, and he withers and disappears. Sarah exits the world of the labyrinth and returns to her home where Toby is sleeping safely and soundly. In Bakhtinian terms, by offering himself to Sarah, Jareth attempts to push carnival past its utility as a safety valve of simply letting off steam in order to reach a utopia where 'carnival envisages a better way for society to be organized',[68] though with Jareth still at the centre. The symbolism behind this reflects Sarah's desire (and the desire

FIGURE 7.8 *The subsequent decrowning of the carnival king.* © The Jim Henson Company.

of the adults for her) to become an adult, yet she is not ready for this chaotic (carnival) way of life, and thus she spurns it. In doing so, diegetically she rejects Jareth, yet she also rejects everything for which Bowie as performer, rock star and sexual icon is a sign – and the carnival comes to an end.

Conclusion

Bowie's capacity to confound expectations of him and to fit perfectly into a film role which has at its core Otherness, the mysterious and the magical are some of the reasons why Jareth and *Labyrinth* have gained in popularity over the years, while interest in several of his other roles and films has waned. His camp, provocative and utterly sexual rendering of Jareth made the character instantly iconic, with an appeal that has lasted over the decades for much more than his bulging crotch or the fantastical nature of his wig and costume. *Labyrinth* deserves to be recognized as an excellent example of Bowie's skills as an actor and songwriter – and further supporting his status as a pop icon – with testament to Jim Henson's foresight in casting him and his efforts to direct Bowie.

The codpiece worn by Bowie in *Labyrinth* has since become popular in its own right, with a Facebook group (*David Bowie's crotch in Labyrinth*)[69] amassing almost 20,000 followers, with much of the content focusing on Bowie's codpiece, as well as drinking games and *Labyrinth*-themed memes. The proliferation of other *Labyrinth*-focused Facebook groups (with content being regularly uploaded) shows that the film – and Bowie's place in it – remains in the public consciousness, despite its lack of success on its initial release; much of the adoration seems to be not for Bowie per se but for Bowie in the persona of Jareth.

There is obviously something special about Jareth and *Labyrinth* that has helped them both to be remembered more than thirty years since the film was released, a something that perhaps needed time to grow in appreciation, and more than Otherness, mystery, magic or a codpiece. Looking at the many musical and film roles that Bowie occupied over his lifetime makes it easier to understand how Jareth fits in there. Due to his singing and dancing, wig, make-up and costume, as well as bespoke songs, it is difficult to separate Jareth from Bowie and Bowie from Jareth, as the character suited the rock star perhaps better than any other film character had during his acting career, many times blurring the line between film and music video, while simultaneously allowing Bowie the chance to act. At the time of writing, a sequel to *Labyrinth* is planned, although it's hard to imagine that any other actor could replace Bowie as Goblin King and still bring a similar level of Otherness, mystery, magic, iconicity and all the other indefinable qualities that made Bowie's Jareth so memorable.

There is a depth not only to *Labyrinth* but also to Bowie's performance which can be made clearer through tools such as Bakhtin's carnival and the performative mask, which highlight the eccentric, transgressive, sexualized and profane basis of Bowie's characterization. In many ways, Bowie *is* carnival, and the masks he wore simply allowed him to showcase his multifaceted abilities in diverse ways, even if they never really gave us a deeper insight into who he was as a human, behind his layers of identity. The character of Jareth and the film *Labyrinth* succeed not only because of Bowie's acting or Henson's directing but also because of the mythology, the shapeshifting and the fantastical nature of David Bowie himself, his carnivalistic essence and the translucent masks he wore, which makes it possible to say that Bowie *is* Jareth, and Jareth *is* Bowie.

Notes

1 Mehdi Derfoufi, 'Embodying Stardom, Representing Otherness: David Bowie in "Merry Christmas, Mr. Lawrence"', in *David Bowie: Critical Perspectives*, ed. Eoin Devereux, Aileen Dillane and Martin J. Power (London and New York: Routledge, 2015), 161.
2 Peter Doggett, *The Man Who Sold the World* (London: Vintage Books, 2011), 45.
3 Ibid., 34.
4 Alison Blair, 'Marc Bolan, David Bowie, and the Counter-Hegemonic Persona: "Authenticity," Ephemeral Identities, and the "Fantastical Other"', *MEDIANZ* 15, no. 1 (2015): 168.
5 Elizabeth McCarthy, 'Telling Lies: the interviews of David Bowie', in *David Bowie and Transmedia Stardom*, ed. Ana Cristina Mendes and Lisa Perrott (London: Routledge, 2020), 91.

6. Nick Deriso, '72 Musicians Who Are Totally Lying About Their Names', 29 March 2018, https://ultimateclassicrock.com/musicians-name-change/, accessed 20 December 2020.
7. Philip Auslander, *Performing Rock: Gender & Theatricality in Popular Music* (Ann Arbor, MI: The University of Michigan Press, 2006), 4.
8. Brad Erickson, 'George Clinton and David Bowie: The Space Race in Black and White', *Popular Music and Society* 39, no.5 (2016): 1.
9. Blair, *Marc Bolan, David Bowie, and the Counter-Hegemonic Persona*, 167.
10. Paula M. Block and Terry J. Erdmann, *Jim Henson's Labyrinth: The Ultimate Visual History* (San Rafael, CA: Insight Editions, 2016), 50.
11. Brian Jay Jones, *Jim Henson* (New York, Ballantine Books, 2016), 369.
12. Block and Erdmann, *Jim Henson's Labyrinth*, 19.
13. Ibid., 53.
14. Brian Jay Jones, *Jim Henson*, 370.
15. Christopher Frayling, Philip Hoare and Mark Kermode, 'David Bowie Then ... David Bowie Now', in *David Bowie Is*, ed. Victoria Broackes and Geoffrey Marsh (London: V&A Publishing, 2013), 299.
16. Dylan Jones, *David Bowie: A Life* (London: Windmill Books, 2018), 339.
17. Ilana Shiloh, *The Double, the Labyrinth and the Locked Room: Metaphors of Paradox in Crime Fiction and Film* (New York: Peter Lang, 2011), 93.
18. Brian Jay Jones, *Jim Henson*, 376.
19. Block and Erdmann, *Jim Henson's Labyrinth*, 53.
20. Jones, *David Bowie*, 339.
21. Block and Erdmann, *Jim Henson's Labyrinth*, 53.
22. Jones, *David Bowie*, 313.
23. Block and Erdmann, *Jim Henson's Labyrinth*, 54.
24. Mikhail Bakhtin, *Problems of Dostoevsky's Poetics*, trans. and ed. Caryl Emerson (Minneapolis: The University of Minnesota Press, 1984), 6.
25. Michael Gardiner, *The Dialogics of Critique: M. M. Bakhtin and the Theory of Ideology* (London: Routledge, 1992), 23.
26. Bakhtin, *Problems of Dostoevsky's Poetics*, 122.
27. Ibid.
28. Ibid.
29. Steven Mills, 'Bakhtin against Dualism: Restoring Humanity to the Subjective Experience', in *Mikhail Bakhtin's Heritage in Literature, Arts and Psychology: Art and Answerability*, ed. Slav N. Gratchev and Howard Mancing (Lanham: Lexington Books, 2018), 259.
30. Yelena Mazour-Matusevich, 'Contextualizing Bakhtin's Intuitive Discoveries: The End of Grotesque Realism and the Reformation', in *Mikhail Bakhtin's Heritage in Literature, Arts and Psychology: Art and Answerability*, ed. Slav N. Gratchev and Howard Mancing (Lanham, MD: Lexington Books, 2018), 138.

31 Bakhtin, *Problems of Dostoevsky's Poetics*, 123.
32 Michael Gardiner, 'Bakhtin's Carnival: Utopia as Critique', *Utopian Studies* 3, no. 2 (1992): 32.
33 Blair, *Marc Bolan, David Bowie, and the Counter-Hegemonic Persona*, 169.
34 Bakhtin, *Problems of Dostoevsky's Poetics*, 124.
35 Mikhail Bakhtin, *Rabelais and His World*, trans. Helene Iswolsky (Bloomington, IN: Indiana University Press, 1984), 39–40.
36 Renate Lachmann, Raoul Eshelman and Marc Davis, 'Bakhtin and Carnival: Culture as Counter-Culture', *Cultural Critique* 11 (Winter, 1988–9): 116.
37 Ibid., 117.
38 Katerina Clark and Michael Holquist, *Mikhail Bakhtin* (Cambridge: The Belknap Press, 1984), 298.
39 Andrea Nightingale, 'Toward an Ecological Eschatology: Plato and Bakhtin on Other Worlds and Times', in *Bakhtin and the Classics,* ed. R. Bracht Branham (Evanston, IL: Northwestern University Press, 2002), 226.
40 Clark and Holquist, *Mikhail Bakhtin*, 299.
41 Philip Auslander, *Theory for Performance Studies: A Student's Guide* (London: Routledge, 2008), 41.
42 Auslander, *Performing Rock*, 111.
43 Shelton Waldrep, *Future Nostalgia: Performing David Bowie* (New York: Bloomsbury, 2016), 1.
44 Auslander, *Performing Rock*, 4.
45 Clark and Holquist, *Mikhail Bakhtin*, 169.
46 Erickson, *George Clinton and David Bowie*, 10.
47 Will Brooker, *Why Bowie Matters* (London: William Collins, 2019), 142–3.
48 Robert Stam, *Subversive Pleasures: Bakhtin, Cultural Criticism, and Film* (Baltimore, MD: The Johns Hopkins University Press, 1989), 126.
49 Blair, *Marc Bolan, David Bowie, and the Counter-Hegemonic Persona*, 172.
50 Justin Myers, 'David Bowie's Official Top 40 Biggest Selling Downloads Revealed!' 11 January 2016, https://www.officialcharts.com/chart-news/david-bowie-s-official-top-40-biggest-selling-downloads-revealed-__2854/, accessed 29 December 2020.
51 Nicholas Pegg, *The Complete David Bowie* (London: Titan Books, 2016), 179.
52 David Hepworth, 'How Performing Starman on Top of the Pops sent Bowie into the stratosphere', *The Guardian*, 15 January 2016, https://www.theguardian.com/music/musicblog/2016/jan/15/david-bowie-starman-top-of-the-pops.
53 Rosalind Galt, 'David Bowie's Perverse Cinematic Body', *Cinema Journal* 57, no. 3 (Spring 2018): 135–6.
54 Ibid., 136.
55 Ibid., 138.

56 Jones, *David Bowie*, 339.
57 Bakhtin, *Rabelais and His World*, 40.
58 Pegg, *The Complete David Bowie*, 692.
59 Wolfgang Kayser, *The Grotesque in Art and Literature*, trans. Ulrich Weisstein (Bloomington, IN: Indiana University Press, 1933). 187.
60 Gary R. VandenBos, ed., *APA Dictionary of Psychology* (Washington, DC: American Psychological Association, 2015), 357.
61 The Archive for Research in Archetypal Symbolism, 'Father-imago', accessed 31 January 2021, https://aras.org/concordance/content/father-imago.
62 Galt, *David Bowie's Perverse Cinematic Body*, 131.
63 Ibid., 138.
64 Ibid.
65 Jones, *David Bowie*, 339.
66 Ibid.
67 Joe Navarro, *The Dictionary of Body Language: A Field Guide to Human Behaviour* (William Morrow, 2018). E-book.
68 David Wiles, 'The Carnivalesque in *A Midsummer Night's Dream*', in *Shakespeare and Carnival: After Bakhtin*, ed. Ronald Knowles (London: Macmillan, 1998), 79.
69 'David Bowie's Crotch in Labyrinth', Facebook, published 24 March 2010, https://www.facebook.com/DavidBowiesCrotchInLabyrinth/.

8

Bowie as actor/Bowie as icon

Authenticity versus iconography in Martin Scorsese's *The Last Temptation of Christ*

Ian Dixon

Introduction

First the megastar's voice – a Gitanes smoking iconic presence more heard than seen – then his horse – symbol of subordination to the empire – then the majesty of Sultan Moulay Ismail's royal stables, the divinity of the Cecile B. de Mille lighting – more Catholic than Romanesque – then, with a theatrical turn, David Bowie – music-recording megastar and crossover film artist – in a toga. By analysing the text of Martin Scorsese's *Last Temptation of Christ* (1988) as star iconography and acting instrument for David Bowie, this chapter closely reads Bowie in the role of Pontius Pilate. In this ostensibly naturalistic cameo performance Bowie synthesizes two contrasting acting styles: Brechtian exteriority and Stanislavskian interiority.

While Stanislavskian naturalism has become the default theory for producing 'quality' film performances in modern narrative cinema, Brechtian principles have either been ignored or appropriated without nuanced understanding. Whether Stanislavskian or Brechtian, the problem begins with poor perceptions of what screen performance *could* be as opposed to the purism of what it *should* be. Plainly stated, Bowie may not be trained as an actor but *Last Temptation* demonstrates a synthesis of these two apparently opposing theories in practice. Bowie's Pilate scene becomes a vehicle for illuminating the gap between those two key concepts: 'conscious signage', including star iconography and the 'presentational' acting of Brecht's epic theatre; and the supposed 'authenticity' of Stanislavskian naturalism as 'representational' performance.

By 'conscious signage' I refer to Bowie's unique exploitation of mask, mime, gesture and iconography, which functions as a chain of signifiers, involving skills that are essentially Brechtian in nature,[1] at least 'presentational' and deliberately performative.[2] By contrast, Stanislavskian 'authenticity' refers to a perceived fidelity to portrayed reality, not only dependent on audience perception but also 'internally' generated by the actor to avoid what Harold Clurman calls mere 'competent stagecraft . . . "performance" fabrication, artifice'.[3] Scorsese's screenwriter Paul Schrader's screenplay helps organize this twofold analysis: at one end of the spectrum is Bowie's conscious Brechtian signage – an embedded performativity; at the other end is his craft of 'authentic' screen performance in the Stanislavskian tradition, which in America became dominated by Lee Strasberg's Method.

Bowie is adept at, and merges, both styles to great effect. His consciously chosen 'signs of performance' prevail in the first half of the scene,[4] up until the 'transition' beat,[5] then Bowie's 'internal' authenticity takes over, while simultaneously merging these two opposing acting styles. By balancing Bowie's wilfully theatrical style against his naturalistic performance, I champion Bowie as an actor who changes his performance mode perhaps more lucidly than a trained actor might, to drift between the 'poles' of twentieth-century performance conventions – a rare achievement for a pop star in modern screen acting.

While the scene's blocking is largely theatrical and conventional, its narrative function works whether one is aware of Bowie's status as a pop icon or not. Nevertheless, I will reference Scorsese's filmic construction and shot proxemics to illuminate Bowie's performance and show how meaning becomes layered and subtle, especially if the viewer invests in Bowie's star status and image. By using contemporary acting theory as a discursive tool to analyse Bowie's performance, I expose the contradictions within cinematic playing conventions and uncover Bowie's eclectic yet effectively naturalistic prowess.

For the purposes of this chapter, all theorists fall under one of the two diametrically opposed acting styles. In addition, the chapter references performance theory, practical acting methodology and semiotic analysis – theoretical modes sometimes considered contradictory[6] but which converge as analytical tools for unpacking screen acting. The chapter also draws upon secondary theorists from Richard Schechner's performance theory to Erving Goffman's *Performance in Everyday Life* Strasberg's Method-based bastardization of Stanislavsky's System, James Naremore's *Acting in the Cinema* and Colin Counsell's *Signs of Performance*. In this 'deep dive' into the scene – and Bowie's performance specifically – I will not labour my outline of theory in the hope that the references tell the untold story. I therefore read the signs at play in this scene from my own analytical perspective as a film and performance theorist as well as a film practitioner to draw attention to previously unnoticed elements in Bowie's performance, to direct the gaze of the spectator, generate specific affects and dispel the commonly held assumption that Bowie merely plays himself on screen. On the one hand, I identify Bowie's performative 'bag of tricks', on the other, I articulate his excellence at signing, miming and playing. My intention for this chapter is therefore not to fix meaning but rather to elucidate how meaning is generated and recognize Bowie's lucid performance acumen. Indeed, Bowie's 'theatrical' interests serve him well as a film actor, particularly in a scene where Pontius Pilate and Jesus Christ cannot exist without David Bowie and Willem Dafoe. At the centre of it all is David Bowie – megastar of stage and screen or rather chameleonic musical talent adopting the guise of screen actor in *Last Temptation* – a film as iconic and iconoclastic as Bowie himself.

Pontius Pilate as British 'bad guy' in Scorsese's *Last Temptation*

Scorsese's production, including the casting of Bowie, had a long and arduous history. Scorsese knew of Nikos Kazantzakis' 1955 book *The Last Temptation of Christ* as an NYU film student but felt the prose was thick, verbose and 'too "poetic"'. However, Scorsese appreciated 'the representation of Christ, stressing the human side of His nature without denying that He is God'.[7] This contravenes Catholic teaching, which stipulates that Jesus was fully divine, not human – a debate emerging from the Council of Chalcedon in 451 CE.[8] Like Scorsese, the Bible casts Pilate as a 'bit part in Jesus's story', but according to Josephus (Jewish historian writing contemporaneously to the Gospels) history was the other way around.[9] Far from Pilate as a weak, unwilling gentile who sensed the divinity of Christ, Pilate was a brave soldier, effective administrator and skilful diplomat who used Christ's condemnation for the Roman state's benefit – as Scorsese's casting of Bowie emphasizes.[10]

Scorsese had wanted to dramatize a Christ story since viewing *The Robe* (Henry Koster, 1953).[11] As precedents to *Last Temptation*, Scorsese also admired the epics: *Quo Vadis* (Mervyn LeRoy, 1951); George Stevens's *The Greatest Story Ever Told* (1965);[12] John Huston's 'beautifully staged' film *The Bible: In the Beginning . . .* (1966)[13] (especially for Christopher Fry's screenplay)[14] and Nicolas Ray's *King of Kings* (1961) – a film the young Catholic Scorsese found originally offensive but later admired for its 'simple iconography'.[15] Scorsese notes that his initial desire to make *Last Temptation* was 'So I can get to know Jesus better'.[16] Accordingly, Scorsese intended to make *Last Temptation*'s Jesus figure accessible to non-believers.[17] After protracted funding rejection,[18] the film was eventually green-lit as a French co-production with Cinema Odeon providing half the budget.[19]

Casting, in direct contrast to Bowie, saw Dafoe securing the lead role as Jesus. Perhaps betraying Scorsese's representational preference (or unconscious prejudice), every actor considered for Jesus was a blue-eyed Caucasian.[20] Similarly, his choice to cast Bowie was a recognizably ideological one and the megastar's mismatched eyes proved effective for generating meaning. However, despite claiming that he always wanted to work with Bowie, Scorsese's first choice for Pilate was Sting. A crucial aspect, therefore, was to engage a British pop star as the legal alien Pilate.[21] Scorsese's decision to associate sin, death and the Devil with iconic English accents included: the serpent the burning bush and David Bowie – by contrast to the goodly Jesus as American. 'When it came to the outside voices, the Romans, and the world of Satan, they had to have a very different accent, but the same language', states Scorsese, so by borrowing from William Wyler's *Ben Hur* (1959), Scorsese betrayed his cultural prejudice by making the 'bad guys' British.[22] This nevertheless demonstrates that Scorsese was well aware of the film's semiotic/ideological construction – especially when involving Bowie.

The Bowie as actor 'story'

In order to examine Bowie as an eclectic actor, I repeatedly watched his single scene from *Last Temptation*. On first viewing, I perceived Bowie's naturalistic performance as an 'instinctual' seamlessness he had not achieved since *The Man Who Fell to Earth* (Nicolas Roeg, 1976). On further analysis of *Last Temptation*, it seemed that Bowie's performative masks – the personae of Ziggy and the Duke – peeled away to reveal a consciously signing performer who nonetheless drew on the codes of performance to appear *like* a naturalistic actor, a credit to his imitative skillset. It became evident that, in this film, Bowie positions himself between the role of actor and the act of performance to achieve this seamless effect. As such, Bowie's performance is a pastiche of imagistic detail more complex and consciously connotative than Dafoe's,[23] as Bowie's alternative methodology reveals the cracks in naturalism's mythology. This is despite Wendy Leigh erroneously opining, 'the truth was that, above all, [Bowie] was a Method actor.'[24] As Counsell suggests, any actor can imitate the Method despite their absence of the internality it claims. This amounts to Bowie's performative 'bag of tricks' rather than any Method acumen as Leigh argues.[25] While Bowie himself describes his performative being as a 'personality' figure',[26] his performance in *Last Temptation* nevertheless paves the way for professional actors to draw on differing methodologies while noting that a persona like Ziggy does not equate to film acting.[27]

Bowie commentators display a myriad of contrasting opinions about the megastar's mime and acting skills. Admitting that his focus in the 1980s was on film acting, Bowie is nevertheless praised by director Nicolas Roeg as an 'extraordinary' artist: 'He can't be singled out, "Ah that is Bowie," because that's the way he always does that. He never appears the same way twice.'[28] Conversely, while tracing Bowie's talent for mimicry and role play from his earliest songs as 'trying on someone else's persona for size', Will Brooker considers that with Bowie's 'larger-than-life persona' he 'tended to play himself as an actor'.[29] By contrast, in *David Bowie Is*, film critic Mark Kermode commends Bowie's 'invisible' acting as he 'didn't appear to be acting at all'.[30] Ava Cherry opines that Bowie 'was either a fabulous actor or a man whose emotions ran deep'.[31] Why Cherry would consider her two categories as mutually exclusive represents another common misconception of acting methodology: such 'fabulous' acting, Strasberg and Stanislavsky might argue, can only rise from psychic depth. While noting Bowie's introversion and complementary extroversion, poetic biographer Paul Morley opines that Bowie 'must continually become someone else' and that his early musical style involved 'the obvious copying of something that is itself an obvious if spunky copy', but that this 'natural mimic' desired to become a 'character' by using his 'body, gesture [and] expression' to communicate.[32] This opposes Ana Leorne's position that Bowie's personae betray a schizophrenic mind in denial. For Leorne, the 'alienesque Cracked Actor' solicits his Eros and Thanatos drives to construct multiple personae as a self-defence mechanism to cover an impossible vulnerability so as not 'to expose either himself or his basic instincts of desire'.[33] Leorne's psychoanalytic study interprets Bowie's masks as summoning a deeper aspect of the questionable self but contrasts with Method acting by stressing that Bowie's theatrical personae were designed to obfuscate, not expose, his internal instincts. Contrary to Leorne's assertion, Bowie's one-time manager Ken Pitt declares the theory of Bowie's chameleonic masks concealing his 'true' personality as simply unconvincing.[34]

After the late 1970s Thin White Duke, Bowie claims to have discarded his infamous stage personae altogether on the premise that he no longer required such characters to hide behind.[35] Nevertheless, Bowie confides his trepidation regarding formal acting: 'It's the most terrifying position I've ever put myself in. I've no legitimate theatre training whatsoever. I've just had a mime thing, which is very different. I went in with a very naïve conception of how one acts.'[36] While these statements may be disingenuous on Bowie's part, they nevertheless indicate that Bowie recognizes the difference between mime as performance art and the contrasting skillset required for psychologically motivated naturalistic film performance.

For my part, I perceive Bowie as a gifted actor whose early skills were fostered by Lindsay Kemp's mime classes, yet a film clip as early as 'When I'm Five' (1968)[37] demonstrates that his talent for 'inhabiting' character went significantly beyond the 'attitude' of mime. I read this obscure clip as a point of entry to Bowie's charisma, mimetic 'attitude' and use of mask in *Last Temptation*. Chris O'Leary describes 'When I'm Five' as a pretentious clip, 'both endearing and embarrassing . . . matched visually by his mime-like performance . . . and perform[ed] without a trace of self-consciousness'.[38] I see 'When I'm Five' otherwise, as an indicator of a burgeoning, yet remarkable acting talent as the twenty-one-year-old Bowie internalizes a four-year-old child through adept imitation, psychologizing through demonstrative gesture and sophisticated use of performative mask.

The juvenile Bowie marches, not like 'the soldiers in the May Day Parade' but like a child imitating a soldier (or rather, Bowie imitating a child who is mimicking a soldier – a boy who is, as Phillip Auslander opines, 'not not David Jones').[39] In a process similar to Stanislavsky's 'emotional memory', the young Bowie lifts his eyeline from an imaginary soldier to take in the whole panorama of May Day – the shift in focus registers in his eyes. In a gesture that breaks his childlike pretension, Bowie then licks his lips a little too lasciviously while apparently picturing 'the magazines on Mummy's shelf'.

After the camera tracks past the giant birthday candle, the child-Bowie breaks the fourth wall by pretending to 'see' the camera for the first time, announcing, 'Yesterday was horrid day [sic] 'cause Raymond kicked my shin', performing the direct (and self-conscious) camera address of Brechtian alienation. Next, in a deliberately performative run-on sentence, he exclaims, 'I dropped my toast at breakfast, And I laughed when Bonzo licked my [gasp] face.' At this point, he moves from 'inhabiting' (or conjuring) this imaginary child to drawing upon an old Russian clowning routine (also used in *The Mask* (Malcolm J. Thomson, 1969)) to 'reveal' his enforced smile, then takes a theatrically deep inhalation like a child out of breath. This demonstrates extraordinary adeptness at changing, not only dramatic beats in the representational Stanislavskian sense but also a rapid change of convention from mimicry to clowning, to presentational Brechtian *Gestus* and ironic statement.

As he sings, 'I wonder why my Daddy cries' he morphs his naïve child's gesture of face touching into a stylized fingertip teardrop as lucidly as his falling glissando melody suggests. He then returns to the child's point of view to evoke, then mime, the act of catching a butterfly and eating it. He segues effortlessly from apparently internal images of sweetshops and bleeding knees to external gestures admonishing Daddy for not washing up then cavorts backwards while disregarding the strict rhythm he sings demonstrating agility both narratively and performatively. In short, though maligned by critics, Bowie demonstrates an arguably natural skillset, honed into a mime-like dance, inhabiting character, mood and mask for dramatic intent, not yet personae, not yet naturalism, but remarkably shamanic.

Key voices on performance convention

Respecting that Bowie's famed complexity 'demands that any critical engagement with his overall work must be interdisciplinary and wide-ranging',[40] I reach to contrasting acting theories largely divided between 'Stanislavskian aesthetics' and Brechtian performativity. For my argument regarding Stanislavsky's naturalism – where playability depends on seeking an 'objective' and performing individualized dramatic 'actions' – this involves Goffman, Naremore, Strasberg and Susan Batson. In Goffman's thesis – which (ironically) draws from theatre practice as a metaphor for everyday performativity – observers 'glean clues from [a performer's] conduct and appearance', which consequently show signs of 'involuntary expressive behaviour'.[41] In this ingrained process, Goffman identifies two radically different sign activities: 'the expression that [the performer] *gives* [conscious signage], and the expression that he *gives off*' (disavowed internality), where the former indicates a conscious intention to affect their listening partner or 'action that others can treat as symptomatic of the actor'.[42] For Bowie, the ability to control others is paramount within his stage concerts and in interviews in which he consciously fabricates,[43] but in screen performance the controlled signs he *gives* also succumb to another subset of signs he *gives off* – like his involuntary eye flutter in *Last Temptation*.

Building upon Goffman's premise, Naremore opines that Western cinematic art is dominated by the psychologizing effects of 'Stanislavskian aesthetics', which denote expressive-realist conventions manifest in most screen performances.[44] According to Naremore, twentieth-century performance divides into two conventions: 'presentational' and 'representational'.[45] Representational acting connotes the inner life of the actor and relies on the illusion of spontaneity; presentational acting, by contrast, means theatrical artifice. As such, rhetorical readings of text espoused by Bertholt Brecht are discouraged in modern screen playability, yet these effects are adapted by Bowie in discontinuity, gestural presentation and star image as icon. This kind of presentational acting is inappropriate in cinema as the camera amplifies any lack of psychological authenticity, which Bowie nevertheless achieves. Naremore suggests that resultant performative codes 'inculcate spontaneity, improvisation, and low-key psychological introspection; they devalue anything that looks stagy' as with Bowie as poseur par excellence, a trait evident in the first half of Scorsese/Schrader's scene. For Naremore, 'Stanislavskian aesthetics' are just over a century old, while rhetorical readings based on gestural lexicon stem back to the Classical Greeks – a stance adopted by Brechtian actors and adapted by Bowie.[46]

Strasberg's Method also derives from Stanislavsky's System. Based on spurious readings of Theodule Ribot and Sigmund Freud, Strasberg's Method reinforces performance internality and generates 'quasi-psychoanalytic rehearsal techniques, inviting the actor to delve into the unconscious mind, searching out ostensibly "truthful" behaviour'.[47] Even untrained actors can imitate the clichés of Method with a complete absence of internal process.[48]

Millenia before Method, the mask as theatrical device derived from Dionysian ceremonial poetry or 'dithyramb' and Grecian 'goat singers'.[49] Cambridge anthropologists contend that Greek theatre is the basis of all theatrical forms, but Schechner asserts that performance might be innate.[50] Despite Schechner declaring its irrelevance to modern theatre,[51] Batson upholds the Greek origin theory,[52] exemplifying the ancient performer Thespis's painted face and first-person vocal delivery as transformative persona: a 'willingness to let his own individuality breathe life from underneath that painted mask'.[53] In this manner, Leorne asserts, Bowie's personae work 'because he always put a part of his innermost drives into them'.[54] In Leorne's sense, Bowie's stage masks connote his 'essential nature' – more 'soul portrait' than extrinsic signage.[55] Similarly, as evidenced in 'q', Kevin Hunt suggests that mask elicits animistic/shamanic images for its audience and argues that mask:

> announces the incarnation of a spirit such as a god, ancestor or other mythological/alien being. Given Bowie's penchant for masks, make-up and characterization, it is interesting to note that masks are historically dualistic: a traditional mask is 'a soul portrait' revealing an image of the wearer's 'essential nature'.[56]

Partly by utilizing mask in film art, Brechtian technique also abounds in Bowie's performances. Bowie was aware of Brechtian theatre having recorded songs penned by Brecht's composer Kurt Weill since 1978,[57] referenced Brecht in his own songwriting methodology and played the lead in Alan Clarke's BBC adaptation of Brecht's first play, *Baal*.[58,59] In *Baal*, Bowie relies on Brecht's 'alienation effect' – or *verfremdungseffekt* – where audiences are encouraged to suspend their emotional engagement for rhetorical purposes. Brecht's *verfremdungseffekt* refers to the formal separation of actor from character and the audience's resulting disengagement with the locus of character and situation.[60] Indeed, 'The very self-consciousness that Stanislavsky sought to eradicate because it hampered the creation of unitary character, Brecht courts in order to fracture that character'.[61] Bowie's performance in *Baal* genericizes Baal's antisociality rather than fully exploiting Brechtian presentational range.

Despite Bowie's performance, the inventive, but overstated camerawork captures the diminutive frame of Bowie gesticulating in a manner more 'rich mist' of Method signs than selective gestural communication in Brechtian manner.[62] According to Leigh, 'Critics were underwhelmed' by Bowie's *Baal*.[63] *Last Temptation*, however, is a naturalistic text in which Bowie imitates Brechtian theatre as a seamless confluence to surpass 'When I'm Five' and *Baal*.

To support his analytical epic theatre, Brecht indicates that the basic actor's tool is the gesture, which he divides into two parts (similar to Goffman's *giving* and *giving off* analysis), which together constitute the *Gestus*. Under the Stanislavsky-inspired realists, claims Brecht, the power of gesture is diminished.[64] By contrast, Brechtian scholar John Willett points out that *Gestus* combines gesture with mimetic 'attitude'. For Willett, 'Brecht's word *Gestus* is best translated by this obsolete English word referring to an actor's "bearing", "carriage" or general "mien"'.[65] As Counsell illustrates, 'Brecht draws attention not just to overt artifice but to the resulting split between the act of telling and what is told – that is, between the actor and his/her role' – a division Bowie never loses sight of (despite the Bowie/Ziggy psychological blur).[66]

Making use of this Brechtian expressionism, Bowie both reciprocates and unmasks the naturalistic acting conventions of Stanislavsky's System and avoids Method acting's 'rich mist of generalised signs of the psyche'.[67] As such, Bowie does not overlook his conscious signage as a serious vehicle for meaning creation: he is too aware of his miming body to fall into the Method fallacy and, as illustrated below, Scorsese's finessed direction enables Bowie's acting 'choices' to shine.

Bowie's performance as 'conscious signage' in *Last Temptation*

Bowie's history as a pop icon allows for a rich analysis of *Last Temptation*, where conscious, even Brechtian, signage is a key aspect of his performativity. At this end of the spectrum stands the iconographic Bowie, once camp, 'slim, sinuous figure[s] of Pre-Raphaelite painting',[68] now transformed into a historically maligned Roman prefect. The Pilate scene involves a nest of significations, which exploit Brechtian *Gestus*, Bowie's star image and conflate his prior personae reaching back to glam rock. In this way, despite Bowie's genuine performance acumen in *Last Temptation*, his degenerate Baudelairean glamour precedes him in a manner Clurman considers mere '"performance" fabrication, artifice'.[69]

Yet it is that very artifice which allows Bowie to consciously sign meaning in surprising ways – a unique exploitation of mask, mime and gesture.

By way of entry into Bowie as Pilate, I draw upon Stanley Dorfman's 'Heroes' (1977),[70] where Bowie's performance forms a pastiche of signage (Figure 8.1, 8.3, 8.5). The following images demonstrate conscious, performative signage and cinematic referentiality: the alien from *Close Encounters of the Third Kind* (1977) (Figure 8.2), Marlon Brando's hypermasculinity in *The Wild One* (1953) (Figure 8.4) and feminized effigies of the Hindu Goddess Parvati (Figure 8.6).

Bowie applies this same capacity for consciously derived signage in *Last Temptation*, but in a more subtle manner. The scene's opening tracking shot features a saddler's exposed leg and his counterpart's 'masturbatory' saddle polishing under an array of phallic swords, which sexualizes the mise en scène prior to the focus pull to Bowie. Thus, even before Bowie's horse tampering, the scene begins with a subtle glam rock/gender-bending overtone. The audiences become aware of Pilate from behind his body in

FIGURES 8.1–8.6 *Bowie's derivations in 'Heroes'*, © Stanley Dorfman; Close Encounters, © EMI Films; Brando, © Stanley Kramer Productions; Hindu Goddess Parvati.

wide shot – accompanied by Bowie's iconic, cigarette husky, English croon. For the American viewer, the Britishness of Bowie's voice invokes a suspicion of Rome and Satan.[71] Comfortable in a toga though he may be, Bowie's conscious imitation of Roman behaviour references Marcus Aurelius (Figure 8.7) while still utilizing the 'degenerate dandyism of Baudelaire' in his star image (Figure 8.8).[72] The self-conscious folding of his hands signs this: he 'never simply stands, he *poses*', which renders his performance more 'stylized and poetically unnatural' than his scene partner, Dafoe.[73]

As the blue heavenly light (borrowed from DeMille) shines down through Moulay Ismail's stables, Bowie gestures his horse away and glides towards Jesus. Indeed, the theatrical lighting 'presents' Bowie by contrast to Dafoe's cinematic/naturalistic camera angle. Scorsese, however, is too good a director not to include some poignant visual oppositions: the flaming torches as fires of hell, the pagan magic of the smoke haze – timeless imagery to supplement the mythology of Jesus with the iconography of Bowie, particularly represented in Bowie's dialogue '. . . good magic or bad magic?', ironically implicating Bowie's immersion in Aleister Crowley's uniform.[74]

The master shot allows the majesty of God's light to reflect in Dafoe's iconic blue eyes, but not into Bowie's mismatched anisocoric eyes ogling the would-be messiah: Jesus faces the light; Pilate turns away from it. Bowie's eyes are only emphasized in the later over-shoulder close-ups, sitting with Dafoe as Pilate declares: 'It simply doesn't matter how you want to change things. We don't want them changed.' Bowie's non-normative iconic eyes render him mad/evil by contrast to the clear blue high-key lighting on

FIGURE 8.7 AND 8.8 *Bowie's Baudelairean Marcus Aurelius, like Charlie Chaplin, he 'never simply stands, he* poses*'.* © *Universal, Cineplex Odeon Films, Ufland Productions.*

Dafoe's pious face.[75] Consequently, Bowie stars as Pontius Pilate: vilified historical figure equated with liminal glam figure and therefore resistant to authenticated readings.

Can Bowie, a figure already maligned for deserting performance authenticity on stage, be trusted to perform as a naturalistic Pontius Pilate? Does the role of imperialist prefect suit Bowie because of the fascist implications of the Thin White Duke as 'Über-Controlling . . . icy Führer' or the Dionysian excess of Ziggy? Or does the double-consciousness of megastar playing tyrant destroy any perceived authenticity from the audience's viewpoint?[76] Reception studies suggest that it cannot: this is a 'clear and dramatic case of the creation and presentation of performance personae' in action, which is why Scorsese shows us Bowie's obvious performativity – heightened by the implication of his past stage personae – before succumbing to the reflective 'evil' of the role.[77] The actor functions as both Bowie and Pilate (and Ziggy, the Duke and 'not David Jones').[78] In the Brechtian sense, the division between actor and role cannot be missed: while Pilate propels the narrative, Bowie conducts the metanarrative (and consequently carries Scorsese's pro-Christian ideological stance). While convincing, Bowie's opening gambit threatens the plausibility of his performance, which is an amalgam of mime, Brechtian gesture and inappropriate staginess. As such, the memory of counterculture's 'antitheatricalism' and rock's 'antiocular bias' render Bowie's performance inauthentic by association in *Last Temptation*.

In addition, the scene witnesses Bowie's accent regress from his manufactured 1980s upper-class Brit to his 1970s South London identification – representing both extremes of his fluid personality. In terms of class, Redmond points out the postcolonial implications of Bowie's whiteness – particularly in the 1980s after his *Let's Dance* video clip – which in this dramatization of Pilate's interrogation holds further power by virtue of his playing against a white blue-eyed Jesus: the 'hyper-white' Bowie is imperial – displaying 'civility' through posture and projected gaze – where the swarthy Dafoe represents humanity.[79] Bowie's well-established musical personae connote a kaleidoscopic perversity – be the audience Christians, fans or cineastes. The 'gender undecidability' of Bowie's star persona,[80] particularly when appearing as the historically damned Pilate, becomes additive.

Donning the archetypal robe of Nikolai Ge's *What Is Truth?* and sporting the questionable comb-down fringe that Roland Barthes lampoons in *The Romans in Films*, Bowie's presence adds to the received mythology of Pilate – especially given Bowie's iconic feminine appearance (Figure 8.9 and 8.10). Bowie sports his Romanesque hairdo, as Barthes opines: 'one of those Roman foreheads, whose smallness has at all times indicated a special mixture of self-righteousness, virtue and conquest'.[81] Slightly hunched in an 'attitude' of power and self-righteousness from mime artistry, Bowie's hands are cupped in fey intellectualism imitating the theatrical conventions

FIGURE 8.9 AND 8.10 *Bowie's comb-down fringe as Barthes's 'self-righteousness, virtue and conquest'.* © Universal, Cineplex Odeon Films, Ufland Productions; *his robes referencing Nikolai Ge's* What Is Truth? *(1831–91).*

of British traditional acting yet signing Brechtian *Gestus*.[82] Also functional is Bowie's use of allusion and ambiguity working together under Braudy's cinematic concept of 'mystery replaces articulation' where the audience second guess an actor's inner psyche. Both known and unknowable, Bowie therefore serves as an enigma when portraying Pilate: his once beautiful face reads as allusion; his wry performance, his cynical eye rolling borrowed from Meryl Streep's melodramatic signage.[83]

Despite his naturalistic performance style, gesture takes precedence in Bowie's acting as deliberate Brechtian presentational artifice. Scorsese's conventional blocking suggests he is aware of this division in performative style between Bowie and Dafoe: Bowie captured in panning/tracking wide, full and mid shots, where Dafoe's predominate stillness is mostly in medium and close-ups, denoting Jesus as protagonist and Pilate as antagonist. Bowie's artificial (performative) gesture of pointing with two fingers with his Aurelius-like extended arm aimed directly at Dafoe while pronouncing, 'You're more dangerous than the Zealots', betrays a performer comfortable with projecting his body to large rock crowds (Figure 8.11). Yet, Bowie is an artist aware of his significance, consciously using the 'elaborate gestures' of 'street-corner mime' and costume as 'conceptual or cognitive "frame"' to make Pilate's rhetorical point.

Even as biblical hagiography, Scorsese's intelligent rendering of the scene favours a more accurate depiction of the historical Pilate. Scorsese's

FIGURE 8.11 *Bowie/Pilate's gest: 'Roman prefects stand like this'.*

point is that Pilate was a soldier and diplomat faithful to the Roman gods and Emperor Tiberius. While Bowie's presence reads as less military, given his emaciated frame, a diplomat he most certainly is – as decades of manipulating the press attests.[84] Bowie also lends his status as pop star to the authority of Pilate along with the silent absence of the epicurean Ziggy or the Duke, Bowie's self-confessed nastiest character.[85] As Pilate, his consciously confident gestures to his minions – not by saying, but by demonstrating – connote authority. With conscious signage, Bowie plays against Christianity's opinion of Pilate as an indecisive coward; Bowie's star image problematizes this – a rich visual contradiction.

Delving deeper into the nature of the scene's first half, I note that the Brechtian actor uses *gestus* to locate 'performance signs capable of indicating social positions and relationships'.[86] A gest might derive from behavioural codes such as an actor altering their proximity or tone of voice, striking poses denoting: 'capitalists stand like this'.[87] Carrying himself with the 'mien' of a Roman prefect, Bowie's two-fingered Zealot comment performs a similar gest as Pilate. His head tilted forward in accusation, his fingers outstretched, his left hand still cupped – using not only British traditional acting – but also *Gestic* signs to convey authority and period – an essentially Brechtian choice. Contrary to any pejorative reading of Bowie's performance as mere imitation, 'Gestic acting [is] more subtle, capable of conveying detailed information to an audience'.[88] In this case, Bowie's gest communicates Pilate's social status and emotional intent to accuse Jesus (the overriding subtext of the scene). Further, as Brecht argues, gestic actors 'do not employ a formal system of signs but select from an existing pool of socially derived gestural conventions'.[89] In this way, Bowie chooses this stance from prevailing tyrannical gestures, just as Goffman observes the mask of a performer selecting, rather than creating, meaning. Curiously for the inauthentic (read Brechtian) Bowie, such a convention does 'not necessarily signify artifice'.[90]

At this point, Bowie's star image and personae insinuate their presence into Pilate's manipulations – an amalgam of the oppressor/oppressed relationship – and are therefore gestic. In combination with his gestic split, this enables the audience a differing stance on the character of Pilate; as Naremore intimates, such a gestic split proposes a stance outside of the character's field of reference, thereby placing their emotions in a new context so as to prevent empathy with them.[91] This would be an unconventional naturalistic approach, but Bowie's fluid gestural eclecticism means he can circumnavigate the 'rich mist of generalised signs' preferred by exclusively Method actors.[92]

While acknowledging the conscious signage in Bowie's performance as Pilate, I suggest that his iconography and fame compliment, rather than negate, his authentic performance with reference to Brechtian technique for the first half of the scene. Bowie's 'overtly theatrical performance' may distract from the film's naturalism and in the wake of countercultural 'disdain for rock theatrics' may seem inauthentic.[93] However, Bowie's work derives from Brechtian codes yet appears as authentic naturalistic performance by cleverly disguising his Brechtian influence. Naturally, his character's 'internality' must be visually communicated and is therefore still signage. This is where Bowie blends his styles most obviously. As with 'When I'm Five', his performance becomes shamanic.

Bowie's performance as 'truthful' naturalism

Once Bowie's Brechtian *Gestus* – even hints of his Thin White Duke stage personae – have been noted, Bowie's naturalistic acting skills gracefully emerge. This largely occurs after the scene's major transition beat: 'We don't want them changed.' As such – and in contrast to Brechtian signage – I now build a picture of Bowie as an internally conscientious actor to investigate his balance of authenticity and performativity. While questioning the 'truth claims' of 'Method madness',[94] I suggest that Bowie is genuinely vulnerable in ways that, like Thespis, render his performance 'truthful' by allowing his individuality to breathe new life into the icy mask of the Duke.[95] As Amedeo D'Adamo points out, Bowie inhabits and transcends his iconography as 'a mask-wearer . . . enacting poetic fantastic performances that inhabit and explode iconography'.[96]

Bowie's 'truth' and performative mask therefore collapse: his ingrained 'true' mask more prevalent than the internality of 'When I'm Five'. Examining Bowie's myriad personalities as mask to his 'true' personality axiomatically engages the hypocritical ideology of Method's 'illusion of the unified self', which in Bowie's case is inappropriate.[97] While not trained as an actor, Bowie nevertheless emulates Stanislavskian acting and imitates Method conventions as Counsell illustrates (contrary to Leigh's claim to Bowie *being* Method). Yet, Bowie does not need to 'act' naturalism as even that textual mimicry precedes him. In this way, Bowie, the eternal cultural vacuum, borrows in screen performance, just as he does in music.

Nevertheless, Bowie subsumes his mask skills into the craft of naturalism in a bifurcated fashion: he uses 'street-corner mime' and gestures that are incrementally too theatrical. Yet, these 'elaborate gestures' in tandem with his Roman costume as 'conceptual or cognitive "frame"' allow the narrative to unfold through accepted conventions of naturalism.[98] While it seems true that Bowie, like Charlie Chaplin, 'never simply stands, he *poses* . . . [in] stylized and poetically unnatural' fashion – true also that he imitates the 'heightened glow' of Marlene Dietrich's expressionist posing[99] – his gestural life nevertheless indicates a Stanislavskian internality. This can be demonstrated through the 'present tense' moment as Bowie glances to the guard, sharing a silent joke to disparage the naivety of Jesus. Bowie's deliberate cocky performativity provides both self-reflexive cinema and active naturalistic listening, as Naremore suggests, a play within a film – 'a tendency to make acting or role playing the subject of their performances',[100] while using costume as 'a conceptual or cognitive "frame"'.

Yet, after his line 'That's disappointing', Bowie's flickering eyes betray an insecure moment and become a serendipitously deferential 'rich mist' within his impression of Pilate – or did he just forget his lines? In either case, as Naremore illustrates regarding Lillian Gish, when the 'present tense' moment defeats even the ingrained masks of Bowie, he adopts 'involuntary expressive behaviour' as serendipitous 'expressive incoherence' within his characterization.[101] Rather than defensively insulating his 'inner selves' as Leorne opines,[102] Bowie lets down his guard in the service of naturalism. The ensuing moments of intimacy from Bowie betray the life of a real prefect refusing to pander to the King of the Jews. As such, Pilate functions as a perturbed Roman authority figure supported by Christianity's expectation of humility in the presence of Jesus's 'Kingdom Come': a cameo in Jesus's greatness, rather than the historically accurate picture of Jesus as bit part within Pilate's reign.

The scene as synthesis: 'Conscious signage' meets naturalism

In this last component, closer analysis of Schrader's screenplay (rewritten by Scorsese in 1983) in action within Scorsese's mise en scène reveals Bowie's iconography in play while highlighting the excellence of his intimate performance. Indeed, the contrast between representational naturalism and presentational Brechtianism is emblematic of the authenticity-versus-performativity paradigm in Bowie's case. Bowie's Pilate never externally condemns Jesus because the scene is written subtextually – in a manner derivative of St John's gospel. In this, Scorsese's rewrite of Schrader's screenplay aligns with Ann Wroe's reference to the Pilate-Jesus interrogation as 'Pinteresque':[103] a series of questions with only deferred answers – like a Harold Pinter screenplay. How Bowie *gives* and *gives off* in Goffman's sense questions, but ultimately bolsters, biblical reality.

Bowie initiates the scene by casually mentioning: 'So, you are the King of the Jews? ... Well, you are Jesus of Nazareth, aren't you?' These are the words Pilate nailed to the cross: the provocation declared with Bowie's lounge lizard, upper-class intellectual star image signing British authority. In this way, the diplomatic Pilate attempts to ensnare Jesus, but Jesus's Pinteresque response denies Pilate his satisfaction: '"King" is your word.' Bowie then switches to Brechtian performativity with 'You're more dangerous than the Zealots' as his self-conscious pointing gesture is counterbalanced against his following naturalistic present tense remark: 'Do you know that?' If, in Goffman's terminology, Bowie 'is manipulating the presumably spontaneous aspects of his behaviour' to affect his audience, then he is doing so convincingly.

Stanislavsky's relationship between scene 'objective' and dramatic 'action' provides Bowie with a nuanced performance: changing his 'action' with each successive beat or verb/adverb relationship.[104] Wryly forcing Jesus with 'You had better say something', his emphasis is on the word 'had', which betrays an outside-in technique of Stanislavskian 'table work', cannily avoiding the obvious emphasis on 'better'. Bowie then displays what Counsell labels 'sustained nodding', a mannered performance trait imitative of Method. He nevertheless plays his next Stanislavskian 'beat' with subtle 'actions' including threatening gently, cajoling and deriding. Though still slim and sinuous, Bowie plays his part with self-convinced authority – not with camp Pre-Raphaelite hysteria. In this way, Bowie renders Pilate a ranking soldier with relaxed dominance in a quintessentially British manner (again relying on the signification of Scorsese's casting). Abiding by the rule 'power never argues', Bowie simply mocks and reasons with empirical, quiet confidence. Bowie then interjects across Dafoe's line to repeat, 'And Rome is the statue, yes', listening and responding in Stanislavskian present tense action.

Asking of Jesus's mystical kingdom, 'Where is it?', Bowie disparages inquisitively with the finesse of a naturalistic actor. Then provoking Jesus's response 'It's not here. Not on earth' with the comedic tone of a private joke, Bowie interjects: 'It wouldn't be, would it?' Here Bowie's outer space association precedes his performance, delivered with sceptical sarcasm to provide further irony.

This brings Bowie to Scorsese/Schrader's transitional beat, which Bowie performs expertly. Bowie sits beside Dafoe in two-shots, Scorsese framing them from behind: two adversaries equidistant from the camera: leper messiah and would-be messiah.[105] It is a moment of class levelling as Bowie politely explains: 'It's one thing to want to change the way that people live ... but you want to change how they think, how they feel', not with histrionic condemnation but with pity, active listening and engaged intelligence. With this response to Jesus's offence against Rome, a lesser actor might have ranted self-righteously (like the melodramatic epics of Scorsese's youth), but Bowie explains gently: 'It simply doesn't matter how you want to change things. We don't want them changed.' Scorsese then cuts to the reverse close-ups to pit evil (Bowie) against good (Dafoe). Despite the subtlety of his performance, Bowie's anisocoria catches the light demonically – connoting the sinister 'evil eye' in Hunt's sense (Figure 8.12).[106] This provides a beautiful visual irony from Bowie's caringly formal tone of delivery to the universal imagery of evil – a credit to Scorsese's direction. Perfect as Dafoe's worthy adversary, Bowie's mismatched irises counterbalance the blue-eyed vulnerability of Christ, the two actors' 'working consensus' captured in close-up as Bowie's weirdness becomes the dominant signifier. As Hunt explains: Bowie's 'discordant eyes'[107] connote not only how he is *seen* but also the way he *sees*, in this case, 'evil eye[-ed]'.[108] British cynical outsider pitted against the naïve idealism of Jesus, yet (also remediating Scorsese's cinematic precedents) both Caucasian.

Contrary to any Chaplinesque posing, Bowie then 'simply stands' to ask: 'You do understand what has to happen?' This is the final condemnation of Christ, again not with histrionics or clichéd handwashing gestures but with an oblique strategy: a Pinteresque reference to Golgotha, its significance already understood by billions. The handwashing gesture is replaced by a look back to Jesus – a mimetic 'attitude' adopted by Bowie, which appears to deny the audience any self-righteous biblical reading. With his understated delivery of this off-the-cuff dialogue, Bowie is more effective a tyrant than Rod Steiger's cowardly hysteria in Franco Zeffirelli's *Gesù di Nazareth* (1977) or the melodrama of Hristo Shopov in Mel Gibson's *The Passion of the Christ* (2004) (Figure 8.13). With the veiled threat of

FIGURE 8.12 *Bowie politely explains: his anisocoric eyes denoting evil/madness in juxtaposition to his gentleness.* © *Universal, Cineplex Odeon Films, Ufland Productions.*

Golgotha, Bowie's naturalistic performance prevails: Bowie plays his Stanislavskian actions with unwavering authenticity when explaining, with embittered pragmatism, that there are 'Three thousand skulls there by now', then switching back to Thin White Duke-inspired British classicism for the ensuing comment: 'I do wish you people would go out and count them some time. Maybe you'd learn a lesson.' In this way, with some well-planned and fluidly executed verb/adverb 'actions', Bowie explains domineeringly, mocks matter-of-factly, enquires innocently then patronizes Jesus with the present tense 'throwaway' line, 'Probably not' and exits, stage left, under Moulay Ismail's theatrical set. Far from a performative 'bag of tricks', with every sentence of this scene, Bowie changes his Brechtian signage and/ or Stanislavskian 'action' with performative finesse. Despite his mix of styles, Bowie nevertheless fosters an 'invisible' form of acting that appears authentic, which by Bethany Usher and Stephanie Fremaux's estimation *is* authentic.[109]

Bowie's role play within Goffman/Naremore's first two performance categories blends and blurs history – projecting his theatrical personae (Ziggy/Duke) while depicting a celebrity inhabiting a theatrical representation of himself (and Pilate). As such, Bowie represents a unique conflation of ideas relating to his star image, but this does not equate to what Brooker calls Bowie's tendency to 'play himself'. Analysing the scene, I perceive the character of Pilate through the lens of David Bowie or at least not not Bowie.[110] While challenging Auslander's 'differences between

FIGURE 8.13 *Hristo Shopov's melodramatic Pilate in Mel Gibson's* The Passion of the Christ *(2004).* © *Icon Productions.*

performers and spectators',[111] Bowie's authenticity prevails – a credit to his acting prowess and confluence of styles.

Bowie's presence renders Pilate 'evil', yet Bowie's naturalistic acting also humanizes him. This paradox suggests two alternative readings of the scene. First, that Bowie is a superman/*Übermensch* who befriends and condemns Scorsese's very human Jesus. Second, Bowie as perverse/vampiric figure fails to recognize the true messiah and condemns himself to eternal hell within the popular imaginary. Either way, the pivotal decision for the audience rests with Bowie's authentic and authenticated (and apparently) naturalistic acting, while harnessing Brechtian rhetorical performativity in tandem. As such, Bowie is both star and 'rich mist' of psychological signage. While Auslander analyses the 1970s Bowie as anti-authentic, this is only half the equation. By 1988, Bowie's conscious signage on film dovetails with his plausible portrayal of Pilate.

Conclusion

I venture that *Last Temptation* is Bowie's most successful naturalistic performance, yet still incorporates conflicting praxis from eclectic sources including Brechtian theory, Stanislavskian table work and delivery, Method imitation, mime and mask. Where he may previously have used his multiple stage personae as 'mechanism[s] of self-defense' to cover his vulnerability, in *Last Temptation* his acting craft incorporates his finessed choices as 'expressive incoherence' and present tense action, while mix-matching performance styles to great effect. While we can never know what motivated Bowie's key moments on screen or what degree of formal analysis he brings to his performances, we can at least use acting theory as a discursive tool to break down the signs of performance in *Last Temptation* and show the aptitude of his delivery. His unique exploitation of mask, mime and gesture, his drawing upon contrasting codes of performance to appear *like* a naturalistic actor and – whether authenticated performance or simply an obvious, spunky copy – Bowie's body, gesture and expression betray an adept and versatile screen performer.[112]

By directing the gaze of the spectator to dispel the assumption that Bowie merely plays himself, I have shown how Bowie's iconic performativity confounds his naturalistic authenticity in *Last Temptation*, yet his performance remains intact. In this way, Bowie helps render *Last Temptation*'s Jesus figure accessible to non-believers by utilizing his past personae in his role as Pilate – even in absence. Further, Bowie's performance allows a misreading of naturalistic conventions to expose the limitations and hypocrisies of Method's 'iconography of neurosis' as well as exploiting and challenging Brecht's epic theatre.[113] As such, Bowie's iconography interplays with his authenticity, often exposing the denied ideology of naturalism. The fluidity of Bowie's star image and gender undecidability inflects his performance, which can never be read through the fresh eyes of the naturalism afforded an unknown player – even if the viewer does not know him. Yet, Bowie works hard to play over and above his iconography to maintain authenticity. This questions Clurman's dissatisfaction with 'competent stagecraft' as mere fabrication and artifice. Indeed, the text itself, which references St John's gospel, effectively enmeshes the mystery of Jesus with the hallowed 'myth of Bowie'.[114]

Notes

1. Ana Leorne, 'Dear Dr. Freud – David Bowie Hits the Couch: A Psychoanalytic Approach to Some of his Personae', in *David Bowie: Critical Perspectives*, ed. Eoin Devereux, Aileen Dillane and Martin J. Power (London and New York: Routledge, 2015), 111–27.
2. James Naremore, *Acting in the Cinema* (Berkeley, CA: University of California Press, 1988), 28.
3. Colin Counsell, *Signs of Performance: An Introduction to Twentieth-Century Theatre* (USA: Routledge, 1996).
4. Ibid.
5. Robert McKee, *Story: Substance, Structure, Style and the Principles of Screenwriting* (Great Britain: Methuen Publishing Limited, 1999).
6. Richard Schechner, *Performance Theory* (London: Routledge, 2003); Counsell, *Signs of Performance*.
7. Ian Christie and David Thompson, *Scorsese on Scorsese* (USA: Farrar, Straus and Giroux, 2004), 128.
8. Ibid., 117.
9. Ann Wroe, *Pontius Pilate* (New York: Random House, 1999).
10. Helen K. Bond, *Pontius Pilate in History and Interpretation* (Cambridge: Cambridge University Press, 2000).
11. Christie and Thompson, *Scorsese on Scorsese*, 116.
12. Ibid., 123.
13. Ibid., 117.
14. Ibid., 126.
15. Ibid., 131–2.
16. Ibid., 120.
17. Ibid., 124.
18. Ibid., 120.
19. Ibid., 124.
20. Ibid., 126.

21 Sting, *Englishman in New York*, A&M Records, 13 October 1987, CD.
22 Christie and Thompson, *Scorsese on Scorsese*, 127.
23 Despite Dafoe's own performance eclecticism, commentary is beyond the present scope.
24 Wendy Leigh, *Bowie: The Biography* (New York: Gallery Books, 2014), 135.
25 Judith Weston, *Directing Actors: Creating Memorable Performances for Film & Television* (California: Michael Weise Productions, 1996).
26 Leigh, *Bowie*, 147.
27 See Lisa Perrott in Chapter 1 for an alternative perspective.
28 Steve Shroyer and John Lifflander, 'Spaced Out in The Desert', *Creem* (December 1975). www.bowiegoldenyears.com/press/75-12-00-creem.html.
29 Will Brooker, *Why Bowie Matters* (Great Britain: William Collins, 2019), 12, 97.
30 Christopher Frayling, Phillip Hoare and Mark Kermode, 'David Bowie Then . . . David Bowie Now', in *David Bowie Is,* ed. Victoria Broackes and Geoffrey Marsh (London: V & A Publishing, 2013), 285.
31 Leigh, *Bowie*, 117.
32 Paul Morley, *The Age of Bowie: How David Bowie Made a World of Difference* (New York: Gallery Books, 2014), 70–1, 126, 161.
33 Leorne, 'Dear Dr. Freud', 114, 123.
34 Paul Trynka, *Starman: David Bowie the Definitive Biography* (Great Britain: Sphere, 2012).
35 Leorne, 'Dear Dr. Freud', 124.
36 Leigh cites Lisa Robinson, *Biography*, 211.
37 David Bowie, *When I'm Five*, Deram, May 1984, CD.
38 Chris O' Leary, *'When I'm Five,' Pushing Ahead of the Dame*, published 2 November 2009, https://bowiesongs.wordpress.com/?s=when+I%27m+five.
39 Philip Auslander, *Performing Glam Rock: Gender and Theatricality in Popular Music* (Ann Arbor, MI: University of Michigan Press, 2006), 5.
40 Eoin Devereux, Aileen Dillane and Martin J. Power, eds, *David Bowie: Critical Perspectives* (London and New York: Routledge, 2015), xiv. 'David Bowie Is One of the Few Artists to Whom the Term ["iconic"] Is Deservedly Ascribed'.
41 Erving Goffman, *The Presentation of Self in Everyday Life* (Middlesex: Penguin Books, 1980), 13–14.
42 Ibid.
43 Brooker, *Why Bowie Matters*, 27, 41.
44 Naremore, *Acting in the Cinema*, 2.
45 Ibid., 28.
46 Ibid., 14.
47 Ibid., 2.

48 Counsell, *Signs of Performance*.
49 Susan Batson, *Truth: Personas, Needs and Flaws in the Art of Building Actors and Creating Characters* (USA: Webster\Stone, 2013), 10.
50 Schechner, *Performance Theory*, 2.
51 Ibid., 7.
52 As does Naremore, *Acting in the Cinema*, 14.
53 Ian Dixon, "So Where's the Moral?': David Bowie becomes *The Elephant Man* (1980) in the Theatre of Disability', in *The Cambridge Companion to David Bowie*, ed. Denis Flannery (Cambridge: Cambridge University Press, forthcoming in 2023).
54 Leorne, 'Dear Dr. Freud', 123.
55 Kevin J. Hunt, 'The Eyes of David Bowie', in *Enchanting David Bowie: Space/Time/Body/Memory*, ed. Toija Cinque, Christopher Moore and Sean Redmond (New York: Bloomsbury Academic, 2015), 175–96. Hunt's citation of Chris Rojek introduces the notion of mask as not only hiding the wearer but also identifying the character.
56 Ibid., 184; Hunt cites Efrat Tseëlon, *Masquerade and Identities: Essays on Gender, Sexuality and Marginality* (London: Routledge, 2001).
57 David Bowie, *Alabama Song*, BOW 5, PB 9510, 1978, compact disc.
58 Joe Gore, 'Changes 2.1: New Digital Stimulation from David Bowie and Reeves Gabrels', *Guitar Player*, June 1997, 46–7.
59 *Baal*, directed by Alan Clarke, aired 9 March 1982 on BBC TV.
60 Counsell, *Signs of Performance*, 102.
61 Ibid, 103.
62 Ibid, 71.
63 Leigh, *Bowie*, 216.
64 Bertolt Brecht, *The Messingkauf Dialogues* (London: Methuen, 1985), 28.
65 Ibid., 46.
66 Counsell, *Signs of Performance*, 96.
67 Ibid., 71.
68 Barney Hoskyns, *Glam!: Bowie, Bolan and the Glitter Rock Revolution* (London: Faber and Faber, 1998), 11.
69 Counsell, *Signs of Performance*.
70 David Bowie, *'Heroes'*, RCA Records, 14 October 1977, CD.
71 Christie and Thompson, *Scorsese on Scorsese*, 127.
72 Hoskyns, *Glam!*, 11.
73 Naremore, *Acting in the Cinema*, 17.
74 Christie and Thompson, *Scorsese on Scorsese*, 118.
75 Hunt, 'The Eyes of David Bowie'.
76 Leorne, 'Dear Dr. Freud – David Bowie Hits the Couch', 114.

77   Auslander, *Performing Glam Rock*, 6.
78   Ibid., 5.
79   Sean Redmond, 'The Whiteness of David Bowie', in *Enchanting David Bowie: Space/Time/Body/Memory*, ed. Toija Cinque, Christopher Moore and Sean Redmond (New York: Bloomsbury Academic, 2015), 217.
80   Shelton Waldrep, *Future Nostalgia: Performing David Bowie* (New York: Bloomsbury Academic, 2015), 29.
81   Roland Barthes, *Mythologies* (London: Vintage, 1993), 26.
82   Naremore, *Acting in the Cinema*.
83   Counsell, *Signs of Performance*.
84   Bethany Usher and Stephanie Fremaux, 'Turn Myself to Face Me: David Bowie in the 1990s and Discovery of Authentic Self', in *David Bowie: Critical Perspectives*, ed. Eoin Devereux, Aileen Dillane and Martin J. Power (London and New York: Routledge, 2015), 56–81.
85   Leorne, 'Dear Dr. Freud', 119.
86   Counsell, *Signs of Performance*, 86.
87   Ibid., 87.
88   Ibid., 86.
89   Ibid., 87.
90   Ibid., 90.
91   Naremore, *Acting in the Cinema*.
92   Counsell, *Signs of Performance*, 71.
93   Auslander, *Performing Glam Rock,* 13; Lauren Onkey, 'Voodoo Child: Jimi Hendrix and the Politics of Race in the Sixties', in *Imagine Nation: The American Counterculture in the 1960s and '70s,* ed. Peter Braunstein and Michael William Doyle (New York: Routledge, 2002), 200.
94   Michael Chekhov, *To the Director and Playwright* (Connecticut: Praeger, 1977).
95   Batson, *Truth*, 11.
96   Amedeo D'Adamo, 'Ain't there One Damn Flag that Can Make Me Break Down and Cry?' in *Enchanting David Bowie: Space/Time/Body/Memory,* ed. Toija Cinque, Christopher Moore and Sean Redmond (New York: Bloomsbury Academic, 2015), 121.
97   Naremore, *Acting in the Cinema*, 4.
98   Ibid., 14.
99   Leo Braudy, *The World in a Frame: What we See in Films* (Chicago, IL and London: University of Chicago Press, 1976), 202.
100 Naremore, *Acting in the Cinema*, 17.
101 Ibid., 80; Goffman, *The Presentation of Self in Everyday Life*, 14.
102 Leorne, 'Dear Dr. Freud', 31.
103 Wroe, *Pontius Pilate*.

104 Weston, *Directing Actors*.
105 Alexander Sun, personal communication.
106 Hunt, 'The Eyes of David Bowie', 176.
107 Ibid., 175.
108 Ibid., 183.
109 Usher and Fremaux, 'Turn Myself to Face Me'.
110 Auslander, *Performing Glam Rock*, 5.
111 Ibid., 13–14.
112 Morley, *The Age of Bowie*.
113 Counsell, *Signs of Performance*, 70.
114 Frayling, Hoare and Kermode, 'David Bowie Then . . . David Bowie Now', 293.

9

The surveillant power of the (a)temporal cameo in *Twin Peaks*

Fire Walk with Me (1992)

Tyne Daile Sumner

>Watching them come and go
>Tomorrows and the yesterdays

From the poetic isolation of astronaut Major Tom in 'Space Oddity' ('And I think my spaceship knows which way to go') to the poised disaffection of 'Fashion' ('They do it over there / But we don't do it here'), the role of the 'outsider looking in' has been a foundation of David Bowie's oeuvre. Numerous critics have described this tendency as Bowie's alienation, while others have used terms such as tourist, voyeur or rogue to describe his capacity to be both inside and outside at once.[1] Of his expertly crafted characterization as an 'other', Bowie himself has commented:

>I do tend to stand on the outside sometimes. I don't know whether it's a failing or whether it's an advantage. My own feeling is that I hope very much that an outsider's viewpoint is as beneficial, if not more beneficial than that of somebody who is completely involved.[2]

As this reflection reveals, Bowie has crafted his distinctive performance style out of the constitutive tension between insider and outsider, a method that

FIGURE 9.1 *Agent Dale Cooper and Phillip Jeffries in the office hallway. Still from* Twin Peaks: Fire Walk with Me *by David Lynch.* © *1992 Twin Peaks productions.*

exemplifies his filmic appearances as much as it does his music, fashion and visual art, all of which feature personas with distinctive and complex positions with regard to observation and knowledge. With this hybrid performance technique as its starting point, this chapter uses Bowie's cameo appearance in David Lynch's 1992 film *Twin Peaks: Fire Walk with Me (Fire)* to explore the contradictory role that internal and external subjectivities play in structuring his work. It shows that, by evading a fixed subjectivity and disrupting the logical sequence of cinematic time, Bowie stages a surveillant perspective that confuses and distorts narrative order, rendering it both atemporal and highly unstable. Surveillant subjectivity in Bowie's performance in *Fire* is thus defined by his ability to play the roles of voyeur and alienated subject at once: always the outsider looking in.

While several critics have already addressed Bowie's role as an outsider in both his music and filmic performances, little has been written to date regarding the extent to which his position as insider/outsider and observed/observer works to disrupt temporal and narrative logic. Ian Chapman has noted how, as a key part of his 'performative palette, Bowie has frequently taken the position of an outsider, and in so doing he has provided something of a rallying call for those who may themselves feel alienated'.[3] Relatedly, Denis Flannery has read the duality and othering that characterizes Bowie's oeuvre through the concept of absence. 'In Bowie's songs', he writes, 'there is often a figure who is addressed, a figure who, like the audience, is moving towards absence and a second figure who is fearfully becoming absent just because the first figure moves away.'[4] Perhaps the most obvious characters in this formulation are Major Tom and Ground Control; however, as recently as 2015 in the stage musical *Lazarus*, Bowie was strategically visually and physically absent, even though his songs were used to structure the performance end to end.

Through a close examination of Bowie's brief but formative cameo in *Fire*, I extend these readings with an attention to the implications that the role of 'outsider looking in' has for the film's depiction of surveillant subjectivity. In the cameo and the film more generally, I explore the technological, temporal and psychological dislocation enacted by Lynch's dramatic use of the mounted surveillance camera, a device that is used both figuratively and literally to develop Bowie's cinematic construction of the surveillant gaze. In this model, both panoptic and synoptic surveillance prevail as viewers experience a scene in which physical and digital surveillance are conflated upon the site of Bowie's body moving through time. To borrow Thomas Mathiesen's theorization in 'The Viewer Society', the surveillant gaze in Bowie's cameo establishes a *synoptic* 'system enabling the many to see and contemplate the few' alongside the *panoptic* model of the few observing the many.[5] To account for this shift, this chapter reads surveillance through Michel Foucault and Gilles Deleuze's models of Panopticism as well as engages with the work of Mary Ann Doane to consider the infiltration of Bowie's body into cinematic time. While Lynch's film is largely concerned with the surveillance strategies of several FBI agents who seek to decode visual clues, understand cryptic dialogue and interpret surrealist dreams, I argue that it is Bowie whose observational powers are ultimately the most discerning because he is able to be both absent and present, and therefore inside and outside, at the same time.

Keep your 'lectric eye on me, babe'

In *Twin Peaks: Fire Walk with Me*, David Bowie plays the mysterious Phillip Jeffries, an agent of the Federal Bureau of Investigation who vanished while on assignment in Buenos Aires, Argentina, in 1987. Occurring near the start of the film, Bowie's cameo scene opens with a shot of Philadelphia's Liberty Bell, an iconic symbol of American independence with its distinctive large crack, said to have been acquired sometime in the early nineteenth century. FBI agent Dale Cooper (Kyle MacLachlan) enters an office and approaches Regional Bureau Chief Gordon Cole (David Lynch) before kneeling at a desk and soberly stating: 'Gordon. It's 10.10 am on February sixteenth. I was worried about today because of the dream I told you about.' By conflating the act of surveillant extrapolation with reference to a cryptic dream, Cooper's statement reflects a common strategy in Lynch's work in which a seemingly straightforward crime narrative is subverted or distorted through supernatural themes. By connecting a fact ('It's 10.10 am on February sixteenth') with a personal anecdote about a dream, Cooper's statement sets up the film's distinct 'philosophical context' in which Lynch ties surveillant forms of knowledge acquisition ('characters searching for clues, accumulating evidence, and making inferences') to dreaming.[6] As a result, viewers are immediately positioned to question the possibility that the scene itself is already part of a dream sequence.

In this formative moment of *Fire*, Cooper's perplexing reference to both the time and a dream foregrounds temporal dislocation as one of the film's central tropes, informing its relationship to the *Twin Peaks* series of which it is a prequel as well as the way that surveillant subjectivity is rendered throughout. Having been told the time of day, Cole looks at his wristwatch yet does not appear to register the ostensible relevance of the information Cooper has arrived to impart. The cut that immediately follows reveals a long corridor, at the end of which a mounted surveillance camera is centrally positioned to maximize a line of sight along the full length of the scene. Cooper abruptly appears in frame before stopping in the middle of the corridor as if instinctively aware of the camera's presence. A succession of brief shots then alternates between Cooper looking directly into the mounted surveillance camera and attempting to verify the camera's digital record of his presence in an adjacent room, described in Lynch's original film script as 'the Surveillance Room', where a bank of screens are being monitored by an unnamed man. In an attempt to be both in front of the camera's gaze (observed) and see himself captured on camera (observer) at the same time, Cooper walks back and forth between the two sites, appearing confused that he is not able to glimpse himself rendered in the surveillance matrix. The indiscernibility of exterior and interior in this sequence is typically Lynchian (as some would argue, Freudian) in that Cooper's voyeuristic witnessing – while an attempt at resolution – only works to further confuse the physical and temporal puzzle.

It is perhaps no surprise, then, that David Bowie would be Lynch's choice for a cameo appearance in this scene. Afterall, Bowie's work is frequently characterized by a similar method in which cryptic messages are communicated from within a conflicted or surrealist dream state or from a position of external omniscient observation. The lyrics of 'Space Oddity', for example ('I've heard a rumour from Ground Control / Oh, no, don't say it's true'), reflect his 'fascination with the interior, unconscious worlds of dreams and ideas that arise and percolate from this state of heightened consciousness'.[7] Similarly, the narrative and aesthetic environment of the *Ashes to Ashes* music video represents a heighted instance of Bowie's deliberate fusion of puzzle, introspection and dream. The apparent lack of logic in *Ashes to Ashes*, combined with its placement of characters in seemingly incongruent settings and its vivid, expressionistic colouring, all point to a surrealist version of interiority in which Bowie – as both Bowie *and* Bowie in character – achieves an all-knowing, all-seeing perspective that exists beyond the viewer's own viewpoint.[8] It is therefore crucial that, prior to Bowie's entrance into the scene, Cooper and Cole are already ostensibly confused by narrative and temporal order.

Cooper subsequently becomes fixated on the boundary between the actual and the recorded as he uses his own appearance on the CCTV camera as a tool for validating space and time. Leo Charney describes this mode of epistemological experimentation in his observation that '[m]odern subjects (re)discovered their place as buffers between past and future by (re) experiencing this condition as film-viewers. Past and future clashed not in a hypothetical zone but on the terrain of the body.'[9] For Cooper, viewing the *absence* of himself on camera becomes the arena in which temporal dislocations are tested and verified insofar as the surveillant gaze implicates his body (the body of the viewer) in experiencing movement in time. Moreover, the temporal boundaries of this corridor scene are estranged from the real time of the bureau office, creating the effect of a conversation taking place in another place and time. This is an archetypal cinematic split that produces 'a simulacrum of time' in which, as May Anne Doane has described, 'temporal continuity is in fact haunted by absence, by the lost time represented by the division between frames'.[10]

Yet while the cameras in the surveillance room at first appear to display a live feed of the nearby corridor, David Bowie's entrance produces an instantaneous rupture in the space and time parameters verified by Cooper's rehearsal in front of the CCTV moments prior. A lift door opens with a loud metallic 'ding!' and the camera rests for about five seconds on the space outside the lift where we expect someone will appear but does not, suggesting an otherworldly or alien presence in the space of the FBI office. Sean Redmond observes that Bowie's peculiar '(dis)appearance' in this scene is akin to 'a classically coded star cameo entrance, the delay a device to build suspense before the blissful surprise'.[11] Yet the figure who emerges from the lift is both familiar and alien at the same time: unmistakably dressed in a loose-fitting pastel suit reminiscent of Bowie's 1983 *Let's Dance* chapter and yet markedly distinct from the officially adorned FBI agents in the office. Fans acquainted with this period in Bowie's career are positioned to immediately recognize a style 'from the period when Bowie became an international superstar and supposedly dropped the masks and costumes along with much of his subversive play and provocation'.[12] This was also the period which marked the beginning of 'Bowie's return to (or invention of) a fitter, happier, healthier self', stripped of all the personas he'd adopted in the previous decade.[13] Lynch's decision to costume Bowie as reminiscent of arguably his most commercially popular incarnation therefore seems a strategic choice in the context of Jeffries's indiscernibility as a character. Even if agent Jeffries is not real and is in fact merely a figure in Cooper's dream, David Bowie is nevertheless unmistakably *Bowie*.[14]

Following this first glimpse of Bowie as the 'businessman'[15] of his most stylistically normative era, the scene cuts back to Cooper staring (once again) into the hallway surveillance camera. Bowie can be partially seen walking towards Cooper's turned back before Cooper abruptly turns again into the surveillance room as Bowie strides concentratedly down the corridor. The following series of cuts add yet another layer to the intensifying temporal and spatial dislocation of the scene as it becomes unclear whether Bowie's character is intended to be the real Philip Jeffries – escaped from the Black Lodge after missing for two years – or a figment of the dream Cooper tells agent Cole about at the beginning of the scene. To verify the situation for himself, Cooper scans the surveillance room TVs to observe the movements captured on the camera moments earlier. 'This time Cooper is amazed to see himself staring into the camera', the stage direction states, 'and behind him is Phillip Jeffries coming towards him and the camera.'[16] Yet unlike the prior surveillant construction in which the CCTV appears to show live events (Cooper cannot be both on camera and in the surveillance room at the same time), this time he observes not only himself on the screen with Jeffries behind but also an event that has not yet occurred in the real: Jeffries passes by Cooper and proceeds to walk into the office.

Time in this scene becomes indexical to observation as the focus remains on Cooper's face and gaze, positioning the viewer to consider time and space through his mind's eye. This staging draws on Freud's theorization of the experience of *unheimlich* ('the uncanny') in which a certain form of unease or fear is experienced through engagement with things unknown or strange. The idea of the familiar turned unfamiliar, expounded by Freud in his 1919 essay, is a useful frame for thinking about the role of observation in this scene. Bowie's (Jeffries's) appearance in the bureau office renders Cooper's experience uncanny, a strangeness that becomes amplified when the use of technology to capture his visage itself appears to deviate from a normative understanding of space and time. In this sense, as Freud acknowledges, our experience of the scene becomes a measure of the extent to which we believe we are seeing through the eyes of the narrator or taking on some other kind of vision, perhaps that of the author.[17] For Cooper, seeing the figure of Bowie exist outside the logical boundaries of space and time generates 'the opposite of what is familiar' and leads him to question the validity of his own observations.[18] In contrast to Cooper's confused body language and facial expressions, Jeffries/Bowie seems oblivious to the fact that he is out of place as he charges boldly into the office. The demonstrable otherness of Bowie's entrance in this scene reflects what Kevin Hunt has described as 'the ethereal aspect' central to his 'star persona' which is 'epitomized in many of his characterisations' including Major Tom, Ziggy Stardust, Aladdin Sane and so on.[19] From the first moment of Bowie's appearance in the cameo, therefore, *Fire* trades on his association with the alienated, all-seeing 'other' to suggest that there are components of the world that he, and only he, can see. Or, as Redmond observes of the way that Bowie's presence works to fragment this moment of the film, 'Cooper is very much experiencing time and space in the age of postmodernity.'[20]

By distorting a normative sequence of time, Lynch creates a gap between the live feed of the surveillance footage and the dislocated (out of place and out of time) Bowie, one that suggests multiple scenes are taking place at once. The temporal and the technological are imbricated via the surveillance apparatus, revealing a parallel narrative in which Phillip Jeffries is ostensibly *ahead* of the real time of the bureau office. 'The experience of classical cinema', observes Will Scheibel, 'follows a common-sense logic of images controlled by the sensory-motor schema, that is, everyday life perceptions of space-time relations, achieving the illusion of verisimilitude.'[21] The processes of montage we see on film or 'movement-images', therefore, 'indirectly represent time as linear and chronological, as physical movement through space'.[22] The extent to which we perceive Bowie's (dis)appearance to disrupt the narrative continuity of the scene is ultimately contingent upon the extent to which we believe he even exists in the real space-time of the scene at all. As Deleuze explains of this kind of bodily and temporal fragmentation in *Cinema 2*: 'Time is out of joint . . . time is no longer subordinated to movement, but rather movement to time.'[23] Bowie's bodily (dis)placement is consistent with the ways in which his body performs (and is performed) across most of his work – a body that 'crosses thresholds and boundaries'.[24] As Cinque, Moore and Redmond write, Bowie's body is 'a body also easily resurrected, god-like in its ability to be reborn and remade, a new character emerging from its transcendental canvas'.[25] Using his body as a vehicle for transcending the space and time of the bureau office, Bowie strategically distorts and confuses the surveillance matrix, leaving the agents charged with monitoring the office to question their own observations.

Foucault's theorization of how individuals are both constituted and constitute themselves as modern subjects is a useful paradigm for considering how Bowie first engages with the 'general gaze' in order to transcend the 'threshold of visibility' that forms the central trope of his cameo appearance.[26] For Foucault, 'the power of normalisation imposes homogeneity; but it individualizes by making it possible to measure gaps, to determine levels, to fix specialities and to render the differences useful by fitting them one to another'.[27] Since the normalizing gaze is central to understanding Foucault's view of how modern power functions, it is doubly useful for thinking about how Bowie's cameo initiates a postmodern break from coercive means of observation by confusing, resisting and controlling the visual formulations of the bureau cameras, as well as distorting Cooper's observational powers as an FBI agent. As Redmond asks of the fragmented narrative sequence in this scene, brought about by Bowie's ability to fracture the surveillant gaze: 'Is this a flash-forward, a fragment or a figment from Agent Cooper's dream(ing), or a ghost walking in plain sight?'[28]

Similarly, Gary Marx's *Windows into the Soul* offers a useful guide to this scenario in its study of surveillant 'interaction – whether face-to-face or remote involving agents and subjects of surveillance'.[29] Marx's methodological approach helps explain Lynch's use of Bowie's disjointed character in its assertion that a 'central task of the sociological tradition of symbolic interaction and dramaturgy is to understand how individuals and organizations present themselves through the control and release of personal information, and how others respond to this'.[30] Surveillance, particularly of the kind we witness agent Cooper enact in this scene is, as Marx explains, about the extraction of information from the 'ubiquitous flow of distinct data points' with the aim of producing a coherent narrative.[31] Yet while this is most certainly Cooper's aim, the insertion of Bowie into the scene – both there and not there, not clearly Jeffries and yet not entirely Bowie – confuses the information flow at precisely the moment it becomes electronically recorded. The disruption to the way information is collected, recorded and analysed in this scene resists the surveillant impulse of the late-twentieth-century Information Age, with which Bowie was intimately familiar.

In fact, many interviews and public comments reveal that Bowie was acutely aware of and responsive to the ideological and technological dimensions of digital surveillance. In a 1999 interview with the BBC's Jeremy Paxman, for example, he eerily predicted the surveillant consequences that mass data use would have for the internet, a phenomenon Shoshana Zuboff would later call 'surveillance capitalism':

> I think the potential of what the internet is going to do to society, both good and bad, is unimaginable. I think we're actually on the cusp of something exhilarating and terrifying . . . the actual context and the state of content is going to be so different to anything that we can really envisage at the moment. Where the interplay between the user and the provider will be so in sympatico it's going to crush our ideas of what mediums are all about.[32]

This remarkably prescient reflection was preceded by the launch of BowieNet in September 1998, an ISP devised by Bowie and entertainment pioneers Robert Goodale and Ron Roy which aimed to offer 'uncensored' access to a dedicated David Bowie website and music archive. The relationship between technology, observation and subjectivity that Bowie touches on in this response is also evident in his music, as shown by songs such as '1984' ('You've read it in the tea leaves, and the tracks are on TV'), 'Sound and Vision' ('Blue, blue, electric blue / That's the colour of my room') and even 'TVC15', a song that is said to chart a hallucinogenic experience Bowie had while in front of a television but which also evokes a sense of the seductive influence of twentieth-century technologies on people's attention spans, perceptions and lifestyles.

I get funny dreams again and again

The tension between interiority and exteriority that mediates agent Cooper's surveillance room experience intensifies as the scene continues, with the thematic focus turning to a surrealist dream. David Bowie ('the long-lost Phillip Jefferies') stumbles into the office in which agent Cole has been sitting at the desk, causing him to rise in alarm and yell: 'Phillip, is that you?' Initiating the dreamlike vortex, an unnerving, atonal sound plays, and a fuzzy blue pixilation appears, creating the effect of the entire scene either teleporting in time or existing in another dimension. This could be described as a 'Lynchian distortion of our conventional understanding of the natural world [that] tends to hone in on a special, seemingly inaccessible location: a dream space (or "another place")'.[33] A distressed-looking Jeffries, speaking in a strong southern drawl, staggers forward and proclaims: 'Well, now, I'm not going to talk about Judy. In fact, we are not going to talk about Judy at all, we're going to keep her out of it.' Bowie's strong accent and jittery, exaggerated tone, while in many ways recognizably *Bowie*, nevertheless comes as a surprise in contrast to the constrained and official enunciation of the other bureau agents. Pointing concentratedly at agent Cooper, who has followed him into the office, Jeffries questions: 'Who do you think this is, there?' The excess of linguistic shifters in this conspicuously strange (rhetorical) question creates a jarring effect for the viewer, one that echoes the 'subversive imitation' that has played out provocatively across Bowie's career through 'costume, make-up, reworking of lyrics, vocal mimicry, musical quotation, bodily gesture and pose'.[34] Lisa Perrott has argued that, as 'is the case with auditory and musical mimicry, the affective intensity of bodily communication through movement, stasis and kinaesthetic recognition is a primal vehicle for transgression'.[35] Bowie is thus the ideal figure for Lynch's effort to establish a subjective fluidity and alienation in the character of Jeffries, not just because of his ability to move his body in peculiar ways but also because of his natural tendency towards unsettling modes of vocal distortion and imitation.

Alongside the performative strangeness of his accent, Jeffries's question suggests that he has information the others do not; pointing sternly at Cooper is perhaps a reference to his prior encounters with him that exist somewhere in a non-linear timeframe. In one sense, the 'this' that Jeffries refers to can also be read as purely fictive, reminding us that even one's experience of external reality and of physical matter itself can be 'every bit as expansive as that of the interior consciousness'.[36] By both evading fixed subjectivity and ostensibly harbouring secret knowledge about Cooper, Jeffries exemplifies modern disciplinary power through the application of a distinct form of hierarchical observation.

This is consistent with Foucault's notion of an embedded surveillance – that of an architecture that 'is no longer built simply to be seen' or 'to observe external space' but rather to facilitate an 'internal, articulated and detailed control'. In *Discipline and Punish* Foucault outlines this model, noting how

> The perfect disciplinary apparatus would make it possible for a single gaze to see everything constantly. A central point would be both the source of light illuminating everything, and a locus of convergence for everything that must be known: a perfect eye that nothing would escape and a centre towards which all gazes would be turned.[37]

While Cooper retains the apparent insight and foreshadowing ability of his dream, Jeffries seems to experience multiple dimensions at once, suggesting a parallel plot into which neither the viewer nor Cooper gain insight but also multiple ways of seeing within a single scene. This reflects Kevin Hunt's observation in 'The Eyes of David Bowie' that '[a]side from having uncanny qualities that affect how Bowie is seen, Bowie's eyes are also part of how *he* sees'.[38] As the scene begins to break up and fragment, it is evident that the static interference that causes it to dissolve in and out of view is somehow produced by Jeffries, who uses his reappearance to tell Cole that he has 'been to one of their meetings' which takes place 'above a convenience store'. While Jeffries's speech is certainly obscured by interfering sounds (most notably electronic static) it is also interwoven with dialogue of the critical meeting in the convenience store, creating a monologue that is, to borrow Michel Chion's expression, 'parasited by another scene'.[39]

Yet while Jeffries's apparent control over the machinations of this scene can be read as a commentary on the disciplinary power of the modern subject, the grammatical strangeness of his question – using 'this' in place of 'that' when pointing at Cooper – could also be an allusion to the self-reflexive status of the Lynchian cameo itself insofar as Bowie is actually asking the viewer to question who *he* is, and not the FBI agent at whom he's pointing. At this critical moment in the film, David Bowie's appearance functions as both celebrity cameo and as a commentary on the illusory nature of surveillance. Cooper, while a trained observer, does not quite believe that David Bowie has walked into the FBI office, as evidenced by his stunned expression and attempts to compel agent Cole to verify the scene unfolding in front of him. Meanwhile, Bowie turns viewers' attention back onto Cooper, positioning us to question whether it is in fact Cooper who should be under close scrutiny and observation. The transgressive nature of Bowie's identity, combined with the mystery behind Jeffries's disappearance and sudden, unexpected reappearance thus undermines bureau logic. Jeffries's cryptic reappearance in this scene, combined with his 'mysteriously unclear location, seemingly outside of the natural world' and his parting message ('We live inside a dream'), ties 'dreams to the supernatural'.[40] Moreover, as Riches astutely observes, the scene 'recalls a question posed by

Donna to Harold, in *Twin Peaks'* "The Orchid's Curse" (season 2, episode 5), when, like her best friend Laura, Donna begins to fall under his spell'.[41] Philosophically questioning the boundaries of perceived reality, Donna asks: 'How do we know that our dreams are not real?'[42]

After Jeffries shouts, 'We live inside a dream!', an eerie scene follows showing a room of people including The Man From Another Place (Michael J. Anderson), Bob (Frank Silva), Mrs Chalfont and her grandson, The Jumping Man, the Electrician and two Woodmen. Several characters speak cryptically before moving into a secondary realm of the Red Room, a montage sequence immediately recognizable by *Twin Peaks* fans. Central to this unnerving sequence is the classically Lynchian trope of the mask, used repeatedly by the grandson who lifts a mask on and off his face stylistically. The mask also functions to critique Bowie's own multi-layered facades, reminding us of the many masks and disguises he has worn and reinvented throughout this career.[43] Some critics have connected Bowie's mask wearing and role playing with his personal experiences, suggesting that they had, to some extent, been an antidote for his emotional numbness.[44] Perhaps supporting this idea, Bowie once told Hubert Saal: 'Offstage I'm a robot. Onstage I achieve emotion. It's probably why I prefer dressing up as Ziggy to being David.'[45] Whatever the connection between the masks in this scene and Bowie's own emotional vicissitudes, Lynch uses them to amplify the effect of multiple identities converging at once, both in the time of the bureau office and the time of the Red Room. Back in the Philadelphia office, Jeffries lets out a loud, tormented scream before suddenly disappearing against the backdrop of haphazardly shot powerlines, an empty wooden chair and a blue sky as news arrives from Dear Meadow that Desmond has also vanished.

This scene exemplifies the way that Lynch's viewers are frequently positioned to decipher complex plots by stitching together coded messages delivered in the form of characters' cryptic speech or dreams. Yet the dream sequence of Bowie's cameo shows that there are also instances in which Lynch's characters must examine their own dreams in order to gain knowledge. Agent Cooper is critical to this surveillant paradox in that, as Chris Rodley has noted, he is 'unique in the detective genre, because he uses his mind, his body and most importantly his intuition'.[46] Staying true to his mantra of 'crack the code, solve the crime', Cooper immediately returns to the surveillance room and replays the camera footage in order to confirm whether Jeffries/Bowie did actually walk up behind him in the hallway. While Cooper ordinarily uses 'the intuitive dimension of his unconscious', a trait that 'distinguishes him from both classical and hard-boiled versions of the detective', he must rely on the electronic recorded image in his attempt to locate Bowie in space and time.[47] By subverting and renegotiating time, Bowie uses his role as a surveillant agent to add yet another layer of shapeshifting to his already unstable identity. As the metatheatricality of this scene shows, when David Bowie 'embodies a cameo role, a series of intersecting star and performance registers are in play that suggest that he is always *in cameo*'.⁴⁸

Spy, spy, pretty girl

In taking on the 'disappearing' role of FBI agent Phillip Jeffries, Bowie's performance in *Twin Peaks: Fire Walk with Me* differs notably from his cameo appearances in other films where he appears as himself.⁴⁹ By playing a bureau agent, Bowie uses his cameo to develop a commentary on the observational paradox that characterizes modern disciplinary surveillance by deliberately confusing the roles of observed and observer as well as via the distortion of the clues, dialogue and other information viewers normally use when trying to interpret Lynch's films. Afterall, the history of surveillance is in many ways tied to the history of bureaucratic information collecting, even if that information does not provide a clear explanation for the human interactions it seeks to surveil. The proliferation of textual and visual documentation about individual citizens by surveillance organizations works in contradictory ways to not only instil fear and accountability in people but also to confuse, deflect and delay. Or, to borrow Valentin Groebner's useful description, 'surveillance achieves its effects not through administrative perfection, but through arbitrariness'.⁵⁰ Other scholars have drawn attention to the ways that surveillance strategies are preoccupied with controlling 'the emotive import of words' by establishing 'an evaluative scale of patriotism and betrayal signified by a security-risk ranking'.⁵¹ We are introduced to this process of code reading and information gathering early in the film before Bowie appears, where Lynch forecasts the language and bodily encryption that is performed by Jeffries in the bureau office scene.

Special Agent Chester Desmond (Chris Isaak) meets agent Cole in a private airfield in Portland, Oregon, where he is introduced to his new partner, Special Agent Sam Stanley (Kiefer Sutherland) and assigned to the murder case of Teresa Banks. At this formative moment a young woman named Lil the Dancer appears in a bright red dress with a blue rose pinned to the top and moves towards the men, writhing and gesturing in an outlandish manner. During the car ride to a nearby town to examine Teresa's body, Desmond decodes the woman's performative semantic display, telling Stanley that is an FBI method developed by Cole to covertly brief incoming agents on what to expect during a murder investigation. 'That was really something. That dancing girl. What did it mean?' asks Stanley. 'Code', replies Desmond, before elaborating:

> Her face had a sour look. That means we're going to have trouble with the local authorities. They are not going to be receptive to the FBI.

Both eyes blinking means there is going to be trouble higher up; the eyes of the local authority. A sheriff and a deputy. That would be my guess. Two of the local law enforcers are going to be a problem. If you noticed she had one hand in her pocket which means they are hiding something, and the other hand made a fist which means they are going to be belligerent.[52]

The interpretive decoding strategies on display here exemplify Lynch's use of cinema as a medium for distorting reality as it conventionally appears to us. While Desmond is able to thoroughly decipher and explain Lil's gestures, facial expressions and dress, he withholds (or simply does not know) the meaning of her blue rose, telling Stanley, 'Very good, but I can't tell you about that.' Through this bureau codebreaking routine Lynch makes it clear that even the most reassuring way of thinking about objects and bodies cannot be entirely trusted because even when it is palpably visible to the naked eye, matter is anything but solid and stable.[53] This filmic effect, in which clues and signs are rehearsed and clarified in such a way as to ironically further confuse their meaning, echoes Bowie's own musical speech acts and use of symbols. Bowie does this, for instance, in the lyrics of 'Young Americans' in which, as Amedeo D'Adamo observes, 'narrator slippage is in fact a form of vocal affect with large implications for anthemic speech-acts, a point that returns us to the concept that an intimacy corridor opens in this song in the final verses between "Bowie himself" and the listener'.[54] The instability (or duality) of character that Lynch constructs through speech acts was also adopted by Bowie's use of facial make-up – the most well-known example being the depiction of split-identity on the album cover of Aladdin Sane, where Bowie's mask-like face is split by a blue and red lightning flash suggestive of schizophrenia or unresolved internal and external states.

Lynch plays on this aspect of Bowie's work by linking Jeffries with the cryptic Judy, who he mentions in the bureau office. While some scholars have connected Judy to various clues and dialogue within the *Twin Peaks* TV series, others have treated her as a recurrent fixture within the broader *Twin Peaks* mythology – a symbol whose real meaning is never fully apparent. Of Judy's relationship to Bowie/Jeffries in *Fire*, however, Miller has intriguingly suggested that Jeffries 'doesn't really want to talk about Judy because that reminds him of whatever happened to him'.[55] In an interview with *Wrapped in Plastic*, Lynch's co-writer Robert Engels remarked:

The thing behind Judy has to do with where David Bowie came from.... He was down there [in Buenos Aires], and that's where Judy is. I think Joan Chen [Josie] is there, and I think Windom Earle is there. It's the idea that there are portals around the world and Phillip Jeffries had one hell of a trip to Buenos Aires and back![56]

Importantly, as many critics have observed, references to Judy also change in different accounts of the script. One of these exists in the expanded version of Bowie's scene and the one that follows it in 'The Missing Pieces', ninety minutes of deleted scenes cut from *Fire* that appeared in the 2014 *Twin Peaks: The Entire Mystery Set*. The feature-length compilation contains, for instance, one scene set in Buenos Aires in which Jeffries enters a cryptic portal and emerges instantaneously in Philadelphia. 'The Missing Pieces' presents Bowie's cameo in Cole's office in full and as such we are given insight into all of Jeffries's dialogue, which in the film becomes fragmented and inaudible as the action moves to the convenience store and Red Room scenes. After stating that he isn't 'gonna talk about Judy', Jeffries asks, 'Who do you think that is there?' before going on: 'I sure as hell want to tell you everything, but I ain't got a whole lot to go on. But I will tell you one little bitty thing, Judy is positive about this. . . . Listen to me carefully. I saw one of their meetings. It was above a convenience store.'

Jeffries's resistance to providing a clear explanation for Judy, both within the film and in the original extended script in 'The Missing Pieces', represents yet another power play at the level of information gathering and observation, confirming the extent to which the dreaming experiences in *Twin Peaks* are not equivalent to 'experience of worldly facts' and are instead 'a supernatural experience of the supposed facts of an otherworldly nonphysical realm'.[57] In this sense, Lynch worked on *Fire* (as he did with many of the other puzzle films), 'in much the same way that a writer of mystery novels might: initially the text contains too many clues or too obvious ones; and these are progressively excised or obscured until a solution is no longer obvious'.[58] Moreover, Nicholas Rombes argues that interpreting the Lynchian dreaming experience requires accepting a task full of contradictions and impossibilities, and nowhere is this more necessary than in tracing the film's explication of the mysterious Judy.[59]

Turn myself to face me

Bowie's long-lost character appears one final time, twenty-five years later in the series' third season, *Twin Peaks: The Return*, which premiered in May 2017 just over a year after his death. A series described by some critics as 'the most perfect and uncanny audiovisual product', *The Return* is filled with split characters, outlandish behaviour and unnatural colouring (red and black) throughout.[60] Matt Fowler, for instance, points out that *Twin Peaks* 'came back as a true artistic force that challenged just about every storytelling convention we know'.[61] When agent Cooper finally meets Bowie again in episode 14, 'We Are Like the Dreamer', he appears not as himself but as a mysterious talking machine – a large, metal-like figure some fans identified as a tea kettle. Others have suggested that Bowie is represented by the white glowing orb that vaporizes out of the mechanical object. In ways similar to the uncanny effect produced by the surveillance camera footage in *Fire*, Bowie is positioned as both familiar and unfamiliar at once: an unsettling, anthropomorphized figure who stares out from the abyss to observe and comment on the scene. In relation to characters who succeed in producing these uncanny effects, Freud quotes his collaborator, the German psychiatrist Ernst Jentsch, who writes:

> In telling a story, one of the most successful devices for easily creating uncanny effects is to leave the reader in uncertainty whether a particular figure in the story is a human being or an automaton, and to do it in such a way that this attention is not focused directly upon his uncertainty, so that he may not be led to go into the matter and clear it up immediately. That, as we have said, would quickly dissipate the peculiar emotional effect of the thing.[62]

This effect is deployed as Jeffries speaks out from the metal casing against a backdrop of puffing smoke and a repetitive, ominous sound of clanging metal.[63] Jeffries plays two realities over one another, tempting the evil doppelganger Cooper with intelligence about Judy but ultimately revealing nothing. 'Phillip, why didn't you want to talk about Judy? Who is Judy? Does Judy want something from me?' asks Cooper into the darkness. 'Why don't you ask Judy yourself', replies Jeffries. After one final attempt to extract the identity of Judy, Cooper receives one final, cryptic reply from Bowie's reincarnated metal pitcher: 'You've already met Judy.'

The factual confusion of this scene, in which Jeffries confuses the logic not only of season 3 but also of the prior *Fire* film reveals the gradual erosion of memory over the course of time as well as the way that Lynch's work distorts the essential facts about experience in order to conflate dreams, facts and reality. This strategy has been described as Lynch's 'deliberate obfuscation and contravention of logic at the diegetic level' and compared to Francis Bacon's (1909–92) artistic approach in which 'aesthetic vision fractures narrative'.[64] Lynch's choice of Bowie to galvanize this filmic tactic is a logical one, especially in light of the way in which Bowie, as an artist, has perfected the inhabiting of 'discrete and contradictory spaces, while creating spaces that fans can travel to, or recognize in their own social life'.[65] By denying Cooper the information he seeks at this final moment in their encounters, Bowie's role in *Twin Peaks* more broadly becomes one of an all-knowing conspirator, a character capable of rearranging narrative on his own terms and in resistance to the often impenetrable obscurity of Lynch. Jeffries, as both Bowie and Tin Machine, functions to confuse, even at the series' end, the FBI's attempt at codebreaking. Of the elimination of these standard narrative boundaries, Angela Hauge observes that we see the dissolution 'of the barriers between past, present, and future; between physical and psychic space; between individual human beings; and between the human and non-human'.⁶⁶

Philip Jeffries's final appearance in *The Return* perhaps therefore functions to confirm a suspicion that viewers had all along: Jeffries was never really there to begin with and is instead Bowie in disguise, observing events unfold under the cover of a cleverly layered performance. As Bowie commented in an interview with *Toppop* in 1977: 'I think I'm a fairly good social observer and I think that I encapsulate areas; maybe every year or so I try and stamp that down somewhere ... My job is as an observer of what is happening.' This craft, one that combines panoptic observation and synoptic insight with surrealist artistic expression, ultimately places Bowie as artist firmly inside the world of Lynchian film. It is his meticulously crafted and performed indiscernibility of interior and exterior – the exemplification of Freudian voyeuristic witnessing – that allows Bowie to participate so convincingly in Lynch's world of the uncanny.⁶⁷

In his surveillant atemporal cameo in *Twin Peaks: Fire Walk with Me*, David Bowie crafts a complex filmic role in which he *sees all*, observing without limits in order to subvert standard paradigms of observation, interpretation and time. By playing the role of an FBI agent, Bowie further complicates the surveillance and information gathering logic of Lynch's film by evading not only interrogation and logical placement in space and time but also a fixed subjectivity. Performing in this way, Bowie comes to both exemplify and resist the formal and aesthetic qualities of Lynchian cinema; he is neither in cameo nor ever really himself. His indiscernible persona and distortion of standard panoptic observation amplifies Lynch's 'cinematic ideals' of 'visual and aural sequences that combine images and sounds liberated from a purely narrative function'.⁶⁸ He exceeds conceptual and linguistic expression in *Fire*, just as he does in his music by defying fixed interpretation, distorting logic and, ultimately, existing beyond and outside of standard narrative and time. By playing the role of 'outsider looking in', Bowie uses his cameo to return to the role of alienated outsider that fans, especially of the Ziggy Stardust era, found transformative in their own lives for negotiating change, isolation and difference. From 'isolating curse to divine celestial calling',⁶⁹ the role of the outsider continues to be a hallmark of Bowie's oeuvre and one that, in our datafied, hurried and socially fragmented age, has more significance than ever.

Notes

1 Will Brooker, 'Time Again: The David Bowie Chronotope', in *Enchanting David Bowie: Space, Time, Body, Memory*, ed. Toija Cinque, Christopher Moore and Sean Redmond (New York: Bloomsbury Academic, 2015), 97.

2 Barry Miles, *Bowie in His Own Words* (London: Omnibus Press, 1984), 61–2.
3 Ian Chapman, 'Ziggy's Urban Alienation: Assembling the Heroic Outsider', in *Enchanting David Bowie: Space, Time, Body, Memory*, ed. Toija Cinque, Christopher Moore and Sean Redmond (New York: Bloomsbury Academic, 2015), 27.
4 Denis Flannery, 'Absence, Resistance and Visitable Pasts: David Bowie, Todd Haynes, Henry James', *Continuum: Journal of Media & Cultural Studies* 31, no. 4 (2017): 549.
5 Thomas Mathiesen, 'The Viewer Society: Foucault's "Panopticon" Revisited', *Theoretical Criminology: An International Journal* 1, no. 2 (1997): 219.
6 Simon Riches, 'Intuition and Investigation into Another Place: The Epistemological Role of Dreaming in Twin Peaks and Beyond', in *The Philosophy of David Lynch*, ed. William J. Devlin and Shai Biderman (Lexington: University Press of Kentucky, 2011), 25.
7 Bethany Usher and Stephanie Fremaux, 'Turn Myself to Face Me: David Bowie in the 1990s and Discovery of Authentic Self', in *David Bowie: Critical Perspectives*, ed. Eoin Devereux, Aileen Dillane and Martin J. Power (New York: Routledge, 2015), 65.
8 Aileen Diliane, Eoin Devereux and Martin J. Power, 'Culminating Sounds and (En)visions: *Ashes to Ashes* and the case for Pierrot', in *David Bowie: Critical Perspectives*, ed. Eoin Devereux, Aileen Dillane and Martin J. Power (New York: Routledge, 2015), 44.
9 Leo Charney, 'In a Moment: Film and the Philosophy of Modernity', in *Cinema and the Invention of Modern Life*, ed. Leo Charney and Vanessa R. Schwartz (Berkley: University of California Press, 1995), 292–3.
10 Mary Anne Doane, *The Emergence of Cinematic Time: Modernity, Contingency, the Archive* (Cambridge, MA: Harvard University Press, 2002), 172.
11 Sean Redmond, 'David Bowie: In Cameo', *Cinema Journal* 57, no. 3 (Spring 2018): 151.
12 Brooker, 'Time Again', 99.
13 Christopher Sandford, *Bowie: Loving the Alien* (London: Little, Brown & Company, 1996), 87.
14 Tanja Stark, 'Confronting Bowie's Mysterious Corpses', in *Enchanting David Bowie: Space, Time, Body, Memory*, ed. Toija Cinque, Christopher Moore and Sean Redmond (New York: Bloomsbury Academic, 2015), 63.
15 Brooker, 'Time Again', 99.
16 *Twin Peaks: Fire Walk with Me*, directed by David Lynch (New Line Cinema and CiBY 2000, 1992).
17 Sandford, *Bowie*, 182.
18 Sigmund Freud, 'The Uncanny', in *The Standard Edition of the Complete Psychological Works of Sigmund Freud*, trans. James Strachey (London: Hogarth Press, 1953), 220.

19   Kevin Hunt, 'The Eyes of David Bowie', in *Enchanting David Bowie: Space, Time, Body, Memory*, ed. Toija Cinque, Christopher Moore and Sean Redmond (New York: Bloomsbury Academic, 2015), 178.
20   Redmond, *David Bowie*, 151.
21   Will Scheibel, 'Gilles Deleuze: On Movement, Time, and Modernism', in *Thinking in the Dark: Cinema, Theory, Practice*, ed. Murray Pomerance and R. Barton Palmer (New Jersey: Rutgers University Press, 2016), 153.
22   Ibid.
23   Gilles Deleuze, *Cinema 2: The Time-Image*, trans. Hugh Tomlinson and Robert Galeta (Minneapolis, MN: University of Minnesota Press, 1989), xi.
24   Toija Cinque, Christopher Moore and Sean Redmond, 'Introduction, Section Three: Body', in *Enchanting David Bowie: Space, Time, Body, Memory*, ed. Toija Cinque, Christopher Moore and Sean Redmond (New York: Bloomsbury Academic, 2015), 171.
25   Ibid.
26   Michel Foucault, *Discipline and Punish: The Birth of the Prison*, trans. Alan Sheridan (New York: Vintage Books, 1995), 191.
27   Ibid., 184.
28   Redmond, *David Bowie*, 152.
29   Gary Marx, *Windows into the Soul: Surveillance and Society in an Age of High Technology* (Chicago, IL: The University of Chicago Press, 2016), 8.
30   Marx, *Windows into the Soul*, x.
31   Ibid., 1.
32   Keith Stuart, 'BowieNet: How David Bowie's ISP Foresaw the Future of the Internet', *The Guardian*, Monday 11 January 2016.
33   Riches, 'Intuition and Investigation into Another Place', 26.
34   Lisa Perrott, 'Bowie the Cultural Alchemist: Performing Gender, Synthesizing Gesture and Liberating Identity', *Continuum: Journal of Media & Cultural Studies* 31, no. 4 (June 2017): 529.
35   Ibid.
36   Martha Nochimson, *David Lynch Swerves: Uncertainty from Lost Highway to Inland Empire* (Austin, TX: University of Texas, 2013), xiv.
37   Foucault, *Discipline and Punish*, 175.
38   Hunt, 'The Eyes of David Bowie', 187.
39   Michel Chion, *David Lynch*, trans. Robert Julian (London: British Film Institute, 2006), 137.
40   Riches, 'Intuition and Investigation into Another Place', 36–7.
41   Ibid.
42   The dreamlike nature of Bowie's cameo exemplifies two other critical themes that recur throughout Lynch's work: the *experience* of dreaming as compared to the experience of reality and the notion of gathering and gaining

information through some form of investigation. By craftily merging these two themes, Jeffries's dream sequence in *FWWM* is exemplary of Lynch's 'puzzle films', a group in which *Lost Highway*, *Mulholland Drive* and *Inland Empire* also belong. In these films we are 'challenged to keep track of recurring elements, whether objects, phrases, colors, or movements, in order to discover associations that have been obscured through narrative or spatial fragmentation or even through visual or sonic interference'. See Jeremy Powell, 'David Lynch, Francis Bacon, Gilles Deleuze: The Cinematic Diagram and the Hall of Time', *Discourse* 36, no. 3 (2014): 137.

43 Redmond also makes this point, invoking Greg Olsen to note how the mask suggests 'a belief in a multifarious reality, in deep truths concealed by facades'. See Redmond, *David Bowie*, 153.

44 See, for example, Shelton Waldrep, *The Aesthetics of Self-Invention: Oscar Wilde to David Bowie* (Minneapolis, MN: University of Minnesota Press, 2004), 17.

45 Sandford, *Bowie*, 129.

46 Chris Rodley, *Lynch on Lynch* (London: Faber and Faber, 1997), 169.

47 Angela Hague, 'Infinite Games: The Derationalization of Detection in *Twin Peaks*', in *Full of Secrets: Critical Approaches to Twin Peaks*, ed. David Lavery (Detroit: Wayne State University Press, 1995), 136.

48 Redmond, *David Bowie*, 150.

49 *Zoolander* (Ben Stiller, 2001) and *Extras* (Ricky Gervais, BBC, 2006).

50 Valentin Groebner, *Who Are You?: Identification, Deception, and Surveillance in Early Modern Europe*, trans. Mark Kyburz and John Peck (New York: Zone Books, 2007), 249.

51 William H. Epstein, 'Counter-Intelligence: Cold War Criticism and Eighteenth Century Studies', *ELH* 57, no. 1 (1990): 77.

52 David Lynch and Bob Engels, *Twin Peaks: Fire Walk with Me*, directed by David Lynch (Lynch/Frost Productions, 1992).

53 Nochimson, *David Lynch Swerves*, xiv.

54 Amedeo D'Adamo, 'Ain't There One Damn Flag that Can Make Me Break Down and Cry? The Formal, Performative and Emotional Tactics of Bowie's Singular Critical Anthem "Young Americans,"' in *Enchanting David Bowie: Space, Time, Body, Memory*, ed. Toija Cinque, Christopher Moore and Sean Redmond (New York: Bloomsbury Academic, 2015), 143.

55 Craig Miller, 'Robert Engels Interview', *Wrapped in Plastic*, April 2002, 8.

56 Ibid., 2–11.

57 Riches, 'Intuition and Investigation into Another Place', 38.

58 Powell, 'David Lynch, Francis Bacon, Gilles Deleuze', 317.

59 Nicholas Rombes, 'Blue Velvet Underground: David Lynch's Post-Punk Poetics', in *The Cinema of David Lynch: American Dreams, Nightmare Visions*, ed. Erica Sheen and Anette Davidson (London: Wallflower Press, 2004), 72.

60 Dominique Chateau, 'The Film That Dreams: About David Lynch's Twin Peaks Season 3', in *Stories*, ed. Ian Christie and Annie van den Oever (Amsterdam University Press, 2018), 119.
61 Matt Fowler, 'Twin Peaks: The Return Review', *IGN*, 12 September 2017.
62 Freud, 'The Uncanny', 227.
63 Receiving news from Lynch of his character's return to the screen, Bowie reportedly asked for Jeffries's voice to be played by a Louisianan actor, having been dissatisfied with his apparently inauthentic accent in *FWWM*.
64 Greg Hainge, 'Weird or Loopy? Specular Spaces, Feedback and Artifice in Lost Highway's Aesthetics of Sensation', in *The Cinema of David Lynch: American Dreams, Nightmare Visions*, ed. Erica Sheen and Annette Davidson (London and New York: Wallflower Press, 2004), 142.
65 Toija Cinque, Christopher Moore and Sean Redmond, 'Introduction, Section One: Space', in *Enchanting David Bowie: Space, Time, Body, Memory*, ed. Toija Cinque, Christopher Moore and Sean Redmond (New York: Bloomsbury Academic, 2015), 9.
66 Hague, 'Infinite Games', 133–4.
67 This is a method Dominique Chateau has described as 'the fantastic ambivalence with regard to reality' that characterizes Bowie's work as much as it does that of Lynch. See Chateau, 'The Film That Dreams', 124.
68 Robert Sinnerbrink, 'Cinematic Ideas/Ideals?' *Film-Philosophy* 9, no. 34 (2005).
69 Michael Lupro Mooradian, 'Keeping Space Fantastic: The Transformative Journey of Major Tom', in *Enchanting David Bowie: Space, Time, Body, Memory*, ed. Toija Cinque, Christopher Moore and Sean Redmond (New York: Bloomsbury Academic, 2015), 14.

10

Loving the alienation

Bowie, *Basquiat*, Brecht

Glenn D'Cruz

Introduction

While he is best remembered for his peerless catalogue of music, David Bowie was always looking to expand his artistic and intellectual capabilities by pursuing a wide range of artistic opportunities. He studied and flirted with the visual and performing arts throughout his life, participating in mime, fashion, theatre, film, video, television commercials and painting. A notable autodidact, Bowie also displayed an impressive grasp of art history and studied avant-garde cinema, especially German Expressionism, during the mid-1970s. These interests helped Bowie become competent in a variety of media. Indeed, his musical oeuvre is compelling because it was consistently enriched by his insatiable curiosity about adjacent art forms and new technologies. Let us not forget that Bowie was one of the first celebrities to embrace the potential of the internet for publicizing his activities and connecting with his fans – BowieNet was also a testament to his entrepreneurial acumen.

That said, it is also possible to see Bowie as a dilettante, especially with respect to his status as a film actor. With a few rare exceptions, critics and academic commentators tend to damn Bowie's acting in the cinema with faint praise. Will Brooker points out that Bowie tended to play himself on the screen[1] and that as 'a dancer, an artist and an actor he was an enthusiastic amateur'.[2] Sir Christopher Frayling states that 'Bowie's best film performances are when he just has to be. When he's Warhol in *Basquiat*, when he's Tesla in *The Prestige* or when he's Mr Newton [in *The Man Who Fell to Earth*], I think he's astonishingly charismatic and enigmatic. But he's not an actorly actor . . . he just is.'[3] What is an 'actorly' actor? And what does Frayling mean when he claims that Bowie is best when 'he just has to be'? In what follows, I will unpack these statements with reference to what we might call 'actor theory', focusing primarily on Bowie's portrayal of Andy Warhol in Julian Schnabel's film, *Basquiat* (1996). In so doing, I hope to demonstrate how this body of scholarship (drawn mostly from theatre and performance studies) might help better understand how Bowie's acting involved more than just being Bowie. Bowie may not have been an 'actorly' actor, but he was, I will contend, something just as interesting: a cracked actor, frequently exposing the gap between actor and role; in short, Bowie's performances often, as we shall see, resonated with key features of Bertolt Brecht's theory of epic theatre.

This paper will read Bowie's performance in *Basquiat* through the lens of what we might call Brecht's dramaturgy of alienation. Brecht regularly exposed the theatrical means of production by making the process of artistic creation visible to the audience. In other words, he developed theories, principles and practical strategies for exposing the theatrical and political cracks and fissures in his work. However, before substantiating my claim about the value in approaching Bowie's performance as Andy Warhol in *Basquiat*, I want to contextualize and situate my argument in relation to scholarly commentary on screen acting, theatricality and actor theory.

Star performers as signs

While there is no clear consensus on the quality of Bowie's acting skills, there appears to be a consensus on the connection between Bowie's star persona and the way he signifies meaning on the screen. Within cinema studies, scholars generally tend to analyse the screen performances of stars like Bowie as signs. For example, Richard Dyer points out, quite correctly, that stars bring the attitudes and values associated with their public personas to their screen roles.[4] He calls this the 'always-already-signifying nature of star images'.[5] So, audiences see *David Bowie* playing Andy Warhol rather than an actor playing Warhol. James Naremore, in his seminal book, *Acting in the Cinema*, acknowledges another system of signification at work in screen performances when he points out that 'all performing situations employ a physics of movement and gesture that makes signs readable; in this sense Nietzsche's observation that actors translate their person into a simplified version still holds true'.[6] While both Dyer and Naremore recognize the importance of acting technique their interest focuses on how these dramaturgical practices function as signs. From this perspective, it is Bowie as sign rather than Bowie as actor that captures our scholarly interest. By focusing on Bowie's star persona, Mehdi Derfoufi takes a similar approach to understanding Bowie's function as an actor. For Derfoufi, Bowie's persona is comprised of the following elements: sexual ambiguity, otherness and stardom; moreover, he is a figure that straddles the avant-garde and the mainstream.[7]

As we have seen, a star's persona can be of the utmost interest to a filmmaker with artistic ambitions. Few actors would have been able to highlight as well as Bowie does in *Merry Christmas, Mr. Lawrence* the richness and complexity of contemporary issues such as the gaze, desire and otherness within the context of a postcolonial, hybridized and globalized world.[8]

The key point in this passage echoes Frayling's opinion that Bowie was at his best as an actor when he played a version of himself or his public persona. This is a problematic proposition since Bowie's public persona was hard to pin down – it changed over time. Nevertheless, Frayling recalls that when the director of *The Man Who Fell to Earth*, Nicholas Roeg, saw 'the "Cracked Actor" documentary on TV, and when he met Bowie it was as if someone was walking towards the part. He just had to *be*, really'.[9] Julian Schnabel, the director of *Basquiat*, makes a similar point when he confesses that 'I needed a pop icon to play a pop icon. I wanted people to say is this David Bowie playing Andy Warhol or Andy Warhol playing David Bowie' (1996).[10]

For now, let me acknowledge that a substantial part of Bowie's appeal in his most successful films, *The Man Who Fell to Earth* and *Merry Christmas, Mr. Lawrence*, owes much to the resonances between his star persona and the characters he plays. However, I think this 'star-centric' approach to understanding Bowie as an actor does a disservice to his talent as an actor. At the risk of pointing out the obvious, it should be clear that not all rock stars with thespian ambitions can act. Look no further than Bob Dylan's supremely awkward performances in films such as *Pat Garrett & Billy the Kid* (1973) or *Hearts of Fire* (1987), a film as bizarre as it is inept. Other notable failures include Neil Diamond in the *Jazz Singer* (1980) and Mick Jagger in *Ned Kelly* (1970). You do not have to search too hard to find other examples to add to this list. Star power alone, I repeat, cannot make an actor out of just any pop icon, and if Bowie is just an enthusiastic amateur actor, he is a damn good one. I want to defend this claim by appealing to actor theory, a body of scholarship devoted to unpacking the art of acting as both an artistic and social practice.

Bowie and theatricality

Even a cursory survey of the critical literature on David Bowie reveals that his name is synonymous with theatricality. David Buckley's observation that Bowie 'took glam rock to new rarefied heights and invented character-playing in pop, marrying theatre and popular music in one seamless, powerful whole' is typical of such commentary.[11] As is well known, Bowie described himself as 'The Actor' on the credits for the *Hunky Dory* album and almost every commentator is compelled to comment on the characters he creates in his music: Major Tom, Ziggy Stardust, Aladdin Sane, The Thin White Duke and so on. Like most good singers, Bowie knows how to sell a song by seducing his audience. Look at his video clips. They are often overtly theatrical and filmic ('Be My Wife', 'Blue Jean', 'China Girl') but even when he's performing to studio cameras, he usually creates the impression of inhabiting his characters.

His early performances on the *Old Grey Whistle Test* (1971) confirm this observation. His performance of 'Five Years' is, if nothing else, actorly in the way he uses facial expressions and exploits an almost conversational vocal phrasing when he sings the lines:

> I think I saw you in an ice-cream parlour
> Drinking milkshakes cold and long
> Smiling and waving and looking so fine
> Don't think you knew you were in this song.[12]

Bowie sings in character while knowing how to work the camera; there's not a trace of awkwardness or self-consciousness in his performance. He takes an attitude to his invisible interlocutor by almost spitting out the lines as his eyes widen with exasperation. He is a consummate performer – a skilled actor, which should come as no surprise since he often acknowledged his early theatrical ambitions. In his interview with Jeremy Paxton, Bowie recalls that as a teenager he wanted to write musicals for Broadway and the West End – an ambition he achieved shortly before his death with *Lazarus* (2015).[13] It should come as no surprise, then, to discover that Bowie's early heroes were musical theatre figures such as Anthony Newly and Lionel Bart. This interest in theatre also goes some way towards explaining his participation in various mime, dance and film projects before he became a star. In short, Bowie, as critics and commentators repeat ad nauseam, is overtly theatrical and his theatricality manifested in his concert performances and video clips.

> I was a character when I performed all those albums . . . and I carried the character into interviews, newspapers, on stage, off stage – whenever there was media around I had to keep those characters concrete. The fabric of my work is using my body, my personality as well as my songs and stage performance . . . rather like a canvas.[14]

This statement confirms Auslander's claim that 'Bowie not only envisioned the rock concert as a staged, costumed, and choreographed theatrical performance, he understood his own performing and his relationship to his audience in actorly terms'.[15]

In 1999, Bowie explained that he killed off his characters so he could focus on being a singer, a good singer-songwriter. Julien Temple's 21-minute promotional film, *Jazzin' for Blue Jean* (1984), has Bowie parodying his early 1970s personas by playing two characters: a hapless everyman who is trying to impress a woman and Screaming Lord Byron, clearly a tongue-in-cheek reference to Bowie's overtly theatrical performances in the 1970s. This repetition of well-known facts about Bowie's theatricality, hopefully, dispels the idea that Bowie was an amateur actor. While researching this chapter, I watched as many of Bowie's film clips as I could find, most were drawn from the excellent *Best of Bowie* DVD (2002); Bowie rarely makes a misstep in those videos with dramatic scenes. A supercut of these cameo performances (the Boss figure in 'Let's Dance' or the lover in 'China Girl' or, more recently, his poignant and often hilarious duet with Tilda Swinton in 'The Stars Are Out Tonight') will confirm that Bowie was an accomplished actor who could perform well beyond the range one might expect of a mere dilettante. After all, he often appears with consummate professionals and holds his own. *Basquiat*, after all, is a star-studded affair with appearances by luminaries such as Jeffrey Wright, Dennis Hopper, Christopher Walken, Gary Oldman, Willem Dafoe and Parker Posey.

Actor theory

That said, Bowie was not a conventional actor, so in order to understand what kind of actor Bowie was and offer an evaluation of his performances in the cinema, we need to get a better understanding of the art of acting itself and remark on some of the differences between stage performances and screen performances. Let us begin with a brief survey of actor theory. On a fundamental level, actors construct characters in order to create and maintain the illusion of inhabiting another world, typically a self-contained, fictional world that is sustained by the audience's suspension of disbelief. Several commentators have observed that there are basically two approaches to understanding how actors achieve this aim. David George provides a succinct account of these apparently antithetical approaches when he writes:

> Acting theory in the West has been dominated for at least the past two hundred years by the ongoing, acrimonious debate between those who claim, on the one hand, that the actor disappears in the character, that he has no identity separate from the role, and those who have countered that claim by arguing that whatever the audience may experience, the actor remains separate from the character, projecting it, manipulating

it, 'playing' it. We may call these the *fusion model* and the *fission model* respectively.[16]

George suggests that Sarah Bernhardt was an exemplar of the fusion model (or what is sometimes known as the inside-out approach to acting). Bernhardt, according to George, apparently described acting as a form of possession – she would become the characters she played through a mystical process that involved being possessed by the spirit of her characters.[17]

A lay understanding of the Stanislavski system mistakenly assumes that it also advocates a fusion of the actor with character and erases the actor's self in performance. In actuality, Stanislavski believed it was important for the actor to identify with the fictional character as part of the rehearsal process.[18] Denis Diderot articulates an opposing view in his oft-quoted essay 'The Paradox of the Actor' (written in 1773) which resonates with the fission or outside-in model of acting. He contends that actors always need to be self-reflexive if they are to know their cues, hit their marks and connect with an audience. He wrote that 'the very moment when he touches your heart he is listening to his own voice [...] He is not the person he represents; he plays it, and plays it so well that you think he is the person; the deception is all on your side; he knows well enough that he is not the person.'[19]

George's perceptive and nuanced argument is too complex to gloss in the context of this paper, but suffice it to say that he believes that both accounts of acting are flawed because they assume a binary split between actor and role. He posits a triadic model of acting that identifies three distinct elements that intersect and overlap in the process of creating a dramatic character: character, actor, person. Let us break this down and see how it might help us understand how Bowie functions as an actor in Schnabel's film. In *Basquiat*, Bowie plays the character of Andy Warhol. We know Warhol was a real person, a public personality with a set of highly recognizable visual and verbal characteristics. Bowie's task is to represent or, as I will argue later in this chapter, present this personage. George points out that acting is a profession and actors, whether they are formally trained or not, develop strategies and techniques for portraying characters. So, in *Basquiat*, Bowie draws on his repertoire of actorly techniques derived primarily from his experience as a highly theatrical singer, although we must also consider his training in mime and his general observations of other performers as being part of his actorly 'bag of tricks'. In short, he comes to the role of Warhol with an extensive body of experience on stage and in front of cameras (in his previous films, TV appearances and promotional videos). The triadic model's final element is the person.

Presumably this refers to Mr David Jones, a real flesh-and-blood person. In George's account, successful acting occurs when a role is personalized; that is, acting becomes compelling when the actor gives something of their 'real', unique selves to the role. George's paper is not only about the art of acting.

His triadic model also seeks to save the sovereign self from those theories that suggest that the self is an illusory effect of discourse, consciousness or some other phenomena. George's main rival is the sociologist Erving Goffman whose seminal book *The Presentation of Self in Everyday Life* (1959) argues that we are nothing more than our social roles.[20] In other words, we play a number of different parts in everyday life without there being a single essential part that gives us our sense of self. Today, the concept of the unique self is undermined by a variety of sources (for relatively new ideas about the status of the self, see works about the philosophy of the mind and the biology of the brain). Bowie, the champion of inauthenticity, apparently confounds George's thesis regarding the personal dimension of acting. As Buckley points out:

> Bowie was living proof that our personalities are constantly in flux, constantly being made and remade, not fixed in stone by age, class or gender. His changes of character in the 70s, which began with Ziggy, were media-produced manifestations of how we all sift through ourselves, rummaging through the baggage to produce new, hopefully improved, versions for public consumption.[21]

Philosopher and hardcore Bowie fan, Simon Critchley, also casts doubt on the coherence of human identity when he writes that 'identity is a very fragile affair. It is at best a sequence of episodic blips rather than some grand narrative unity.'[22] And let us not forget that it is possible to be authentically inauthentic in the manner of Oscar Wilde – a key precursor to the likes of Warhol, Bowie and Basquiat.[23] The essential 'Person', a key component of the triadic model, is not easy to identify, but George suggests, following the sociologist, Benita Luckmann, that it is that entity that enables us to shift between our social roles and part-time existences in 'small life-worlds' – Luckmann's key idea is that we are always juggling competing roles (mother, actor, friend, sibling and so on).[24]

Persona and theatricality

While the triadic model does expose the limitations of the actor/role binary it does not seem capable of helping understand the complexities involved in Bowie's acting career since it ignores the concept of persona. As we have already seen, it is the Bowie persona, not the person David Jones, that plays a crucial role making Bowie a viable proposition as an actor. Auslander recognizes the importance of persona in understanding Bowie as a performer when he writes that Bowie's stage characters are 'defined by three layers: the real person (the performer as human being), the performance persona (the performer's self-presentation) and the character (a figure portrayed in a song text)'.²⁵ The actor pole of George's triadic model is not part of Auslander's account, which is why the two models complement each other since George neglects the importance of persona while Auslander pays scant attention to acting as a profession that develops specific performance strategies and techniques.

When we start to break things down, though, we find that understanding acting with reference to models is really difficult. Neither George nor Auslander considers the crucial role of ineffable factors such as charisma and stage presence as integral parts of a successful performance.²⁶ I saw David Bowie on stage in 1983 as part of his *Serious Moonlight* tour. This was his greatest hits show, but I've never forgotten how Bowie managed to project a palpable sense of energy through his songs and theatrical set pieces, which involved the use of simple and elaborate props. He kept me enthralled and focused by projecting energy and charisma throughout his performance (which was not an easy task given the cold, cavernous confines of the concert venue, the now-defunct Perth Entertainment Centre). Live performance is one thing; screen performances, however, are, in many ways, significantly different.

For instance, the process of focalization in the cinema is the result of framing, editing and mise en scène. In the theatre, lighting and blocking can go some way towards directing the gaze of the audience, but the actor drives the performance, which must be sustained over the course of the duration of the play. Cinema acting, as is often remarked, is significantly shaped by technical apparatuses and acting occurs in bursts of activity. This is perhaps why most trained actors profess a love of the theatre over the cinema, for the theatre is primarily an actor's medium. While the focus of this volume is on Bowie as a film actor, it is important to acknowledge that his approach to acting owed a lot to his stage performances as a singer and his deep interest in the theatre. Geoffrey Marsh confirms this when he writes:

> In 1967, aged 20, Bowie discovered The Stage. Not the tatty stages, feeble PA systems and basic lighting of the ballrooms and clubs he had toured in recent years. Rather, the vast 'philosophical' stages of the theatre thinkers such as Stanislavski, Artaud and Brook, where there is no beginning or end, and the limits are solely those of the devisor – stages that could become any sort of space.²⁷

But I have delayed my encounter with Bowie as Warhol for long enough. It's finally time to break down this performance and make a few observations about the power of Bowie's performance in this small but crucial role.

Character and identification

Fusion or fission? Outside in or inside out? There's no way of telling how Bowie actually approached playing Warhol beyond the few insightful remarks he made in a televised conversation about the film with Julian Schnabel and Charlie Rose.[28] Actors often speak about the need to find a point of identification with the characters they create. It could not have been hard for David Bowie to identify with Warhol. First, he admired Warhol as an artist – it is not difficult to see why. In Warhol, Bowie saw a figure who transcended his humble beginnings through art. Warhol, like Bowie, turned to face the strange and in so doing revised the idea of what art could be in the postmodern world. Warhol struggled to conform to the social codes and conventions of small-town America and was further alienated from the mainstream by his homosexuality and Polish ethnicity. His artistic ambitions motivated his move to New York City in 1949 at the age of twenty. He thrived in the city and eventually established himself as one of the most influential artists of the twentieth century by immersing himself in pop culture and consumer society. He made a virtue out of repetition, reproduction and found glamour in the worlds of advertising and film. This put him at some remove from the individualistic concerns of prevailing artistic trends. Warhol's art was antithetical to the abstract expressionism of celebrated artists such as Jackson Pollock. In short, it is not hard to find resonances between Warhol and Bowie: they both promoted an aesthetic of otherness, artifice and transformation. Further, they both explored the connections between art and commerce and in so doing became stars and pop icons.

Of course, there were significant differences between the two. Shy, awkward and frail, Warhol managed to find fame and celebrity despite his anxieties about his physical appearance whereas Bowie exuded confidence and was a paragon of physical beauty. Perhaps this key difference partially explains why Bowie and Warhol never became friends and collaborators. They did meet once, but things did not go well. Their meeting was documented on a grainy black-and-white video (readily available on YouTube). If we are to be frank, Bowie performs a rather ordinary mime for Warhol – clearly, his mime training with Lindsay Kemp did not make him a virtuoso.[29] Although it is hard to gauge much from the silent documentary record, it appears that Warhol was unimpressed by Bowie and, according to some accounts, insulted by Bowie's song, 'Andy Warhol':

Andy Warhol looks a scream
Hang him on my wall
Andy Warhol, Silver Screen
Can't tell them apart at all.[30]

Simon Critchley provides another compelling explanation for Bowie's identification with Warhol:

After Andy Warhol had been shot by Valerie Solanas in 1968, he said, 'Before I was shot, I suspected that instead of living I'm just watching TV.

Since being shot, I'm certain of it.' Bowie's acute ten-word commentary on Warhol's statement, in the eponymous song from *Hunky Dory* in 1971, is deadly accurate: 'Andy Warhol, silver screen / Can't tell them apart at all.' The ironic self-awareness of the artist and their audience can only be that of their inauthenticity, repeated at increasingly conscious levels. Bowie repeatedly mobilizes this Warholian aesthetic.[31]

He goes on to note the prevalence of cinematic references in Bowie's lyrics, noting that Bowie often gives the impression of being 'stuck inside his own movie'.[32] So, the belief that the boundary between life and art is porous – or perhaps impossible to absolutely determine – is another key commonality between Warhol and Bowie. I think there's also a sense in which Bowie probably identified with Jean-Michel Basquiat, too.

Basquiat began as a street artist in the Soho district of New York in the late 1970s, tagging his spray-painted work SAMO. By 1984, he was a well-established artist and his work was selling for large sums of money.[33] By this time, the celebrated 'downtown' artist was also part of Warhol's circle, a feat Bowie, despite his fame and celebrity, never managed to emulate. Basquiat belonged to a generation and an art scene that embraced many of Bowie's innovations. The so-called downtown scene within which Basquiat flourished embraced a multimedia aesthetic, which saw all manner of artists producing work for a variety of mediums: visual artists made films, actors painted and almost everyone played in a band. Basquiat himself was part of a band called 'Gray' that played in venues like the famous Mudd Club and lofts like A's.[34] According to Alexis Adler, one of Basquiat's girlfriends, Basquiat was a Bowie fan who enjoyed *Low* and the second side of *Heroes*.[35] Basquiat also acted in the unfinished film, *Downtown 81*, a Warhol project that attempted to capture the vibrancy of the downtown scene in the late 1970s and early 1980s. As an artist Basquiat is often described as a neo-expressionist who embraced primitivism. His work also explored racial identity and Black history, which gave many of his paintings an overtly political edge. Unfortunately, Basquiat met a typically rock and roll demise, joining the 27 club in 1988, thereby cementing his celebrity status and the monetary value of his work. Bowie, an avid and knowledgeable connoisseur of art, actually bought a few Basquiat paintings after participating in Schnabel's film; these purchases turned out to be shrewd financial investments.

Bowie/Warhol/Brecht

David Bowie obviously loved New York City. He lived there longer than any other city that hosted his animal grace. He described himself as a New Yorker, so it should come as no surprise that he could easily identify with Warhol and Basquiat, artists who also lived in the great metropolis and took inspiration from its manic energy and frenetic pace. Identifying with these characters is one thing, but how does an actor – any actor – embody a character like Warhol? And how do we evaluate the success of the characterization? Clearly, David Bowie does not resemble Andy Warhol. So, Bowie's performance fails if judged purely in terms of mimesis, although some people believe his portrayal of Warhol was uncannily accurate. When I watch the film, I see the pop icon David Bowie wearing one of Andy's wigs and some of his clothes; I certainly do not register any kind of fusion. Bowie does not become Andy Warhol and he certainly does not disappear into the role (as an unknown or 'character' actor might). At this point it might be useful to cite Dyer's account of the signs of performance, which include

> facial expression; voice; gestures (principally of hands and arms, but also of any limb, e.g., neck, leg); body posture (how someone is standing or sitting); body movement (movement of the whole body, including how someone stands up or sits down, how they walk, run, etc.).[36]

Bowie's expressions and gestures are mannered and writ large, especially in those scenes that involve him interacting with the other characters. At best, he provides a broad imitation of Andy, but this is not necessarily a bad thing since it keeps the malleability and fragility of identity in play. Bowie as Andy doesn't smile; he nods his head, like a fey *Thunderbird* puppet, and often contorts his mouth in a way that suggests a mild sneer (as in the café scene which shows Basquiat's first encounter with Andy and the scene that depicts Basquiat's first solo show). Bowie's gait and posture suggests awkwardness (body skewed, hands on hip), but I can't help seeing through these studied movements to the thin, lithe body of David Jones (the person) but I also see the 'alien' Bowie persona (the freak, the outcast) and this is what makes Bowie's performance credible: his characterization of Warhol makes visible traces of the physicality of other Bowie personas (Jones/Bowie/Ziggy/the Thin White Duke and so on). Bowie's voice is one of the most intriguing things about his performance in this film. Bowie loved playing with accents (he apparently mimicked the Derek and Clive accent almost every time he spoke to Brian Eno, for instance). Bowie's vocal flexibility and facility with accents are most evident in his singing, which, especially in the early days of his career, took on a broad cockney brogue, which was distinct from his default South London voice (a result of his often-remarked obsession with Anthony Newly, no doubt).[37]

Bowie's voice morphs throughout his career – he could croon, rock and scream with a rare degree of control – and his vocal prowess as a singer bled into his acting. He could, if he chose, pull off a hammy New York accent or a histrionic southern drawl – see his reading from *The Diary of Nathan Adler*, the story that provided the inspiration for his 1995 concept album, *1. Outside,* for an example of the former and his cameo in David

Lynch's *Fire Walk with Me* (1992) for an example of the latter. In *Basquiat*, Bowie mimics the rhythms and cadences of Andy Warhol's distinctive speech patterns, but his attempts at an American accent are inconsistent at best. In fact, he plays Warhol with a discernible British tone of voice, one fairly close to Bowie's speaking voice (or one of his voices, anyway). This further exposes the gaps between person, actor, character and persona.

And these gaps convey a palpable affinity between Bowie's performance in *Basquiat* and Brechtian dramaturgy, though this is not the place to provide an extensive account of Brecht's theories. Suffice to say that Brecht developed an aesthetic designed to dispel the spectator's suspension of disbelief. Put differently, Brecht's approach to theatre attempted to reveal the forces and relations of theatrical production by foregrounding artifice and breaking the narcotic effects of performance. As is well known, Brecht, a Marxist, attempted to find a way to combat Nazism, which used radio, film and spectacle to seduce the German nation. Brecht's often strident political agenda nevertheless inspired a series of formal innovations for theatrical performance. His famous alienation effects[38] attempted to distance the audience from the dramatic characters and the stage spectacle, so they could make critical judgements about the scenarios he depicted in his plays. Brecht articulates some of the key elements of what he calls 'epic theatre' in his essay 'The Street Scene', which suggests that his preferred model of acting is analogous to an eyewitness explaining the cause of an accident to other bystanders, so they can form an opinion about what took place. Brecht underscores that

> it is important that he [the actor] should not be too perfect. His demonstration would be spoilt if the bystanders' attention were drawn to his powers of transformation. He has to avoid presenting himself in such a way that someone calls out 'What a lifelike portrayal of a chauffeur!' He must not 'cast a spell' over anyone. He should not transport people from normality to 'higher realms'. He need not dispose of any special powers of suggestion.[39]

Brecht explicitly rejects the actorly actor's 'transformation' into character, so the audience cannot mistake the representation of an event for the unassailable truth of an event. The A-effect has been incorporated into mainstream theatre practice for many years, yet there is a paucity of commentary that demonstrates that Brecht's theories succeeded in realizing his political aims; the relationship between formal aesthetic innovations and political change is difficult to quantify, but this is not my concern in the present context. My rather modest claim is simply this: rather than transform into Warhol, Bowie takes an *attitude* towards Warhol.

This enables him to convey the character's vulnerability and lack of confidence, especially in the scene depicting his artistic collaboration with

Basquiat, of which I will say more later. For now, it is sufficient to note that the Warhol character's arc, as Bowie represents it, manages to convey the shifting power dynamics between mentor and mentee, partially because of Bowie's lack of 'actorly' acting – I see Bowie's *gestic attitude* to Andy. I can't be sure that Bowie actually thought of Brecht while creating this interpretation of Warhol, but I am sure that Bowie was acquainted with Brechtian ideas, having played the lead role in a BBC TV production of Brecht's first play, *Baal* (1982) – the production is a little staid and the script is not among Brecht's best work. That said, Bowie turns in a compelling performance as the titular character: a prototype rock star poet who is feted by corrupt bourgeois patrons. Baal was certainly another role Bowie could identify with, given his exploitation by managers such as Tony Defries.[40]

In a fascinating and sometimes testy three-way conversation between Bowie, Julian Schnabel and Charlie Rose, Bowie actually describes his approach to the role of Andy Warhol. Among various topics, he speaks about how having access to some of Andy's possessions (his wig and leather jacket) helped him build the character. He admits that he only knew Andy superficially and relied on research to get an understanding of Andy's character. Most tellingly, for my purposes, Bowie overtly states that he never intended to impersonate Andy: 'I didn't go much beyond having noted what his *spirit* was – the way he moved and stuff – just his *attitude*. It was more of an interpretation than anything else.'[41] Bowie's aim to *represent* Warhol's attitude and spirit was an astute dramaturgical choice since his physicality alone would most probably have foiled any attempt to transform himself into the iconic artist. So, Bowie adopts a *gestic* attitude to the *representation* of Warhol's attitude towards life; it is important to clarify the distinction between these two uses of the word 'attitude' in this context.

Brecht's concept of *Gestus* provides a useful way of further unpacking Bowie's approach to the role of Warhol, which, as I have already implicitly suggested, is more presentational than representational. Put simply, *Gestus* is best understood as a practical strategy for actors, which enables them to show how relationships between characters are shaped by signifiers of social status. In Brecht's words:

> The realm of attitudes adopted by the characters towards one another is what we call the realm of gest. Physical attitude, tone of voice and facial expression are all determined by a social gest: the characters are cursing, flattering, instructing one another, and so on.[42]

The realm of gest resonates with Dyer's catalogue of signs cited earlier in this chapter, but gests are more than mere signs of performance. Brechtian scholar Meg Mumford provides a more expansive account of the term when she writes:

> We find Brecht using *Gestus* in a rather slippery way throughout his writings to mean one or all of the following: social(ized) gesticulation as opposed to psychological facial expression; contextualized and alterable comportment; and the rhetorical crafted gestures of a performer. From the late 1920s Brecht repeatedly combined these meanings, contriving a rich amalgam of ideas that formed the core of his political theatre. To 'show the *Gestus*' came to mean *to present artistically the mutable socio-economic and ideological construction of human behaviour and relations.*[43]

In the film, the dynamic between Warhol and Basquiat shifts and mutates as Basquiat's star rises. Clearly, Bowie's Warhol occupies a position of power in relation to Jeffrey Wright's Basquiat during the film's early scenes. We first encounter Bowie's character in a point-of-view shot: Basquiat spies Warhol as he is looking through the window of an art gallery populated by stylishly dressed men and women. Basquiat is literally on the outside looking into the rich and rarefied world of New York's elite art world. His clothes, hairstyle and race mark him as an outsider, and his gaze is occluded by the gallery's opaque window, but he glimpses Warhol's world through the window's transparent signage – the eyeline match allows the spectator to share the character's experience. In other words, the spectator's field of vision, like Basquiat's, is also partial and distanced. We see Bowie's Warhol, for the first time, in a wide shot: he raises his left hand to his mouth in a rhetorical gesture of studied contemplation as he appraises the paintings on the gallery wall. Bowie, resplendent in one of Andy's wigs, also has a polaroid camera around his neck, which further reinforces what I have suggested is an essentially presentational approach to playing Warhol (objects play an important role in Brecht's *gestic* dramaturgy as signifiers of social status). The scene ends as Warhol/Bowie allows himself to be guided through the assembled throng by a sharply dressed man who appears to be upsetting Dennis Hopper's art dealer character, Bruno Bischofberger, by commanding Warhol's attention.

Basquiat/Wright moves away from the gallery and paints some graffiti on what looks like a corrugated garage door. At this point, the social division between Warhol and Basquiat is conveyed through a set of oppositions: inside/outside, white/black, rich/poor, young/old. Thus, the full significance of the scene's social context is evident as we see that Basquiat's studio and gallery are located on the street whereas Warhol occupies conventionally prestigious spaces. This is the way things are, but not necessarily how things will always be, for the film's political subtext is about the variability and vulnerability of human existence and human relationships.

As the film progresses, Basquiat becomes the dominant partner in his relationship with Warhol. He audaciously breaks into Andy's world and eventually becomes one of Warhol's most esteemed collaborators. While the oppositions are not entirely reversed during the course of the film, Basquiat/Wright becomes a celebrity artist whose critical reputation and commercial value eclipse and move past Warhol's. The film, then, is also about the mutability of social status, acclaim and success, which is why a *gestic* reading of Bowie's performance resonates with Schnabel's presentation of the *trajectory* of Basquiat's relationship with Warhol: one star ascends as another declines.

'Oh, gee, Jean, that was my favourite part', says Warhol/Bowie as Basquiat paints a large white stripe across a large canvas depicting the winged horse, Pegasus. Those familiar with Basquiat and Warhol's collaborative work will recognize the painting as a reproduction of a work titled, *Amoco* (1984), in its nascent form. 'It needed more white, that's better', says Basquiat/Wright. 'You make me feel so worthless. You're so famous now', says Warhol/Bowie in a despondent tone. As the scene progresses, it is clear that Warhol is second guessing himself and he concedes that Basquiat possesses the greater talent – the reversal is complete. Bowie maintains his low-key, presentational approach to playing Warhol in this key scene – his performance is admirably consistent. He retains the distinctive cadences of Warhol's voice without attempting to totally conceal his own accent and he strikes several distinctive poses that accentuate his lithe physicality. This is especially evident when he stares at the canvas, left hand on hip, right hand clasping the left: 'I can't even see what's good anymore.' Bowie maintains an even tone as he speaks; he does not emote so much as he lets his body, posture and flat vocal tone convey his attitude to the painting and to Basquiat, his collaborator and usurper. There's not a trace of malice or resentment in the way Bowie delivers his lines. In short, he does not rely on a psychological, inside-out approach to the role; rather, he strikes a series of revealing poses, *gestic* poses, if you will. For me, it is as though Bowie is showing the audience that he is deliberately taking an *attitude* towards his character rather than trying to disappear into the character in stark contrast to Jeffrey Wright's approach to representing Jean-Michel Basquiat.

After learning of Andy's death, late in the film, Basquiat consoles himself by watching old black-and-white video tapes of Warhol in the studio and on vacation. This is a crucial scene since Schnabel cuts images of the real Warhol with those of Bowie as Warhol, thereby further exposing the gap between presentation and impersonation. Tears stream from Jeffrey Wright's eyes as he plays the scene. The medium close-up of Basquiat/Wright reveals a more conventional, psychological approach to screen performance: Wright's performance closes the gap between actor and role, exemplifying, perhaps, David George's fusion model.

Conclusion

I have not provided the definitive account of Bowie as Warhol, for there are always other ways of understanding and evaluating performances, but

I think the Brechtian framework I have sketched in this paper provides a compelling approach to assessing the strength of Bowie's presentation of Andy Warhol in *Basquiat*. That said, there are no guarantees that spectators will read Bowie's performance in *gestic* terms or with reference to Brechtian alienation. In many ways, this is beside the point, for there is something poignant about watching *Basquiat* today, decades after it was released. Basquiat, Warhol, Bowie and Brecht are all dead, but their work and aesthetic ideals continue to circulate in a variety of media. These twentieth-century pop art icons continue to haunt the twenty-first century as spectres who remind us, among other things, of the social and political tensions that marked their time on earth. Bowie may provide another way of unpacking his screen performance as Warhol by paying tribute to the *spirit* of experimentation and risk once embodied by Basquiat, Bowie and Warhol, but that would require taking another, not unrelated, approach to unpacking our understanding of Bowie as actor. For now, let us be content with using Bertolt Brecht's dramaturgy of alienation as a mechanism for appreciating David Bowie's prowess as a non-actorly actor, a cracked actor who managed, in *Basquiat*, to skilfully exploit the gaps between character, actor and person.

Notes

1 Will Brooker, *Why Bowie Matters* (London: William Collins, 2019), 12.
2 Ibid., 73.
3 Christopher Frayling, 'David Bowie Then . . . David Bowie Now', in *David Bowie Is*, ed. Victoria Broackes and Geoffrey Marsh (London: V&A Publishing, 2013), 285.
4 Richard Dyer, *Stars* (London: British Film Institute, 1998), 126.
5 Ibid., 129.
6 James Naremore, *Acting in the Cinema* (Berkeley, CA: University of California Press, 1988), 34–67.
7 Mehdi Derfoufi, 'Embodying Stardom, Representing Otherness: David Bowie in *Merry Christmas, Mr. Lawrence*', in *David Bowie: Critical Perspectives*, ed. Eoin Devereux, Aileen Dillane and Martin J. Power (London: Taylor & Francis Group, 2015), 165.
8 Ibid., 175.
9 Frayling, 'David Bowie Then . . . David Bowie Now,' 285.
10 Julian Schnabel and David Bowie, interview by Charlie Rose, *Charlie Rose*, PBS, 9 August 1996, https://www.youtube.com/watch?v=ZRWbM42P-1U, accessed 21 July 2020.
11 David Buckley, *Strange Fascination: David Bowie: The Definitive Story* (London: Virgin Books, 2005), 2.

12 David Bowie, 'Five Years' RCA Records, 1971.
13 David Bowie, Interview with Jeremy Paxton.
14 David Bowie quoted in Buckley, *Strange Fascination*, 139.
15 Philip Auslander, *Performing Glam Rock: Gender and Theatricality in Popular Music* (Ann Arbor, MI: The University of Michigan Press, 2006), 106.
16 David E. R. George, 'Letter to a Poor Actor', *New Theatre Quarterly* 2, no.8 (November 1986): 353.
17 Ibid., 353.
18 Constantin Stanislavski, *An Actor Prepares*, trans. Elizabeth Reynolds Hapgood (New York: Routledge, 1989), 14.
19 Denis Diderot, 'The Paradox of the Actor', in *Actors on Acting: The Theories, Techniques, and Practices of the World's Great Actors, Told in Their Own Words*, ed. Toby Cole and Helen Chinoy (New York: Crown, 1970), 165.
20 Erving Goffman, *The Presentation of Self in Everyday Life* (New York: Anchor Books, 1959).
21 Buckley, *Strange Fascination*, 6.
22 Simon Critchley, *Bowie* (New York: OR Books, 2014), 64.
23 See Shelton Waldrep, *The Aesthetics of Self-Invention: Oscar Wilde to David Bowie* (Minneapolis, MN: University of Minnesota, 2004).
24 Benita Luckmann, 'The Small Life-Worlds of Modern Man', *Social Research* 37, no. 4 (1970): 580–96.
25 Auslander, *Performing Glam Rock*, 4.
26 See Jane Goodall, *Stage Presence* (London: Routledge, 2008) for a fuller account of this crucial topic.
27 Geoffrey Marsh, 'Astronaut of Inner Spaces: Sundridge Park, Soho, London . . . Mars', in *David Bowie Is*, ed. Victoria Broackes and Geoffrey Marsh (London: V&A Publishing, 2013), 38.
28 Julian Schnabel and David Bowie, interview by Charlie Rose, *Charlie Rose*, PBS, 9 August 1996, https://www.youtube.com/watch?v=ZRWbM42P-1U, accessed 21 July 2020.
29 See Toija Cinque, '"Canvas of Flesh": David Bowie, Andy Warhol in *Basquiat*', *Cinema Journal* 57, no. 3 (Spring 2018): 158–66 for a detailed account of the meeting between Bowie and Warhol.
30 David Bowie, 'Andy Warhol' *Hunky Dory*, RCA Records, 1971.
31 Critchley, *Bowie*, 23.
32 Ibid., 24.
33 Marvin. J. Taylor, 'Playing the Field', in *The Downtown Book: The New York Art Scene 1974–1984*, ed. Marvin J. Taylor (Princeton, NJ: Princeton University Press, 2006), 35.
34 Bernard Gendron, 'The Downtown Music Scene', in *The Downtown Book: The New York Art Scene 1974–1984*, ed. Marvin J. Taylor (Princeton, NJ: Princeton University Press, 2006), 63.

35 Ekow Eshun, 'Bowie, Bach and Bebop: How music powered Basquiat', *Independent*, 25 September 2017, https://www.independent.co.uk/arts-entertainment/art/bowie-bach-and-bebop-how-music-powered-basquiat-a7966541.html, accessed 20 July 2020.
36 Dyer, *Stars*, 134.
37 For a detailed account of the role of Bowie's voice played in the construction of his personas see Kevin Holm-Hudson, '"Who Can I Be now?": David Bowie's Vocal Personae', *Contemporary Music Review* 37, no. 3 (2018): 214–34.
38 Also known as V-effects since Brecht used the German word, *Verfremdungseffekt*, to describe his dramaturgy. The word is most commonly translated as alienation or distancing in English.
39 Bertolt Brecht, 'The Street Scene: A Basic Model for Epic Theatre', in *Brecht on Theatre: The Development of an Aesthetic*, trans. John Willett (London: Eyre Methuen, 1978), 121.
40 David Buckley, *Bowie*, 2005, for an account of Bowie's relationship with Tony Defries.
41 David Bowie, 'Interview with Charlie Rose', 1996.
42 Brecht, *Brecht on Theatre*, 198.
43 Meg Mumford, *Bertolt Brecht* (London: Routledge, 2018), 54.

11

Performative emotional symbolism and stylistic gesture in Christopher Nolan's *The Prestige*

Toija Cinque

Introduction: *Essence and Gesture* – 'are, you watching, closely?'

A single ray of light from a distant star falling upon the eye of a tyrant in bygone times may have altered the course of his life, may have changed the destiny of nations, may have transformed the surface of the globe, so intricate, so inconceivably complex are the processes in Nature. In no way can we get such an overwhelming idea of the grandeur of Nature than when we consider, that in accordance with the law of the conservation of energy, throughout the Infinite, the forces are in a perfect balance, and hence the energy of a single thought may determine the motion of a universe.

– Nikola Tesla, 1893

Set against the backdrop of nineteenth-century London, the Christopher Nolan-directed 2006 film *The Prestige* showcases the significance of David Bowie in the pivotal role of Nikola Tesla. The chapter undertakes a critical examination of *The Prestige* and in so doing will specifically analyse David Bowie's role in the film as Nikola Tesla, a theatrical sign. For perspective, Nikola Tesla was a Serbo-Croatian-born electrical engineer and successful inventor. As a young man with ambition and self-directed learning in physics, he immigrated to New York to advance his research, such as his 'wireless lighting' which he would unveil theatrically at public events. Before Marconi (who had the ultimate success in signal transmission), Tesla was one of the first in the then emerging field of telecommunications to predict and work on wireless receiver technologies – running out of funds before his vision was realized. Undeterred, Tesla proceeded to devise several experiments in early X-ray production, discovering and patenting the rotating magnetic field, the basis of most alternating current (AC) machinery.[1] With undoubtable global impact, Tesla introduced the concept of AC generated with his Tesla coil (used later in radio, telephony and televisions) and electricity supply with successful patents used by Westinghouse Electric. Tesla was in direct competition with his colleague and peer, Thomas Edison, who had invented the direct current (DC) light bulb. With greater funding and production systems to support him, however, Edison flourished while Tesla (a great futurist) saw little commercial success by the end of his days. Tesla's important technological insights have, however, laid the foundation for later communications systems and modern power. Many years later, recognition of the impact of his work saw Martin Eberhard and Marc Tarpenning establish in 2003 the electric car and clean energy storage company, Tesla Motors, using his name by way of tribute.

Tesla remains an enigma and visionary, who also occupies his own mythic niche in the cultural and historical consciousness of the West. While a detailed exploration of this would be beyond the scope of the chapter, there is a certain synthesis between the mythic auras of Tesla and Bowie, both thus elevating the symbolism of the character on-screen. Nikola Tesla's biography of great career highs and lows can be understood here as that form of unfolding and refolding that Soussloff calls our attention to which acts to generate his own mythic aura. As a result, *The Prestige* holds a vibration of one mythic aura (David Bowie) entwined with another (Nikola Tesla) as Nolan and the audience place faith in Bowie's charisma to inhabit that role. Even though he is seen for little more than five minutes, I will argue that Bowie's presence is at the heart of Nolan's overarching narrative: a call for the audience to actively consider the complexity of the formation processes contributing to one's identity. As we will see hence, Nolan's filmography holds to a stylistic coherence typified by complex characters and a scaffolding of tropes, plots and perplexing endings.

The question of what defines us as individuals is not new. On the one hand, for Plato in *Parmenides*: 'A man [sic] must be gifted with very considerable ability before he can learn that everything has a class and an absolute essence; and still more remarkable will he be who discovers all these things for himself, and having thoroughly investigated them is able to teach them to others.'[2] Counter to the rationalist position, John Locke's thesis is that understanding is neither innate nor is identity distinct to the individual but are acquired through direct experience formed from sensory experiences then progressed by reflection. In this context and in accord with Locke's premise, *The Prestige*'s interest in illusion rouses the audience to deeply consider identity as defined by the function one performs. By following this thread, Nolan presents the provocation that one's identity is not predesigned by the stars, or of God-given soul or essence as in Plato's proposal, but by the function that we execute (such as the diligent worker, the creative artist, the loving parent, etc.). The philosophical excursion in *The Prestige* is undertaken using various disciplines that, when drawn together, congeal the action to both endorse and discredit the binary proposition of absolute essence versus direct experience. While the visual/aural narrative is important to understanding Nolan's intent by film's end, so too is the movement of the actors' bodies with artistic and illustrative intentions. Examined from this perspective, Nolan's film-philosophy appears to be approaching the creative process in accord with Bertolt Brecht's early work through *gest* and the motif of the dialectical circumstance between instinct and reason typified in his plays. Of these works, Brecht states:

> I hope in *Baal* and *Dickicht* I've avoided one common artistic bloomer, that of trying to carry people away. . . . The spectator's 'splendid isolation' is left intact: . . . he [sic] is not fobbed off with an invitation to feel sympathetically, to fuse with the hero and seem significant and indestructible as he watches himself in two simultaneous versions. A higher type of interest can be got from making comparisons, from whatever is different, amazing, impossible to take in as a whole.[3]

There is much to be found from Brecht's work that is applicable to David Bowie and *The Prestige*. This includes an interpretation of realism as a way of connoting the reasons behind why people behave as they do in order to critically explore what might be done to solve a problem or issue; the audience must, however, be actively involved. In accord with Locke's theory of direct experience, the Brechtian theatre's manifesto takes as its prime motivation a process aimed directly at facilitating the audience's internal self-reflection and individual change for the betterment of the surrounding world. Found in Brecht's aesthetic is that reality is critical and changeable, and every emotion comes with a set of social relations. 'For it is what happens between people', Brecht says, 'that provides them with all the material that they can discuss, criticize, alter.'[4]

David Bowie brings his own 'back catalogue' of theatrical works and performances to the role of Nikola Tesla. Specifically, Bowie's use of *stylistic gesture* in acting[5] is rendered here as *performative emotional symbolism* and significant, as unpacked further below. The *gesture* by human action is what Vilém Flusser explains to be 'a movement of the body or of a tool attached with the body, for which there is no satisfactory causal explanation' for its significance.[6] That is, a gesture is characterized by what can be understood from its symbolic meaning as opposed to any instrumental purpose. The performative emotional symbolism – comprising the stylistic gesture Bowie referred to, drawing emotions such as the sharp vicissitudes of love, desire, despair or anger – is aimed at calling forth feelings in the listening/viewing audience in contrast to dully luring 'the audience into the emotional content of what you are doing'.[7] With similar provenance is Michael Chekhov's Psychological Gesture proposed as an acting method for expressing the essence of an archetype.[8] Chekhov found that genuine actors hold within themselves the aptitude to inhabit (but not be) the internal process of performance.[9] Even though Chekhov does contend with the notion of realism on intra-actor communication, his technique recognizes the Platonic 'essence', given the actor's own nature. Following Chekhov is the effort to recreate then express the 'realism' of how people actually behave and speak to each other, and to translate it to the screen or stage to manifest the human condition as accurately as possible in the hope of making the audience reflect upon their own definition of what it means to be human.

With not little allusion to Chekhov's Psychological Gesture in acting, Bowie has explained: 'I want to portray emotions symbolically.'[10] Grasping the diversity and complexity of life, Bowie does so by appearing to represent 'reality'. His are intentional motions that draw on combinations of meanings that are revealed across time in the process of aspiring towards the realization of a future, but unfixed, condition.

David Bowie is appreciated as a consummate artist, with many contradictions across forms from music, acting and fine arts. In performance, his showmanship is tightly choreographed, affording professionally controlled experiences and intentional performances.[11] Bowie has a unique understanding of the audience and when he sings 'I never done good things, I never done bad things. I never did anything out of the blue' in 'Ashes to Ashes' on the 1980 album *Scary Monsters . . . and Super Creeps* – undertaken to purge past identities in an effort to work through internal conflicts, eradicate feelings he was uncomfortable with and better understand them – he is most certainly conscious of what he intends but also aware of what is being received, and how.[12] Contemplating the good/bad binary in his music's lyrics above, to be found is the tone of purposeful becoming not one necessarily impelled by their innate intentions. The 'good things' and 'bad things' might be read scripturally as the essence in/of the human condition versus the exertion of direct, learned experience. The song draws on a Brechtian architecture, being punctuated in a seemingly random fashion by past memories, unanswered questions and a jarring of metaphoric rhythms imparted as a challenge to the patterns of our own engagement so that we too might be forced to confront the vehicle for our own discomfort.[13] From narrative forms materialized to interpretive art and, specifically, acting, Bowie uses a countervailing performative emotional symbolism to draw the essence of an emotion he wishes to portray. This works to free himself from the constraints of merely depicting the 'real' world to re-evaluate it instead in new ways by breaking accepted associations between language, movement and things. This causes fissures to be created whereby new and multiple meanings are rendered possible and valid, going beyond both the creator and audience across time.

The metanarrative that David Bowie gives *The Prestige* is one that sensations of incongruence in the audience are essential to the effect of Nolan's overarching creative execution. This is delivered in part by a seemingly cut-up story but in fact is an attempt to structure drama as *deliberately* meaningful through juxtaposition so that the plot remains hidden until the end. Even then, the plot is only revealed if one dares to confidently reject the surface of carefully constructed truths. Using the 'cut-up' technique borrowed from the Dadaists of the early twentieth century (via William S. Burroughs) relies on rejecting reason and logic in favour of irrationality and intuition, to assemble what could be words or images or sounds that (seemingly) render any 'real' narrative obsolete.[14] Along these lines, the plot reveals a process whereby images are being ambiguously juxtaposed to facilitate polysemic interpretation. As I argue in this chapter, in parallel with his other works, Bowie's performance in *The Prestige* is imbued with thoughtful and carefully controlled intimacies – perhaps counterintuitively informed by both Chekhov (via an approach to acting) and Brecht (via thoughts on theatre) – between the character and others on-screen and affectively between Bowie and his audience. As unravelled hence, we are neither completely one thing nor another across time but an amalgam of competing and complementary forces.

Significant against the film's use of science fiction (featuring an electric machine that can duplicate an unlimited number of identical animate and inanimate objects) is that Bowie has himself drawn creatively on the genre in films such as *The Man Who Fell to Earth* and music.[15] David Bowie embodies certain identity positions that are alien, alternative and transgressive as related to the outsider via metaphor and alter egos that render him essentially strange.[16] An alien, seemingly cold apartness and science fiction's 'examination of the meaning of human existence and identity enter his creative output and inform his fluid identity as a performer' through multiple stage, film and music personae: Major Tom, Ziggy Stardust, Aladdin Sane, Halloween Jack, Thomas Jerome Newton and The Thin White Duke.[17] These personae are Bowie's metaphors for conveying the didactic and are as much the result as they are the essence of his work, and a personal aesthetic he applied in artistic spheres beyond music. David Bowie assembles these 'roles' with his own style of 'splendid isolation'[18]: a cold apartness tinged with deep trauma is applied throughout his works. For a number, David Bowie represents a rethinking of how knowledge is created in the context of artistic practice.

The neologism *mythic aura* is used then as the theoretical framing to consider the myth of the artist.[19] This follows the assertion that considered together the epistemologies of myth and artist reveal them to be structures greater and more enduring than 'reality'[20] – creating replicas of sorts, as opposed to notions of complete falsehoods. Catherine Soussloff explains compellingly that the figure of the artist in historical contexts has been produced by way of biographies and anecdotes that work up and reinforce the myths associated with the artist,[21] and to varying degrees, audiences have put their faith in the 'myth'. Undoubtedly, for this reason, Nolan flew to New York to personally pitch the Nikola Tesla role to Bowie, telling him, 'No one else could possibly play the part.'[22]

While a complete annotated review is beyond the scope of this chapter, some examples of the impacts of his works with the consequent forming of his *mythic aura* are necessary towards understanding the symbolic inclusion of David Bowie in Nolan's picture that transcends the boundaries of the film. In regard to challenging 'established' societal norms, via his output Bowie has influenced the Punk movement,[23] mid-1980s Grunge – typified by Nirvana's performance of 'The Man Who Sold the World' on MTV Unplugged in New York[24] – and reflected in Lorde emotionally singing 'Life on Mars' in tribute at the BRIT awards held in London soon after Bowie's death. As a proponent of individualism and materialized in costume form, his styles have seen him inserted forever into the story of modern art such that those so affected by his especial sensibilities have exerted similar influence as designers and fashion editors in their own ensuing careers. Hints of Bowie's consequence are seen regularly in contemporary fashion including Dries Van Noten men's fall 2011, Jean-Paul Gaultier spring 2013, Haider Ackermann spring 2016 collections, to a neo-Glam acknowledgement by Lady Gaga at the 2016 Grammy Awards in the United States. There is also a growing body of critical academic work,[25] and David Bowie has exacted a particular mythic status as a result (as a genius, an icon, an auteur), as ever new generations of fans come to partake in his artistic oeuvre. I conclude with the provocation that David Bowie cast in the role of a real-life inventor finds audiences placing their faith in his charisma – videlicet, his *mythic aura*.

The greatest magic trick

'This is the truth, isn't it?'

As the opening sequence of the film begins, the camera tracks slowly in close-up over a collection of black silk, flat-crowned top hats scattered in a darkened, foggy, autumn woodland. There is only the merest diegetic hint of an unseen wind. This sets up everything that comes after. The fleeting image is soon lost, and the camera now moves with similar pace past a series of small cages, side by side, each with an identical canary within. Led in by an older magician, Cutter, the audience is told what a magician does – their function:

> The magician shows you something ordinary – a deck of cards, a bird, or a man. He [*sic*] shows you this object, perhaps he asks you to inspect it to see that it is, indeed, real.

Unbeknownst to the first-time viewer, the film begins with the story's ending in medias res and does not adhere to a chronological structure throughout but presents a complex time-jumping narrative. We hear a disembodied male voice with a cockney accent, typical of the working class in the East End of London, ask: 'are you watching closely?' At a distance from the diegetic contexture from the start, this question is not rhetorical but calls the audience to awareness. This metaphysical question is delivered for all and not just the educated classes. Building on Locke's thesis, it is a question that demands that those in the audience pay critical attention, that is, to self-reflect upon whether they want either merely to be entertained by the film's magic tricks (read as life's illusions) or instead be existentially challenged to address the version of reality and the account of ourselves we choose to live with, and thus exert one's individual agency. Below the surface, the film is far less about magic and deception and uses the frame of illusions and misconception to create a complex story that is also about filmmaking's processes for cleverly entertaining the audience with its capacity for challenging the viewer/listener to be a more skilled participant in its unfolding events.

In the opening scene that lasts a little over one minute, Nolan has identified the themes of his film. The first is *identity*, represented by the sleek black top hat. In the film the hat denotes a magician (which could well be the wizard inventor, Nikola Tesla) as well as gentlemen from the middle and upper classes (Angier/Lord Caldlow). Identity is unpicked through the key characters' assumed roles, obscured identities and replication. There are twin boys born into the working class, Albert and Fredrick (this detail from the book of the same name).[26] They combine their names to 'Alfred Borden' to become a single identity. Another assumed identity is that of 'Robert Angier', the name a pseudonym for a wealthy British aristocrat, Lord Caldlow. The ostensibly American magician, Robert Angier, himself adopts a further onstage identity, as The Great Danton. Angier goes on a quest to find his own double to perform a magic trick which might be read as the deeper search to become his true self or a better version of it. The use of different identities by single characters might appear in line with Brecht's interest in the attitudes which people adopt towards one another, wherever they are socio-historically typical or noteworthy. The actors present characters with an attitude of such a sort that the social laws under which they are acting come into stark relief for the effect that '[h]uman behaviour is shown as alterable, man [sic] as dependent on certain political and economic factors and at the same time capable of altering them'.[27] In the film, neither 'Alfred Borden' nor 'Angier' is a single man simply using multiple identities but a notional single identity using multiple men to perform different functions. Through them 'the spectator is given the chance to criticize human behaviour from a social point of view' because they can comparatively examine and consider everything that influences the way in which people behave.[28]

The second theme is *sacrifice*, as a small bird seems to die rendering a leitmotif for consideration over and over again through various losses in the film including of love, life and purpose. Robert Angier loses his wife and, seeing his nemesis with his own happy family, feelings resonate internally so that grief for what he no longer has in turn becomes a different mindset: one of anger, rage, jealousy and obsession. As Angier becomes smaller in his driving to be the better showman in the minds of audiences, Borden seems to grow in stature, tirelessly working to improve, indeed perfect his performed shows. Tesla, in his own life, possessed a similar lifelong professional drive, one that was matched by David Bowie's own. Bowie, who strove to perfect 'the star performer', ultimately came to the despairing need in the 1970s to 'kill off' Ziggy Stardust and then later leave for Berlin to escape the world that had grown around Thomas Jerome Newton (the lead character in *The Man Who Fell to Earth*); they had respectively grown psychologically all-consuming as onstage/on-screen personae bleeding into his everyday lived experience.[29] For Bowie and Tesla (and Borden), this self-directed (essential) motivation to strive became a compulsion to be better, to become more. Indeed, Bowie, Borden and Tesla are all sacrificing glory, family, friendship and love for the trick by giving all to their art. In life and consumed by professional motivation, Tesla never married and died alone in a hotel. At a career high point from the 1970s, David Bowie's marriage began unravelling and he divorced in the early 1980s. The emphasis on one's sacrifice will be a point of contention in a conversation that Bowie-as-Tesla has with Angier.

The third theme is *reality* and what we might want to believe. The opening comprises images out of sequence, and the story unfolds via edited collections whereby not one piece gives anything in and of itself but needs to be related to all the others. Through a Brechtian lens, this works to keep the audience confused, perplexed and asking questions until the very end. The film is circular, starting with the objectively final scenes, but multiple viewings render new understandings. Narratively, the film is a story of the reading of two notebooks, one written by ambitious magician Robert Angier and the other by his equal peer and later rival, Alfred Borden. Both journals were created by unreliable sources for the express purpose to manipulate the other. They are connivingly compiled from falsehoods and misleads but with some semblances of truths to be believable. The film's plot follows two people reading two subjective diaries and the parallel entanglements that ensue. The camera gives us objective views of the protagonists while shifting around whose story is actually being told. Taken chronologically, these two magicians work together but when a trick goes wrong, killing Angier's wife, it appears that Borden might have been responsible. This event sets the two irrevocably apart with Angier layering the path of anger, jealousy and obsession. One day, Angier sees Borden perform on stage a trick that he cannot fathom or perform convincingly, and he resolves to discover its true secret. It is through reading Borden's diary that his character arc shifts importantly when he locates the cypher 'Tesla' and feels impelled to contact the inventor as the likely solution.

Nolan's film, like myths themselves, can neither be interpreted nor understood as formed from a continuum that might progress in neat order from a beginning to end with a set destination. Rather, the film must be taken as *gestalt* in that the whole story is made up of the sum of the individual parts and subplots – as we are. Each story element is sewn together in overlapping, rhizomatic layers to form, in this instance, the complete film. For structural anthropologist Claude Lévi-Strauss, myths are 'bundles of events' that might arise at different points in time in a story; this conceit finds fertile ground when Bowie-as-Tesla is woven into the tale.[30] Bowie proceeds as a composite meaning-carrying (floating) signifier for the fluidity of identity propositions. He depicts sacrifice as an essential/innate call, one that is cultivated and refined. The 'reality' of these themes is unpicked through critical realism.[31]

'They are all your hat, Mr Angier'

The challenge presented for the 'actor' on stage – and equally extrapolated to the human condition in (struggling through) life – is that one 'must perform the structure laid out ... yet freely improvise within the structure, making discoveries and decision moment by moment' in order to render a truth.[32] Axiomatic to the Bowie-as-Tesla role is the moment when Tesla agrees to build for Angier at great cost a fantastical machine that allows him to enact 'The Transported Man' trick – simply seen, one person enters a box and swiftly emerges from another that is set apart at a distance. Angier is not content to accept the obvious explanation: that Borden might have a secret twin, a double who could be used to perform the extraordinary magical feat. Angier will create human clones of himself instead, choosing a dreadful fate for each.

The first encounter with Bowie-as-Tesla is via an interior shot which finds Angier standing in a dimly lit, concrete and steel warehouse. A ball hangs from a central point in the ceiling, shooting crackling shards of electricity in all directions towards the raised stage below it. Angier's facial expression is incredulous as he looks up at Bowie-as-Tesla who has made his theatrical entrance and emerged as if materialized from the lightning rainstorm (49:55) – the electricity perhaps symbolizing the light of awareness that would soon be Angier's by film's end. Bowie-as-Tesla holds the air of a prophet with one eyebrow raised and hands behind his back. Here, too, his *mythic aura* alludes to the explorative journey one might embark upon through the questioning of sociopolitical obstacles that bind many to a version of reality that handicaps potentially sincerely lived experiences. At the very point Bowie-as-Tesla speaks the electricity stops. Bowie performs Tesla with precision timing, thus proving his (and Nolan's) demonstrated control of the meaning he generates.

Extracting David Bowie's myth is not an endpoint in itself, for myths are not static but open to polysemic interpretation and reinterpretations (unfolding and refolding) over time and in different places, changing with the telling and retelling as underscored in the sections above. The motifs arising around David Bowie's stories have simply not been produced through a unidirectional process, prepared by a public relations agent for the fans by way of example. The stories of Bowie – his myths, if you will – have evolved (like our own) in iterative processes affording mutually constitutive opportunities for construal and interpretation.[33] This premiss connects to Chekhov's contention in regard to *intra*-actor communication, for Bowie-as-Tesla conveys a Platonic-like 'essence' given the actor's own nature so that the filmic act emerges and meaning materializes *from within* the relationship, not outside of it.[34]

Standing with the sombre countenance of a school master with square-set shoulders and hands clasped behind his back at the edge of his stage, Bowie-as-Tesla dramatically delivers the line 'So . . . this is The Great Danton' (49:59). Bowie-as-Tesla then walks – chin up, back straight – down the stairs towards the camera, this movement a strong gesture in a Chekhovian sense. It is also demonstratively typical of Bowie's own 'single-minded, fuck-the-lot-of-you mind-set' and a perspective that Tesla surely shared as he faced his multiple setbacks yet kept generating marvellous ideas.[35] This scene cuts to a close-up of Bowie-as-Tesla and his gaze momentarily but potently seems to pierce Angier knowingly (50:08). The eyes are the central focus in the close-up shot: they are the windows to the soul. But these eyes are Bowie's strange eyes, one blue and one green – unearthly, preternatural. In accord with Locke, and as one who has cultivated by force the capacity to suffer, Bowie-as-Tesla senses that Angier is prepared to face any danger to realize his goal.

Seen together now in mid shot, Bowie-as-Tesla asks Angier to give him his hand and in a seeming act of magic, he puts a light bulb in one as he holds his other and their bodies conduct enough power to shine the globe brightly. The pair are seen in shot-reverse-shot, and Bowie-as-Tesla explains in a softly spoken voice that people can both conduct and produce energy. As soon as he releases the hand of Angier the light goes out with a flourish as if to say 'on your own you are in the dark' – unenlightened. The interaction between the two characters is in accord with Brecht's teaching, providing the critical audience with all the material they require for contemplation. We then hear Bowie-as-Tesla ask if Angier has eaten, and with the slightest of gestures we see his fingers curl sharply in the air. The refocusing of conversation and that they are in what appears to be a sparsely furnished laboratory, aside from Tesla's 'magnifying transmitter' (in Figure 11.1), seems incongruous to a place people would meet to really enjoy a meal together. The food to which he refers (and the subsequent depiction of a formal luncheon) is perhaps a metaphor for the sustenance of life.

The scene cuts to a mid shot of them in another perplexing state: we see them in mid shot seated on the side of a mountain, floating clouds hanging at head height, yet their table is fashionably set with cut crystal glasses, china teacups and saucers and delicate, cut sandwiches. The scene depicts a duality: the civility of social circumstance set hard against the rawness of nature. Balanced on a tripod is a telescope at the table's edge denoting the affordances of increased knowledge through new scientific discoveries during the so-called enlightened turn to the observable sciences. In this setting, the crystal claret pitchers might easily be borosilicate glass beakers and the tea standing in for francium, caesium, gallium and rubidium liquefying at slightly elevated temperatures. The scene is calling on the viewer to quickly understand the historical march of time from basic human survival and simple needs being met to individual actualization and social enculturation. By way of speeding up the continuous time series, Bowie-as-Tesla performs softly this melodramatic beat to impart that 'society only accepts one change at a time' (50:49), as he personally knows to his chagrin. For Bowie-as

FIGURE 11.1 *Bowie-as-Tesla on stage.*

Tesla summarizes that it is not the capacity that one is born with that sees greatness but how brave one is to chance the seeming impossible. The depth of emotion fleetingly conveyed through his facial expression alone demands and finds a level of combined intensity and perspicuity. In close-up, Bowie-as-Tesla uses his steady eyes and slightly quivering mouth to convey his inner turmoil, paying close attention to conveying humility and vulnerability while in parallel he asks Angier (yet rhetorically as both are obsessively goal oriented) to seriously consider the cost one takes on in pursuit of ambition. By way of performative emotional symbolism through Psychological Gesture, the hesitations and slight pauses in vocal delivery communicate a constant sense of personal inner reflection in the way Bowie plays Tesla. In a steadfast glare, the eyes that see are barely moving from the other man's face. Bowie-as-Tesla stings Angier to self-reflexively ponder what he is willing to lose in order to advance and what is to be gained in the process.

Upon his departure from Colorado under pressure that the truly extraordinary is not permitted and difference little appreciated, Bowie (long the 'outsider') playing Tesla writes in a note to Angier that what is sought can be found in 'the box'. This promise is tied to another allegory to explain that that which Angier seeks might not be what he expected, as Pandora found too late in the box she possessed (the artefact in this pertinent Greek story is a device from mythology called upon to highlight that which is not working or is problematic to bring about its end). As Bowie-as-Tesla recommends, 'we need to try different material. It might provoke a different result' (1:24:20). Just as each Angier reproduced in the box is killed as a result of every performance, multiple identities are shed in the process of change, refinement and alteration during the film. For the audience, both Borden and Angier have *become* something unexpectedly different by the film's end.

Run out of town, Bowie-as-Tesla is seen in mid shot looking out a carriage window (1:30:46). His unbodied voice implores Angier, however, to drop 'the box' – the cause of consternation but also renewal – into the deepest ocean and destroy it in fear of what it might bring about. Yet the story of Pandora's box holds the tenet that Hope alone remained inside waiting to be set free. When Bowie-as-Tesla decries to Angier that 'exact science is not an exact science, the machine simply does not operate as expected. It requires further examination' (1:22:01), a parallel is drawn that neither is a human life predictable nor is it controllable despite the intended function a number might want or expect of it. As a metaphor for the human, initially Tesla's machine does not operate as he expected it to, needing further examination. Again, the careful audience is called to engage in a form of self-examination all prepared to pull oneself apart and be humbled by the mysteries. Drawing the arc back to the beginning and Nolan's opening scene of black top hats in a grove, we see them now on Bowie-as-Tesla's table-as-chemistry bench as identically reproduced artefacts from 'the box'.

Bowie-as-Tesla reminds Angier: 'don't forget your hat' (1:26:21). Confused, Angier asks: 'well, which one is mine?' To which Bowie-as-Tesla responds Chekhovian-like via a convergence between Platonic 'essence' and Lockean 'direct experience' through his rendering of performative emotional symbolism with an oblique assertion: 'they are all your hats, Mr Angier' (1:26:25), and we see the slightest knowing smile at the corners of his mouth for the first time as he does so.

One interpretation is that the hat, like one's identity, is a working composite applied to its function. We might conversely understand the multiple hats not, however, as an identically formed item each with a preset function but each instead as an individual outcome of striving for the impossible. Thus, when Bowie-as-Tesla overtly states that 'they are all your hat, Mr Angier', he is implying that commitment and struggle with great endeavour regardless of anguish, via the sign of the hats in this context, portends the extraordinary and can be had. The action here tracing Nietzsche's prototypical philosopher's aesthetic contemplation whereby humankind is assisted in the 'vivisections on our own souls' that we might dissect them and 'heal ourselves afterwards; we have no doubt that being ill is instructive, even more instructive than being well'.[36] Bowie asks us – as Tesla petitions Angier – to be 'nutcrackers' of our own soul, making us question and questionable and thus 'more deserving [appreciative?] – of life . . . ?'[37]

Conclusion

Where the top hat in *The Prestige* might imply effort in identity construction, the replication machine presented in the film by Bowie-as-Tesla intimates that the possibility of self-completion or self-perfection is always already deferred by the fact that the mechanical process of self-reproduction allows for any object, including a human, to be endlessly unfolded, reproduced and refolded. But the process and quality of replication, and effort in doing so, are what are being lit up. It is not merely in regard to replication in and of itself. Like Bowie's stage personae, it is continual refinement in the Lockian context whereupon each version of one's self is fashioned with improvements upon the last. What Nolan accomplishes in *The Prestige* by highlighting the constructed nature of the magic trick as a theatrical event is to demonstrate the artifice of 'the show' by revealing 'art' as an event on a stage. The stories of Bowie that unfold and refold assist in the journeying. His myths are in iterative processes and find accord with Brecht, for the multiple contradictions 'are all absorbed into a glorious fluidity, both clear and indecipherable, crystallised, perhaps in the notion of Bowie as simultaneously *sui generis* and an amalgam of multiple influences'.[38] Working metaphorically, if life (its enduring struggle and sacrifice) is our 'stage' and we are all 'actors' upon it,[39] then art and its forms are the comments upon life – and, from a Brechtian point of view, are not fixed but ours to shape.

Notes

1. Margaret Cheney, *Tesla: Man Out of Time* (Hoboken: Prentice Hall, 1981).
2. Plato, *Parmenides* (South Bend: Infomotions, Inc., 2000), 9.
3. Bertolt Brecht, *Brecht on Theatre: The Development of an Aesthetic*, ed. John Willett (London: Methuen, 1964), 9.
4. Ibid.
5. Joe Gore, 'Changes 2.1: New Digital Stimulation from David Bowie and Reeves Gabrels', *Guitar Player*, June 1997, 46–7.
6. Vilém Flusser, *Gestures*, trans. Nancy A. Roth (Minneapolis, MN: University of Minnesota Press, 2014), 3.
7. Gore, 'Changes 2.1'.
8. Michael Chekhov, *Lessons for the Professional Actor*, trans. Deirdre Hurst du Prey with an introduction by Mel Gordon (New York: Performing Arts Journal Publications, 1985).
9. Ibid.
10. Gore, 'Changes 2.1'.
11. Patricia Mackay, 'Serious – and stunning – moonlight', in *The Bowie Companion*, ed. Elizabeth Thomson and David Gutman (Cambridge, MA: Da Capo Press, 1996), 195–8.
12. Nicholas Pegg, *The Complete David Bowie*, 6th ed. (London: Titan Books, 2011), 360.
13. Toija Cinque, 'Semantic Shock: David Bowie', in *Enchanting David Bowie: Space/Time/Body/Memory*, ed. Toija Cinque, Christopher Moore and Sean Redmond (New York: Bloomsbury, 2015), 199–211.
14. Ibid.
15. Ian Dixon, 'Always Crashing on the Same Synth: Voice/Synth Counterpoise in David Bowie's *Low*', in *Interpreting the Synthesizer: Meaning Through Sonics*, ed. Nick Wilson (Newcastle upon Tyne: Cambridge Scholars Publishing, 2020), 21–35.
16. Cinque, 'Semantic Shock', 199.
17. Angela Ndalianis, 'Bowie and Science Fiction/Bowie as Science Fiction', *Cinema Journal* 57, no. 3 (Spring 2018), 139–49.
18. Brecht, *Brecht on Theatre*, 9.
19. Catherine Soussloff, *The Absolute Artist: The Historiography of a Concept* (Minneapolis: University of Minnesota Press, 1997).
20. Roland Barthes, *Mythologies*, trans. Annette Lavers (London: Vintage Books, 2000), 142.

21 Soussloff, *The Absolute Artist*.
22 Donald Clarke, 'Tricks of the Trade', *Irish Times*, 10 November 2006.
23 John Rob, *Punk Rock: An Oral History* (Great Britain: Ebury Press, 2006).
24 See 'Nirvana – The Man Who Sold The World (MTV Unplugged)', Nirvana, published 17 June 2009, https://www.youtube.com/watch?v=fregObNcHC8.
25 See for example the respective critical academic works: Eoin Devereux, Aileen Dillane and Martin J. Power, eds, *David Bowie: Critical Perspectives* (Routledge: London, 2015); Toija Cinque, Christopher Moore and Sean Redmond, eds, *Enchanting David Bowie: Space/Time/Body/Memory* (New York: Bloomsbury, 2015); Will Brooker, *Forever Stardust: David Bowie Across the Universe* (New York: Bloomsbury, 2017); Ana Cristina Mendes and Lisa Perrott, eds, *David Bowie and Transmedia Stardom* (London: Routledge, 2020).
26 Christopher Priest, *The Prestige* (New York: Touchstone, 1995), 404.
27 Brecht, *Brecht on Theatre*, 86.
28 Ibid.
29 David Buckley, *Strange Fascination: Bowie* (London: Random House, 2005).
30 Claude Lévi-Strauss, 'Myth and Music', in *Myth and Meaning* (Toronto, ON and Buffalo: University of Toronto Press, 1978), 45.
31 Roy Bhaskar, *Reflections on Meta-Reality: Transcendence, Emancipation, and Everyday Life* (Thousand Oaks: Sage Publications, 2002).
32 Leslie Bennett, 'Inspired States: Adapting the Michael Chekhov Technique for the Singing Actor', *Theatre, Dance and Performance Training* 4, no.2 (2013): 146–61.
33 Toija Cinque, 'Chapter Nine: Ghostly Pilgrimages', in *The Fandom of David Bowie: Everyone Says "Hi"*, ed. Toija Cinque and Sean Redmond (Switzerland: Palgrave, 2019), 177–200.
34 Karen Barad, 'Posthumanist performativity: Toward an understanding of how matter comes to matter', *Signs: Journal of women in culture and society* 28, no.3 (2003): 801–31.
35 Buckley, *Strange Fascination*, 259.
36 Friedrich Nietzsche, *On the Genealogy of Morals: A Polemic*, ed. Robert C. Holub, trans. Michael A. Scarpitti (London: Penguin Books, 2013), 99.
37 Ibid.
38 Mark Readman, 'Editorial – David Bowie', *Journal of Media Practice* 17, no.1 (2016): 3.
39 Erving Goffman, *The Presentation of Self in Everyday Life* (New York: Doubleday, 1959).

12

'Just like the films'

Lazarus and cinematic melancholia

Denis Flannery

A. A pathological state of despondency; severe depression (now, *Medicine*) severe endogenous depression, with loss of interest and pleasure in normal activities, disturbance of sleep and appetite, feelings of worthlessness and guilt, and thoughts of death or suicide.

B. In extended use: gloominess, a theatrical or aesthetic indulgence in reflective or maudlin emotion.
– Definition of 'Melancholia', *OED Online*[1]

> If my love song
> Could fly over mountains
> Could laugh at the ocean
> Just like the films
>
> – David Bowie and Enda Walsh, 'Absolute Beginners'
> (*Lazarus* version)[2]

Introduction

Lazarus (2015) depends for its existence on a melancholic relationship to cinema. David Bowie and Enda Walsh's tightly written, emotionally driven and coarsely energizing musical dream play has an attachment to being 'just like the films', and to being like one particular film, Nicolas Roeg's 1976 *The Man Who Fell to Earth*, in a way for which the word 'melancholic' feels right, at least to me. I use the phrase 'feels right' because words like 'melancholic', 'melancholy' and 'melancholia' do not appear in Bowie and Walsh's text. Yet one viewing of the show, one reading of its published text or a little time spent listening to its original cast recording would demonstrate how it traffics in what the OED definition of melancholia terms 'pathological states of despondency'.[3] The dictionary provides a second definition of melancholia as a form of theatrical or aesthetic indulgence in reflective or maudlin emotion, also at work in *Lazarus*. On many levels, I will be arguing that cinema enables many of *Lazarus*'s melancholic impacts; how it does so and what the play might help us to value in melancholia are my preoccupations in this chapter.

I pursue these preoccupations with my eye on the text of Bowie and Walsh's play, on my memories of having seen it many times and on the particularities of both Roeg's film and the 1963 novel which inspired it. It may seem odd that a book devoted to Bowie as a film performer ends with a consideration of a play and one, furthermore, in which Bowie did not appear. But *Lazarus* is, as I have claimed, passionately attached to the film of *The Man Who Fell to Earth*. *Lazarus* also depends for its theatrical force on the interaction between the moving bodies of live performers with pre-recorded, moving images. Whatever theatrical space might hold a performance of this play is required to take on some of the basic features of cinema. Revisiting the plot of Roeg's film (in which Bowie the singer appeared but did not sing), *Lazarus* is full of Bowie songs which, though not actually sung by him, inevitably invoke recollections of his force as a singer and performer. In the wake of his death, just over a month after the play premiered, these recollections, for many people, took on haunted and melancholic aspects.

I also write as a literary scholar formed by very traditional critical protocols (particularly close reading) and as someone whose writing, especially in more recent years, has been impassioned and broadened by encounters with both critical theory (particularly queer theory and work on temporality) and contemporary European theatre. Close reading has also been central to the operations of queer theory and, as I've argued elsewhere, the ethos and practice of Ivo van Hove (who directed the first production of *Lazarus*) are driven by the kinds of attentive revisitations of texts without which close reading cannot operate.[4]

Reading and remembering *Lazarus*, I draw on Judith Butler's rereading of Sigmund Freud's 1917 writing on melancholia, both at the significant moment when, in 1990, she brought Freudian melancholia into the realms of queer theory and in her more recent work. I also draw on writers whose work considers the relationship between melancholia, representation, affect and temporality as it is manifest in Shakespeare and the Renaissance (Drew Daniel and Lee Edelman), in the odes of John Keats (Anahid Neressian) and as it is revalued in Henry James's writing on history (David McWhirter).

Further, 'Cinema and its Ghosts', an interview with Jacques Derrida, emphasizes two aspects of cinema which are vitally important to *Lazarus*. The first is what he calls 'the thoroughly spectral structure of the cinematic image'.[5] To experience cinematic melancholia is to experience a mournful, ambivalent and haunted attachment to a cultural form constituted by spectral images that are caught between life and death – to be haunted by a haunting form. The second aspect relates to a word 'free' that, as I show, is repeated in *Lazarus*. Derrida makes clear in this interview that for his younger self, cinema (especially in its American manifestations) came to embody what he calls a 'sensual, free expedition'.[6] In being attached to cinema, a cultural form that necessarily inhabits a state between life and death, *Lazarus* is also attached to a cultural form that (for the young Derrida) embodied the state of being 'free' in which the play invests so much.

Lazarus was first performed at the New York Theatre Workshop in December 2015. 'Inspired by *The Man Who Fell to Earth* by Walter Tevis' are words we read on the published play's front cover.[7] These words give no emphasis to the fact that Tevis's 1963 science-fiction novel had been made into a film in which Bowie had played the protagonist Thomas Jerome Newton, a humanoid alien who comes to earth to obtain water for his dying planet. His plans to enable his home world's salvation by building his own space mission are destroyed by politics, love and alcohol. The film *The Man Who Fell to Earth* is broadly faithful to the novel's plot but is much more fragmented; its editing and visual style(s) are dazzling. For Susan Compo, Tevis's novel is written in 'a hospitable, intimate style that . . . comforts the reader'; Roeg's film is much more stylish, image-driven and disorientating.[8] Although tightly plotted, its sense of causality is rarely rational and hardly ever linear – *Lazarus* echoes all this.

The front-cover blurb of the play's published text announces that it is inspired by a novel and not by a film. On the back cover, we encounter a slightly different claim: *Lazarus*, we are now told, is 'inspired by the book by Walter Tevis *and its cult film adaptation* starring David Bowie' (my emphasis).[9] The blurb goes on: '*Lazarus* brings the story of Thomas Newton to its devastating conclusion.'[10] That promise of a 'devastating conclusion' signals that, rather than being an adaptation of Roeg's film or inspired by Tevis's novel, *Lazarus* is more accurately viewed as a kind of sequel. But to what? To Tevis's novel? I prefer to imagine *Lazarus* as a stage adaptation (with music by Bowie) of the screenplay for that film's imaginary sequel, an adaptation whose staging, as specified in Bowie and Walsh's text, requires that theatre take on the sensory dimensions of going to – being in – the cinema.

While *Lazarus* is marked by all the promises, dangers, embarrassments (and melancholia) of sequels, it is also doing something disruptive and peculiar to the promises of repetition, return and variation that inhere in the sequel as a phenomenon. A term that might better capture its relationship to its originating material is the French word *survie*, defined as the noun 'survival'.[11] Kristin Ross, though, defines *survie* as

> A kind of afterlife that does not exactly *come after* but in my view is part and parcel of the event itself . . . a life beyond life. Not the memory of the event or its legacy, although some form of these are surely already in the making, but its *prolongation*, every bit as vital as the initial acts of insurrection in the streets of the city. It is a continuation of the combat by other means. . . . Actions produce dreams and ideas, and not the reverse.[12]

The 'initial acts of insurrection in the streets of the city' to which Ross refers are the early moments of the 1871 Paris Commune, a context which is, I admit, quite remote from that of *Lazarus*. There is a world of difference between, on the one hand, an 1871 mass, insurrectionary reordering of the city of Paris and, on the other, a 2015 late-career musical play co-written by a rock icon and an Irish playwright. But Ross's *survie* provides a vocabulary that helps me better grasp *Lazarus*'s relationship to its originating 'actions' (the writing and making of *The Man Who Fell to Earth*, the novel and the film). Read with Ross's formulation, *Lazarus* is best understood not as a sequel, nor as part of a legacy, but as part and parcel of those events – it shares their initial vitality. In this context it is telling that Newton's salvational plans in both Tevis's novel and Roeg's film are themselves focused on enabling the survival of his dying home planet.

Tevis's novel is itself saturated in the cinema. Throughout, its narrator continually reminds us of the role that films had in providing Newton with a blueprint for the humanity among whom he was obliged to live. Even in the book's final pages, Newton, blinded and drunk in New York, asks Nathan Bryce, his former employee (and betrayer), if he remembers 'a motion picture, shown on television, called *A Letter to Three Wives*?' Bryce replies that he doesn't and Newton says, 'Well, I learned to write English long-hand from a photograph of that letter, twenty years ago.'[13] Newton says this having given Bryce, quite literally, a blank cheque – one that he signs to the tune of one million dollars.

In Tevis's novel, Newton's self-making emerges from his relationship to films. Newton's lack of self-regard in the passage I quoted earlier – his drinking, his readiness to give the man who has betrayed him a blank cheque – is to be maintained in the opening minutes of *Lazarus*. 'But this isn't living for a man like you', Michael says to him early in the play, 'eating Lucky Charms, living on gin and fucking Twinkies'.[14] In saying this, Michael begins *Lazarus*'s project of ousting Newton from his melancholia. The passage in Tevis's novel makes clear, however, that Newton's distanced contact with cinema (in the form of 1949's *A Letter to Three Wives* (Joseph L. Mankiewicz)) has given him the representational skills – notably the capacity to write longhand in English – that have enabled the partial success of his mission; yet those same skills are also part of his failure. On a very basic level, cinema has enabled Newton's melancholic lack of self-regard, but not just melancholia represented in fiction that was later to be adapted into cinema. This is melancholia for which cinema has provided the basic building blocks – Roeg's 1976 adaptation kept this alive. 'I loved the fact', Paul Mayersberg, the film's screenwriter, said in an interview, 'that he [Newton] was getting his stuff from mostly old movies, great classic movies.'[15]

Like a theatre actor, Bowie's Newton was costumed, had learnt his lines, was uneven, alive and obliged to respond to the particular conditions of the place and time of his performance. Part of the film's (and the novel's) suspense was derived from wondering if or when the performance (or Newton) could survive. So, the theatre was built into the DNA of the novel and the film, first on the level of plot; everything Newton does before he is exposed and captured (this is true of both the novel and the film) is theatre. Casting Bowie, whose contribution to rock 'n' roll had been a massive injection of the theatrical – one that was spectacularly critical of what Philip Auslander calls rock 'n' roll's 'ideology of authenticity' – highlighted the fundamental theatricality of Tevis's novel, whose narrator at one point compares Newton to 'an ageing Hamlet'.[16] Hence a theatrical outcome for *The Man Who Fell to Earth*, an outcome like *Lazarus*, can be seen as a *survie* of both the novel's and the film's action, a continuation by other means.

Finally, there is the 'place' of Bowie's music and musicianship in the film. There are two scenes where Bowie's status as a singer is referenced or invoked: The first is when, as Newton, he tries – and fails – to sing along in a church's congregation with 'Jerusalem'. The second is when, towards the film's end, a slow panning shot inside a record shop casually takes in an advertising display for *Young Americans* (1975), his then most recent album. Again, the making of a piece which prolongs the narrative of *The Man Who Fell to Earth* on stage and does so with Bowie's music can be seen as a *survie* in Ross's sense: not a legacy, not an add-on, but a prolongation, a continuation of its action by other means.

Thinking about *Lazarus* in terms of *survie* also enables me to understand levels on which it does not quite 'add up' as a sequel to either Tevis's novel or Roeg's film. First, Newton, at the end of both the novel and the film, has been blinded; Bowie and Walsh's Newton can see. In both the novel and film of *The Man Who Fell to Earth*, Newton, like Dorothy in *The Wizard of Oz* (1939, Victor Fleming), has three 'helpers': his lawyer Oliver Farnsworth; a research scientist called Nathan Bryce; and a woman whose name is Betty-Jo in the novel (and Mary-Lou, played by Candy Clark, in the film). In *Lazarus*, Newton also has three 'helpers': the first is Michael, a new character who, the play implies, had worked in some capacity with Newton and who is clearly in love with him; the second is Girl, a character referred to in the published text's blurb as a 'lost soul'[17]; and finally, there is Elly, his assistant, who, like Michael, is in love with Newton and fixated on his love of Mary-Lou.

There are also murderous forces at work in the film, a rather comically designated FBI, two of whose agents (in the film, though not in the novel) murder Farnsworth. A major character in the play is a mass murderer named Valentine; murder is also a key part of the play's narrative prehistory. In the play's backstory, Girl has been murdered and caught between life and death (a ghost of a certain kind), she gets 'stuck' in Newton's New York apartment. Girl has physical sensations (she doesn't like the way Newton's apartment smells, she feels pain), and her first (prophetic) words in the show are 'A little piece of you/The little piece in me/Will die', the first lines of 'This is Not America', one of the two songs in *Lazarus* which Bowie originally wrote and performed for film soundtracks.[18]

Besides a ghostly young girl who mysteriously appears singing a Bowie soundtrack song, the figure of Mary-Lou is another, even more obvious mode in which the play enacts its cinematic melancholia. Despite its avowed attachment to Tevis's novel, *Lazarus* hangs onto the film's name for this character, dispensing with her name in the novel. Housekeeper, lover, mother and in part betrayer, Mary-Lou is not, strictly speaking, a character in the play; she is, though, an often-mentioned force and object of obsession for Newton and for others. In different ways, both Elly and Girl 'become' her. 'I can feel Mary-Lou walk over and claim me as hers', Elly says, 'I'm dressing in her clothes and she's taking my voice'.[19] As a form of what she calls 'therapy' for Newton, Girl stages a little play based on his 'last conversation with Mary-Lou'.[20] This play-within-a-play repeats a scene in the film, though not one that occurs in the novel. The very first piece of music in *Lazarus* is not a song by Bowie but a recording of Ricky Nelson's 'Hello Mary-Lou (Goodbye Heart)', a song which had, towards the end of the film, accompanied a violent sex scene between Bowie's Newton and Mary-Lou.[21] This same song provides the soundtrack to Girl's would-be therapeutic play.

Established as a sonic and musical force, Mary-Lou is also established, just before 'Lazarus', the play's first Bowie song, as a visual force. Michael asks Newton, 'So you never see her? Do you ever see Mary-Lou?', to which the latter replies, 'Only in my head'.[22] Moving images of her are later specified in the stage directions for the singing of 'Where Are We Now?': 'Faint images appear on the walls around NEWTON – of a repeated image of Mary-Lou slowly turning and looking towards him.'[23] Many accounts of melancholia emphasize its status as a mournful, awkward and partly disavowed attachment to someone or something that is gone. Reading *Lazarus* or seeing it onstage involves being a witness to such an attachment (Newton's love for Mary-Lou), but in a theatrical form that derives power from its attachment to the cinematic layers of the play's source material and, more simply, to moving images themselves.

Melancholia

The intensity with which cinema is knotted into melancholia's existence across Tevis's novel, Roeg's film and, inevitably, *Lazarus* is at odds with a major strand of the play, which is to oust Newton from his melancholia. The strand is first embodied by Michael who asks Newton if he can 'remember the person' he once was. The following dialogue ensues:

NEWTON: That was before.

MICHAEL: And it's gone? All of it?

NEWTON: Of course it's gone.

MICHAEL: But this isn't living for a man like you – eating Lucky Charms, living on gin and fucking Twinkies . . .

NEWTON: There's nothing of the past. It left. This is it now.[24]

In this exchange, it would appear that Newton is claiming that he has gone from melancholia to mourning; his past is, he claims, 'gone', though his drinking would suggest otherwise. Michael then asks Newton if he ever sees Mary-Lou; Newton's response – 'only in my head' – indicates that what we are witnessing is a scene of melancholy attachment. No sooner has Newton uttered these words than the music to 'Lazarus' – the play's first Bowie song – begins. Girl's agenda with Newton works in a similar way: 'You're stuck here heartbroken over Mary-Lou', she counsels him. 'You forget about her and you can start making something else.'[25]

I have used the word 'melancholia' so far rather hazily, relying on the definitions from the *OED* online that constitute my first epigraph. For Freud, writing in 1917, we enter into melancholic states in response to the 'loss of a beloved person, or an abstraction taking the place of the person, such as one's fatherland, freedom, an ideal, and so on'.[26] In the moments I have quoted, Newton would be a textbook instance of the state Freud outlines.

For Freud, melancholia is distinguished by 'a profoundly painful depression, a loss of interest in the outside world, the loss of the ability to love, inhibition of any kind of performance and a reduction in the sense of self'.[27] He also claims that it has 'three preconditions . . . the loss of the object, ambivalence and the regression of libido into the ego'.[28] Loss, inhibition, reduction, regression – melancholia is, at first look, a state of varied depletion. All these features are present in the plot of *Lazarus*: Newton has lost not just a 'fatherland' but a whole planet, and persons in abundance. Lost, too, is the goal of his mission to save his home planet.

Freud also observed a manic strand in melancholia, one that he connects with the 'suggestion, accomplished by toxins, of the expenditure of repression' brought about by drinking alcohol – something that is very pertinent to

Lazarus.²⁹ Writing recently of the relationship between melancholia and mania, Butler has considered melancholia's manic dimensions in more political terms, observing that mania's '"unrealism" . . . suggests a refusal to accept the status quo, and it draws upon, and intensifies, a desire to live on the part of one who is battling against forms of heightened self-beratement'.³⁰ Several songs and moments in *Lazarus* – especially 'Killing a Little Time', one of its 'new' songs – forcefully embody this manic dimension; such mania both emerges from and merges with sorrow. Anahid Neressian has recently written that, for Freud, 'the melancholic's "complaints are really 'plaints' in the old sense of the word" – a musical lamentation or beating of the breast'.³¹ Many of *Lazarus*'s songs, from 'Life on Mars?' to 'Where Are We Now?', were not only plaintive in their original forms but also have, in the context of the play, their plaintive dimensions highlighted.

For Freud, melancholia is both incomplete and mobile. In mourning, one eventually slowly overcomes the loss of the loved one; in melancholia, that loss is internalized and mourning feels eternal – any sense of an ending is deferred. Freud notes that even during the days when one is stuck in melancholia, the condition is regularly alleviated in the evening.³² So, however wedded to depletion melancholia might be, it holds out, however grimly, a certain potential for completion, a potential perhaps signalled by its capacity to change with the day. The work of mourning, Freud claims, is completed when 'the ego is left free and uninhibited once again' after an experience of loss.³³ 'This way or no way, you'll know, I'll be free', Newton sings at the outset of *Lazarus*; 'We're free now', both Newton and Girl sing in a rewritten version of 'Heroes' at the show's very end.³⁴ The play enacts exactly such a process for Newton; it also enacts a resistance to that process.

For Freud, as we've seen, melancholia can occur in response to the loss of 'a beloved person or an abstraction taking the place of the person'.³⁵ More recently, Butler has argued that masculinity can melancholically incorporate the femininity from which its ways are barred and that heterosexuality can yearn for homosexual possibility. 'In the case of a prohibited homosexual union', Butler writes, 'it is clear that both the desire and the object require renunciation and so become subject to the internalizing strategies of melancholia.'³⁶

Both melancholia's mania and its fondness for lament are operative in *Lazarus* and we can also see different modes of desire yearning for their purported opposites. It is easy to claim that Elly becomes fixated on Newton but it is more accurate to say that she is fixated on his love for Mary-Lou, and therefore on Mary-Lou herself. 'What's it like', she asks Newton, 'to feel that much love for someone and to be loved back?'³⁷ Since Mary-Lou is only present in the play as a name or a moving image, Elly's erotic melancholia is as queer as it is cinematically tinged.

Earlier, I claimed that the character of Michael is 'clearly in love' with Newton. Michael doesn't last long; he is the first victim of the killer Valentine.

Prior to Michael's offstage murder, Valentine inveigles his way into his apartment, claiming to be an old friend from his hometown. 'I stood by you', Valentine further claims, 'when you told your family that you were a gay man.' 'I'm fucking straight!' Michael fiercely replies.[38] But the situation between the two men – which is to result in Michael's murder – becomes progressively sheltering and flirtatious. However offstage that murder might be, its aftermath is the spectacular performance of Bowie's 2013 song 'Love Is Lost'. During this song, Newton is onstage, witnessing the murder's aftermath, as are Valentine and the dead Michael who, nonetheless, 'suddenly gets up – his shirt bloody – and leaves the apartment'.[39] Onstage, too, are Elly and Zach and the three ghostly Teenage Girls who (like a Greek chorus or the witches in *Macbeth*) observe, comment on and sometimes partake in *Lazarus*'s action. There is an abrupt transition from Elly's question 'what's it like to feel that much love?' to the sight of Valentine putting on the jacket of the dead Michael, the 'gay man' he has just murdered as this song begins. During this performance the man who is to be Valentine's second victim, the lovestruck (and more emphatically 'straight') Ben, is introduced and there are more moving 'images from inside a packed bar . . . images of people kissing' that 'appear on the walls'.[40] Again, there is a combination of the cinematic and the sexual with different erotic and gendered categories in ambivalent relations with each other. For Butler, forms of desire can almost anthropomorphically yearn for and incorporate each other; such yearning and incorporation are violently present throughout *Lazarus*, and they are always associated with moving images.

So far, I have made melancholia sound like a mostly lonely affair. In his work on affect and epistemology in (and after) the English renaissance, Drew Daniel has encouraged a move away from understanding melancholia as a 'private trait', preferring to see it as 'a kind of dynamic relationship of assemblage which solicits interpretation, ascription, and diagnosis in exchange for the teasing revelation of a rhetorically charged interior'.[41] Anything that solicits interpretation must be aware of some actual or potential individuals or groups who can do the interpreting. The teasing promise that, at some point, a 'rhetorically charged interior' will be revealed presupposes, again, the existence of some actual or potential individuals or groups on whom such a revelation can have an impact. However withdrawn he may be from the world, Newton is from the outset an alluring magnet; others interpret him, ascribe motives to him and diagnose him. The play begins in the midst of an uninvited visit from Michael. Zach, Elly's husband, is fascinated by what she has to tell him about her employer and more than ready to interpret and diagnose him. 'Cut down . . . buried in the ground' and 'not properly dead', though she may be, Girl nonetheless claims that, even in her partially post-mortem state, she was sufficiently magnetized by the sight of Newton at his window to wish to enter his apartment.[42]

Witnessing and perceiving together in bodily proximity are central, of course, to theatre, and it is famously through writing for the theatre that melancholia has made its presences felt over the centuries. Central to Daniel's arguments about melancholy assemblages is a reading of William Shakespeare's *Hamlet*, a line from which turns up in *Lazarus*. 'In this sleep of death – what dreams may come', Newton says, after he has fallen on the ground and, as the stage directions specify, 'the music to "This Is Not America" begins'.[43] Like Hamlet's father, as described by Maud Ellman, Girl has been murdered in the play's prehistory. The subsequent murders in *Lazarus* – of Michael, then of Ben and then of Girl again – are re-enactments of that first 'unwitnessed and unverifiable' killing in the same way that both staged and 'real' murders in Shakespeare's play can be read as re-enactments of the murder of Hamlet senior.[44] 'Good night, sweet prince,'/And flights of angels sing thee to thy rest' are famously the last lines spoken by Horatio to Denmark's melancholy, dead prince; the final stage direction in *Lazarus* simply reads 'Newton finds rest'.[45] As Lee Edelman has pointed out, there is a play in *Hamlet* on the word 'rest', a word readable as 'repose' but also readable as that which remains ('life's restless remnant' as Edelman puts it, responding to Hamlet's utterance 'the rest is silence').[46] Allusively and in terms of its structure, *Lazarus* reaches back into the Shakespearean strand of melancholia's history. Newton can be said to have found 'rest', indicating that he has been ousted from his melancholia. Or Newton can be said to have found 'the rest', that which (restlessly) remains, that which can be considered under the heading of *survie*.

Freud assumed that the objects grieved for are persons or abstractions. Butler, as we've seen, went on to broaden this assumption, claiming that melancholia's objects can be modes of gendered being and modes of desire, existing in an almost anthropomorphic relationship to each other.[47] If heterosexuality can have a melancholic relationship to its foreclosed homosexual possibilities, then there is no reason why different representational modes – theatre and cinema, say – cannot have similarly melancholic, yearning, foreclosed relationships to each other. If, to draw on the title of Paul Young's book, the cinema can dream its rivals, then the theatre, at least in the case of *Lazarus*, can also yearn for (and imitate) the cinema.[48] This yearning process slows down and questions any movement to be free from melancholia. Playing the role of Thomas Newton in *Lazarus* requires an actor to work almost as a kind of living screen (or projector), to be susceptible to things that can come to him 'in these pictures', as he puts it.[49]

In his recent work on melancholia and history in the writing of Henry James, David McWhirter has claimed that melancholia is 'an affective structure especially appropriate to, even productive for, modern lives.' Given that modernity (and its aftermaths) has brutally elevated 'moving on' and its attendant obliterations to something like an ethical duty.[50] Both Michael and Girl articulate this kind of wish to move on. There is a tension, though, in *Lazarus* between melancholy as a pathology – something to be moved through – and melancholy as resource – something to be cherished. This dynamic is particularly evident in the play's relationship to cinema, to being 'just like the films'.

'Just like the films'

Lazarus is a play studded with Bowie's songs (played, with one exception, by an onstage band and sung by members of the cast), but one for which his physical and visual presence was not a requirement. In the original production, directed by Ivo van Hove, and performed (albeit with differing personnel) in New York, London and Amsterdam, Bowie's visual presence was manifest through a stack of albums, seven-inch singles and CD covers, visible behind and around a record deck on the stage left floor. These records included *Aladdin Sane*, *Scary Monsters (and Super Creeps)* and *Diamond Dogs*. The stunning video work for this production also included blink-and-you'll-miss-them fragments of images of Bowie in performance, most notably from the videos of 'Boys Keep Swinging' and 'Little Wonder'. These visual features were, however, not a requirement of Bowie and Walsh's text. Other productions no doubt have, and no doubt will, done/do things differently. In a sense, nothing could have been more 'Bowie' than this playing with absence given that, throughout his career, Bowie's work had trafficked in absence, whether sudden or slowly approaching, intimate or apocalyptic.[51]

Of the show's eighteen Bowie songs, four were new compositions.[52] The advance publicity for *Lazarus* tended to distinguish between these four new songs and well-known 'classics' such as 'Life on Mars?', 'Changes' and 'Heroes'. The inclusion of two songs – 'This is Not America', written for John Schlesinger's 1985 film *The Falcon and the Snowman*, and 'Absolute Beginners', written for Julian Temple's 1986 film of that name – also reminds its audience that writing music for films was a key part of Bowie's artistic endeavours. Of course, one of the reasons Bowie found himself being commissioned to write songs for films was that a (frequently melancholy) relationship to cinema had featured in his songwriting. There is, as Nigel Smith has pointed out, a film at the heart of 'Life of Mars?'[53]

I derive the title of this essay – and its second epigraph – from the second of these film songs. In 'Absolute Beginners', the speaker voices a yearning wish that his song could have magical, personified and corporeal powers: that it could fly or laugh. The banal phrase 'just like the films' sets out to encapsulate this transcendental push of desire. The lyrics of the *Lazarus* 'Absolute Beginners' are also rewritten. The first line I quote in my epigraph reads 'If my love song'; the original goes 'If our love song'. The move away from the original contains and enacts senses of separation and loss which are foundational to Bowie and Walsh's play. The appeal of the phrase 'just like the films' lies partly in its openness to failure; the agenda set is so huge, the speaker's sense of what, precisely, constitutes 'the films' is so romantically, delightfully imprecise. This simile resembles the lines 'You know, I'll be free/just like that bluebird' in 'Lazarus' (the opening song in the play) or the lines 'I, I wish you could swim/Like the dolphins/like dolphins can swim' in 1977's 'Heroes' (a rewritten and very melancholically rearranged version of which ends it).[54] In all three instances, there is a sense of possibility (flying, laughing, being free, swimming) attached to precisely worded though vaguely designated entities: 'the films', 'that bluebird', 'the dolphins'. In all three instances, the line between triumph and failure is blurred; the aesthetic and emotional force of these songs – and indeed of *Lazarus* – is dependent on that blurring. The wish for freedom and transcendence in all three songs is matched by countervailing senses of stasis and stuckness.

'Absolute Beginners' is the ninth of the eighteen Bowie songs that form, in Susan Bennett's words, the play's 'interpretive spine', and it is important and exceptional in many ways.[55] In this musical, songs tend to interrupt or play over dialogue. 'You hear that!?', Newton asks the character of Girl early on, just as 'The Man Who Sold the World' (sung by Michael in, ostensibly, another space and time) begins. 'What?', Girl replies, to which Newton responds, 'Music'.[56] Rather differently, *Lazarus* 'Absolute Beginners' starts with Newton singing a cappella, to himself, the lines 'I've nothing much to offer/There's nothing much to take'. A stage direction which reads 'the music to "Absolute Beginners" is heard' follows.[57] These lines conform rather strictly to the definition of melancholia outlined in my essay's first epigraph, embodying 'despondency, depression, feelings of worthlessness and guilt'. They can, especially in the context of this scene, be described as 'a theatrical or aesthetic indulgence in reflective or maudlin emotion'.[58] These lines also correspond to Freud's description of melancholia as dejection, cessation of interest and inhibition of activity; singing them, Newton invites interpretation, ascription, even diagnosis.

Whether, in musical theatre, songs exist to amplify and throw light on narrative or whether the narrative aspects of musical exist to create pretexts for the performance of its songs is a question that, especially in the context of *Lazarus*, is worth considering. Traditionally, one reason (or pretext) for the very existence of songs in musical plays is that the former set out to articulate aspects of the characters' interiority that are otherwise unavailable to the audience. A stage direction in Conor McPherson's Bob Dylan-fuelled musical, *Girl from the North Country* (2017), occurring just as two of that play's characters are about to sing 'I Want You', reads: 'We see what their souls are doing despite everything that's just been said.'[59]

In his preface to *Lazarus*'s published text, Walsh emphasizes how the show's songs enable a process for the characters of 'accessing their souls'.[60] This is true of many songs in the show, both new and 'classic': it's true of the title song; it's true of 'The Man Who Sold the World' (which becomes a love song from Michael to Newton); and of 'Changes', as sung by Elly.

These moments wherein the audience and/or the characters can 'access their souls' are pauses in the action or they tend to throw new interpretive and emotional light on action that has already taken place. D. A. Miller caustically refers to this as the 'dramatic model' of Broadway musical describing it as the 'narrative naturalism from whose tedium and tyranny [the Broadway musical's] real merit was to keep alive ... the prospect of a liberation'.[61] *Lazarus* flirts with narrative naturalism but escapes its tyranny through a ritualistic narrative (and musical) fury that is a characteristic of much of Walsh's writing, most notably *The Walworth Farce* (2006).

'Absolute Beginners' functions as both song *and* narrative. Neither a solo performance nor an articulation of what the characters' souls are doing (which would entail in both cases a pause in the action), the song constitutes a populous, dramatic moment of narrative force, alteration and separation. It is sung first by Newton on his own, then in a duet by Newton and by Elly, his assistant. Her participation in the song is motivated by her love for Newton and her fixation on his own melancholic attachment to the departed Mary-Lou. Part of the song's chorus is sung by one of the play's three ghostly Teenage Girls, all three of whom provide the 'ba-ba-ba ooo' backing vocals.

The text requires the onstage presence of Valentine the murderer and Girl, the 'lost soul' during the singing of 'Absolute Beginners'. One of the few songs in the play that isn't an interruption of dialogue – pointing back to the opening ('Lazarus') and to the ending ('Heroes') – 'Absolute Beginners' requires the presence and interaction of all of the play's major characters and it sets them all in fateful directions.

Together Girl and Newton begin to forge their intuitive mutual death pact in which Valentine will play a major part. For Newton, this will enable a resolution that can be figured either as his death, a return home to the stars from where he first came or, at least, some respite from the stuck state of being, in his words, 'a dying man who can't die'.[62] For Girl, this will be a ritual and very problematic re-enactment of her first murder, this time at Newton's hands. The motivational push is towards a transition into a second 'proper' death and an eventual remembering of the name that, all the way through the play, she has been unable to recall.[63] There is a parallel here to the strand in the play that is about ousting Newton from his melancholia. This schema's adherence to a distinction between 'proper' and 'improper' death is complicated, though, by the fact that no sooner has Girl been killed a second time than she is summoned out of that state by Newton's pleading.[64]

Newton's decision to reject the replicating, melancholy love offered to him by Elly is enacted during the singing of 'Absolute Beginners': 'He turns away from her and looks towards the GIRL', the stage directions read, and 'the GIRL turns and looks at NEWTON ... ELLY is devastated by NEWTON's rejection of her'.[65] Repeated moving images of Mary-Lou 'turning and looking' at Newton were operative in the singing of 'Where

Are We Now?', the song just before 'Absolute Beginners'.[66] As they sing the latter, the actors are not only singing of being 'just like the films' in an aspirational sense. In turning and looking at each other, they are imitating the moving image of Mary-Lou who is herself a key component of the play's cinematic melancholia. All of this turning, looking, choosing – and devastation – takes place as the song's chorus – of which the line 'Just like the films' is so important a part – is sung.

Repeated twice in the chorus of 'Absolute Beginners', this phrase is a link in an image chain in the play that equates one genre (the pop song) with often-romanticized, symbolic animals (bluebirds and dolphins) and with a drive of transcendental desire. The phrase also makes that genre's wish to be 'just like the films' central to the dream-driven, melancholy subjectivity – one often formed by the force of violence – that much of Bowie's work (and certainly *Lazarus*) celebrated and enacted. Bowie's writing of music for a film (in this case *Absolute Beginners*) and a complex and partly disavowed aspiration to being 'just like the films' are therefore at this play's affective, narrative and dramatic heart.

The text of *Lazarus* tersely compels anyone making a production of the play to reckon with the extent to which they are required to turn theatrical space into something like cinema – an auditorium where people look at pre-recorded, moving images projected onto a screen. I've already noted the presence of moving images on the walls during the singing of 'Love Is Lost' and that moving images of Mary-Lou are a key component of the play's staging of 'Where Are We Now?' During the song 'Killing a Little Time', the stage directions require that 'An image of Newton fills the wall – it thrashes the apartment'.[67] Just before the character of Ben is murdered by Valentine, 'the walls fill with images of a raucous night'.[68] Repeatedly, the text of *Lazarus* requires that the audience's experience of the show becomes akin to the experience of watching cinema. All of the images I have mentioned are moving images: the figures in bars enacting their raucousness; Mary-Lou turning and looking at Newton; Newton's image thrashing his own apartment. It is also a requirement of the text that this cinematic aspect oversteps any initial boundaries. Bowie and Walsh's stage directions require that these images 'fill the wall(s)'. If the theatre holds onto the cinema in a melancholic mode, then the cinematic takes advantage of that holding and often threatens to dominate the mode which aspired to contain it.

Deferred endings

Lazarus opened in New York in December 2015, Bowie died just over one month later and the London performances began in October 2016. For those who were in the audience after Bowie's death, their encounter with the play would have been connected with the loss of 'a beloved person' (to repeat

Freud's formulation), a person who had, over decades, come to incarnate a number of complex and emotive abstractions: sexuality, liberty, style, wit, the capacity to change, freedom from rigid categorization and so on.

Comparing the first New York performances with the later London performances, Susan Bennett has written of 'the uncanny resemblance of Michael C. Hall's voice to Bowie's'. Hall played the role of Newton in both New York and London, and his singing of seven of the show's eighteen Bowie songs had, for Bennett, amounted to the channelling of the voice of the recently dead man. In her view, this 'gave the London performance a haunting quality . . . sustained and underscored' by what she claims is 'the only significant change made to the production'.[69] This change consisted in fact that

> At the end of the show a large headshot of Bowie was projected onto the centre-stage screen. . . . After the curtain call, many spectators wandered down to the front of the house to take selfies and group shots in the company of this last trace of David Bowie, a Lazarus that even the most devoted fans could not raise from the dead.[70]

In New York, I remember, the same screen had remained stolidly blank at the play's end. When, in December 2019, a Dutch-language version of the show – also directed by Ivo van Hove and with the same set, video work and musical arrangements – opened in Amsterdam, that large final headshot of Bowie also appeared. As they took their selfies and group shots, the audience members, Bennett describes, were also putting photography to one of its most time-honoured uses: prolonging the fleshly existence of a lost person or ideal – in this case, Bowie.[71]

Like many commentators (myself included) Bennett connects the play's title with the figure of Lazarus, the friend that Christ, as recounted in the Gospel of St John, brings back from the dead.[72] But the title has other sources: In his preface, Walsh recounts Bowie's early wish that their play feature a woman who 'thought she might be Emma Lazarus . . . the American poet whose poem "The New Colossus" is engraved on the base of the statue of Liberty'.[73] This one woman envisaged by Bowie is, in *Lazarus*, split into two characters: Elly (the first two letters of whose name replicate Emma Lazarus's initials) and Girl. In the published text, Emma Lazarus's sonnet appears in its entirety, one turn of the page after the words 'The End'. Like the post-show photograph of Bowie on the video screen in London and Amsterdam – an image that functioned as a visual postscript – her poem therefore registers as a second ending, keeping the ending itself at bay.

'The New Colossus' is a sonnet that is itself split in two. Its first eight lines anthropomorphically describe the statue of Liberty: 'a mighty woman with a torch whose flame/is the imprisoned lightning'. The last six lines are uncannily spoken 'by' this monument as she addresses the old world, or 'ancient lands', famously demanding that they 'give me your tired, your poor,/Your huddled masses, yearning to breathe free'.[74] For a reader of Bowie and Walsh's published text, that word 'free', as encountered in the poem, amounts to a repetition of a crucial word that had occurred in the play's opening and closing songs, 'Lazarus' and 'Heroes'.

The presence of Bowie's image on the screen at the end of the London and Amsterdam performances can be considered melancholic because it keeps present the face of the lost, 'beloved person or an abstraction taking the place of the person', even as the possibility of seeing that face in the flesh has gone.[75] The eight-foot screen had, for the two intense and unbroken hours of the show, fulfilled the role of a cinema screen in the most basic sense: it had been the blank space onto which moving images (what Bennett describes as the show's 'extraordinary and poetic video work') had been projected in a darkened auditorium.[76] The London audience members grouped around Bowie's photo image can also be considered as open to 'cinematic' melancholia because of *Lazarus*'s deep affiliation with a particular film (*The Man Who Fell to Earth*). Furthermore, those images had broken their bounds and, often, filled the walls. If, both in the text of *Lazarus* and in its manifestations after Bowie's death, processes of completion, closure and ousting from melancholia are energetically enacted, then they are also resisted. The passage from melancholia to mourning, however theoretically desirable or however convenient for others, clearly came at a cost which *Lazarus* – in itself and in its *survie* – was not prepared to pay.

Notes

1. 'Melancholia', Oxford English Dictionary Online, accessed 22 June 2021, https://www.oed.com/view/Entry/115994?redirectedFrom=melancholia#eid.
2. David Bowie and Enda Walsh, *Lazarus: A Musical* (London: Nick Hern Books, 2016), 36.
3. 'Melancholia', Oxford English Dictionary.
4. For a discussion of the relationship between close reading and queer theory, see Elizabeth Freeman, *Times Binds: Queer Temporalities, Queer Histories* (Durham, NC and London: Duke University Press, 2010), xvi–xvii. See also Denis Flannery, 'Ivo van Hove: Celebrity and Reader', in *Contemporary European Theatre Directors*, 2nd ed., ed. Maria Delgado and Dan Reballato (London and New York: Routledge, 2020), 275–98, 285.
5. Antoine de Baecque and Thierry Jousse, 'Cinema and Its Ghosts: An Interview with Jacques Derrida', trans. Peggy Kamuf, *Discourse* 37, no.1–2 (Winter/Spring 2015): 22–39, 26.
6. Ibid., 24.
7. Bowie and Walsh, *Lazarus*, front matter.

8   Susan Compo, *Earthbound: David Bowie and The Man Who Fell to Earth* (London: Jawbone, 2017), 20.
9   Bowie and Walsh, *Lazarus*, back matter.
10 Ibid.
11 'Survie', Oxford Reference, accessed 23 June 2021, https://www.oxfordreference.com/view/10.1093/acref/9780191739545.001.0001/b-fr-en-00003-0018037?rskey=zY7sLX&result=1.
12 Kristin Ross, *Communal Luxury: The Political Imaginary of the Paris Commune* (London and New York: Verso, 2015), 6–7.
13 Walter Tevis, *The Man Who Fell to Earth* (London: Penguin, 2005), 184.
14 Bowie and Walsh, *Lazarus*, 6.
15 *The Man Who Fell to Earth* (40th Anniversary Collector's Edition), directed by Nicolas Roeg (1976; Paris: Studiocanal, 2016), Blu-Ray.
16 Philip Auslander, *Performing Glam Rock: Gender and Theatricality in Popular Music* (Ann Arbor, MI: University of Michigan Press, 2006), 13; Tevis, *The Man Who Fell to Earth*, 80.
17 Bowie and Walsh, *Lazarus*, back matter.
18 Ibid., 11.
19 Ibid., 38.
20 Ibid., 33.
21 Ibid., 4.
22 Ibid., 6.
23 Ibid., 27.
24 Ibid., 6.
25 Ibid., 26.
26 Sigmund Freud, *On Murder, Mourning and Melancholia*, trans. Shaun Whiteside with an introduction by Maud Ellman (London: Penguin, 2005), 203.
27 Ibid., 204.
28 Ibid., 217.
29 Ibid., 214.
30 Judith Butler, *The Force of Non-Violence: An Ethico-Political Bind* (London: Verso, 2020), 170.
31 Anahid Nersessian, *Keats's Odes: A Lover's Discourse* (Chicago, IL and London: Chicago University Press, 2021), 82.
32 Freud, *On Murder, Mourning and Melancholia*, 213.
33 Ibid., 205.
34 Bowie and Walsh, *Lazarus*, 7, 62.
35 Freud, *On Murder, Mourning and Melancholia*, 203.
36 Judith Butler, *Gender Trouble: Feminism and the Subversion of Identity* (New York and London: Routledge, 1999), 75.

37 Bowie and Walsh, *Lazarus*, 20.
38 Ibid., 16.
39 Ibid., 20.
40 Ibid.
41 Drew Daniel, *The Melancholy Assemblage: Affect and Epistemology in the English Renaissance* (New York: Fordham University Press, 2013), 142.
42 Bowie and Walsh, *Lazarus*, 56.
43 Ibid., 10.
44 Freud, *On Murder, Mourning and Melancholia*, xiv.
45 William Shakespeare, *Hamlet*, edited by Robert S. Miola (New York and London: W. W. Norton and Company, 2011).
46 Lee Edelman, 'Hamlet's Wounded Name', in *Shakesqueer*, ed. Madhavi Menon (Durham, NC and London: Duke University Press, 2011), 97; Shakespeare, *Hamlet*, 5. 2, l. 331.
47 Butler, *Gender Trouble*, 75.
48 Paul Young, *The Cinema Dreams its Rivals: Media Fantasy Films from Radio to the Internet* (Minneapolis, MN: University of Minnesota Press, 2005).
49 Bowie and Walsh, *Lazarus*, 5.
50 The phrase is David McWhirter's, from his 'Feeling Backwards with Henry James: The Melancholy of History', *The Henry James Review* 41, no.1 (2020): 1–14, 9.
51 On this, see my 'Absence, Resistance and Visitable Pasts: David Bowie, Todd Haynes, Henry James', *Continuum: Journal of Media and Cultural Studies* 31, no. 4 (2017): 542–551.
52 The four (then) new songs were 'Lazarus', 'No Plan', 'Killing a Little Time' and 'When I Met You'. Bowie's own versions of them were released with the *Lazarus* OCR in 2016 and, separately, as the *No Plan* EP in 2017. The show also features four songs from *The Next Day*, Bowie's 2013 album. These songs are 'Love is Lost', 'Where are We Now?', 'Dirty Boys' and 'Valentine's Day'.
53 Nigel Smith, 'Songs and their Lyrics: Any Room at the Feast?' in *Evaluations of US Poetry since 1950, Volume 1: Language, Form, and Music*, ed. Robert von Hallberg and Robert Faggen (Albuquerque: University of New Mexico Press, 2021), 283–300, 296.
54 Bowie and Walsh, *Lazarus*, 7, 62.
55 Susan Bennett, 'A Tale of Two Cities: *Lazarus* in New York and London', in *Ivo van Hove: From Shakespeare to Bowie*, ed. Susan Bennett and Sonia Massai (London: Bloomsbury, 2018), 200–5, 201.
56 Bowie and Walsh, *Lazarus*, 13.
57 Ibid., 36.
58 'Melancholia'.
59 Conor McPherson, *Girl from the North Country* (London: Nick Hern Books, 2017), 48.

60 Bowie and Walsh, *Lazarus*, ix.
61 D. A. Miller, *Place for Us: Essay on the Broadway Musical* (Cambridge, MA: Harvard University Press, 1998), 2.
62 Bowie and Walsh, *Lazarus*, 12.
63 'I've found out my name's Marley', Girl says towards the end – echoing the names of singer Bob Marley (1945–81) and of Charles Dickens's Jacob Marley, Scrooge's dead colleague in *A Christmas Carol* (1843), 61.
64 I discuss this moment and its aftermath at length in 'Apostrophe', in *The Oxford Research Encyclopaedia of Literature*, https://doi.org/10.1093/acrefore/9780190201098.013.1048.
65 Bowie and Walsh, *Lazarus*, 37.
66 Ibid., 27.
67 Ibid., 43.
68 Ibid., 48.
69 Bennett, 'A Tale of Two Cities', 204. There was in fact another significant change. An entire scene, one where Girl's murderer (played by Alan Cummings) speaks with her from the video screen, was part of the New York production and cut from the London production. But that is a topic for another essay.
70 Ibid., 205.
71 For Jay Prosser, 'Photography Is a melancholic Object . . . A memento mori', in *Light in the Dark Room: Photography and Loss* (Minneapolis: University of Minnesota Press, 2005), 1–2.
72 I make this connection in my 2015 essay 'Why We Should Expect Great Thing from David Bowie's New Musical Play', https://theconversation.com/why-we-should-expect-great-things-from-david-bowies-new-musical-play-39946.
73 Bowie and Walsh, *Lazarus*, viii.
74 Ibid., 65.
75 Freud, *On Murder, Mourning and Melancholia*, 203.
76 Bennett, 'A Tale of Two Cities', 201.

FILMOGRAPHY

Edel, Uli, director. *Christiane F. – Wir Kinder vom Bahnhof Zoo*. Neue Constantin Film, 1981.
Henson, Jim, director. *Labyrinth*. Tri-Star Pictures, 1986.
Lynch, David, director. *Eraserhead*. Libra Films, 1977.
Lynch, David, director. *Twin Peaks: Fire Walk with Me*. AMLF and New Line Cinema, 1992.
Nolan, Christopher, director. *The Prestige*. Buena Vista Pictures Distribution and Warner Brothers Pictures, 2006.
Oshima, Nagisa, director. *Merry Christmas, Mr. Lawrence*. Universal Pictures, 1983.
Pennebaker, Donn, director. *Ziggy Stardust and the Spiders from Mars*. 20th Century Fox, 1983.
Roeg, Nicolas, director. *The Man Who Fell to Earth*. British Lion Films, 1976.
Roeg, Nicolas, director. *The Man Who Fell to Earth (40th Anniversary Collector's Edition)*. Studiocanal, 2016. Blu-ray.
Scott, Tony, director. *The Hunger*. MGM, 1983.
Scott, Tony, director. *The Hunger*. Warner Home Video, 2004. DVD.
Schnabel, Julian, director. *Basquiat*. Miramax Films, 1996.
Scorsese, Martin, director. *The Last Temptation of Christ*. Universal Pictures and Cineplex Odeon Films, 1988.
Scott, Tony, director. *The Hunger*. Metro-Goldwyn-Mayer, 1983.

Television

Baal. Directed by Alan Clarke. Aired 2 March 1982, on BBC TV.
Bowie, David. Interview by Brett Hansen. *Radio with Pictures*. TVNZ, 1981.
Bowie, David. Interview by Cees van Ede. *Cinevisie*. Dutch Broadcasting Corporation, 1983.
Bowie, David. Interview by Dick Cavett. *The Dick Cavett Show*. ABC, 5 December 1974.
Bowie, David. Interview by Kerry O'Brien. *7.30 Report*. Australian Broadcasting Corporation, 2004.
Bowie, David. Interview by Russell Harty. *The Russell Harty Show*. ITV, 28 November 1975.
Cracked Actor. Directed by Alan Yentob. Aired 26 January 1975, on BBC TV.

The Hunger. Season 2, episode 1. 'Sanctuary'. Directed by Tony Scott. Aired 10 September 1999, on Showtime.
Twin Peaks. Created by Mark Frost and David Lynch. Aired 1990–1, on ABC.
Twin Peaks: The Return. Created by Mark Frost and David Lynch. Aired 21 May 2017 to 3 September 2017, on Showtime.
Will Kenny Everett Make It to 1980? Show. 'The Kenny Everett Video Show'. Directed by David Mallett. Aired 31 December 1979 on Thames TV.

Short films/Music videos

Mallet, David, director. 'Black Tie White Noise'. BMG Video, 1993.
Rock, Mick, director. 'Life on Mars'. Promotional Film, 1973.
Rock, Mick, director. 'John I'm Only Dancing'. Promotional Film, 1972.
Thomson, Malcolm J., director. 'Love You till Tuesday'. Promotional Film: Produced 1969, released 1984.

DISCOGRAPHY

Bowie, David. 'Andy Warhol'. Recorded Summer 1971. Side 2, track 2 on *Hunky Dory*. RCA, 1971.
Bowie, David. *Black Tie White Noise*. Savage, 1993.
Bowie, David. *Blackstar*. ISO, Columbia and Sony, 2016.
Bowie, David. 'Five Years'. Recorded November 1971. Track 1 on *The Rise and Fall of Ziggy Stardust and the Spiders from Mars*. RCA, 1972.
Bowie, David. *"Heroes"*. RCA, 1977.
Bowie, David. *Hunky Dory*. RCA, 1971.
Bowie, David. 'It's No Game (No.1)'. Recorded 1980. Track 1 on *Scary Monsters and Super Creeps*.
Bowie, David. 'Lazarus'. Recorded 2015. Track 3 on *Blackstar*. ISO Columbia, 2016.
Bowie, David. *Outside*. Arista/BMG, 1995.
Bowie, David. *The Rise and Fall of Ziggy Stardust and the Spiders from Mars*. RCA Records, 1972.
Bowie, David. *Scary Monsters (and Super Creeps)*. RCA, 1980.
Bowie, David. *Scary Monsters Interview Promo Disc*. RCA, 1980. Promotional CD.
Bowie, David. 'Telling Lies'. Recorded 1996. Arista BMG, 1996. Downloadable single.
Bowie, David. *When I'm Five*. Deram, May 1984, CD.
Murphy, Peter, David Haskins, Kevin Haskins and Daniel Ash. 'Bela Lugosi's Dead'. Recorded January 1979. Single. Small Wonder, 1979.
Pop, Iggy and David Bowie. 'Funtime'. Recorded 1976. Track 3 on *The Idiot*. RCA, 1977.
Strummer, Joe and Allen Ginsberg. 'Ghetto Defendant'. Recorded 1981. Track 4, side 2 on *Combat Rock*. CBS, 1982.
Springsteen, Bruce. *The Wild, the Innocent & the E Street Shuffle*. Columbia, 1973.

BIBLIOGRAPHY

A

Ackermann, Hermann, Steffen R. Hage and Wolfram Ziegler. 'Brain Mechanisms of Acoustic Communication in Humans and Nonhuman Primates: An Evolutionary Perspective.' *Behavioural and Brain Sciences* 37, no. 6 (Dec 2014): 529–46.
Agamben, Giorgio. *Homo Sacer: Sovereign Power and Bare Life*. Stanford, CA: Stanford University Press, 1998.
Agamben, Giorgio. 'Kommerell, or on Gesture.' In *Potentialities: Collected Essays in Philosophy*, Edited and Translated by Daniel Heller-Roazen, 77–85. Stanford, CA: Stanford University Press, 1999.
Agamben, Giorgio. *Means Without End: Notes on Politics*. Translated by Vincenzo Binetti and Cesare Casarino. Minneapolis, MN: University of Minnesota Press, 2000.
Andreyev, Leonid. 'Lazarus.' In *Leonid Andreyev: Selected Stories*, Translated by Dmitry Fadeyev, 10. Boston: The Stratford Company, 1918.
Arnal, Luc H., Adeen Flinker, Andreas Kleinschmidt, Anne-Lise Giraud and David Poeppel. 'Human Screams Occupy a Privileged Niche in the Communication Soundscape.' *Current Biology* 25, no. 15 (Aug 2015): 2051–6.
Auslander, Phillip. 'Musical Personae.' *TDR*, The MIT Press 50, no. 1 (Spring 2006): 100–19.
Auslander, Philip. 'Musical Persona: The Physical Performance of Popular Music.' In *The Ashgate Research Companion to Popular Musicology*, Edited by Derek B Scott, 303–16. Farnham, Surrey; Burlington, VT: Ashgate, 2009.
Auslander, Phillip. 'The Performativity of Performance Documentation.' *PAJ: A Journal of Performance Art* 28, no. 3 (2006): 1–10.
Auslander, Phillip. *Performing Glam Rock: Gender and Theatricality in Popular Music*. Ann Arbor, MI: University of Michigan Press, 2006.
Auslander, Phillip. *Theory for Performance Studies: A Student's Guide*. London: Routledge, 2008.
Auslander, Philip. 'Watch That Man David Bowie: Hammersmith Odeon, London, July 3, 1973.' In *Performance and Popular Music: History, Place and Time*, Edited by Ian Inglis, 70–80, London: Routledge, 2006.
Austin, J. L. *How to Do Things with Words*. Edited by J. O. Urmson and Marina Sbisà. Cambridge, MA: Harvard University Press, 1975.

B

Baecque, Antoine de and Thierry Jousse. 'Cinema and Its Ghosts: An Interview with Jacques Derrida.' Translated by Peggy Kamuf. *Discourse* 37, no. 1-2 (Winter/Spring 2015): 22-39.

Baer, Hester. 'Producing Adaptations: Bernd Eichinger, Christiane F., and German Film History.' In *Generic Histories of German Cinema: Genre and Its Deviations*, Edited by Jaimey Fisher, 173-96. Camden House: Boydell & Brewer, 2013.

Bakhtin, Mikhail. *Problems of Dostoevsky's Poetics*. Edited and Translated by Caryl Emerson. Minneapolis, MN: University of Minnesota Press, 1984.

Bakhtin, Mikhail. *Rabelais and His World*. Translated by Helene Iswolsky. Bloomington, IN: Indiana University Press, 1984.

Barad, Karen. 'Posthumanist Performativity: Toward an Understanding of How Matter Comes to Matter.' *Signs: Journal of Women in Culture and Society* 28, no. 3 (Spring 2003): 801-31.

Barbas, Samantha. *Movie Crazy: Stars, Fans, and the Cult of Celebrity*. New York: Palgrave, 2001.

Barthes, Roland. *Mythologies*. Selected and Translated by Annette Lavers. London: Vintage Books, 2000.

Batson, Susan. *Truth: Personas, Needs and Flaws in the Art of Building Actors and Creating Characters*. USA: Webster\Stone, 2013.

Baylis, Nicola. 'Making Visible the Invisible: Corporeal Mime in the Twenty-first Century.' *Theatre Quarterly: NTQ, Cambridge* 25, no. 3 (Aug 2009): 274-88.

Beattie, Keith. 'It's Not Only Rock and Roll: "Rockumentary", Direct Cinema and Performative Display.' *Australasian Journal of American Studies* 24, no. 2 (2005): 21-41.

Beattie, Keith. 'Reworking Direct Cinema: Performative Display in Rockumentary.' In *Populäre Musikkulturen im Film. Film und Bewegtbild in Kultur und Gesellschaft*, Edited by Carsten Heinze and Laura Neibling, 131-52. Wiesbaden: Springer VS, 2016.

Benjamin, Walter. *Illuminations*. Edited by Hannah Arendt. Translated by Harry Zohn. New York: Schocken Books, 1969.

Bennett, Leslie. 'Inspired States: Adapting the Michael Chekhov Technique for the Singing Actor.' *Theatre, Dance and Performance Training* 4, no. 2 (2013): 146-61.

Bennett, Susan. 'A Tale of Two Cities: *Lazarus* in New York and London.' In *Ivo van Hove: From Shakespeare to Bowie*, Edited by Susan Bennett and Sonia Massai, 200-5. New York and London: Bloomsbury, 2018.

Bhaskar, Roy. *Reflections on Meta-Reality: Transcendence, Emancipation, and Everyday Life*. Thousand Oaks: Sage Publications, 2002.

Bittorf, Wilhelm. 'Irgendwas Irres muß Laufen.' *Der Spiegel*, 6 April, 1981.

Blair, Alison. 'Marc Bolan, David Bowie, and the Counter-Hegemonic Persona: "Authenticity", Ephemeral Identities, and the "Fantastical Other".' *MEDIANZ* 15, no. 1 (2015): 167-86.

Block, Paula M. and Terry J. Erdmann. *Jim Henson's Labyrinth: The Ultimate Visual History*. San Rafael, CA: Insight Editions, 2016.

Blumenberg, Hans. 'Besonders Wertvoll.' *Die Zeit*, 6 April 1981.
Bond, Helen K. *Pontius Pilate in History and Interpretation*. Cambridge: Cambridge University Press, 2000.
Bordwell, David, Janet Steiger and Kristin Thompson. 'The Classical Hollywood Cinema - Cap 5.' *Leyendocine*, 1 May 2007. http://leyendocine.blogspot.com/2007/05/classical-hollywood-cinema.html.
Bowie, David and Mick Rock. *Moonage Daydream: The Life and Times of Ziggy Stardust*. Bath, UK: Doppelganger, 2002.
Bowie, David and Enda Walsh. *Lazarus: A Musical*. London: Nick Hern Books, 2016.
Bradley, Laura J. R. *Brecht and Political Theatre: The Mother on Stage*. Oxford: Clarendon Press, 2006.
Bradley, Peri and James Page. 'David Bowie – the Trans who Fell to Earth: Cultural Regulation, Bowie and Gender Fluidity.' *Continuum: Journal of Media & Cultural Studies* 31, no. 4 (2017): 583–95.
Braudy, Leo. *The World in a Frame: What we See in Films*. Chicago, IL and London: University of Chicago Press, 1976.
Brecht, Bertolt. *Brecht on Art and Politics*. Edited by Tom Kuhn and Steve Giles. London: Methuen, 2003.
Brecht, Bertolt. *Brecht on Theatre: The Development of an Aesthetic*. Edited and Translated by John Willett. London: Methuen, 1964.
Brecht, Bertolt. *Brecht on Theatre: The Development of an Aesthetic*. Edited and Translated by John Willett. New York: Hill and Wang, 1964.
Brecht, Bertolt. *The Messingkauf Dialogues*. Edited by John Willett. London: Methuen Drama, 1985.
Brecht, Bertolt. 'A Short Organum for the Theatre.' In *Brecht on Theatre: The Development of an Aesthetic*, Edited and Translated by John Willett, 179–208. New York: Hill and Wang, 1964.
Brecht, Bertolt. 'The Street Scene: A Basic Model for Epic Theatre.' In *Brecht on Theatre: The Development of an Aesthetic*, Edited and Translated by John Willett. London: Eyre Methuen, 1978.
Brooker, Will. *Forever Stardust: David Bowie Across the Universe*. New York: Bloomsbury, 2007.
Brooker, Will. 'Time Again: The David Bowie Chronotype.' In *Enchanting David Bowie: Space, Time, Body, Memory*, Edited by Toija Cinque, Christopher Moore and Sean Redmond, 27–47. New York: Bloomsbury Academic, 2015.
Brooker, Will. *Why Bowie Matters*. London: William Collins, 2019.
Brooks, Peter. *The Melodramatic Imagination: Balzac, Henry James, Melodrama and the Mode of Excess*. New Haven, CT: Yale University Press, 1984.
Brown, Geoff. 'Down a Drink and Drug Drain.' *The Times Preview*, 11–17 December 1981.
Brown, Tina. 'The Bowie Odyssey.' *The Sunday Times Magazine*, 20 July 1975.
Bruzzi, Stella. 'Documentary, Performance and Questions of Authenticity.' *ZDOK*. Published 2011. https://blog.zhdk.ch/zdok/files/2017/11/A_Bruzzi_120311.pdf.
Bruzzi, Stella. *New Documentary: A Critical Introduction*. London and New York: Routledge, 2006.
Buckley, David. 'Revisiting Bowie's Berlin.' In *David Bowie: Critical Perspectives*, Edited by Eoin Devereux, Aileen Dillane and Martin J. Power, 215–20. New York: Routledge, 2015.

Buckley, David. 'Still Pop's Faker?' In *The Bowie Companion*, Edited by Elizabeth Thomson and David Gutman, 3-11. New York: Da Capo Press, 1996.

Buckley, David. *Strange Fascination: David Bowie: The Definitive Story*. London: Virgin Books, 2005.

Bukatman, Scott. *Terminal Identity: The Virtual Subject in Postmodern Science Fiction*. Durham, NC and London: Duke University Press, 1993.

Burke, Andrew. 'The Perfect Kiss: New Order and the Music Video.' In *Music/Video: Histories, Aesthetics, Media*, Edited by Gina Arnold, Daniel Cookney, Kirsty Fairclough and Michael Goddard, 79-90. New York: Bloomsbury, 2017.

Burns, Rob and Wilfried van der Will. 'The Federal Republic 1968 to 1990: From the Industrial to the Culture Society.' In *German Cultural Studies: An Introduction*, Edited by Rob Burns, 257-323. Oxford: Oxford University Press 1995.

Burroughs, William S. *The Adding Machine: Collected Essays*. London: John Calder, 1985.

Butler, Judith. *The Force of Nonviolence: An Ethico-Political Bind*. London: Verso, 2020.

Butler, Judith. *Gender Trouble: Feminism and the Subversion of Identity*. London and New York: Routledge, 1990.

Butler, Judith. *Gender Trouble: Feminism and the Subversion of Identity*, 2nd ed. London and New York: Routledge, 1999.

Butler, Judith. 'Performative Acts and Gender Constitution: An Essay in Phenomenology and Feminist Theory.' *Theatre Journal* 40, no. 4 (1988): 519-31.

C

Chapman, Ian. 'Ziggy's Urban Alienation: Assembling the Heroic Outsider.' In *Enchanting David Bowie: Space, Time, Body, Memory*, Edited by Toija Cinque, Christopher Moore and Sean Redmond, 87-102. New York: Bloomsbury Academic, 2015.

Chare, Nicholas and Liz Watkins. 'Introduction: Gesture in Film.' *Journal for Cultural Research* 19, no. 1 (2015): 1-5.

Charney, Leo. 'In a Moment: Film and the Philosophy of Modernity.' In *Cinema and the Invention of Modern Life*, Edited by Leo Charney and Vanessa R. Schwartz, 279-97. Berkley, CA: University of California Press, 1995.

Chateau, Dominique. 'The Film That Dreams: About David Lynch's Twin Peaks Season 3.' In *Stories*, Edited by Ian Christie and Annie van den Oever, 119-41. Amsterdam: Amsterdam University Press, 2018.

Chekhov, Michael. *Lessons for the Professional Actor*. From a Collection of Notes Transcribed and Arranged by Deirdre Hurst du Prey; Introduction by Mel Gordon. New York: Performing Arts Journal Publications, 1985.

Chekhov, Michael. *On the Technique of Acting*. New York: HarperCollins, 1991.

Chekhov, Michael. *To the Actor: On the Technique of Acting*. Connecticut: Martino Publishing, 2014.

Chekhov, Michael. *To the Director and Playwright*. Connecticut: Praeger, 1977.

Chion, Michel. *Audio-Vision: Sound on Screen*. New York: Columbia University Press, 1994.
Chion, Michel. *David Lynch*. Translated by Robert Julian. London: British Film Institute, 2006.
Christie, Ian and David Thompson. *Scorsese on Scorsese*. USA: Farrar, Straus and Giroux, 2004.
Cinque, Toija. '"Canvas of Flesh": David Bowie, Andy Warhol in *Basquiat*.' *Cinema Journal* 57, no. 3 (Spring 2018): 158-66.
Cinque, Toija. 'Chapter Nine: Ghostly Pilgrimages.' In *The Fandom of David Bowie: Everyone Says "Hi"*, Edited by Toija Cinque and Sean Redmond, 177-200. Switzerland: Palgrave, 2019.
Cinque, Toija. 'Semantic Shock: David Bowie.' In *Enchanting David Bowie: Space/Time/Body/Memory*, Edited by Toija Cinque, Christopher Moore and Sean Redmond,197-214. New York: Bloomsbury, 2015.
Cinque, Toija, Ndalianis Angela and Sean Redmond. 'David Bowie On-Screen.' *Cinema Journal* 57, no. 3 (Spring 2018): 126-30.
Cinque, Toija, Christopher Moore and Sean Redmond (eds). *Enchanting David Bowie: Space/Time/Body/Memory*. New York: Bloomsbury, 2015.
Clark, Katerina and Michael Holquist. *Mikhail Bakhtin*. Cambridge, MA: Belknap Press, 1984.
Clarke, Donald. 'Tricks of the Trade.' *Irish Times*, 10 November 2006.
Compo, Susan. *Earthbound: David Bowie and The Man Who Fell to Earth*. London: Jawbone Books, 2017.
Constantineau, Wayne. 'Mime and Media: The Parallel Worlds of Étienne Decroux and Marshall McLuhan.' *Dalhousie French Studies* 71 (Summer 2005): 115-34.
Counsell, Colin. *Signs of Performance: An Introduction to Twentieth-Century Theatre*. London and New York: Routledge, 1996.
Cramer, John. 'The Transactional Interpretation of Quantum Mechanics.' *Reviews of Modern Physics* 58, no. 3 (Jul 1986): 647-88.
Critchley, Simon. *Bowie*. New York: OR Books, 2014.
Crowe, Cameron. 'Ground Control to Davy Jones.' *Rolling Stone*, 12 February 1976, 78-83.
Crowe, Cameron. 'Candid Conversation: An Outrageous Conversation with the Actor, Rock Singer and Sexual Switch-hitter.' *Playboy*, September 1976, 32-4.

D

D'Adamo, Amedeo. 'Ain't There one Damn Flag that Can Make Me Break Down and Cry?: The Formal, Performative & Emotional Tactics of Bowie's Singular Critical Anthem "Young Americans".' In *Enchanting David Bowie*, Edited by Toija Cinque, Christopher Moore and Sean Redmond, 119-51. New York: Bloomsbury Academic, 2015.
D'Adamo, Amedeo. 'Dantean Space in the Cities of Cinema.' In *Media and the City: Urbanism, Technology and Communication*, Edited by Simone Tosoni, Matteo Tarantino and Chiara Giaccardi. 244-58. Newcastle Upon Tyne: Cambridge Scholars Press, 2013.

D'Adamo, Amedeo. *Empathetic Space On Screen: Constructing Powerful Place and Setting*. London: Palgrave Macmillan Press, 2018.

D'Adamo, Amedeo. 'Freedom vs. Possibility: Bowie, Kierkegaard, and Stages of Time.' In *The Cambridge Companion to David Bowie*, Edited by Denis Flannery. Cambridge: Cambridge University Press, Forthcoming 2023.

D'Adamo, Amedeo. 'Is Bowie Our Kierkegaard? - A Theory of Agency in Fandom.' In *David Bowie and Transmedia Stardom*, Edited by Ana Cristina Mendes and Lisa Perrott, 57–71. London and New York: Routledge, 2019.

D'Adamo, Amedeo. 'Urgently Communicating the Unintelligible: Bowie's Screaming Techniques on It's No Game.' *Talk*, Australian Centre for the Moving Image, 2015.

Daniel, Drew. *The Melancholy Assemblage: Affect and Epistemology in the English Renaissance*. New York: Fordham University Press, 2013.

Darby, Helen. 'I'm Glad I'm Not Me: Subjective Dissolution, Schizoanalysis and Post-Structuralist Ethics in the Films of Todd Haynes.' *Film-Philosophy* 17, no. 1 (Dec 2013): 330–47.

davidbowie.com. 'Bowie's Elephant Man Debut 40 Years Ago Today.' Published 29 July 2020. https://www.davidbowie.com/blog/2020/7/29/bowies-elephant-man-debut-40-years-ago-today.

Deleuze, Gilles. *Cinema 2: The Time-Image*. Translated by Hugh Tomlinson and Robert Galeta. Minneapolis, MN: University of Minnesota Press, 1989.

Deleuze, Gilles and Felix Guattari. *A Thousand Plateaus Capitalism and Schizophrenia*. Minneapolis, MN: University of Minnesota Press, 1987.

Deleuze, Gilles and Felix Guattari. *Anti-Oedipus: Capitalism and Schizophrenia*. Minneapolis, MN: University of Minnesota Press, 1983.

Derfoufi, Mehdi. 'Embodying Stardom, Representing Otherness: David Bowie in "Merry Christmas Mr. Lawrence".' In *David Bowie: Critical Perspectives*, Edited by Eoin Devereux, Aileen Dillane and Martin J. Power, 160–77. London: Routledge, 2015.

Deriso, Nick. '72 Musicians Who Are Totally Lying About Their Names.' *Ultimate Classic Rock*. Published 29 March 2018. https://ultimateclassicrock.com/musicians-name- Change/.

Derrida, Jacques. 'Signature Event Context.' In *Limited Inc.*, 1–25. Evanston, IL: Northwestern University Press, 1988.

Desjardins, Mary. 'The Incredible Shrinking Star.' *Camera Obscura* 19, no. 3 (Jan 2004): 22–55.

Devereux, Eoin, Aileen Dillane and Martin J. Power (eds). *David Bowie: Critical Perspectives*. London and New York: Routledge, 2015.

Diderot, Denis. 'The Paradox of the Actor.' In *Actors on Acting: The Theories, Techniques, and Practices of the World's Great Actors, Told in Their Own Words*, Edited by Toby Cole and Helen Chinoy, 162–70. New York: Crown, 1970.

Dillane, Aileen, Eoin Devereux and Martin J. Power. 'Culminating Sounds and (En)visions: *Ashes to Ashes* and the Case for Pierrot.' In *David Bowie: Critical Perspectives*, Edited by Eoin Devereux, Aileen Dillane, and Martin J. Power, 35–55. New York: Routledge, 2015.

Disaster Centre. 'New York Crime Rates 1960-2019.' Published 2019. https://www.disastercenter.com/crime/nycrime.htm.

Dixon, Ian. 'Always Crashing on the Same Synth: Voice/Synth Counterpoise in David Bowie's *Low*.' In *Interpreting the Synthesizer: Meaning Through Sonics*, Edited by Nick Wilson, 21–35. Newcastle Upon Tyne: Cambridge Scholars Publishing, 2020.

Dixon, Ian. 'Your Face is a Mess: Desecrating David Bowie's Face-as-commodity in "*Diamond Dogs*".' *Celebrity Studies* 11, no. 1 (Mar 2020): 140–3.

Doane, Mary Ann. *The Emergence of Cinematic Time: Modernity, Contingency, the Archive*. Cambridge, MA: Harvard University Press, 2002.

Dodds, Georges T. 'Piercing the Darkness: Undercover with Vampires in America Today (Review).' *SF Site*. Published 1998. https://www.sfsite.com/12b/pier47.htm.

Doering-Manteuffel, Anselm. 'Amerikanisierung und Westernisierung, Version: 2.0.' *Docupedia-Zeitgeschichte*. Published 19 August 2019. http://docupedia.de/zg/Doering-Manteuffel_amerikanisierung_v2_de_2019.

Doggett, Peter. *The Man Who Sold the World: David Bowie and the 1970s*. New York: Harper Perennial, 2013.

Dolan, Josephine. 'Crumbling Rejuvenation: Archetype, Embodiment and the Aging Body Myth.' In *The Happiness Illusion: How the Media Sold us a Fairytale*, Edited by Luke Hockley and Nadi Fadina, 75–88. London and New York: Routledge, 2015.

Douglas, Mary. *Purity and Danger: An Analysis of Concepts of Pollution and Taboo*. London: Routledge, 1966.

Dresslein, Detlef and Anne Lehwald. *Bernd Eichinger. Eine Biografie*. Munich: Wilhelm Heyne Verlag, 2011.

Dyer, Richard. 'A Star is Born and the Construction of Authenticity.' In *Stardom: Industry of Desire*, Edited by Christine Gledhill, 136–44. London and New York: Routledge, 1991.

Dyer, Richard. *Heavenly Bodies: Film Stars and Society*. New York: St. Martin's Press, 1986.

Dyer, Richard. *Stars*. London: BFI Press, 1998.

E

Edelman, Lee. 'Hamlet's Wounded Name.' In *Shakesqueer*, Edited by Madhavi Menon, 97–105. Durham, NC and London: Duke University Press, 2011.

Edmonds, Ben. 'Bowie Meets the Press: Plastic Man or Godhead of the Seventies?' *Circus*, 27 April 1976, 24–30.

Eichinger, Katja. *BE*. Hamburg: Hoffmann und Campe, 2012.

Elam, Keir. *The Semiotics of Theatre and Drama*. London: Methuen, 1980.

Epstein, William H. 'Counter-Intelligence: Cold War Criticism and Eighteenth-Century Studies.' *ELH* 57, no. 1 (Spring 1990): 63–99.

Erickson, Brad. 'George Clinton and David Bowie: The Space Race in Black and White.' *Popular Music and Society* 39, no. 5 (2016): 1–16.

Eshun, Ekow. 'Bowie, Bach and Bebop: How Music Powered Basquiat.' *Independent*, 25 September 2017. https://www.independent.co.uk/arts-entertainment/art/bowie- Bach-and-bebop-how-music-powered-basquiat-a7966541.html.

Esslin, Martin. *Artaud*. London: J. Calder, 1976.

F

F. Christiane, With Kai Hermann and Horst Rieck. *Wir Kinder vom Bahnhof Zoo*. Hamburg: Carlsen, 2009.

'Father-imago.' *The Archive for Research in Archetypal Symbolism*. Accessed 12 August 2021. https://aras.org/concordance/content/father-imago.

Felscherinow, Christiane and Sonja Vukovic. *Christiane F. Mein Zweites Leben*. Berlin: Deutscher Levante-Verlag, 2014.

Fisher, Jaimey. 'Introduction: Toward Generic Histories – Film Genre, Genre Theory, and German Film Studies.' In *Generic Histories of German Cinema: Genre and Its Deviations*, Edited by Jaimey Fisher, 1–25. Camden House: Boydell & Brewer, 2013.

Fisher, Mark. 'Gothic Materialism.' *Pli: The Warwick Journal of Philosophy* 12 (2001): 230–43.

Fitch, Richard. 'In This Age of Grand Allusion: Bowie, Nihilism and Meaning.' In *David Bowie: Critical Perspectives*, Edited by Eoin Devereux, Aileen Dillane and Martin J. Power, 19–34. London: Routledge, 2015.

Flannery, Denis. 'Absence, Resistance and Visitable Pasts: David Bowie, Todd Haynes, Henry James.' *Continuum: A Journal of Media Studies* 31, no. 4 (Jul 2017): 542–51.

Flannery, Denis. 'Apostrophe.' In *The Oxford Research Encyclopaedia of Literary Theory*, Edited by John Frow, 1–23. New York: Oxford University Press, 2020.

Flannery, Denis. 'Why we Should Expect Great Things from David Bowie's New Musical Play.' *The Conversation*. Published 10 April 2015. https://theconversation.com/why-we- Should-expect-great-things-from-david-bowies-new-musical-play-39946.

Fluck, Winfried. 'The Americanization of German Culture? The Strange, Paradoxical Ways of Modernity.' In *German Pop Culture: How 'American' Is It?*, Edited by Agnes C. Mueller, 19–39. Ann Arbor, MI: University of Michigan Press, 2004.

Flusser, Vilém. *Gestures*. Translated by Nancy Ann Roth. Minneapolis, MN: University of Minnesota Press, 2014.

Foucault, Michel. *The Birth of the Clinic: An Archaeology of Medical Perception*. Translated by A. M. Sheridan. London: Taylor & Francis, 2003.

Foucault, Michel. *Discipline and Punish: The Birth of the Prison*. Translated by Alan Sheridan. New York: Random House, Vintage Books, 1979.

Fowler, Matt. 'Twin Peaks: The Return Review.' *IGN*, 12 September 2017. https://www.ign.com/articles/2017/09/11/twin-peaks-the-return-review.

Frayling, Christopher, Phillip Hoare and Mark Kermode. 'David Bowie Then . . . David Bowie Now.' In *David Bowie Is*, Edited by Victoria Broackes and Geoffrey Marsh, 282–301. London: V&A Publishing, 2013.

Freeman, Elizabeth. *Time Binds: Queer Temporalities, Queer Histories*. Durham, NC and London: Duke University Press, 2010.

Freud, Sigmund. *On Murder, Mourning and Melancholia*. Translated by Shaun Whiteside with an Introduction by Maud Ellman. London: Penguin, 2005.

Freud, Sigmund. 'The Uncanny.' In *The Standard Edition of the Complete Psychological Works of Sigmund Freud*, Edited and Translated by James Strachey, 219–52. London: Hogarth Press, 1953.

Furby, Jacqueline. 'New Killer Star.' *Cinema Journal* 57, no. 3 (Spring 2018): 167-74.

G

Gallagher, Brian. 'Some Historical Reflections on the Paradoxes of Stardom in the American Film Industry, 1910-1960.' *Images: Journal of Film and Popular Culture*. Published 3 March 1997. http://www.imagesjournal.com/issue03/infocus/stars1.htm.
Galt, Rosalind. 'David Bowie's Perverse Cinematic Body.' *Cinema Journal* 57, no. 3 (Spring 2018): 131-8.
Gardiner, Michael. 'Bakhtin's Carnival: Utopia as Critique.' *Utopian Studies* 3, no. 2 (1992): 21-49.
Gardiner, Michael. *The Dialogics of Critique: M. M. Bakhtin and the Theory of Ideology*. London: Routledge, 1992.
Gendron, Bernard. 'The Downtown Music Scene.' In *The Downtown Book: The New York Art Scene 1974-1984*, Edited by Marvin J. Taylor, 41-65. Princeton, NJ: Princeton University Press, 2006.
George, E. R. David. 'Letter to a Poor Actor.' *New Theatre Quarterly* 2, no. 8 (Nov 1986): 352-63.
Gledhill, Christine. 'Introduction.' In *Stardom: Industry of Desire*, Edited by Christine Gledhill, xiii-xiv. London and New York: Routledge, 1991.
Glennie, Jay and Darryl Webber. *The Man Who Fell to Earth*. London: Unstoppable Editions, 2016.
Goddard, Michael. 'Audiovision and Gesamtkunstwerk: The Aesthetics of First and Second Generation Industrial Music Video.' In *Music/Video: Histories, Aesthetics, Media*, Edited by Gina Arnold, Daniel Cookney, Kirsty Fairclough and Michael Goddard, 163-80. London: Bloomsbury Academic, 2017.
Goffman, Erving. *Frame Analysis: An Essay on the Organization of Experience*. Cambridge, MA: Harvard University Press, 1974.
Goffman, Erving. *The Presentation of Self in Everyday Life*. Middlesex: Penguin Books, 1980.
Goffman, Erving. *The Presentation of Self in Everyday Life*. New York: Anchor Books, 1959.
Goffman, Erving. *The Presentation of the Self in Everyday Life*. London: Allen Lane, 1969.
Goodall, Jane. *Stage Presence*. London: Routledge, 2008.
Gore, Joe. 'Changes 2.1: New Digital Stimulation from David Bowie and Reeves Gabrels.' *Guitar Player*, June 1997, 45-56.
Gribbin, John. *Schrodinger's Kittens and the Search for Reality: Solving the Quantum Mysteries*, London: Weidenfeld and Nicolson, 1995.
Groebner, Valentin. *Who Are You?: Identification, Deception, and Surveillance in Early Modern Europe*. Translated by Mark Kyburz and John Peck. New York: Zone Books, 2007.
Gussow, Mel. 'Roeg: The Man Behind The Man Who Fell to Earth.' *New York Times*, August 22, 1976.

H

Haden-Guest, Anthony. 'Bowie: The Wild Side.' *Radio Times*, 25–31 January 1975, 6–7.

Hague, Angela. 'Infinite Games: The Derationalization of Detection in *Twin Peaks*.' In *Full of Secrets: Critical Approaches to Twin Peaks*, Edited by David Lavery, 130–43. Detroit: Wayne State University Press, 1995.

Hainge, Greg. 'Weird or Loopy? Specular Spaces, Feedback and Artifice in Lost Highway's Aesthetics of Sensation.' In *The Cinema of David Lynch: American Dreams, Nightmare Visions*, Edited by Erica Sheen and Annette Davidson, 136–50. London and New York: Wallflower Press, 2004.

Hauptfuhrer, Fred. 'Rock's Space Oddity, David Bowie Falls to Earth and Finds His Feet in Film.' *People*, 6 September 1976.

Hepworth, David. 'How Performing Starman on Top of the Pops Sent Bowie into the Stratosphere.' *The Guardian*. Published 15 January 2016. https://www.theguardian.com/music/musicblog/2016/jan/15/david-bowie-starman-top-of-the-pops.

Hilburn, Robert. 'Bowie: Now I'm a Businessman.' *Melody Maker*, 28 February 1976.

Hirsch, Joshua. *Afterimage: Film, Trauma and the Holocaust*. Philadelphia: Temple University Press, 2004.

Hodenfield, Chris. 'Bad Boys in Berlin: David Bowie, Iggy Pop and the Terrible Things an Audience Can Make You Do.' *Rolling Stone*, 4 October 1979, 41–5.

Hollinger, Karen. *The Actress: Hollywood Acting and the Female Star*. London: Routledge, 2006.

Holm-Hudson, Kevin. '"Who Can I Be Now?": David Bowie's Vocal Personae.' *Contemporary Music Review* 37, no. 3 (Aug 2018): 214–34.

Hoskyns, Barney. *Glam!: Bowie, Bolan and the Glitter Rock Revolution*. USA: Faber and Faber, 1998.

Hunt, Kevin. 'The Eyes of David Bowie.' In *Enchanting David Bowie: Space, Time, Body, Memory*, Edited by Toija Cinque, Christopher Moore and Sean Redmond, 175–96. New York: Bloomsbury Academic, 2015.

J

Jackson, Earl Jr. 'Desire at Cross (-Cultural) Purposes: *Hiroshima, Mon Amour* and *Merry Christmas, Mr. Lawrence*.' *Positions* 2, no. 1 (1994): 133–74.

Jaynes, Julian. *The Origin of Consciousness in the Breakdown of the Bicameral Mind*. Boston: Houghton Mifflin, 1976.

Johnson, Kathryn. 'David Bowie Is.' In *David Bowie: Critical Perspectives*, Edited by Eoin Devereux, Aileen Dillane and Martin Power, 1–18. New York: Routledge, 2015.

Jones, Brian J. *Jim Henson*. New York, Ballantine Books, 2016.

Jones, Dylan. *David Bowie: A Life*. London: Windmill Books, 2018.

K

Kayser, Wolfgang. *The Grotesque in Art and Literature*. Translated by Ulrich Weisstein. Bloomington, IN: Indiana University Press, 1933.

King, Barry. 'Articulating Stardom.' In *Star Texts: Image and Performance in Film and Television*, Edited by Jeremy G. Butler, 125-53. Detroit: Wayne State University Press, 1991.

Klevan, Andrew. 'What is Evaluative Film Criticism.' *Film Criticism* 40, no. 1 (Jan 2016). https://doi.org/10.3998/fc.13761232.0040.118.

Koenig, Peter. 'The Laughing Gnostic: David Bowie and the Occult.' Published 1996, Updated in 2020. https://www.parareligion.ch/bowie.htm.

Krasniewicz, Louise and Michael Blitz. 'The Replicator: Starring Arnold Schwarzenegger as the Great Meme-Machine' In *Stars in Our Eyes: The Star Phenomenon in the Contemporary Era*, Edited by Angela Ndalianis and Charlotte Henry, 21-44. Westport: Praeger, 2001.

Kubernik, Harvey. 'D.A. Pennebaker on David Bowie.' *Cave Hollywood*. Published 12 January 2016. http://cavehollywood.com/d-a-pennebaker-on-david-bowie/.

L

Lachmann, Renate, Raoul Eshelman and Marc Davis. 'Bakhtin and Carnival: Culture as Counter-Culture.' *Cultural Critique* 11 (Winter 1988-1989): 115-52.

Laing, R. D. *The Divided Self: An Existential Study in Sanity and Madness*. London: Penguin Books, 1965.

Lajosi, Krisztina. 'Wagner and the (Re)mediation of Art: Gesamtkunstwerk and Nineteenth Century Theories of Media.' *Frame* 23, no. 2 (2010): 42-60.

Large, David Clay. *Berlin*. New York: Basic Books, 2000.

Leigh, Wendy. *Bowie: The Biography*. New York: Gallery Books, 2014.

Leorne, Ana. 'Dear Dr. Freud – David Bowie Hits the Couch: A Psychoanalytic Approach to Some of His Personae.' In *David Bowie: Critical Perspectives*, Edited by Eoin Devereux, Aileen Dillane and Martin J. Power, 111-27. London and New York: Routledge, 2015.

Lévi-Strauss, Claude. 'Myth and Music.' In *Myth and Meaning: Five Talks for Radio by Claude Lévi-Strauss*, 44-54. Toronto, ON and Buffalo: University of Toronto Press, 1978.

Leys, Ruth. 'The Turn to Affect: A Critique.' *Critical Inquiry* 37, no. 3 (Spring 2011): 434-72.

Lobalzo-Wright, Julie. 'The Extraordinary Rock Star as Film Star.' In *David Bowie: Critical Perspectives*, Edited by Eoin Devereux, Aileen Dillane and Martin J. Power, 230-44, New York and London: Routledge, 2015.

Loder, Kurt. 'Straight Time.' *Rolling Stone*, 12 May 1983, 22-9.

Long Star Biographies, Davidson Dalling Associates Information Folder. London: Davidson Dalling Associates, 1975.

Loxley, James. *Performativity: The New Critical Idiom*. London: Routledge, 2007.

Luckmann, Benita. 'The Small Life-Worlds of Modern Man.' *Social Research* 37, no. 4 (1970): 580-96.

M

MacCormack, Patricia. 'Perversion: Transgressive Sexuality and Becoming-monster.' *Thirdspace* 3, no. 2 (2004). https://journals.sfu.ca/thirdspace/index.php/journal/article/view/maccormack/174.

Mackay, Patricia. 'Serious – and Stunning – Moonlight.' In *The Bowie Companion*, Edited by Elizabeth Thomson and David Gutman, 195–8. Cambridge, MA: Da Capo Press, 1996.

MacKinnon, Angus. 'The Future Isn't What It Used to Be.' *NME*, 13 September 1980, 31–8.

Maltby, Richard. *Hollywood Cinema*, 2nd ed. Malden: Blackwell, 2003.

Marsh, Geoffrey. 'Astronaut of Inner Spaces: Sundridge Park, Soho, London . . . Mars.' In *David Bowie Is*, Edited by Victoria Broackes and Geoffrey Marsh, 27–46. London: V&A Publishing, 2013.

Marquie, Elizabeth. 'Conceptualizing Documentary Performance.' *Studies in Documentary Film* 7, no. 1 (2013): 45–60.

Marx, Gary. *Windows Into the Soul: Surveillance and Society in an Age of High Technology*. Chicago, IL: The University of Chicago Press, 2016.

Mast, Gerald. *A Short History of the Movies*, 5th ed. New York: Macmillan, 1992.

Mathiesen, Thomas. 'The Viewer Society: Foucault's "Panopticon" Revisited.' *Theoretical Criminology: An International Journal* 1, no. 2 (1997): 215–32.

Mazour-Matusevich, Yelena. 'Contextualizing Bakhtin's Intuitive Discoveries: The End of Grotesque Realism and the Reformation.' In *Mikhail Bakhtin's Heritage in Literature, Arts and Psychology: Art and Answerability*, Edited by Slav N. Gratchev and Howard Mancing, 137–56. Lanham, MD: Lexington Books, 2018.

McCarthy, Elizabeth. 'Telling Lies: The Interviews of David Bowie.' *Celebrity Studies* 10, no. 1 (2019): 89–103.

McCarthy, Elizabeth. 'Telling Lies: The Interviews of David Bowie.' In *David Bowie and Transmedia Stardom*, Edited by Ana C. Mendes and Lisa Perrott, 89–103. London: Routledge, 2020.

McKee, Robert. *Story: Substance, Structure, Style and the Principles of Screenwriting*. London: Methuen, 1998.

McLuhan, Marshall. *Understanding Media*, 2nd ed. London: Routledge, 2001.

McPherson, Conor. *Girl From the North Country*. Music and Lyrics by Bob Dylan. London: Nick Hern Books, 2017.

McWhirter, David. 'Feeling Backwards with Henry James: The Melancholy of History.' *The Henry James Review* 41, no. 1 (2020): 11–14.

Mendes, Ana Cristina and Lisa Perrott. *David Bowie and Transmedia Stardom*. London and New York: Routledge, 2019.

Menninghaus, Winfried. *Disgust: Theory and History of a Strong Sensation*. New York, SUNY Press, 2003.

Merleau-Ponty, Maurice. *Phenomenology of Perception*. Translated by Donald A. Landes. London: Routledge Press, 2012.

Miles, Barry. *Bowie In His Own Words*. London: Omnibus Press, 1984.

Miller, Craig. 'Robert Engels Interview.' *Wrapped in Plastic*, April 2002, 2–11.

Miller, D. A. *Place for Us: Essay on the Broadway Musical*. Cambridge, MA and London: Harvard University Press, 1998.

Miller, William Ian. *The Anatomy of Disgust*. Cambridge, MA: Harvard University Press, 1998.
Mills, Steven. 'Bakhtin Against Dualism: Restoring Humanity to the Subjective Experience.' In *Mikhail Bakhtin's Heritage in Literature, Arts and Psychology: Art and Answerability*, Edited by Slav N. Gratchev and Howard Mancing, 255-77. Lanham, MD: Lexington Books, 2018.
Milne, Tom. 'The Man Who Fell to Earth.' *Sight & Sound*, Summer 1976, 146.
Mitter, Shomit. 'Inner and Outer: "Open Theatre" in Peter Brook and Joseph Chaikin.' *Journal of Dramatic Theory and Criticism*, vol. III, no. 1, (Fall 1988): 47-69.
Mooradian, Michael Lupro, 'Keeping Space Fantastic: The Transformative Journey of Major Tom,' In *Enchanting David Bowie: Space, Time, Body, Memory*, Edited by Toija Cinque, Christopher Moore and Sean Redmond, 13-26. New York: Bloomsbury Academic, 2015.
Morley, Paul. *The Age of Bowie: How David Bowie Made a World of Difference*. New York: Gallery Books, 2014.
Mumford, Meg. *Bertolt Brecht*. London: Routledge, 2018.
Myers, Justin. 'David Bowie's Official Top 40 Biggest Selling Downloads Revealed!' *Official Charts*. Published 11 January 2016. https://www.officialcharts.com/chart-news/david-Bowie-s-official-top-40-biggest-selling-downloads-revealed-__2854/

N

Naremore, James. *Acting in the Cinema*. Berkeley, CA: University of California Press, 1988.
Navarro, Joe. *The Dictionary of Body Language: A Field Guide to Human Behaviour*. William Morrow, 2018. E-book.
Ndalianis, Angela. 'Bowie and Science Fiction/Bowie as Science Fiction.' *Cinema Journal* 57, no. 3 (Spring 2018): 139-49.
Ndalianis, Angela and Charlotte Henry. *Stars in Our Eyes: The Star Phenomenon in the Contemporary Era*. London: Praeger Publishers, 2002.
Neressian, Anahid. *Keats's Odes: A Lover's Discourse*. Chicago, IL and London: Chicago University Press, 2021.
Nichols, Bill. 'How Can We Describe the Observational, Participatory and Performative Modes of Documentary Film?.' In *Introduction to Documentary*, 3rd ed., 132-58. Bloomington, IN: Indiana University Press, 2017.
Nietzsche, Friedrich. *On the Genealogy of Morals: A Polemic*. Edited by Robert C. Holub. Translated by Michael A. Scarpitti. London: Penguin Books, 2013.
Nightingale, Andrea. 'Toward an Ecological Eschatology: Plato and Bakhtin on Other Worlds and Times.' In *Bakhtin and the Classics*, Edited by R. Bracht Branham, 220-49. Evanston, IL: Northwestern University Press, 2002.
Nochimson, Martha. *David Lynch Swerves: Uncertainty from Lost Highway to Inland Empire*. Austin, TX: University of Texas, 2013.
Nussbaum, Martha. *Hiding From Humanity: Disgust, Shame and the Law*. Princeton, NJ: Princeton University Press, 2006.

O

O'Leary, Chris. *Rebel Rebel*. Winchester, UK; Washington, USA: Zero Books, 2015.

O' Leary, Chris. 'When I'm Five.' Pushing Ahead of the Dame. Published 2 November 2009. https://bowiesongs.wordpress.com/?s=when+I%27m+five.

October, Dene. 'The [becoming Wo]Man Who Fell to Earth.' In *David Bowie: Critical Perspectives*, Edited by Eoin Devereux, Aileen Dillane and Martin J. Power, 245–62. New York and London: Routledge, 2015.

October, Dene. 'Between Sound and Vision: Low and Sense.' In *Enchanting David Bowie: Space/Time/Body/Memory*, Edited by Toija Cinque, Christopher Moore and Sean Redmond, 275–304. New York: Bloomsbury Academic, 2015.

October, Dene. 'Can You Hear Me?' *David Bowie Studies*. https://davidbowiestudies.wordpress.com/can-you-hear-me/.

October, Dene. 'David Bowie: Ooh Fashion!' Panel Discussion, Victoria and Albert Museum, 22 March 2016.

October, Dene. 'Is it Any Wonder I Reject You First?' *David Bowie Studies*. Published 2018. https://davidbowiestudies.wordpress.com/is-it-any-wonder-i-reject-you-first/.

October, Dene. 'The Man Who Fell to Earth.' In *Bloomsbury Encyclopedia of Film and Television Costume Design*, Edited by Deborah Nadoolman Landis. New York: Bloomsbury, Forthcoming 2022.

October, Dene. 'Shooting Stars: Filming the Jodie Whittaker Era of *Doctor Who*.' In *Doctor Who: New Dawn*, Edited by Brigid Cherry, Matthew Hills and Andrew O'Day. Manchester: Manchester University Press, 2021.

October, Dene. 'Transition Transmission: Media, Seriality and the Bowie-Newton Matrix.' In *David Bowie and Transmedia Stardom*, Edited by Ana Cristina Mendes and Lisa Perrott, 104–18, London and New York: Routledge, 2020.

Oursler, Tony. 'David Bowie.' *Artforum*. Accessed 1 March 2020. https://www.artforum.com/print/201603/David-bowie-58102.

P

Paget, Derek, and Jane Roscoe. 'Giving Voice: Performance and Authenticity in the Documentary Musical.' *Jump Cut: A Review of Contemporary Media* 48 (Winter 2006). https://www.ejumpcut.org/archive/jc48.2006/MusicalDocy/.

Paglia, Camille. 'Theatre of Gender: David Bowie at the Climax of the Sexual Revolution.' In *David Bowie Is*, Edited by Victoria Broackes and Geoffrey Marsh, 69–92. London: V&A Publishing, 2013.

Pateman, Matthew. 'Structuring Stardom: Identity and the Transmigration of Image in the Work of David Bowie.' In *TechKnowledgies: New Imaginaries in the Humanities, Arts, and TechnoSciences*, Edited by Mary Valentis with Tara P. Monastero and Paula Yablonsky, 130–45. New Castle: Cambridge Scholarly Publishing, 2007.

Pegg, Nicholas. *The Complete David Bowie*, 6th ed. London: Titan Books, 2011.

Pegg, Nicholas. *The Complete David Bowie: Revised and Updated 2016 Edition*. London: Titan Books, 2016.
Peraino, Judith A. 'Plumbing the Surface of Sound and Vision: David Bowie, Andy Warhol, and the Art of Posing.' *Qui Parle* 21, no. 1 (Jan 2012): 151-84.
Perkins, Victor Francis. 'Must We Say What They Mean? Film Criticism and Interpretation.' *Movie* 34, no. 35 (1990): 1-6.
Perrott, Lisa. 'Bowie the Cultural Alchemist: Performing Gender, Synthesizing Gesture and Liberating Identity.' *Continuum: Journal of Media & Cultural Studies* 31, no. 4 (Jun 2017): 528-41.
Perrott, Lisa. 'The Alchemical Union of David Bowie and Floria Sigismondi: Dialogic World- Building, "Transmedia Surrealism", and "Loose Continuity".' In *Transmedia Directors: Artistry, Industry and New Audiovisual Aesthetics*, Edited by Carol Vernallis, Holly Rogers and Lisa Perrott, 194-220. New York: Bloomsbury, 2019.
Pettigrew, Jason. 'Goth Inventors Bauhaus Recall the Night They Met David Bowie.' Alternative Press. Published 23 January 2018. https://www.altpress.com/features/bauhaus_undead_met_david_bowie_the_hunger/.
Plato. *Parmenides*. Translated by Benjamin Jowett. South Bend: Infomotions, Inc., 2000.
Pop, Andrei and Mechtild Widrich (eds). *Ugliness*. London: I.B Tauris & Co, 2014.
Powell, Jeremy. 'David Lynch, Francis Bacon, Gilles Deleuze: The Cinematic Diagram and the Hall of Time.' *Discourse* 36, no. 3 (2014): 309-39.
Priest, Christopher. *The Prestige*. New York: Touchstone, 1995.
Prosser, Jay. *Light in the Dark Room: Photography and Loss*. Minneapolis, MN: University of Minnesota Press, 2005.

R

Ramsland, Katherine M. *Piercing the Darkness: Undercover with Vampires in America Today*. New York: Harper Prism, 1998.
Rauch, Andreas M. With Bernhard Matt. *Bernd Eichinger und Seine Filme*. Frankfurt am Main: Haag + Herchen, 2000.
Ray, Robert B. *The ABCs of Classic Hollywood*. Oxford: Oxford University Press, 2008.
Readman, Mark. 'Editorial - David Bowie.' *Journal of Media Practice* 17, no. 1 (2016): 1-3.
Redmond, Sean. 'David Bowie: In Cameo.' *Cinema Journal* 57, no. 3 (2018): 150-7.
Redmond, Sean. 'Sensing Film Performance.' In *Performance Phenomenology*, Edited by Matthew Wagner, 165-83. London: Palgrave Macmillan, 2019.
Redmond, Sean. 'The Whiteness of Stars: Looking at Kate Winslet's Unruly White Body.' In *Stardom and Celebrity: A Reader*, Edited by Sean Redmond and Sue Holmes, 264-74. London: Sage Publications, 2007.
Rentschler, Eric. 'Film der Achtziger Jahre. Endzeitspiele und Zeitgeistszenerien.' In *Geschichte des Deutschen Films*, Edited by Wolfgang Jacobsen, Anton Kaes and Hans Helmut Prinzler, 285-322. Stuttgart: Verlag J. B. Metzler, 1993.

Rice, Anne. *Interview With the Vampire*. New York: Knopf, 1976.
Riches, Simon. 'Intuition and Investigation into Another Place: The Epistemological Role of Dreaming in Twin Peaks and Beyond.' In *The Philosophy of David Lynch*, Edited by William J. Devlin and Shai Biderman, 25-44. Lexington, KY: University of Kentucky Press, 2011.
Rinke, Andrea. 'Liminal Bodies in Liminal Spaces: The Depiction of Drug Addicted Youth in the Films *Christiane F* and *Drifter*.' *Global Media Journal: Australian Edition* 4, no. 1 (2010): 1-12. https://www.hca.westernsydney.edu.au/gmjau/archive/v4_2010_1/andrea_rinke_RA.html.
Ritman, Alex. '"The Man Who Fell to Earth" Cinematographer on David Bowie's "Defining Role".' *Hollywood Reporter*. Published 19 September 2016. https://www.hollywoodreporter.com/news/man-who-fell-earth-cinematographer-930640.
Rob, John. *Punk Rock: An Oral History*. Great Britain: Ebury Press, 2006.
Robinson, Lisa. 'The First Synthetic Rock Star. There is No Other.' *New Musical Express*, 7 March 1976.
Rombes, Nicholas. 'Blue Velvet Underground: David Lynch's Post-Punk Poetics.' In *The Cinema of David Lynch: American Dreams, Nightmare Visions*, Edited by Erica Sheen and Anette Davidson, 61-76. London: Wallflower Press, 2004.
Rook, Jean. 'Waiting for Bowie and Finding a Genius Who Insists He's Really a Clown.' *Daily Express*, 5 May 1976.
Rosenbaum, Jonathan. 'The Man Who Fell to Earth.' Review of *The Man Who Fell to Earth*, Directed by Nicolas Roeg. *Monthly Film Bulletin*, April 1976.
Roscoe, Jane. 'Real Entertainment: Real Factual Hybrid Television.' *Media International Australia* 100 (2001): 9-20.
Ross, Kristin. *Communal Luxury: The Political Imaginary of the Paris Commune*. London and New York: Verso, 2015.
Rubridge, Sarah. 'Does Authenticity Matter? The Case for and Against Authenticity in the Performing Arts.' In *Analysing Performance*, Edited by Patrick Campbell, 219-33. London: Reaktion, 2001.
Rüther, Tobias. *Heroes: David Bowie and Berlin*. London: Reaktion Books, 2014.

S

Sandford, Christopher. *Bowie: Loving the Alien*. Da Capo Press, 1996.
Schechner, Richard. *Between Theatre and Anthropology*. Philadelphia: Pennsylvania University Press, 1985.
Schechner, Richard. *Environmental Theatre*. New York: Hawthorn Books, 1973.
Schechner, Richard. *Performance Theory*. London: Routledge, 2003.
Scheibel, Will. 'Gilles Deleuze: On Movement, Time, and Modernism.' In *Thinking in the Dark: Cinema, Theory, Practice*, Edited by Murray Pomerance and R. Barton Palmer, 150-61. New Jersey: Rutgers University Press, 2016.
Schnabel, Julian and David Bowie. *Charlie Rose*. Edited by Charlie Rose. PBS, 9 August 1996. Accessed 15 July 2020. https://www.youtube.com/watch?v=ExDfj-_D6Sk.

Schober, Siegfried. 'Idol des Letzten Rock.' *Der Spiegel*, 11 April 1976.
Schubart, Rikke. 'Birth of a Hero: Rocky, Stallone, and Mythical Creation.' In *Stars in Our Eyes: The Star Phenomenon in the Contemporary Era*, Edited by Angela Ndalianis and Charlotte Henry, 149-64. Westport: Praeger, 2002.
Sedgwick, Eve Kosofsky. *Tendencies*. Durham, NC and London: Duke University Press, 1993.
Seigworth, Gregory J. and Melissa Gregg. 'An Inventory of Shimmers.' In *The Affect Theory Reader*, Edited by Gregory J. Seigworth and Melissa Gregg, 1-26. Durham, NC: Duke University Press, 2010.
Shakespeare, William. *Hamlet*. Edited by Robert S. Miola. New York and London: W. W. Norton & Company, 2011.
Sharpe, Alex. 'Scary Monsters: The Hopeful Undecidability of David Bowie (1947-2016).' *Law and Humanities* 11, no. 2 (2017): 228-44.
Shaviro, Steven. 'Post-Continuity: An Introduction.' In *Post-Cinema: Theorizing 21st Century Film*, Edited by Shane Denson and Julie Leyda. Falmer: REFRAME Books, 2016.
Shiloh, Ilana. *The Double, the Labyrinth and the Locked Room: Metaphors of Paradox in Crime Fiction and Film*. New York: Peter Lang, 2011.
Shroyer, Steve and John Lifflander. 'Spaced Out in The Desert,' *Creem*, December 1975.
Silverman, Kaja. *The Acoustic Mirror: The Female Voice in Psychoanalysis and Cinema*. Bloomington, IN: Indiana University Press, 1998.
Sinnerbrink, Robert. 'Cinematic Ideas/Ideals?' *Film-Philosophy* 9, no. 34 (2005): 1-15.
Sinyard, Neil. *The Films of Nicolas Roeg*. London: Charles Letts, 1991.
Smith, Nigel. 'Songs and Their Lyrics: Any Room at the Feast?' In *Evaluations of US Poetry Since 1950, Volume 1: Language, Form, and Music*, Edited by Robert von Hallberg and Robert Faggen, 38-58. Albuquerque: University of New Mexico Press, 2021.
Sontag, Susan. 'Notes on Camp.' In *Camp: Queer Aesthetics and the Performing Subject-A Reader*, Edited by Fabio Cleto, 53-65. Ann Arbor, MI: University of Michigan Press, 1999.
Soussloff, Catherine M. *The Absolute Artist: The Historiography of a Concept*. Minneapolis, MN: University of Minnesota Press, 1997.
Spotts, Frederic. *Hitler and the Power of Aesthetics*. New York: Overlook Press, 2003.
Stam, Robert. *Subversive Pleasures: Bakhtin, Cultural Criticism, and Film*. Baltimore, MD: John Hopkins University Press, 1989.
Stanislavski, Constantin. *An Actor Prepares*. Translated by Elizabeth Reynolds Hapgood. New York: Routledge, 1989.
Stark, Tanja. 'Confronting Bowie's Mysterious Corpses.' In *Enchanting David Bowie: Space, Time, Body, Memory*, Edited by Toija Cinque, Christopher Moore and Sean Redmond, 61-77. New York: Bloomsbury Academic, 2015.
Stephan, Alexander. 'A Special German Case of Cultural Americanization.' In *The Americanization of Europe: Culture, Diplomacy, and Anti-Americanism*, Edited by Alexander Stephan, 69-88. New York: Berghahn Books, 2006.
Stott, Andrew McConnell. 'Clowns on the Verge of a Nervous Breakdown: Dickens, Coulrophobia, and the Memoirs of Joseph Grimaldi.' *Journal for Early Modern Cultural Studies* 12, no. 4 (Fall 2012): 3-25.
Strieber, Whitley. *Communion: A True Story*. New York: Beech Tree Books, 1987.
Strieber, Whitley. *The Hunger*. New York: William Morrow & Co, 1981.

Stuart, Keith. 'BowieNet: How David Bowie's ISP Foresaw the Future of the Internet.' *The Guardian*, 11 January 2016. https://www.theguardian.com/technology/2016/jan/11/david-bowie-bowienet-isp- Internet.

T

Tanaka, Shogo. 'The Notion of Embodied Knowledge and its Range.' *Encyclopaideia: Journal of Phenomenology and Education* 37 (2013): 47–66.

Tangney, June Price, Rowland S. Miller, Laura Flicker and Deborah Hill Barlow. 'Are Shame, Guilt, and Embarrassment Distinct Emotions?' *Journal of Personality and Social Psychology* 70, no. 6. (1996): 1256–69.

Tatlow, Antony and Wong Tak-Wai (eds). *Brecht and East Asian Theatre: The Proceedings of a Conference on Brecht in East Asian Theatre*. Hong Kong: Hong Kong University Press, 1982.

Taylor, Marvin J. 'Playing the Field.' In *The Downtown Book: The New York Art Scene 1974- 1984*, Edited by Marvin J. Taylor, 17–39. Princeton, NJ: Princeton University Press, 2006.

Tesla, Nikola. 'On Light and Other Frequency Phenomena.' In *The Inventions, Researches and Writings of Nikola Tesla*, 2nd ed., Edited by Thomas Commerford Martin. New York: The Electrical Engineer, 1894.

Tevis, Walter. 'Letter.' *Circus*, 30 December 1975.

Tevis, Walter. *The Man Who Fell to Earth*. Greenwich: Fawcett Publications, 1963.

Tevis, Walter, *The Man Who Fell to Earth*. London: Penguin, 2009.

The Daily Register. 'People.' *Column*, 18 October 1977.

Trainer, Adam. '"Well, I Wouldn't Buy the Merchandise": David Bowie as Postmodern Auteur.' *Senses of Cinema*. Published October 2003. https://www.sensesofcinema.com/2003/cinema-and-music/bowie_postmodern_auteur/.

Trynka, Paul. *David Bowie | Starman*. New York: Little, Brown and Company, 2011.

Trynka, Paul. *Starman: David Bowie the Definitive Biography*. Great Britain: Sphere, 2012.

U

Usher, Bethany and Stephanie Fremaux. 'Turn Myself to Face Me: David Bowie in the 1990s and Discovery of Authentic Self.' In *David Bowie: Critical Perspectives*, Edited by Eoin Devereux, Aileen Dillane and Martin J. Power, 56–81. London and New York: Routledge, 2015.

V

VandenBos, Gary R. *APA Dictionary of Psychology*. Washington, DC: American Psychological Association, 2015.

Verano, Frank. 'D.A. Pennebaker and the Politics and Aesthetics of Mature Period Direct Cinema.' PhD Thesis. University of Sussex, 2015. https://core.ac.uk/download/pdf/74226234.pdf.
Virillo, Paul. *City of Panic*. Oxford; New York: Berg, 2005.

W

Wagner, Richard. *Das Kunstwerk der Zukunft (The Artwork of the Future)*. Translated by Emma Warner. London: The Wagner Journal, 2013.
Waldrep, Shelton. *The Aesthetics of Self-Invention: Oscar Wilde to David Bowie*. Minneapolis, MN: University of Minnesota Press, 2004.
Waldrep, Shelton. *Future Nostalgia: Performing David Bowie*. New York: Bloomsbury Academic, 2015.
Watts, Michael. 'Bowie's Mainman.' *Melody Maker*, 18 May 1974, 40–1.
Weston, Judith. *Directing Actors: Creating Memorable Performances for Film & Television*. California: Michael Weise Productions, 1996.
Wetherell, Margaret. *Affect and Emotion: A New Social Science Understanding*. London: Sage, 2012.
Wheatley, Helen. *Spectacular Television: Exploring Televisual Pleasure*. London: I. B. Tauris, 2016.
White, Timothy. 'David Bowie: Who Am I This Time?' *Musician*, July 1990.
Wiles, David. 'The Carnivalesque in *A Midsummer Night's Dream*.' In *Shakespeare and Carnival: After Bakhtin*, Edited by Ronald Knowles, 61–82. London: Macmillan, 1998.
Wroe, Ann. *Pontius Pilate*. New York: Random House, 1999.

Y

Yentob, Alan. '*Cracked Actor* Talk for *David Bowie Is* Exhibition.' Presentation, Victoria and Albert Museum, 5 April 2013.
Young, Paul. *The Cinema Dreams its Rivals: Media Fantasy Films from Radio to the Internet*. Minneapolis, MN: University of Minnesota Press, 2006.

Z

Zanetta, Tony. 'The Week David Bowie Met Lou Reed, Iggy Pop and Andy Warhol: An Inside Look.' *Bedford + Bowery*. Published 11 January 2016. https://bedfordandbowery.com/2016/01/an-inside-look-at-the-week-david-bowie-met-lou-reed-iggy-pop-and-andy-warhol-in-nyc/.
Zuboff, Shoshana. *The Age of Surveillance Capitalism: The Fight for a Human Future at the New Frontier of Power*. New York: Public Affairs, 2019.

INDEX

8 ½ (1963)   90
1871 Paris Commune   256
'1984' (song)   206

Absolute Beginners (1986)   12, 13, 15, 155
'Absolute Beginners' (song)   263–6
abstract expressionism   227
AC/DC concert   102
Ackermann, Haider   242
Acting in the Cinema (Naremore)   7, 55, 175, 220
acting skills   27, 177, 187, 220
acting style   18, 59, 102, 173, 174
acting technique   220
acting theory   7, 9, 56, 174, 192
acting training
   in posed tradition   76–7
   in unposed tradition   77–8
actorly acting   231
actor theory   220, 223–5
Adler, Alexis   228
Adler, Stella   78
aesthetics   1, 26, 29, 74, 76, 179, 239
Aesthetics of Self-Invention: Oscar Wilde to David Bowie; David Bowie Is, The (Waldrep)   2, 5
affective assemblage   116
agency friction   86–8, 92, 93
Age of Bowie, The (Morley)   4
aggressive phallus   162, 165
Aladdin Sane (1973)   263
Alberoni, Francesco   8
alienation   199, 200, 207, 220, 234
Americanization   17, 98, 100, 101, 105, 106, 108, 109, 110
Anglo-American pop culture   17, 98–102, 104–6, 108–10

Anglo-American whiteness   104
anti-realism   102
antithetical approaches   223
Argento, Dario   155
Armstrong, Michael   11
Arquette, Rozanne   14
Artaud, Antonin   132, 134, 147
art forms   1, 4, 9, 16, 26, 27, 47
Arthur and the Invisibles (2006)   15
artificiality   14, 46, 47, 57, 100, 102, 107
artistic practice   47, 241
artistic strategy   44, 46
A's   228
'Ashes to Ashes' (song)   83–6, 134, 135, 202, 240
'As the World Falls Down' (song)   164
August (2008)   15
Auslander, Philip   3, 7, 9, 26, 32, 46, 47, 152, 158, 178, 191, 192, 222, 225, 226, 257
Austin, J. L.   54, 62
Australian Centre for the Moving Image   2
authenticity   3, 5, 8, 152, 174, 179, 184, 187, 188, 191–3
autobiography   63
avant-garde   29, 219, 221

Baal (1982)   12, 57, 83, 145, 146, 180, 181, 230, 231, 239
Bachelor and the Bobbysoxer, The (1947)   160
Bacon, Francis   213
Baer, Hester   100
'bag of tricks'   175, 176, 191, 224
Bakhtin, Mikhail Mikhailovich   9, 18, 152, 155–61, 167, 169

Bandslam (2009) 15–16
Barry Lyndon (1975) 140
Bart, Lionel 222
Barthes, Roland 8, 9, 38, 184
Basquiat (1996) 14, 19, 83, 220, 223, 224, 230, 232–4
Basquiat, Jean-Michel 228
Batson, Susan 179, 180
Bauhaus 138, 139
Baylis, Nicola 41
BBC 11, 12, 57, 58, 180, 206, 231
Beardsley, Aubrey 100
Bed, The (1968) 11
behind-the-scenes shots 33, 34
'Bela Lugosi's Dead' (song) 138, 139
Bell, Edward 137
'Be My Wife' (song) 222
Ben Hur (1959) 176
Benjamin, Walter 55
Bennett, Susan 264, 267, 268
Berkeley, Busby 13
Bernhardt, Sarah 224
Besson, Luc 15
Best of Bowie DVD (2002) 223
Between Theater and Anthropology (Schechner) 56
Bible: In the Beginning..., The (1966) 175
Birdwhistell, Ray 9
Black American music 100
Blackstar (2016) 16
'Blackstar' (song) 134
Blair, Alison 152
Blanks, Tim 61
'Blue Jean' (song) 222
Blumenberg, Hans C. 98
body language 160, 204
Bolan, Marc (Mark Feld) 152
Bolder, Trevor 42
Booth Theatre 145
Bordwell, David 38, 39
Bowie, Angie 34
Bowie, David (David Jones) 3, 53, 79, 131, 133, 179–80. *See also individual entries*
  act of self-preservation 132
  as actor 'story' 18, 176–9
  artificiality of rock music 46

  and Bakhtin 158–9
  in cameo appearance as Philip Jeffries 200–14
  constructing personae 151–2, 159, 166
  costume change 35–7
  death 242, 266, 268
  developing stage and screen performance skills 30–2
  documentary performance 32–4, 37, 47
  and his character construction 62–6
  and his personae Thin White Duke 11, 99, 103–8, 110, 187
  as John Merrick 17, 73–5, 80, 85–91, 93, 132, 145, 146, 154
  as Major Tom 65, 83, 85, 126, 134, 199
  mime performance 2, 41, 44
  monstrous skins 141–3
  performance as Andy Warhol in *Basquiat* 14, 220–1, 224, 226–34
  performance as 'conscious signage' 181–7
  performance as Major Jack Celliers 12, 17, 115–28, 159
  performance as Thomas Jerome Newton 16, 54, 55, 60, 61, 64, 65, 146, 244, 255, 257
  performance as 'truthful' naturalism 187–8
  performance as Ziggy Stardust 25–6, 28–30, 151, 244
  performance catalogue 145–6
  performance in *Christiane F.* 12, 98–110
  performing for different audiences 38–41
  persona and identity performance 46
  posed and unposed tradition of performance 75–8, 81–3, 85, 91–3
  press and media performances 65–6

role as Jareth the Goblin King 18, 151–5, 157–69
role as John Blaylock 12, 18, 133–47
role as Nikola Tesla 15, 19, 237, 239, 241–9
role as outsider 200, 201
in role of Pontius Pilate 14, 18, 173–8, 182–93
role of Vendice Partners 13
screaming in songs 86–8
as signs 220–1
stage and screen performance, and collaboration 1, 2, 5–8, 11, 27–30, 35, 47, 48, 58, 188, 220, 223, 226, 234
stardom and star image 5, 6, 16, 19, 58–62, 66, 99, 100, 109, 124, 125, 127, 146, 153, 174, 181, 183, 184, 187, 191, 193, 220, 221
and theatricality 221–3
as transmedia actor 26, 29
unmasking actor 55–8
use of microphone 106
voice-over performance 15
Bowie: Loving the Alien (Sandford) 6
BowieNet 206, 219
Bowie Symposium: The Stardom and Celebrity of David Bowie (2015) 2
'Boys Keep Swinging' (song) 102, 263
Bram Stoker's Dracula (1992) 147
Brando, Marlon 101, 182
Braudy, Leo 185
bravura screaming 88
Brecht, Bertolt 6, 8, 12, 19, 38, 57, 77, 102, 173, 174, 179–81, 186, 192, 220, 228–34, 239, 241, 247, 249, 250
Brechtian theatre 180, 181, 239
Brel, Jacques 29, 30, 36
BRIT awards 242
Broackes, Victoria 2, 61
Broadway 17, 65, 73, 85, 88, 132, 154, 222, 265
brooding authenticity 82

Brooker, Will 4, 9, 177, 191, 219
Brooks, Peter 128
Broughton, James 11
Bruzzi, Stella 32–4
Buckley, David 103, 221, 225
Buñuel, Luis 103
Burretti, Freddie 60
Burroughs, William S. 65, 142, 241
B.U.S.T.E.D. (1998) 14
Butler, Judith 19, 26, 32, 33, 54–6, 254, 260, 262

Cabaret (1972) 90, 104
Caen, Herb 53
candid backstage filming 58
capitalist consumer culture 99
Capote, Truman 62, 63
caricatures 13, 76, 78, 80, 83, 90–2
carnival 152, 155–69
carnivalesque 18, 152, 155
carnivalistic acts 157
carnivalistic mésalliances 156, 157, 159, 163–5
Cavett, Dick 53, 63, 64, 136
chameleonic masks 177
'Changes' (song) 263, 264
chaos cinema 147
Chaplin, Charlie 55, 56, 60, 188
Chapman, Ian 200
character(s) 76, 78, 83, 90–2, 163, 222, 231
construction 53, 54, 56, 62–6
and identification 226–8
Charney, Leo 203
Chekhov, Michael 19, 240, 241, 246
Cherry, Ava 177
'China Girl' (song) 222, 223
Chion, Michel 126, 208
choreography 28, 29
Christiane F. Wir Kinder vom Bahnhof Zoo (1981) 12, 17, 97–100, 102–10
Cinema 2: The Time-Image (Deleuze) 205
cinema acting 226
'Cinema and its Ghosts' (Baecque and Jousse) 255
Cinema Odeon 176

cinematic melancholia   19, 253, 255, 257, 258
Cinéma Verité   31
Cinque, Toija   2, 4, 6, 9, 205
Clark, Candy   57, 58
Clarke, Alan   12, 180
Clinton, George   152
Close Encounters of the Third Kind (1977)   182
close film textual analysis   116
close-up shots   31, 33–5, 59, 119–26, 183, 185, 190, 246, 248
clowns   76, 78–80, 91, 178
Clurman, Harold   174, 181, 193
codpiece   162, 165, 168, 169
Cold War West Berlin   97, 109
collaborative performance   30, 44
colonialism   101
commedia dell'arte tradition   79
Communion (Strieber)   147
Compo, Susan   255
concert films   47, 81
concert performances   76, 222
Connelly, Jennifer   155, 164
conscious signage   174, 176, 181–92
Constantineau, Wayne   41
consumption   99, 109, 110
Conti, Tom   117
Continuum: Journal of Media & Cultural Studies   4
Coppola, Francis Ford   147
corporeal mime   41
costumes   103–4
Counsell, Colin   3, 6–8, 18, 175, 176, 181, 187, 189
Cracked Actor (1975)   11, 53, 56, 58, 60, 62, 64, 65
"Cracked Actor" (documentary)   221
Critchley, Simon   225
critical theory   9, 75, 254
Crowley, Aleister   183
Croydon School of Art   81
culture
  assemblage   135
  borrowing   29
  colonization   106
  form   255
  German   110
  prejudice   176
cut-up techniques   65, 241

Dadaists   241
D'Adamo, Amedeo   187, 211
Dafoe, Willem   175, 176, 183–5, 189, 190, 223
Dalí, Salvador   103
Daltrey, Roger   154
Damski, Mel   158
Daniel, Drew   261, 262
Dark Crystal, The (1982)   153
dark dystopianism   2
darting technique   87
Das Cabinet des Dr. Caligari (1920)   2
David Bowie: Critical Perspectives (Devereaux, Dillane and Power)   2, 5
David Bowie Is (exhibition)   10
David Bowie: Living on the Brink (Tremlett)   6
David Bowie's crotch in Labyrinth (Facebook group)   168
deathly shadow   134, 138, 141, 143, 145, 147
Dean, James   100, 101, 104–6, 110
Decroux, Étienne   41, 44
Defries, Tony   60, 132, 145, 231
Deleuze, Gilles   9, 16, 18, 201, 205
Deneuve, Catherine   136–40, 145
De Niro, Robert   76
Derfoufi, Mehdi   5, 123, 125, 221
Derrida, Jacques   9, 16, 255
Der Spiegel   100
Desjardins, Mary   63
Devereaux, Eoin   2
Diamond, Neil   221
Diamond Dogs (1974)   2, 64, 65, 263
Diary of Nathan Adler, The (1995)   229
Dick Cavett Show, The (TV show, 1974)   63
Im Dickicht der Städte (1923)   239
Diderot, Denis   224
Dietrich, Marlene   11, 12, 29, 188
Die Zeit   98
digital surveillance   201, 206

Dillane, Aileen 2
Direct Cinema 16, 31–4, 37, 38, 47, 48 n.4
Discipline and Punish (Foucault) 208
Doane, Mary Ann 18, 201, 203
documentary performance 32–3, 37, 47
Doggett, Peter 3, 151
doppelganger 53, 55, 61
Dorfman, Stanley 182
Dostoevsky, Fyodor 152, 155, 156
Downtown 81 (film) 228
dramatic model 265
dramaturgy 12, 206, 220, 230, 234
Dream On (1991) 14
du Gay, Paul 4
Dune (1984) 154
Dyer, Richard 5, 8, 54, 58, 60–2, 220, 229, 231
Dylan, Bob 221

Eberhard, Martin 238
Ebert, Roger 98
eccentricity 156, 161–3, 169
Edel, Uli 98, 101, 104, 109, 110
Edelman, Lee 262
Edison, Thomas 238
Eichinger, Bernd 97, 99–101, 104, 109, 110
Ekman, Paul 9
Elam, Keir 58
Elephant Man, The (1980) 10, 12, 16, 17, 73–6, 80, 83, 85, 93, 132, 154
Ellman, Maud 262
embedded surveillance 207
emotional immediacy 83
emotionalism 102
empathetic roles 83
empathy 76, 83, 86, 90–1, 93
empathy funnels 90–1, 93
Enchanting David Bowie: Space/Time/Body/Memory (Cinque, Moore and Redmond) 2, 4, 9
Engels, Robert 211
entangled agencies 54
entanglements 58, 65, 66

epic theatre 57, 174, 181, 192, 220, 230, 239
expressionist posing 188
expressive techniques 102
exteriority 173, 207, 214
externality 17, 99, 102, 107
Extraordinary Rock Star as Film Star, The (Dyer) 5
Extras (TV show) 15
'The Eyes of David Bowie' (Hunt) 208
Eyewitness News 62

facial expressions 107, 109, 110, 167, 204, 222, 229, 232
Falcon and the Snowman, The (1985) 263
'Fame' (song) 60, 132
fandom 5, 6
'Fashion' (song) 79, 84, 140, 199
feature films 1, 2, 6, 10, 16, 33, 66
Federal Republic of Germany (FRG) 17, 98–101, 106, 109
Fellini, Federico 90
Felscherinow, Christiane 17, 97–9, 101–3, 108–10
feminine appearance 184
femininity 29, 260
feminism 165
figurative art practice 76
film acting 10, 17, 18, 38, 39
Fisher, Mark 132, 134, 142, 144, 147
fission model 19, 224
Fitch, Richard 132, 144, 146, 147
Fitzsimmons, Tom 90
'Five Years' (song) 222
Flannery, Denis 200
Fleming, Victor 257
'flicker of authenticity' 35–8, 47
Fluck, Winfried 101
Flusser, Vilém 239
focalization 59, 226
folk culture 157
Followspot lights 33, 35, 42
Fosse, Bob 90
Foucault, Michel 18, 132, 141, 143, 201, 205, 207, 208
Fowler, Matt 212

Frankenstein (Shelly) 80
Frayling, Christopher 219–21
free and familiar contact among people 156, 160
Fremaux, Stephanie 5, 191
Freud, Sigmund 19, 163, 164, 180, 204, 213, 254, 259, 260, 262
Friesen, Norm 4
frontality 27, 38, 39
Froud, Brian 153, 155
Froud, Wendy Midener 153
Fry, Christopher 175
Furby, Jacqueline 127, 137
fusion model 19, 224, 233
Future Nostalgia (Waldrep) 5, 12, 46

Galt, Rosalind 162, 165
Garbo, Greta 8, 29
Gaultier, Jean-Paul 242
gay sexuality 46
Ge, Nikolai 184
gender 32, 33
   identity 27
   norms 159
   undecidability 193
gendered performance 26
genre framing 26
George, David 19, 223–6, 233
Geraghty, Christine 9
German Expressionism 2, 219
German films 97
Gesamtkunstwerk ('total work of art') 16, 27, 28, 33, 44, 46, 47
gest 19, 186, 231, 239
gestic acting 102, 107, 186
gestic attitude 231
gestic poses 233
gestural artificiality 82
gestures 8, 27, 29–31, 36, 37, 42, 46, 47, 78, 107, 108, 110, 116, 119, 121, 124, 128, 160, 167, 174, 181, 183, 185, 186, 188, 192, 229, 232, 239–40, 247
gesturing dust scene 116–28
Gestus 19, 102, 178, 181, 185–7, 231, 232
Gesù di Nazareth (1977) 190
Gibson, Mel 190

Girl from the North Country (2017) 264
Gish, Lillian 188
glam rock 3–5, 26, 81, 181, 222
Gledhill, Christine 60
Glen, John 162
glitting 63, 64
'God' (song) 132
Goffman, Erving 7, 9, 18, 27, 54, 56, 89, 174, 179, 186, 189, 191, 225
Goldblatt, Stephen 137, 140
Goldcrest 13
Goldene Leinwand 97
Goodale, Robert 206
gothic iconography 139
'Gothic Materialism' (Fisher) 132, 147
gothic textures 147
Grammy Awards, 2016 242
Grant, Cary 160
Gray 228
Greatest Story Ever Told, The (1965) 175
Greek theatre 180
Grey, Joel 76, 104
Grimaldi, Joseph 79
Groebner, Valentin 210
grotesque laughter 162
grotesque realism 156
grotesques 76, 78–80, 90, 91, 93
Grunge 242
Guattari, Pierre-Félix 9

Hagen, Uta 78
Hall, Michael C. 267
Hamlet (Shakespeare) 262
Hammersmith Odeon, London 10, 25, 28, 33, 65
Hartnett, Josh 15
Harty, Russell 53, 64
Hauge, Angela 213
Hearts of Fire (1987) 221
Heaven nightclub, London 138–40
Heckel, Erich 81
Heinlein, Robert 64
Heller-Nicholas, Alexandra 11
'Hello Mary-Lou (Goodbye Heart)' (song) 258

Hemmings, David   11
Henson, Brian   154, 162, 165
Henson, Jim   18, 153, 154, 164, 165, 168, 169
Henson, John   154
Hepburn, Katharine   59
Heroes (1977)   81–3, 182, 228, 263, 264, 268
heterosexuality   46
Hofsiss, Jack   1, 17, 90
Hollywood   100, 135, 147
Holmes, Su   8
Hopper, Dennis   223, 232
Hoskyns, Barney   3
Hudson, Hugh   13
Hudson, Ola   64
Hunger, The (1983)   12, 18, 83, 132–47
Hunger, The (TV series, 1997)   14
Hunky Dory (1971)   29, 222, 228
Hunt, Kevin   180, 190, 204, 208
Hurrah nightclub, Manhattan   140
Huston, John   175
hypermasculinity   182

iconicity   1, 5, 10, 18, 19, 162, 169
iconography   29, 174, 187, 188, 192, 193
identity   54–6, 65, 152, 155, 158, 159, 169, 208, 225, 229, 239, 241, 243
  construction   55, 65, 249
  matrixed   54
  racial   228
  social   61
Il mio West/Gunslinger's Revenge (1998)   2, 14
Image, The (1969)   11
'In Focus: David Bowie On-Screen' (Cinque, Ndalianis and Redmond)   3, 5
inhabited clown   79, 83, 85
inhabited grotesque   80, 83, 85–6
interiority   75, 78–80, 82–6, 88, 92, 93, 173, 207, 214
intermedia practice   27
Intersecting David Bowie (Cinque and Redmond)   4

Interview with a Vampire series   136
Into the Night (1985)   12
Isaak, Chris   210
Isolar (1976)   103, 104, 108
'It's No Game (No.1)' (song)   17, 83, 87–9
'It's No Game (No.2)' (song)   83
'I Want You' (song)   264

Jackson, Michael   154
Jagger, Mick   29, 30, 154, 221
James, Henry   254, 262
Jaynes, Julian   65
Jazzin' for Blue Jean (1984)   13, 158–9, 223
Jazz Singer (1980)   221
Jentsch, Ernst   213
John, I'm Only Dancing (1972)   31
Jojo Rabbit (2019)   90
Jones, Brian (Lewis Brian Hopkins-Jones)   152
Jones, Duncan   2
Jones, Dylan   61
Jung, Carl   164
Just a Gigolo (1978)   11

kabuki   4, 26, 29, 41, 104
Kazantzakis, Nikos   175
Keaton, Buster   57
Keats, John   254
Keitel, Harvey   14
Kemp, Lindsay   2, 4, 11, 28–30, 41, 47, 76, 81, 102, 178, 227
Kermode, Mark   3, 177
Kether and *Malkuth*   107
Kid Auto Races at Venice (*The Pest*, 1914)   55
Kierkegaard, Søren   144
'Killing a Little Time' (song)   260, 266
King, Barry   8, 59
'Kingdom Come' (song)   84
King of Kings (1961)   176
Kleven, Andrew   9, 17, 116
Knight, Nick   61
Konsumgesellschaft (consumer society)   17, 98, 99
Korniloff, Natasha   11

Koster, Henry 175
Kraftwerk 103

Labyrinth (1986) 6, 12, 18, 151–69
Lady Gaga 242
Laing, R. D. 65
Lajosi, Krisztina 27
Lang, Fritz 2
La Roche, Pierre 29
Last Temptation of Christ, The (1988) 14, 18, 173–9, 181–7, 192
Last Temptation of Christ, The (Kazantzakis) 175
Lazarus (2015) 10, 16, 19, 65, 201, 222, 253–68
Lebensgefühl (lifestyle) 99
Un Chien Andalou (1929) 103
Lecoq, Jacques 77
Lee Strasberg's Method 8, 57, 58, 174, 176, 177, 180, 181, 187, 189
Lehrman, Henry 55
Leigh, Wendy 6, 176, 181, 187
Lennon, John 18, 60, 132, 141, 143
Leone, Sergio 155
Leorne, Ana 177, 180, 188
LeRoy, Mervyn 175
Let's Dance (1983) 4, 110, 119, 125, 158, 184, 203, 223
Letter to Three Wives?, A (1949) 256
Lévi-Strauss, Claude 245
Life of Gargantua and Pantagruel, The (Rabelais) 158
'Life on Mars' (song) 31, 242, 260, 263
lighting 26, 28, 29, 33, 102, 103
liminal corporeality 116
liminality 17, 19, 56, 58, 80, 116, 124
Linguini Incident, The (1991) 14
linguistic gaps 116
'Little Wonder' (song) 263
live performance 226
Locke, John 19, 238, 239, 243, 249
Lodger (1979) 83, 137
'London Bye Ta-Ta' (song) 11
Long Island Expressway, NYC 133–4

'Look Back in Anger' (1979) 79
Looking Glass Murders, The (1967) 11
'Love Is Lost' (song) 261, 266
Love You till Tuesday (1969) 31
The Lower Third 151
Low (1977) 83, 228
Luckmann, Benita 225
Lynch, David 14, 18, 19, 154, 200–3, 205–7, 209, 210–14, 216–17 n.42, 218 n.63, 229–30

MacInnes, Colin 12
MacLachlan, Kyle 201
McLuhan, Marshall 4, 41, 62
McPherson, Conor 264
McWhirter, David 262
Macy, William H. 76
magic 168, 169
'Magic Dance' scene 156, 160, 162
MainMan 131, 132, 147
make-up 26, 29, 30, 211
Mallet, David 134
mania 260
Mankiewicz, Joseph L. 256
Mann, Michael 140
Man Who Fell to Earth, The (1976) 4, 6, 11, 14, 16, 19, 53–5, 57–60, 62–6, 100, 146, 176, 220, 221, 241, 244, 254–8, 260–1, 268
Man Who Fell to Earth, The (Tevis) 255–8
'The Man Who Sold the World' (song) 242, 264
Marceau, Marcel 41, 50 n.47
Marcus Aurelius 183
Marsh, Geoffrey 2, 226
Marshall, P. David 8
Marx, Gary 206
Masayoshi Sukita 81
Mascia, Tony 59
masculinity 105, 260
Mask, The (1969) 3, 10, 178
'The Mask Maker' (song) 50 n.47
masks 15, 27, 28, 30, 41, 106, 152, 155–9, 169, 174, 176, 177, 180, 187, 188, 192, 209
Mast, Gerald 64

materiality 57, 128
Mathiesen, Thomas 18, 201
Mayersberg, Paul 146, 257
mechanical reproduction 55
media constructions of stars 61
Media Craft studies 75
melancholia 19, 254, 257, 259–64, 268
melisma 86
Melody Maker 64
Mercury, Freddie 154
Merry Christmas, Mr. Lawrence (1983) 3, 5, 6, 12, 14, 17, 83, 115–28, 145–7, 159, 221
metaphors 17, 54, 60, 145, 147, 179, 240, 241
metatheatricality 209
Metropolis (1927) 2
Miami Vice (1984–9) 140
Miller, Craig 211
Miller, D. A. 265
Milne, Tom 59
mimes 2, 4, 5, 26, 27, 29, 30, 35, 41, 42, 47, 75, 102, 174, 177, 178, 192, 224
mimesis 229
mimicry 26, 29, 178
mock crowning 156, 157, 166
modelling techniques 81
Monroe, Marilyn 101
montage 205, 209
'Moonage Daydream' (song) 35
Moore, Christopher 2, 4, 9, 205
Moorecock, Ronald 14
Morley, Paul 4, 10, 97, 177
movement-images 205
movement vocabulary 107, 109
Mr. Rice's Secret (2000) 15
MTV 140
Mudd Club 228
multimodal performance 27, 44, 46, 47
Mumford, Meg 231
Murphy, Peter 139
musical genres 60, 77
musical speech acts 211
music videos 30, 76, 81, 164
mute gesture 128

'My Death' (song) 36, 39
mystery 103, 107, 169, 208
mythic aura 19, 238, 241, 242, 246

Name of the Rose, The (1986) 99
Naremore, James 7, 8, 17, 18, 38, 54, 55, 57, 60, 75, 102, 104, 106–8, 110, 175, 179, 187, 188, 191, 220
narrative dialogue 95–6 n.26
narrative naturalism 265
Nathan Barley (TV series, 2005) 15
naturalism 173, 174, 176, 179, 187–93
naturalistic performance 18, 58, 174, 176, 177, 185, 187, 191, 192
Navigating with the Blackstar: The Mediality of David Bowie (Mendes and Perrott) 4
Ndalianis, Angela 4
Ned Kelly (1970) 221
Nelson, Ricky 258
Neressian, Anahid 260
"The New Colossus" (poem) 267
Newly, Anthony 29, 30, 222
New Musical Express 63
Newton, Helmut 136
New York Theatre Workshop 255
Nichols, Bill 32, 34
Nietzsche, Friedrich 220, 249
Nirvana 242
Noh mask 26, 29
Nolan, Christopher 1, 15, 16, 237–9, 243, 245, 246, 249
normalizing gaze 205
Notes on Camp (Sontag) 3
Nugent, Ted 154

Oedipus Complex 163
Ogilvie, Cyrus 15
Old Grey Whistle Test (1971) 222
Oldman, Gary 223
O'Leary, Chris 132, 140, 178
Omikron: The Nomad Soul (1999) 14–15
One Flew Over The Cuckoo's Nest (1975) 94 n.14
onstage costume 29

onstage performance 26, 28, 35
Ooh Fashion! 61
Ōshima, Nagisa 17, 147
Otherness 1, 54, 59, 65, 161, 169, 221
O'Toole, Peter 59
1. Outside (1995) 229

Pacino, Al 13
Pagliacci (Opera by Ruggero Leoncavallo) (1892) 79
Panopticism 201
panoptic model 201, 214
'The Paradox of the Actor' (Diderot) 224
Parmenides (Plato) 6, 238
Passion of the Christ, The (2004) 190
Pat Garrett & Billy the Kid (1973) 221
Paxman, Jeremy 206
Paxton, Jeremy 222
Penn, Irving 136
Pennebaker, Donn 10, 16, 25, 27, 28, 31, 33–4, 36, 39, 47
Peraino, Judith 62
performance conventions 18, 179–81
Performance in Everyday Life (Goffman) 174
performance signs 6, 174, 192, 229, 231
performance style 77, 78, 81, 199
performance theory 9, 76, 174
performance zones 34–41
performative emotional symbolism 19, 239, 240, 248, 249
performativity 12, 26, 33, 47, 56, 179, 184, 187–9, 192
Performing Glam Rock (Auslander) 3
Perkins, V. F. 9, 17, 116
Perrott, Lisa 207
persona 26, 30, 44, 46, 56, 63, 110, 152, 155, 225–6
  public 16, 54, 62, 66, 221
  stage 1, 104, 135, 137, 177, 184, 187, 192, 249
  star 60, 62, 65, 126, 221
phenomenological presence 86–9, 93

physical contortions 87–9
physicality techniques 76
physical virtuosity 88, 93
Pierrot in Turquoise (1969) 10, 11
Pinter, Harold 189
Pitt, Ken 177
Piwitt, Hermann Peter 101
Plato 6, 19, 238, 239
Poe, Edgar Allen 147
Pollock, Jackson 227
polyphony 155
polysemic performance 8, 16, 55, 57
Pop, Iggy 137
popular culture 29, 99
popular music 27, 29
posed and unposed performance 27, 29, 31, 36, 37, 41, 47, 75–8, 81–3, 90–3
Posey, Parker 223
posing 39, 58, 60–2
Power, Martin J. 2
precision *vs.* moment-by-moment work 90–1
presentational acting 7, 179, 180, 185, 188
Presentation of Self in Everyday Life, The (Goffman) 225
Presley, Elvis 101
Prestige, The (2006) 6, 15, 16, 19, 220, 237–9, 241–9
primary carnivalistic act 156, 157, 166
Prince 154
Problems of Dostoevsky's Creative Art (Bakhtin) 155
Problems of Dostoevsky's Poetics (Bakhtin) 155, 156
profanation 157, 165, 169
promotional interviews 62
psychoanalytical approaches 61
psychoanalytic theory 163, 164
Psychological Gesture 240, 248
punctum 38
Punk movement 242
puzzle films 217 n.42

queer theory 254
Quo Vadis (1951) 175

INDEX

Rabelais, François 152, 156
Rabelais in the History of Realism (*Rabelais and His World*, Bakhtin) 157, 158
Radio Times 62
Rainbow Theatre 28
Ray, Nicolas 176
RCA Records 33, 131, 145
realism 98, 99, 240
Rebel without a Cause (1955) 104
Redmond, Sean 2, 4, 8, 9, 61, 108, 184, 203–5
Reed, Lou 29, 30
representational acting 7, 8, 174, 179, 188
Resident Evil (2002) 99
'The Return of the Thin White Duke' (song) 63
Revolution (1985) 13
Ribot, Theodule 180
Rice, Anne 136
Richard, Little 81
Riches, Simon 208
Richmond, Tony 57, 59
Riefenstahl, Leni 29
Robe, The (1953) 175
Robinson, Lisa 63
Rock, Mick 28, 30–1, 47
rock and roll 1, 7, 63, 101, 152, 257
rock culture 46
rock music 3, 35, 46
rock musicians 3, 135, 152
Rodley, Chris 209
Roeg, Nicolas 11, 16, 19, 56–61, 64, 176, 177, 221, 254–7, 259
Rolling Stone (magazine) 62, 90, 147
The Rolling Stones (Rock band) 152
Romans in Films, The (Barthes) 184
Rombes, Nicholas 212
Ronson, Mick 35, 36, 42, 46
Roquairol (Heckel) 81
Roscoe, Jane 34
Rose, Charlie 227, 231
Rosenbaum, Jonathan 59
Ross, Kristin 256
Roth, David Lee 154
Roy, Ron 206

Russell Harty Show (TV show, 1975) 64

Saal, Hubert 209
Sakamoto, Ryuichi 17, 115, 123
SAMO 228
Samuel, Martin 58
Sandford, Charles 6
San Francisco Chronicle 53
Sarandon, Susan 140
Satz, Wayne 62
Scary Monsters and Super Creeps (1980) 17, 74, 76, 83–7, 90, 93, 132, 135, 137, 147, 240, 263
Schechner, Richard 3, 9, 54, 56, 174, 180
Scheibel, Will 205
Schlesinger, John 263
Schnabel, Julian 19, 220, 221, 224, 227, 228, 231, 233
Schrader, Paul 18, 174, 179, 188, 189
Schubart, Rikke 65
science fiction 26, 29, 241
Scorsese, Martin 1, 18, 173, 174–6, 179, 181, 184, 185, 188–90, 192
Scott, Ridley 136
Scott, Tony 14, 18, 133, 135–40, 142–4, 146, 147
screaming 86–8, 127–8
'Scream Like A Baby' (song) 84
screen acting 146, 174, 220
'SelectaVision VideoDisc' technology 33
self 54, 99, 102, 159, 225
self-Americanization 101
self-construction 1, 62
semiotics 6–9, 18, 174, 176
Sensing Film Performance published in *Performance Phenomenology: To the Thing Itself* (Redmond) 9
sensory-motor schema 205
Serious Moonlight (1983) 226
set designs 28, 29, 103
sexual ambiguity 221
sexual connotations 165
sexual norms 159
sexual symbology 164
Shakespeare, William 141, 254, 262

Sharpe, Alex   141
Shelly, Mary   80
Shiloh, Ilanah   154
Shopov, Hristo   190
shot-reverse-shot   59, 120, 246
Sight & Sound   59
Signs of Performance (Counsell)   7, 8, 175
Sikora, Jack   2
silences   17, 116, 121
simple clowns   91, 92
simple grotesque   80
Sinatra, Frank   100
Smilla's Sense of Snow (1996)   99
Smith, Nigel   263
Snowman, The (1982)   12
social scripts   89
Solanas, Valerie   227
Sontag, Susan   3
'Sound and Vision' (song)   206
Soussloff, Catherine   19, 238, 242
'Sowing the Seed' (song)   123, 127
'Space Oddity' (song)   65, 134, 199, 202
spacey strobe effect   34
spatial awareness   38
'speech act' theory   54
split-identity   211
SpongeBob SquarePants (2007)   15
Spotts, Frederic   29
Springsteen, Bruce   82
Stage (1978)   97
Stanislavskian actions   189, 191
Stanislavsky, Konstantin   6, 8, 57, 77, 78, 102, 173, 174, 177, 178, 180, 181, 189, 224
Stanislavsky's System   57, 175, 180, 181, 224
star authenticity   60, 61
star-centric approach   221
'Starman' (song)   161
Starman: David Bowie - The Definitive Biography (Trynka)   6
'The Stars Are Out Tonight' (song)   223
Station to Station (1976)   63, 100–2, 109
Steiger, Rod   190

Stern   97
Stevens, George   175
Stewart, Rod   154
Stiller, Ben   15
Sting   154, 176
Stranger in a Strange Land (1961)   64
Strasberg, Lee   8, 57, 177, 179
Streep, Meryl   76, 185
street-corner mime   188
'The Street Scene' (Brecht)   230
stretched-out reactions   82
Strieber, Whitley   133, 135, 136, 142, 147
Stroszek (1977)   94 n.14
structured polysemies   61
studio techniques   81
stylistic gesture   19, 239, 240
subversive strategy   46, 47
surrealist opera   136, 147
surveillance capitalism   206
surveillant gaze   201, 203, 205
surveillant subjectivity   200–2, 206
survie ('survival')   256, 257, 262, 268
Sutherland, Kiefer   210
Sutton Park, NYC   135–8, 142, 144
sweet annihilation   145
Swinton, Tilda   223
Sylvia Scarlett (1935)   59
synoptic surveillance   201, 214

table work   189, 192
Tarantino, Quentin   109
Tarpenning, Marc   238
Taylor, Vince   81
'Teenage Wildlife' (song)   84
Temple, Julien   12, 13, 155, 158, 223, 263
Temple, Shirley   160
Tesla, Nikola   237–8
Tesla Motors   238
Tevis, Walter   59, 64, 255–7, 259
'That's Motivation' (song)   13
Theatre 625 (1968)   10
theatricality   3, 220–3, 225–6
theatrical performance   3, 11, 16, 30, 33–5, 187, 230
theatrical style   174, 175
Thespis   180, 187

INDEX

'This is Not America' (song)   262, 263
Thompson, Jack   115
Thomson, Malcolm J.   3, 178
Tin Machine   213
Tomei, Concetta   90
Tonight Show with Johnny Carson, The (TV show, 1980)   105
Tony Award   85
Top Gun (1986)   147
Top of the Pops (TV Show, 1972)   161
Toppop   214
Torn, Rip   55
transgressive allure   100, 110
transitional beat   189
'Transition Transmission' (October)   65
trauma   74, 86, 117, 142, 241
Tremlett, George   6
triadic acting model   19, 224–6
Triumph of the Will (1935)   29
True Romance (1993)   147
Trynka, Paul   6, 104
'TVC15' (song)   206
Twin Peaks: Fire Walk with Me (1992)   14, 18, 200–14, 230
Twin Peaks: The Entire Mystery Set (2014)   212
Twin Peaks: The Missing Pieces (2014)   212
Twin Peaks: The Return (2017)   212, 214

uncanny effect   213
unheimlich ('the uncanny')   204
United States   100
Usher, Bethany   5, 191

V&A   61
van Hove, Ivo   254, 263, 267
Vanilla, Cherry   63
Van Noten, Dries   242
Vaudeville   77, 100
Velvet Underground   100
verfremdungseffekt (V-effekt/'alienation effect')   13, 38, 57, 180, 230
Victoria and Albert Museum   10
video clips   1, 4, 16, 140, 222

Videodrome Discotheque (TV show)   85
Vietnam War   101
'The Viewer Society' (Mathiesen)   18, 201
View to a Kill, A (1985)   162
Virgin Soldiers, The (1969)   11
vocal intonation   29
voice morphs   229

Wagner, Richard   27
Waititi, Taika   90
Waldrep, Shelton   2, 5, 7, 10, 12, 46, 47, 54, 62, 107, 158
Walken, Christopher   223
Walsh, Enda   19, 253–5, 257, 263–8
Walworth Farce, The (2006)   265
Warhol, Andy   19, 62, 63, 100, 137, 227–8
Wayne, John   105
'We Are Like the Dreamer' (2017)   212
Weber, Max   8
Weigel, Hermann   99, 110
Weill, Kurt   180
Wenders, Wim   101
West End   222
Western cinematic art   179
Western narrative tradition   78
West Germans   101, 109
West German society   108, 109
West Germany   17, 99, 101, 109
What Is Truth? (Ge)   184
'When I Live my Dream' (song)   11
'When I'm Five' (song)   178, 181, 187
'Where Are We Now?' (song)   260, 265–6
Why Bowie Matters (Brooker)   4
'The Width of a Circle' (song)   41–4, 46
Wiene, Robert   2
Wild, the Innocent & the E Street Shuffle, The (1974)   82
Wilde, Oscar   62, 225
Wild One, The (1953)   182
Willett, John   181

Williams, Linda   163
*Will Kenny Everett Make It To 1980?
   Show* (1979)   134
Wilson, Owen   15
Windows into the Soul (Marx)
   206
Wizard of Oz, The (1939)   257
Wrapped in Plastic   211
Wright, Jeffrey   223, 232, 233
Wright, Julie Lobalzo   5, 60
Wyler, William   176
Wyman, Bill (William George
   Perks Jr.)   152

Yamamoto, Kansai   26, 29, 37
Yankee colonization   101, 109

Year of Living Dangerously, The
   (1982)   94 n.14
Yellowbeard (1983)   12, 158
Yentob, Alan   11, 56, 62
'Yet San and the Eagle' (mime
   sequence)   47
Young, Paul   262
Young Americans (1975)   257
'Young Americans' (song)   211

Zeffirelli, Franco   190
*Ziggy Stardust and the Spiders from
   Mars* (1973)   10, 16, 25–30, 32,
   33, 34–42, 46–8, 65
Zoolander (2001)   15
Zuboff, Shoshana   206

Printed in the USA
CPSIA information can be obtained
at www.ICGtesting.com
LVHW010318090324
773943LV00001B/64